# A COMPLETE HISTORY OF GUAM

# A COMPLETE HISTORY OF

# GUAM

*by*

PAUL CARANO, M.A.

*Assistant Professor of Social Science, College of Guam*

*and*

PEDRO C. SANCHEZ, Ph.D.

*Peace Corps, former President of the College of Guam*

CHARLES E. TUTTLE COMPANY

*Rutland, Vermont     Tokyo, Japan*

*Representatives*
*Continental Europe: BOXERBOOKS, INC., Zurich*
*British Isles: PRENTICE-HALL INTERNATIONAL, INC., London*
*Australasia: PAUL FLESCH & CO., PTY. LTD., Melbourne*


*Published by the Charles E. Tuttle Co., Inc.*
*of Rutland, Vermont and Tokyo, Japan with*
*Editorial offices at Suido 1-chome, 2–6, Bunkyo-ku*
*Tokyo, Japan*

*Copyright in Japan by the Charles E. Tuttle Co., Inc.*

*Library of Congress Catalog Card No. 64–21619*

*First edition, 1964*


*Printed in Japan*

# TABLE OF CONTENTS

# LIST OF ILLUSTRATIONS

GUAM DURING AND AFTER WORLD WAR II
*Following page 368*

# *FOREWORD*

Prior to World War II, Guam, an American territory since 1898, was virtually unknown to most Americans—a mere coaling station almost lost in the vastness of the Pacific. However, with the dropping of Japanese bombs on December 7, 1941, and the United States' entry into the War, Guam was transformed from a relatively unknown island into occupied American soil to be reclaimed—whatever the cost—from the invader's hands. Wars are not won cheaply, and thousands of lives were lost before Guam was wrested from the enemy. The price paid by the United States foretold the important role which was envisioned for Guam in the prosecution of the war in the Pacific, and soon thereafter Guam and her sister islands to the north became the springboard for the invasion of Iwo Jima and the Ryukyus, and the bombing of the Japanese homeland which culminated in the capitulation of the enemy.

Guam, our westernmost bastion on American soil, today still plays an important and undiminished role in our national defense. The entire island, although under civilian administration, is for practical purposes a fortress where now live seventy thousand Americans. It can no longer be said that Guam is an area unknown to Americans in view of the thousands of American servicemen who have served on Guam or paused there momentarily on their way to or from other areas. Yet what do we or they really know of Guam? Is it not the Guam of yesterday or last month or ten years ago that we know? Even to those whose entire lives have been spent

xiii

on Guam, an island no more than 35 miles in length and 10 miles in width, the history of Guam is no more than what this generation can remember and, prior to this volume, would in the future be no more than this generation could pass on by word of mouth to its children.

Certainly it is not that Guam has no history, for it does. The people of Guam are an old people whose origin is shrouded in uncertainty and who, over the centuries, have been host, both willing and unwilling, to a variety of foreign cultures which have markedly influenced the development and history of the island and its people.

Heretofore, fragments of the history of Guam have been recorded, but these documents have all too often found their final resting place in dust-encrusted files in obscure libraries or remote government vaults, inaccessible and therefore unread. The authors of this work have, for a decade, searched for, located, sorted, and compiled these fragments, augmenting the result with their own knowledge of their island, in order to provide the reader with a single volume encompassing the history of Guam. This volume is not definitive, for much history remains to be recorded, but it capably fills a vacuum which has existed for too long, and I sincerely commend it to the children and students of Guam and to all those, wherever they may live, who share my interest in the history of the United States and its citizens.

RICHARD F. TAITANO
Director, Office of Territories
Department of the Interior

# PREFACE

IN THE YEAR 1952 Dr. Erik K. Reed, regional archeologist with the Region 3 Office of the National Park Service in Santa Fe, New Mexico, prepared a report entitled *Archeology and History of Guam*. His report, written at the request of Guam Governor Carlton Skinner, contained several recommendations concerning the writing of the island's history. With regard to publication needs, he recommended the preparation of a work dealing with Guam's ancient and recent past. Such a work, he wrote, should be "sufficiently complete and correct to be of some value, but so clearly and simply written as to be of wide understandability and general interest." Through this recommendation, Dr. Reed gave expression to the fact that for many decades, but especially since the American reoccupation of Guam in 1944, there has been an urgent and continually growing need for a book concerned with the historical development of the Guamanian people. In an attempt to meet that need, the authors have written the present book. No claim is made to a definitive character for the book. Indeed, it is intended to be an introduction to the study of the history of Guam.

The book has been designed for reading by the general public and for possible use as a textbook in the schools of Guam. It is a narrative account designed to present a picture of the periods of historical development through which the island has passed. The discussion of each period contains some information related to political, economic, and social events that occurred during that period. In view of the fact that much of Guam's history has been determined by the actions of Spanish and American governors, the administrations of a number of outstanding governors have been dealt with at length. The development of Guam as a great military base has been touched upon lightly and only incidentally.

To this date, no successful attempt has been made to write a history covering developments in Guam from pre-Spanish times to the present. Lack of source materials has thus far discouraged any serious attempt along such lines. The lack of materials has been aggravated by the fact that most of Guam's historical records were destroyed during the Pacific war. Consequently, available information is extremely limited and fragmentary. This is especially true of the period extending from the time of the discovery of Guam by Europeans to its emergence as an American possession in 1898. Despite these limitations, it is believed that most of the available historical sources have been studied and used in the preparation of this book. The account of Guamanian history from pre-Spanish times to 1898 has been derived from the writings of the many foreign explorers, adventurers, missionaries, and traders who visited Guam after its discovery in 1521. In view of the paucity of available references and the fragmentary nature of appropriate information which they contain, this book, wherever possible, has made extensive use of direct quotations from such references. This has been done deliberately in order to provide Guamanian readers with access, albeit limited, to otherwise unavailable references and authorities. Throughout the work, and especially in those sections dealing with events after 1898, information from standard references has been reinforced with material gathered from periodicals, government documents, and the oral or written statements of competent Guamanian leaders.

For assistance rendered in the preparation of this book, the authors express their most heartfelt thanks to the many Guamanians and statesiders without whose help the writing would have been an immeasurably more difficult task. Special thanks are extended to the following: To the Honorable Richard F. Taitano, Director, Office of Territories, United States Department of the Interior, for writing the foreword. To Mr. Richard Barrett Lowe, former Governor of Guam; His Excellency the Most Reverend Apollinaris William Baumgartner, O.F.M., Cap., D.D., Bishop of Guam; the late Rear Admiral William B. Ammon, former Commander Naval Forces Marianas; and Rear Admiral Waldemar F. A. Wendt, also former Commander Naval Forces Marianas, for the encouragement arising from their expressions of interest. To the Very Reverend Monsignors Oscar L. Calvo and Felixberto C. Flores, and former Superintendent of Schools Simon A. Sanchez for their constructive criticism and for the use of significant historical data. To Rear Admiral Charles A. Pownall, former Governor of Guam, for the dispatch of an official request to Washington, D.C., urging the compilation of certain official documents for the authors' use. To Mr. William F. Knowland, former United States senator from California, for his interest and timely assistance, which made possible the securing of important microfilms from the National Archives. To the Honorable Harlan Hagen, Congressman, 18th California District, for aid in securing materials from various branches of the United States armed forces. To Lieutenant General Randolph M. Pate, former Commandant, United States Marine Corps, for an official account of the role played by the Marine Corps and the Navy in the reoccupation of Guam. To Dr. Erik K. Reed, to the Library of Congress, to the Essex Institute of Salem, Massachusetts, and to the Stanford University libraries, for the furnishing of much useful material. And, finally, to the following publishers, who have given their permission for the use of quoted material: Appleton-Century-Crofts, Inc.; Bernice P. Bishop Museum; Chapman and Hall, Ltd.; Chicago Natural History Museum; the John Day Company, Inc.; Dorrance and Company, Inc.; E. P. Dutton and Company, Inc.; Henry Holt and Company, Inc.; Alfred A. Knopf, Inc.; Little, Brown and Company; George Philip and Son, Ltd.; Princeton University Press; Tongg Publishing Company, Ltd.; the Viking Press, Inc.; and John Wiley and Sons, Inc.

PAUL CARANO
PEDRO C. SANCHEZ

*CHAPTER ONE*

# THE ISLAND AND ITS PEOPLE

THE SOCIAL, economic, and political development of all peoples is determined, in large measure, by the geographical location of the lands in which they live and by their nearness to or distance from other peoples. These factors have been unusually important in the historical development of the Guamanian people. Because Guam is isolated from the rest of the world by vast stretches of the Pacific Ocean, its history, at least until World War II, was one of physical and cultural stagnation. Since World War II, however, Guam has become a busy center for activities which affect not only the lives of Guamanians but also those of other peoples in the Pacific islands and in Asia. Such activities have drastically altered the way of life of the Guamanian people. To furnish clearer insights into Guam's history, this chapter deals with the island and its people—as they are today and as they were in centuries past.

## THE LAND

Guam, America's farthermost outpost in the Pacific Ocean, is an unincorporated territory of the United States. As such, it is one of America's most important bastions of defense. A glance at a map of the Pacific area shows how strategically Guam is located with reference to Japan, the Philippines, Australia, and the mainland of Asia. Indeed, its strategic location and its value as a base for future naval operations were principal reasons for acquiring

1

it from Spain. While he was Assistant Secretary of the Navy, Franklin Delano Roosevelt stated that the "real value of the Island of Guam to this nation lies in its use as a naval base in the case of operations in the Pacific, and in this respect its importance cannot be overestimated."[1] With equal certainty, it might also be stated that in an age of jet planes and guided missiles Guam's value cannot be overestimated.

Guam is the largest island in the North Pacific Ocean between Hawaii and the Philippines and between Japan and New Guinea. It lies at the southernmost end of a chain of fifteen islands called the Marianas.* These islands are situated between the 13th and 20th parallels of north latitude, and along the 145th meridian east of Greenwich. The distance from Guam to the northernmost island of the Marianas is 420 miles.

Because its narrow waist divides it roughly into two equal parts, Guam's irregular shape may be said to resemble a peanut or a human footprint. Covering an area of approximately 225 square miles, the island is about 30 miles long and from 4 to 9 miles wide. It lies almost directly north and south, with the southern half set slightly to the westward of the northern half. Except for openings at harbors and the mouths of streams, the entire island is surrounded by a coral reef ranging from 20 to 700 yards in width.

The southern part of Guam is high and mountainous. The principal feature of its terrain is a ridge of hills, ranging in altitude from 700 to 1,300 feet. This ridge begins near Pago Bay, crosses to the west coast near Agana, and follows that coast to the extreme southern part of the island. Starting in these hills or mountains, numerous streams wend their way across the entire width of the island and empty into the sea on the east coast. Principal mountains in the region are Mt. Tenjo, with an elevation of 1,013 feet; Mt. Lamlam, 1,334 feet; and Mt. Sasalaguan,

---

* Beginning at the north, the names of the islands of the Marianas are: Farallon de Pájaros, Las Urracas (Maug), Asunción (Asomsom), Agrigan, Pagan, Alamagan, Guguan, Sariguan, Anatahan, Farallon de Medinilla, Saipan, Tinian, Aguigan, Rota (Luta), and Guam.

1,110 feet.[2] Most of the mountains are covered with various grasses, shrubs, and trees. Among them are sword grass, a species of hedge plant called *tangantangan* by the Guamanians, and a tree of the casuarina family commonly called ironwood. In the valleys, grasses and shrubs are overshadowed by a great variety of trees. Among them are the giant banyan (*nunu*), breadfruit, ifil, coconut palm, pandanus (*aggak* and *kafo*), and a species of areca palm (*Palma braba*). These plants are not confined to the southern part of the island alone; many of them are also found on the northern plateau.

The topography of the northern part of the island is quite different from that of the southern part. It is a high plateau, ranging from 200 to 600 feet in elevation, with no permanent rivers or streams. There are, however, a few small brooks that rise on Mt. Santa Rosa and disappear in the coral rock at its base. Steep cliffs, reaching a height of 600 feet above the sea, are found along the north and northeast sides of the island. Their lower levels are usually broken by deep crevasses and cracks. At a higher level, numerous caves are found. Sheer drops of 200 feet or more are quite common along the cliffs. At their base lie coconut groves bordered by narrow strips of white beach sand. In many places, especially along the northeast coast, the cliffs drop abruptly into the sea.

Guam, as well as the other islands of the Marianas, is of volcanic origin. Indeed, some of the northern islands still have active volcanoes, while others show evidence of recent volcanic activity. Geologically, Guam is a young island. As time is reckoned, however, it is extremely old. Remnants of limestone formations found in the southern mountains have been identified as belonging to the Miocene age. This is a geologic period that prevailed more than seven million years ago.[3]

It would appear that Guam was built up from the ocean floor by volcanic action. Originally, only some of the southern mountains and a very small part of Mt. Santa Rosa appeared above the water. When vulcanism ceased, millions of coral polyps attached themselves to the exposed rocks, and the formation of coral reefs

3

was begun. Later, different parts of the island were alternately raised and lowered by strong earth movements. This process, plus steady coral growth, has built up the island to its present state.

The northern plateau of Guam consists almost entirely of some form of coral limestone, commonly called *cascajo*. Sea shells and coral fragments found there suggest that, at one time, most of the plateau was under water. Where erosion has exposed the sides of some of the southern mountains, layers of coarse sandstone, flint quartz, and clay can be seen. Scattered over much of the area are heavy lava rocks called *homun*.

Erosion has had serious effects on the surface appearance of Guam. A series of rounded hills south of Talofofo has been deeply cut by ravines. Their sides are covered by a thin layer of reddish soil that will support almost no vegetation other than clumps of sword grass. In other parts of the island, limestone masses that once covered the sides of mountains have decomposed and been washed down into the valleys. There the soils run together during the rainy season and pack very tightly. Newly broken topsoil, which is usually very thin, is not productive until some months after being broken.

As part of an underwater mountain range which extends from Japan southward through the Marianas, Guam is surrounded by waters which attain great depth. At a point a short distance east of the island, the water reaches a depth of almost six miles. This chasm in the ocean is called the Nero Deep. It received its name from the USS Nero, a vessel which made extensive soundings late in 1899 for the purpose of selecting a cable route across the Pacific. South of Guam is the seven-mile-deep Marianas Trench, the deepest ever discovered. The descent was made by Swiss scientist Jacques Piccard and U.S. Navy Lieutenant Don Walsh in the bathyscaphe *Trieste* in January 1960. For thirty minutes they rested on the bottom of the ocean, 35,800 feet deep, where the water pressure was eight and one-half tons per square inch.

Though Guam lies within the tropics, its climate is tempered throughout the greater part of the year by a brisk trade wind, blowing from the northeast and east. As a result, Guam's climate

4

is generally healthful and, on the whole, pleasant. From July to December the rainy season prevails. Influenced by the southwest monsoon, it is the period of greatest rainfall and is called *fanuchanan* by the islanders. *Fanumnagan* prevails from January to June and is referred to as the dry season. The average yearly rainfall is about 90 inches. In some years as much as 65 per cent of the rain may occur during the six months of the rainy season. Guam's mountains are not high enough to cause differences in the distribution of rainfall on the island, and its area is too small to cause land and sea breezes. Lying, as it does, within the typhoon belt, Guam is sometimes struck by violent storms which occur most frequently during the rainy season. The worst of these typhoons almost completely devastated the island in November 1962.

Although the temperature of Guam may vary from a minimum of 70°F. to a maximum of 91 degrees, the mean annual temperature is about 80 degrees. May and June are the hottest months, and December is the coolest. While variations in temperature are not very great, the rainy months are so definitely marked that certain wasps, which during the summer ordinarily make their nests in the open fields, invade houses and buildings to hibernate.[4]

Taking the area of Guam as 225 square miles and the average yearly rainfall as 90 inches, computations have been made which show that about 375 billion gallons of rain fall on the island in an average year.[5] If the rainfall were evenly distributed it would amount to roughly one billion gallons a day. However, the rainfall is not evenly distributed; on some days no rain falls at all. Nevertheless, during a month having only one-half inch of rain, about 33 million gallons of rain may fall on the island each day.

## ANIMALS OF THE ISLAND

When the ancient Chamorros first came to Guam, they brought no livestock or domestic animals with them—apparently not even dogs.[6] During the long period of Spanish rule, however, domesticated animals commonly found in other parts of the world were imported. Among the animals introduced to the island

5

were cattle, horses, mules, pigs, cats, dogs, goats, and carabao (water buffalo). Except for horses and mules, most common domestic animals are found in Guam today in fairly large numbers. Dogs, especially, are so numerous that they are somewhat of a nuisance. The carabao, a large, ungainly, great-horned animal, was introduced from the Philippines. Its flesh is seldom eaten by present-day Guamanians, and its milk, which is of excellent quality, is seldom used. Until World War II, the carabao was used for carrying burdens, drawing carts, and plowing rice paddies. Postwar changes, however, have lessened the economic value of the animal.

A species of Philippine spotted deer was introduced by Governor Mariano Tobias in the 1770's. It multiplied rapidly and soon became a nuisance. After the general introduction of firearms into the island, however, its numbers diminished rapidly—so much so, in fact, that game laws were enacted to prevent its extinction. Since World War II comparatively few deer remain in a wild state. From time to time, however, one is struck down by an automobile on the island's busy highways. Others are seen occasionally in captivity.

The only mammals of pre-Spanish times were two species of bats, the large fruit-eating "flying fox," called *fanihi* by the Guamanians, and a smaller insectivorous species called *fanihin toyo*. The *fanihi* rarely flies about during the daytime, but when it does, it can be seen flapping its wings slowly like a large bird. It is either shot or caught in the jungle at night by means of nets attached to long poles. Although it has a strong odor, the *fanihi*, boiled or roasted, is eaten as a rare delicacy. The smaller bat flies about very much like the common species found in other parts of the world. It remains in caves during the day and comes out only at night.

The Norway or brown rat, called *chaka* by the Guamanians, is a great pest. It is very abundant and does extensive damage to crops and goods. Following World War II, when vast supply dumps were scattered through the jungle, rats swarmed over the island. Traps and poison are used as weapons in a never-ending

6

struggle against the brown rat. The common mouse and shrews are also found on the island, although they do little harm. Both pests probably reached Guam aboard visiting ships.

There are few reptiles in Guam. The only snake native to the island is a small harmless species which has microscopic eyes and mouth and is covered with tiny scales. It is sometimes called blindworm because, in general appearance, it looks like a large earthworm. It is usually found in damp places, under stones and logs. To prevent the introduction of dangerous reptiles to the island, special care is taken in the unloading of cargo from visiting vessels. In recent years, nevertheless, a number of poisonous snakes have been found on the island.

The most notable reptile in Guam is the large iguana. It oftentimes attains a length of four feet. Called *hilitai* by the islanders, these lizards invade henhouses, where they eat eggs and young chicks. Due to the importation of toads, a natural enemy, this member of the lizard family is rapidly disappearing.

Four species of geckos inhabit Guam. These small lizards, called *gualiig*, are often seen on window screens and on the rafters of buildings. They are harmless creatures which prey on insects. Their toes are so constructed as to enable them to run upside-down on the ceiling. From time to time they make chirping sounds, which have won for them the name "island canary birds."[7]

The giant African snail (*Achatina fulica*) is extremely abundant in Guam and is one of the island's principal agricultural pests. Originating on the east coast of Africa, the snail gradually found its way to India and southeast Asia. In 1933 it was introduced into Japanese-controlled Formosa to supplement the food supply. The Japanese not only used the snail as food but also believed that it possessed unusual medicinal qualities. It is thought that when the war broke out in 1941, the Japanese brought some of the snails with them to the Marianas to provide a "good source of wild food to supplement the scheduled rations or take their place in the event that supply lines were cut."[8] Although they were introduced into the Marianas during the early phases of

World War II, the snails did not spread profusely over Guam until after the war. One account suggests that the snails did not reach Guam until 1946.[9]

Lacking natural enemies in Guam, the snails developed rapidly and soon swarmed over the island, devouring plants and crops in their path. Because they are bisexual, each snail is an egg producer and may lay as many as 300 eggs in a single batch. The snails must have lime in order to live. Unfortunately, limestone and coral formations in Guam provide them with an ample supply.

## THE PEOPLE

Present-day Guamanians are, as a rule, of good physique and pleasing appearance. They do not, however, possess the stature and robust health which characterized the ancient Chamorros, their remote ancestors. Because of their mixed blood, their complexion varies from white to dark brown. The various shades of skin color which prevail among them result from extensive intermarriage between Guamanian women and men of many ancestral backgrounds, among them being Spanish, Italian, French, English, Scotch, German, Japanese, Chinese, Mexican, Filipino, and American. Since World War II, especially, Guamanian-American marriages have become quite numerous.

While it is probably true that there are no longer any fullblooded Chamorros in Guam, a strong native strain runs through present-day Guamanians. Most of the natives who survived the Spanish-Chamorro wars were women. After the conquest they married Spaniards and other off-islanders. Through them much of the Chamorro heritage, especially the language, was passed on from generation to generation. Thus the language has been preserved, although in modified form, and the children, regardless of the fathers' origin, are thought of as being Guamanians.

"The various races," wrote Safford, "have amalgamated thoroughly. Among the principal families on the island are found the names of Anderson, Robert, Wilson, and Millechamp, as well as those of Torres, Palomo, Martinez, Cruz, Perez, Herrero, and others of Spanish and Mexican origin, names all prominent in the archives of the island. In these archives are copies of official orders of the captain-general of the Philippines directing that all for-eigners be sent away from Guam and, in reply, petitions from a number of worthy men stating that they had adopted this little island for their home and begging the captain-general that they might be allowed to remain with their wives and little ones. Some of them even went to Manila and were granted permission to return, becoming useful members of the community and rendering great assistance to the governor as interpreters, captains of the port, and pilots. Many of their descendants inherit their sterling qualities, but are true Chamorros in language, in manners, and in heart."[10]

The amalgamation process has continued to the present. Indeed, since World War II it has been greatly accelerated.

In present-day Guam the term Chamorro is generally used to identify the native language. The people themselves are called Guamanians. The terms Guamians and Guamese are sometimes used by newcomers to the island. They quickly learn, however, that Guamanian is the term officially and commonly used by the islanders themselves.

Since the end of World War II, the Guamanian people have experienced many changes in their customs and way of life. After the war Guam was "overwhelmed by the influx of countless numbers of outsiders who brought with them new techniques, new ideas, and an abundance of cash. Many changes followed in their wake. An excellent network of highways was built, electrical power plants were established, and sanitary facilities were in-stalled. The bull cart was replaced by the jeep; the once obedient child, in order to escape parental authority, went to live with his cousin; and the beer can became the most popular symbol on the island. Guam became indeed an outpost of democracy—a fron-tier area having all the aspects of the wild and woolly west."[11] As a result, old values were gradually replaced by new ones. In matters of speech, dress, and manner of living, the Guamanians, especially the youth, became more and more like mainland Americans. The Americanization process is continuing today at an ever-increasing pace.

English is the official language of Guam. It is the language of instruction in the schools and is spoken by most Guamanians. In their homes and in their own social groups, however, the islanders usually speak Chamorro. Indeed, Chamorro is the first language spoken by most of the children. Consequently, many Guamanians are unable to speak English with fluency and ease. There are others, however, who have an almost perfect command of the English language. Whether fluent or otherwise, most Guamanians speak English in a manner that is readily understood.

Generally speaking, clothing worn by Guamanians is the same as that worn by other Americans. Some older women, however, continue to dress in the Filipino *mestiza* style, especially on festive occasions. The *mestiza* style of dress consists of a starched *pina* blouse with bell sleeves and a long brightly colored cotton skirt. Girls and younger women of Guam dress in American style, as do men and boys.

Guamanian houses are somewhat like those found in the United States. They are usually built of wood, have corrugated tin roofs, are high off the ground, and have "tropical partitions" to permit the free passage of air. Furniture in the house of the average Guamanian is about the same as that found in other American homes. Some old-style houses have a kitchen or cooking area separate from the main house. Because of the tropical heat, most houses do not have glass windows. Hinged shutters and louvers are used to keep out the rain.

By 1950, five years after the end of World War II, approximately 60,000 persons resided in Guam. Although exact figures are difficult to determine, it would seem that the population consisted of about 23,000 Guamanians, 20,000 statesiders, and 15,000 to 17,000 Filipinos. The statesiders, as those from the United States are called, represent several groups. The principal group consists of members of the armed forces and their dependents. "Armed forces personnel and their families," wrote Stevens, "live completely apart from the civilian community. They shop in service

10

stores and commissaries, swim at service beaches, attend service-operated clubs and circulate socially within their own group. Their attitude toward Guam is completely different from that of all others, and they are little concerned with the civil affairs of the island. Their children attend schools of the local system, both public and private, but transportation to and from schools is provided by the services. Every effort is expended toward complete segregation and independence, and although the civilian and military components of the population are not antagonistic toward one another, there is a mutual desire to deal at arm's length. Armed forces personnel almost without exception live on military reservations."[12] Other statesiders consist of thousands of construction workers and civil service personnel. They were recruited from the United States and are employed on armed forces construction projects.

Filipinos comprise one of the largest foreign groups in the island's population. They are, in the main, contract laborers employed by the armed forces and by civilian employers as well. Most of their earnings are spent in Guam. Thus they contribute very materially to the island's economic well-being. Although, in theory, they are not permitted to compete with Guamanian business establishments, in certain fields they have done so nevertheless. Moreover, ever-increasing numbers of them are marrying Guamanian women and are establishing families.

At the present time, Guam is struggling to rebuild itself from the ruins and devastation of war. Like the phoenix of the Egyptians, it is attempting to rise in youthful freshness from its own ashes. The combined efforts of all its people must surely result in success.

The population of Guam, according to the 1960 census, was 67,044. This figure included Guamanian residents, aliens, and military personnel. The following tables present population statistics for Guam from 1901 to 1960.[13]

## ISLAND-WIDE CENSUS AS OF JANUARY 1960
(Excluding transients residing in military reservations)

| MUNICIPALITY OR DISTRICT | GUAMANIANS | | OTHERS | | TOTAL | | TOTAL PERSONS |
|---|---|---|---|---|---|---|---|
| | Male | Female | Male | Female | Male | Female | |
| Agana | 421 | 495 | 331 | 107 | 752 | 602 | 1,354 |
| Agana Heights | 966 | 1,061 | 319 | 248 | 1,285 | 1,309 | 2,594 |
| Agat | 1,375 | 1,414 | 130 | 82 | 1,505 | 1,496 | 3,001 |
| Asan | 653 | 733 | 54 | 49 | 707 | 782 | 1,489 |
| Barrigada | 1,704 | 1,738 | 160 | 134 | 1,864 | 1,872 | 3,736 |
| Chalan Pago-Ordot | 765 | 843 | 69 | 33 | 834 | 876 | 1,710 |
| Dededo | 1,077 | 1,141 | 127 | 55 | 1,204 | 1,196 | 2,400 |
| Inarajan | 836 | 886 | 25 | 17 | 861 | 903 | 1,764 |
| Mangilao | 589 | 673 | 80 | 64 | 669 | 737 | 1,406 |
| Merizo | 682 | 636 | 25 | 10 | 707 | 646 | 1,353 |
| Mongmong-Toto | 810 | 854 | 179 | 160 | 989 | 1,014 | 2,003 |
| Piti | 480 | 497 | 99 | 93 | 579 | 590 | 1,169 |
| Santa Rita | 843 | 888 | 43 | 17 | 886 | 905 | 1,791 |
| Sinajana | 2,114 | 2,265 | 233 | 168 | 2,377 | 2,433 | 4,810 |
| Talofofo | 677 | 617 | 32 | 31 | 709 | 648 | 1,357 |
| Tamuning | 1,191 | 971 | 1,346 | 665 | 2,537 | 1,636 | 4,173 |
| Umatac | 367 | 360 | 1 | 0 | 368 | 360 | 728 |
| Yigo | 462 | 450 | 35 | 13 | 497 | 463 | 960 |
| Yona | 894 | 983 | 136 | 132 | 1,030 | 1,115 | 2,145 |
| TOTAL | 16,936 | 17,505 | 3,424 | 2,078 | 20,360 | 19,583 | 39,943 |

## AREA AND POPULATION OF GUAM BY ELECTION DISTRICTS : 1960

| ELECTION DISTRICT | LAND AREA IN SQUARE MILES | POPULATION | |
|---|---|---|---|
| | | Total | Per square mile |
| Guam | 209 | 67,044 | 321 |
| Agana | 1 | 1,642 | 1,642 |
| Agana Heights | 1 | 3,210 | 3,210 |
| Agat | 11 | 3,107 | 282 |
| Asan | 6 | 3,053 | 509 |
| Barrigada | 9 | 5,430 | 603 |
| Chalan Pago and Ordot | 6 | 1,835 | 306 |
| Dededo | 30 | 5,126 | 171 |

12

| | | | |
|---|---|---|---|
| Inarajan | 19 | 1,730 | 91 |
| Mangilao | 10 | 1,965 | 197 |
| Merizo* | 6 | 1,398 | 233 |
| Mongmong, Toto, Maite | 2 | 3,015 | 1,508 |
| Piti | 7 | 1,467 | 210 |
| Santa Rita | 16 | 12,126 | 758 |
| Sinajana | 1 | 3,862 | 3,862 |
| Talofofo | 17 | 1,352 | 80 |
| Tamuning | 6 | 5,944 | 991 |
| Umatac | 6 | 744 | 124 |
| Yigo | 35 | 7,682 | 219 |
| Yona | 20 | 2,356 | 118 |

* Includes Cocos Island.

## POPULATION OF CITIES AND VILLAGES IN GUAM:
### 1960 AND 1950
Minus sign ( − ) denotes decrease

| CITY OR VILLAGE | ELECTION DISTRICT | 1960 | 1950 | INCREASE 1950 to 1960 Number | Percent |
|---|---|---|---|---|---|
| Agana city | Agana | 1,642 | 1,330 | 312 | 23.5 |
| Agana Heights village | Agana Heights | 3,210 | 858 | 2,352 | 274.1 |
| Asan village | Asan | 543 | 620 | −77 | −12.4 |
| Barrigada village | Barrigada | 1,729 | 1,666 | 63 | 3.8 |
| Dededo village | Dededo | 2,247 | 997 | 1,250 | 125.4 |
| Inarajan village | Inarajan | 761 | 812 | −51 | −6.3 |
| Merizo village | Merizo | 508 | 511 | −3 | −0.6 |
| Mongmong village | Mongmong, Toto, Maite | 2,285 | 663 | 1,622 | 244.6 |
| New Agat city* | Agat | 2,596 | 1,340 | 1,256 | 93.7 |
| Santa Rita village | Santa Rita | 1,630 | 1,410 | 220 | 15.6 |
| Sinajana village | Sinajana | 2,861 | 3,069 | −208 | −6.8 |
| Talofofo village | Talofofo | 947 | 618 | 329 | 53.2 |
| Tamuning village | Tamuning | 5,380 | 1,053 | 4,327 | 410.9 |
| Toto village | Mongmong, Toto, Maite | 730 | 526 | 204 | 38.8 |
| Umatac village | Umatac | 393 | 387 | 6 | 1.6 |
| Yona village | Yona | 1,105 | 997 | 108 | 10.8 |

* New Agat city returned as Agat village in 1950.

## POPULATION OF GUAM, 1901 TO 1960
## AGANA CITY, 1920 TO 1960

| GUAM | | AGANA CITY | |
|---|---|---|---|
| Census Date | Population | Census Date | Population |
| 1960 (Apr. 1) | 67,044 | 1960 | 1,642 |
| 1950 (Apr. 1) | 59,498 | 1950 | 1,330 |
| 1940 (Apr. 1) | 22,290* | 1940 | 10,004 |
| 1930 (Apr. 1) | 18,509** | 1930 | 8,690 |
| 1920 (Jan. 1) | 13,275*** | 1920 | 7,432 |
| 1910 | 11,806 | | |
| 1901 | 9,676 | | |

\* Includes 213 persons on United States naval vessels in Apra Harbor.

\*\* Includes 1,118 persons on United States naval reservations and on United States naval vessels stationed at Guam.

\*\*\* Includes native men enlisted in United States Navy but excludes United States naval station personnel (319).

Statistics in these tables are compiled from *United States Census of Population, 1960,* U.S. Department of Commerce, Bureau of the Census.

## THE ANCIENT CHAMORROS

Little is known about the origin of the ancient Chamorros, remote ancestors of the present-day Guamanians. Limited information that is available seems to indicate that they were a Malaysian people who came originally from southeast Asia. It is believed that they might have been expert seamen who migrated slowly, in canoes, from Asia to the Philippines and the western Carolines. From there, they moved eastward to Guam and the Marianas.[14] Despite the lack of definite information, it appears that the first settlements in Guam resulted from mass migrations that occurred earlier in both Europe and Asia.

At the close of the last glacial period, the land area of southeast Asia was much larger than it is now. The continent of Asia and the islands of the present-day Indonesian Republic were, it is believed, joined together. Thus a "land bridge" extended almost to Australia. Across this bridge, Negroid peoples are believed to have moved into Indonesia, Australia, and the islands of Mela-

14

nesia. It seems rather certain that the Negroid peoples entered this region at a very early time. Moreover, they were well settled there long before large-scale migrations into Polynesia and Micronesia began.

During neolithic times, believed by some authorities to extend from 20,000 to 12,000 B.C., Caucasoids began mass migrations from the region of the Caspian Sea. They spread out in all directions. Some moved up the Danube valley to central and western Europe. Others migrated to Syria, Palestine, Egypt, and north Africa. Still others moved eastward to Afghanistan, India, China, and Japan. Those who settled in the west were the forerunners of the present-day Europeans. Those who moved eastward mixed with the Negroids and Mongoloids of Asia. The Mongoloids had originated in northeast Asia, in the region of Outer Monogolia. At an unknown time they had moved southward and spread over China. The mixing that occurred among some of the people of the yellow, white, and black races in Asia produced a new Mongoloid-Caucasoid-Negroid type. These people established an agricultural civilization that was centered primarily in southeast Asia. Later, other Mongoloids, "who had also learned about agriculture, moved southward and invaded what is now Burma, Siam and Indo-China. This movement reached out into the islands so that by the time of Christ, Sumatra, Java, Bali, Borneo, and the Philippines, to name but a few, had become populated by an essentially Mongoloid people. Others, having mixed with the Australoid, or Ainu-like, aborigines of these islands, continued on out to the Pacific and sired the Micronesians and Polynesians."[15]

Authorities on the subject are not certain why these people left their established homes and moved out into the Pacific islands. However, they might have done so for several reasons, one of the most plausible being that overpopulation in their homelands forced them to move to other areas in search of food. Still another is that, while they were searching for food, some of their canoes were driven out to the islands by great storms. Whatever their reasons for doing so, these great seafaring people established island homes throughout the entire Pacific region. Malayo-Polynesian-speaking people even sailed as far as Easter Island, only about 2,000 miles from the coast of South America. Some of these people, according to Linton, "used great double canoes, sometimes as much as 150 feet long, made of planks sewed together with coconut fiber. The space between the two hulls was decked over and bore a small house. There were either one or two masts with sails of pandanus matting. They are probably to be credited with the introduction of the lateen sail, which made it possible for them to run closer to the wind than the best European square-rigged ship.

"Their stores were baked bread-fruit paste, sweet potatoes, and coconuts. They caught the bonito and other fish of the open sea. Water was carried in gourds and wooden vessels, but they relied mostly upon rain. They steered by the stars and by the long Pacific swell, and were experts at holding a course. Whole tribes sometimes set out in search of new homes, taking with them their gods and the plants and animals which would be needed to found a colony. On such expeditions the fleet spread out into a great crescent with four or five mile intervals between the canoes, thus sweeping a wide expanse of sea. A sharp lookout was kept, and particular attention was paid to the flight of birds. Those which were known to sleep on land were sometimes caught, fed and released, the voyagers following the direction of their homeward flight. If the first land encountered by the fleet was undesirable, perhaps a barren atoll, they would rest for a time and replenish their food supplies and then put out to sea once more."[16]

The greatest period of migration seems to have begun around 2,000 B.C. and to have ended by A.D. 500. It would seem that the first settlers in the Pacific islands were Polynesians. They probably entered the region from Melanesia and settled in Samoa, Tonga, and the Cook, Austral, Society, and Tuamotu groups. It seems fairly certain, however, that they did not reach Hawaii. These people were followed by a second Mongoloid-Negroid type who were probably the first to settle in the Marquesas and Hawaii.

The third race to settle in the islands was probably of Caucasic stock. It appears that they were proto-Malays who came from the fringes of southeast Asia. They were brown-skinned and strongly built. Moreover, they were straight-eyed and had thick black hair. In general, they had features much like Europeans. After entering the Pacific between New Guinea and the southern Philippines, they apparently split into two streams. One stream moved southward through the islands near New Guinea. The other continued eastward and settled throughout Micronesia. It would seem that the ancient Chamorros, remote ancestors of the present-day Guamanians, came from among these people.

The ancient Chamorros, according to early reports, were tall, robust, well built, and apparently of great strength.[17] The women, too, were tall, "good looking and delicately formed, and lighter-complexioned than the men; and wear their hair, which is exceedingly black, loose and hanging quite down to the ground."[18] García, in an early description of the Chamorros, wrote: "The Marianos are in color a somewhat lighter shade than the Filipinos, larger in stature, more corpulent and robust than Europeans, pleasant and with agreeable faces. They are so fat they appear swollen. They remain in good health to an advanced age and it is very normal to live ninety or one hundred years."[19]

Early reports stress the physical strength and the athletic prowess of the Chamorros. According to Mendoza, the natives were light-complexioned people like Europeans, "although in their bodies they do not resemble the latter for they are as large as giants, and of such great strength, that it has actually happened that one of them, while standing on the ground, has laid hold of two Spaniards of good stature, seizing each of them by one foot with his hands, and lifting them thus as easily as if they were children."[20] They were also expert swimmers who spent much of every day in the water. A Spanish sailor, stationed with sword in hand to guard one of the early ships that anchored in Umatac Bay, had occasion to learn at first hand of the aquatic skill of the Chamorros when "one of the natives plunged under the water and swam to where he was, quite unconscious of anything of the sort, and without his seeing it, snatched the sword from his hand and swam back with it. At the cry of the sailor, proclaiming the trick practiced on him by the islander, several soldiers with their

17

arquebuses were stationed to shoot the native when he should emerge from the water. The islander, on seeing this, emerged from the water, holding up his hands and making signs that he had nothing in them. For this reason those who were on the point of shooting him refrained. After a few moments of rest, the native dived once more, and swam under water, until out of range of the arquebuses, where, assured of safety, he took the sword from between his legs where he had hidden it, and commenced to make passes with it, jeering the while at our men whom he had deceived so easily."[21] They were such excellent swimmers that they could catch fish with their bare hands. Their strength and agility were further revealed by the skill with which they handled their swift sailing canoes and by the manner in which they hurled their slingstones, which were thrown with such force that they were frequently buried in the trunks of trees.

No full-blooded natives of the pre-Spanish type are to be found in Guam today. There are, however, many islanders possessing some physical characteristics resembling those of the ancient Chamorros.

The temperament of the ancient Chamorros, according to early accounts, may be described as being compounded of playful friendliness mixed with stubborn persistence and violence. A Franciscan missionary who, in 1596, lived in the Marianas and had an opportunity to observe the early Chamorros at first hand, related that they were "a tractable and kindly people" who "regaled him and his companion and showed them much respect."[22] Although they could be serious when the occasion demanded, they were in general a happy, fun-loving people, fond of festivities, dancing, singing storytelling, and contests of strength and skill. They also took great delight in jokes, playing tricks, mockery, and ridicule. While they appeared, at first glance, to be simple, humble people, they were in reality "inordinately vain, considering themselves to be men of the greatest genius and wisdom in the world, in comparison with whom all other nations were contemptible."[23]

The ancient Chamorros, it would seem, were, in their competitive playfulness, inclined to take advantage of early visitors to

Guam. As a result, the label of *ladrones* (thieves) was frequently applied to them. Padre García, however, felt "called upon to say that although they have been called ladrones, on account of the pilfering of a few pieces of iron from our ships, they do not deserve the name, for though they leave open their houses it is very seldom that anything is missed."

Accounts of the early missionaries relate that the Chamorros were ingenious and quick to learn anything to which they applied themselves. The missionaries were especially impressed by the remarkable intelligence shown by the children in learning the Christian doctrine.

When angered, the ancient Chamorros were inclined to become violent and vengeful. This was amply demonstrated by their prolonged resistance to the Spaniards. According to García:

> Their nature and disposition, although at first appearing simple and bare of deceit as of clothing, gained the praise of the fathers of the Company, and they trusted the generosity and hospitality that were offered. After they experienced more of this, however, they knew them to be deceitful and traitorous. They will cover with pleasant words and appearances any feeling of injury for perhaps two years, until they find an opportunity for vengeance.[24]

According to all accounts, men among the ancient Chamorros wore no clothing whatsoever, not even a breech clout. Some women, however, wore "a cord tied about the waist, and to the cord they hang some grass or leaves from the trees." Others wore little aprons or "mats made from palm leaves."[25] While fishing, the men sometimes wore small conical hats and eyeshades of pandanus leaves, and occasionally they protected their feet with sandals of palm leaf.[26]

On festive occasions the women wore wreaths of flowers in their hair. They also wore necklaces of tortoise shell or red spondylus shells, which they prized very highly. To complete their gala attire, they sometimes encircled their waists with strands of small coconuts suspended from pandanus belts and nicely fitted over skirts of grass or leaves. The only vanity of some men, on the other hand, was an elaborate walking stick. According to García, "the un-

19

married men, for some reason of their own, were accustomed to carry walking sticks which they called *tunas*, which were curiously carved and colored with the root of a plant called *mangu*, at the head of which they affixed three streamers half a yard in length made from the soft bark of trees, with heavy threads as a trimmings."[27]

The hair of the ancient Chamorros was their crowning glory. Accounts of the Magellan and Legazpi expeditions state that both men and women wore their hair long and loose, but sometimes they gathered it up behind the head and even "made up and tied with a knot on the crown and some with two knots." After Father Sanvitores arrived in Guam, he wrote that the men did not wear their hair long but shaved their heads, leaving only a small topknot on the crown. "The women, however, wore it very long and bleached white, apparently with the lime used in other parts of Oceania."[28]

Rank and class consciousness were important factors in the lives of the ancient Chamorros. The highest ranking nobles or chiefs among them were called *chamorri*. In discussing the relationships that existed between the mass of the Chamorros and their leaders, it was said: "Their barbarity is not in keeping with the great esteem they have for their nobility and their observation and discretion of lineage—high, low, and middle class. . . . For nothing in the world would one of their chiefs. . .marry the daughter of a plebeian, even if she were very rich and he very poor. Formerly parents killed sons who married daughters of low-class families."[29]

The highest class in the native society was called *matua*. They had the most privileges, were the principal landowners, and controlled most of the wealth of the island. Occupations having the highest prestige value were reserved for them exclusively. They were the warriors, sailors, fishermen, professional canoe builders, and traders. When a member of the lowest class passed a *matua*, he had to do so in a crouching position with head lowered and eyes averted. Lower class people, furthermore, could never eat or drink in the houses of the *matua* or even come too close to them. If they wished to talk to them they had to do so in a squatting

20

position and always from a distance.[30] The nobles of highest rank lived in Agana, and it was there, especially, that rules of behavior were rigidly enforced. Because of their high rank and power, the nobles of Agana were feared and respected by the people of the entire island.

The middle class consisted of a lesser nobility called *atchaot*. They were usually members of the family or near relatives of the *matua*. Their social privileges were very much the same as those of members of the highest class, and they were permitted to assist the *matua* in their occupations of honor.

The *manachang*, or members of the lowest class, lived almost as slaves. They were set apart from the rest of the society, and their lives were completely governed by restrictions and tabus. They were not allowed to become warriors, sailors, or canoe builders, and their fishing was restricted to the rivers, where they could only catch eels with wooden-tipped spears. Furthermore, they could never, regardless of skill or ability, rise out of their class. According to Thompson, available evidence suggests that "the lowest class were descendants of the aborigines of the Marianas, reduced to a depressed caste by immigrant maritime warriors, who established themselves in prehistoric times in a position of dominance. Their short stature, in contrast to that of the nobles, may be indicative of malnutrition due to a low standard of living rather than to a marked difference in racial type."[31]

The Chamorros of pre-Spanish times were organized into matrilineal clans—that is, kinship groups in which descent was reckoned through the female line. Under this system the women exercised great influence in all matters related to family life, property, and inheritance. Moreover, the children took the surnames of their mothers rather than of their fathers. Each clan was composed of several families, with the family usually consisting of a married couple, their children, and other near relatives. The families that made up the clan were bound together by strong social, economic, and ceremonial ties and obligations.

At the time of the discovery of Guam, the Chamorro clans were grouped in villages that were located either on the beach near a

21

small bay, on the banks of a river for the sake of a constant supply of fresh water, or on a high and rugged hill for the sake of security from attack. When Father Sanvitores established his mission in Guam, he stated that the natives along the coast lived in villages of 50 to 150 huts. In the interior they lived in hamlets of 6 to 20 huts. He estimated that there were 180 such local groups in Guam at that time.

Although the early Chamorros had no king or defined code of laws, they did have a simple form of district government. The island was divided into districts composed of one or more neighboring villages. In each district the nobles, both men and women, formed a kind of council or assembly. The highest-ranking male, namely the oldest noble, was the leader. He was called *magat-lahe*, and his wife was called *maga-haga*.\* The people in one district were loyal to their leader and to their district. Moreover, they were intensely jealous and suspicious of people who lived in other districts. As a result the districts were frequently engaged in warfare.

The early Chamorros engaged in a primitive sort of warfare in which rival villages or districts tested their strength against one another. An imagined insult or the slightest injury was sufficient cause for war. A village would prepare for war with another village with great bustle and an exaggerated show of bravado. After engaging in battle, however, they very soon made peace. One side considered itself defeated when one or two of its men were killed. In a description of native warfare, it was said:

> They are barbarous warriors, quick to anger and easily calmed, laggards in fighting, quick to flee. One village rises against another with a big hurrah, but without a leader, without order and without discipline. They are customarily on a campaign several days without actually meeting in battle, each group observing the movements of the other, and when they arrive at the moment of battle, peace is quickly adjusted, for one side, having lost two or three warriors, gives up the fight and sends messengers to the enemy bearing the shell of a turtle as a sign of submission. The winners celebrate the victory with satirical songs in which they praise themselves and make fun of the losers.

\* *Magat-lahe* is translated as first-born son and *maga-haga* as first-born daughter. The island's governor is still referred to today as *magat-lahe* in the vernacular.

22

Their arms are stones and lances with points of human bones in place of metal. These are made of three or four sharp tines which, puncturing the flesh, break off, causing certain death.

They use these weapons from boyhood and are very skillful in handling them. . . . They do not use bow and arrow, nor sword. They have only a kind of cutlass and some knives obtained from our ships in exchange for fruits. They have never used buckler or other means of defense, depending only on their quick movements to escape the blows of an adversary.[32]

Spears and slings were the principal weapons used by the Chamorros. The slingstones were of oval shape, fashioned out of stones or made of baked clay. According to Thompson, "slingstones have been found in caches of 12 to 40 stones of uniform size, shape, color, material, and workmanship, buried to a depth of 3 feet. This suggests that they were made by specific groups of warriors and stored for ammunition."[33]

In their warfare the Chamorros relied on strategy and hit-and-run tactics. To gain an advantage in battle, they sometimes resorted to fire, burning the grass and trees around the positions of their enemies and throwing burning lances upon the thatched roofs of their buildings. They also used hidden obstacles, thorns, and ambuscades and, if necessary, even dug trenches. Although their battles were usually brief engagements, the methods of fighting employed by the early Chamorros indicate that they were skillful and ingenious warriors.

Little is known of the religion of the ancient Chamorros. According to early accounts, however, it can be seen that, from the time of their arrival in the Marianas, the Spaniards were interested in learning about the religious practices of the natives. In 1586 Mendoza reported that "these islands are extremely healthful and fertile, and will be very easy to win to the faith of Christ. . . . Their rites and ceremonies are not known yet, because no one understands their speech. . . . It is understood, from some signs that we saw them make, that they are all pagans and that they worship idols and the devil, to whom they sacrifice the booty obtained from their neighbors in war."[34]

The ancient Chamorro religion had no organized priesthood, no temples, and no defined creed. It seemed, primarily, to be a religion of myths, superstitions, and ancestor worship. The report of the Loiasa expedition states that they worshipped the bones of their ancestors. These they carefully kept in their houses, anointed with coconut oil. According to Sanvitores, the Chamorros worshipped the spirits of the dead, called *aniti*. They believed that the *aniti* were sacred and powerful spirits who could help them. If angered, however, they could do a great deal of harm. As a result, the spirits and relics of the dead, especially of one's ancestors, were feared and venerated.

While the ancient Chamorro religion had no organized priesthood, there was, nevertheless, a class of professional sorcerers called *makahna*. The people believed that the *makahna* had the power to communicate with the spirits of the dead. They also believed that they could cause sickness and death, could produce rain, and bring good luck in fishing. Of the *makahna*, one account says: "There are *macanas* [sic] who promise health, good fishing and smiilar benefits by means of invoking the dead whose skulls they keep in their houses with no altar, niche, or adornment except a basket in which they are left about the house, forgotten until the time comes when they want to ask some favor of the *aniti*."[35]

In all probability the *makahna* practiced some form of black magic. This was done by using their enemy's "dirt," such as his spittle, a bit of his hair, nails, refuse of his food, or other objects closely connected with him. Because of their superstitious fear of the *makahna*, the Chamorros took care to spit when no one was looking and they did not spit near the house of another.

A later class of sorcerer, known as *kakahna*, survived into recent times. It was believed that they possessed powers of causing and curing sickness. Such powers could be passed on to their children. Another group, called *suruhana*, were herb doctors. Thompson says: "Although *suruhana* are not mentioned in the early reports, it is probable that they existed in olden times. They treated illness with herbs, whereas the *kakahna* apparently used supernatural means."[36]

Belief in the *taotaomona*, men of superhuman strength, appears to have sprung up after the Spaniards settled in Guam.

The ancient Chamorros conducted elaborate burial ceremonies for their dead. Funerals were usually occasions for demonstrations of intense grief. They were accompanied by prolonged weeping, fasting, and the clattering of shells and trumpets.

> Their demonstrations of grief at funerals are very singular, many tears, fasting and a great clattering of shells. Weeping customarily continues for six or eight days, according to their affections or obligations toward the departed. They spend their time singing lugubrious songs, giving parties around the catafalque on which they have placed the defunct, adorned with flowers, palms, shells and other things they consider suitable.
>
> The mother of the dead man cuts off a lock of his hair and keeps it as a memento, and counts the days after his death by tying a knot each night in a cord which she wears around her neck.[37]

When a chief or woman of high rank died, the demonstrations of grief were much greater. Then, in addition to the usual demonstration, they would decorate the streets with garlands of palms and would build arches and other funeral structures as signs of mourning. At the same time they would destroy coconut trees, burn houses, and break up their boats and hang the torn sails in front of their houses as a sign of grief. For many days and nights, friends of the deceased would join in the chanting of songs and prayers, called *tinaitai*, exclaiming with many tears that henceforth life would not be worth living, since he who was the life of all, their sun, their moon, and their stars, was no longer with them.

Three methods of burial were used, namely burial in *latte* or house sites, in caves, and in earthenware urns. At times, spearheads, fishhooks, axes, and other implements were buried with or near the body. Although there is no evidence to indicate that such was the case, perhaps the implements were added in order that the deceased might have them for use in his paradise in the underworld, which, the ancient Chamarros believed, was overflowing with bananas, coconuts, sugar cane, and other fruits of the earth.

## ARTS AND CRAFTS

The skill with which the ancient Chamorros built houses and canoes indicates that they were expert craftsmen. Many of the early visitors to Guam were so impressed by the craftsmanship of the Chamorros that they wrote lengthy accounts in their journals about the skill of the natives. Concerning their houses, it was said: "The houses are the cleanest that have yet been found among Indios; built of coconut and maria wood with roofs of coconut leaves curiously woven. They have four rooms, with doors or curtains of the same matting. One serves as a sleeping room, another for storing goods, one as kitchen, and the fourth is large enough in which to build and store boats."[38]

In one of the accounts of the Legazpi expedition it was said that some houses, supported on large stone pillars, served as sleeping quarters, while others, built on the ground, were used for cooking and other work. Besides these there were large buildings that served as storehouses for an entire village. In such buildings, boats, canoes, and community property were kept. These larger buildings, in most cases, were built on strong pillars made of either stone or masonry. Some of these pillars, arranged in double rows, are still to be found on the island. They are called *latte* or *casas de los antiguos* by present-day Guamanians, who tend to regard them with fear. With regard to the construction of Chamorro houses, Thompson has written:

> ... There were evidently at least two types of houses built on stone pillars in the Marianas, namely pile houses and canoe sheds.... Concerning the pile houses, we know that the roofs were thatched. The floors were raised above the ground and the floor space was divided into compartments which probably served as sleeping rooms, kitchens, storage, carpentry shops, etc. The walls of some houses at least had openings which served as windows. The ground under the houses was used for burials.... We may safely assume that at least some of the pile houses served as men's clubs.... Moreover, it is probable that canoe sheds in the Marianas resembled sheds built for housing war canoes in the Pelews [Palau Islands] except that the thatched roof was supported by capped stone uprights instead of wooden posts.[39]

The small outrigger canoes of the Chamorros were the admiration of all the early navigators. Indeed, more was written in their journals about the canoes of the natives than on any other aspect of Chamorro culture. Pigafetta, one of the first Europeans to describe the Chamorros and their canoes, said of them:

> Their amusement, men and women, is to plough the seas with those small boats of theirs. Those boats resemble *fucelere*, but are narrower, and some are black, some white and others red. At the side opposite the sail, they have a large piece of wood pointed at the top, with poles laid across it and resting on the water, in order that the boats may sail more safely. The sail is made from palm leaves sewn together and is shaped line a lateen sail. For rudders they use a certain blade resembling a hearth shovel which has a piece of wood at the end. They can change stern and bow at will, and those boats resemble the dolphins which leap in the water from wave to wave.[40]

Because of the great speed attained by these small canoes, early writers called them "flying praos."

The Chamorros also used a type of canoe that was much larger than the prao. These large canoes, sometimes 30 to 40 feet in length, were used for commerce, ceremonial occasions, and warfare. The building of large sailing canoes was a highly prized privilege of the *matua*, who prided themselves on their skill at carpentry. Sometimes they were assisted in the work by members of the middle class, but members of the lowest class were forbidden to engage in such work. The privilege of steering such canoes was held exclusively by the chiefly class and was jealously guarded by them.

The early Chamorros, in spite of the lack of metal, were highly skilled as stoneworkers and masons. This is amply demonstrated by the skill with which they made stone implements, such as axes, chisels, knives, flint scrapers and spearheads, hammers, mortars and pestles, and slingstones. Examples of their most important stonework, however, are probably revealed in the stone and masonry pillars of the numerous *latte* sites still to be found in various parts of Guam. Such pillars, called *halege*, were often times uprights of carefully cut slabs of coral limestone. These were set securely in the ground and capped by rough cuplike heads of coral, called *tasa*. Such pillars were sometimes mass-produced at a distance from the sites where they were to be used. Thompson has said that "on the island of Rota in 1925, Hornbostel[41] discovered a quarry at As Nieves where uprights and caps for *latte* had been partially cut out of solid limestone. Here were also found nine uprights and caps completely finished and ready to be moved. Hornbostel assumed that the limestone for each unit had been fired in order to convert it into lime, then scraped out with a stone adz until the unit was isolated and could be moved."[42]

Trade between the various islands of the Marianas, and with the Carolines as well, was carried on regularly by the ancient Chamorros. To make the exchange of goods or services easier, several types of shell "money" were used. Concerning the manufacture and use of such money, Chamisso, noting that "we have seen ourselves the objects we describe," wrote:

> On a coarse cord of cocoa-bast are strung pieces of tortoise shell, of the form of a button, but as thin as paper, pressed to each other, and extremely polished by rubbing. The whole forms a pliable roll or cylinder about the thickness of a finger and several feet in length.
>
> These cords are said to have been current as a means of commercial intercourse, and but a very few chiefs had the right to manufacture and issue them.
>
> Plates of tortoise shell, of the large sea turtle, are differently pierced in the middle with a large hole, and on the broad thin edge with several smaller holes, or they have only one hole in the middle.
>
> Whoever, probably in swimming, had killed a turtle (in reality a very hazardous adventure), brought a plate of the mail to the chief, who, according to the circumstances of the deed and the assistance received in performing it, bored holes in it; the fewer of them, the greater was the value. Such trophies then gave the owner a certain right to exchange them, according to established customs, for other property, and passed in a certain manner as means of commerce and signs of value.[43]

Shell money and iron were the principal items of barter used by the Chamorros in their trade relations with the Carolinians. Such trade was carried on both before and after the discovery of Guam by Europeans. After the Spanish conquest of the Marianas, the Carolinians discontinued the trade. It was not renewed until 1788, when a large group of them sailed to Guam to trade for iron. In exchange for iron, they gave the Chamorros canoes, woven cloth, pots, wooden boxes, shells, and other articles. Moreover, the men of Yap traded for stone as well, which, according to Thompson, "they made into perforated disks 12 inches in diameter, used as money in Yap."[44]

The early Chamorros made most of their money from tortoise shell. These disks were usually strung together and worn around the neck. Thompson has written a description of two types of shell-disk necklaces. They were "(1) the *guini*, a string of thin, regular, perforated disks, in width slightly less than the little finger and in length such that it hung down to the navel, after having passed twice around the neck; and (2) the *lukao-hugua*, a string of thin, regular, perforated disks about the width of a thumb and the length such that, when hung around the neck, it reached the hip."[45]

Another type of shell money was called *guineha fumaguon*. It was a chest ornament worn by men, and it had the highest value of any shell object used as money by the ancient Chamorros.

At the time of the discovery of Guam, Pigafetta wrote that some Chamorro women wore little aprons that consisted of "a narrow strip of bark as thin as paper, which grows between the tree and the bark of the palm."[46] This would seem to indicate that the early Chamorros were familiar with the process for making tapa cloth. Safford, however, states that the Chamorros were not tapa makers like the Polynesians. Since the paper mulberry did not grow in the Marianas, and since the early Chamorros were unfamiliar with the loom, it is quite likely that their weaving was limited to the plaiting of mats, sails, hats, baskets, and other articles from pandanus leaves. According to Thompson, the Chamorros were familiar with "both the technique of diagonal plaiting and that of right-angled plaiting, and they produced a variety of shapes, especially in basketry."[47]

Until recent times it was generally believed that the ancient Chamorros were not pottery makers. Later evidence, however, reveals not only that they made pottery but also that their ware was varied in terms of color, surface finish, shape, and design. Such variety seems to indicate that the early Chamorros might have possessed a highly developed artistic sense. Because evidence that the Chamorros knew how to use the potter's wheel is lacking, it is generally believed that their pottery was made by hand. Regardless of process, however, it is now known that the ancient Chamorros used baked clay for making cooking pots, water jars, burial urns, and slingstones.[48]

SUMMARY: Guam is America's westernmost outpost. Its strategic location makes it an unusually important base for defensive military activities in the Far East. Since World War II, especially, the island's social, economic, and political life has undergone many changes. Such changes have hastened the development of American attitudes and ideals. In matters of speech, dress, and manner of living the Guamanian people have become pretty much like their fellow Americans on the mainland.

In terms of ancestral background, present-day Guamanians represent many racial strains. They are so different from their remote ancestors, the ancient Chamorros, that almost no relationship now exists. The ancient Chamorros, strongly built proto-Malays, had established settlements in the Marianas by at least 1500 B.C. They were expert seamen and skilled craftsmen. In addition to being skillful house and canoe builders, they were also familiar with the arts of weaving and pottery making. Moreover, they had a clan and district government supported and reinforced by a rigid class system. For unknown thousands of years they lived on their islands in almost complete isolation from the rest of the world. Before the Spaniards arrived in the Marianas, the Chamorros cultivated their crops, swam and fished in the ocean, developed their arts and crafts and, in spite of their intermittent warfare, lived out their lives in comparative security and peace. Meanwhile, in Europe and Asia, events were occurring that would eventually bring about important changes in their way of life. In the next chapter some of the events and movements that led to the discovery and control of Guam by Europeans will be discussed.

## NOTES

1.   Earl S. Pomeroy, *Pacific Outpost* (Stanford University Press, Stanford, California, 1951), p. 53.

2.   L. M. Cox, *The Island of Guam* (U.S. Navy Department, Washington, 1926), p. 2.

3.   Erik K. Reed, *General Report on Archeology and History of Guam* (National Park Service, U.S. Department of the Interior, Washington, 1952), p. 3.

4.   William Edwin Safford, "Our Smallest Possession: Guam," *National Geographic*, Vol. XVI, No. 5 (National Geographic Society, Washington, 1905), p. 233.

5.   Preston E. Cloud, Jr., *Reconnaissance Geology of Guam and Problems of Water Supply and Fuel Storage* (prepared by Military Geology Branch, U.S. Geological Survey, for Intelligence Division, General Headquarters, Far East Command, 1951), p. 31.

6.   Reed, *op. cit.*, p. 11.

7.   William Edwin Safford, *The Useful Plants of the Island of Guam, with an Introductory Account of the Physical Features and Natural History of the Island, of the Character and History of Its People, and of Their Agriculture* (contributions from the U.S. National Herbarium, U.S. National Museum, Washington, 1905), p. 81.

8.   Albert R. Mead, "The Giant Snails," *Atlantic Monthly*, Vol. 184, No. 2 (Boston, 1949), p. 39.

9.   Reed, *op. cit.*, p. 12.

10.   Safford, *The Useful Plants of the Island of Guam*, p. 119.

11.   Paul Carano, "The Old Order Changeth," *Guam Examiner* (October, 1951), p. 11.

12.   Russell L. Stevens, *Guam, U.S.A.: Birth of a Territory* (Tongg Publishing Co., Ltd., Honolulu, 1953), pp. 46–47.

13.   Statistics in the first three of these tables are compiled from *United States Census of Population, 1960* (Bureau of the Census, U.S. Department of Commerce); those in the fourth are from the island-wide census of January 1960 taken by the municipal commissioners.

14.   Laura Thompson, *Guam and Its People* (Princeton University Press, Princeton, New Jersey, 1947), p. 30.

15.   Carleton S. Coon, *The History of Man, from the First Human to Primitive Culture and Beyond* (Lowe and Brydone, Ltd., London, 1955), p. 199.

16.   Ralph Linton, *Ethnology of Polynesia and Micronesia* (Field Museum Press, Chicago, 1926), pp. 17–18.

17.   Emma Blair and James A. Robertson, eds., *The Philippine Islands,*

*1493–1898* (Arthur H. Clark Co., Cleveland 1903), Vol. II, p. 110.
18.  *Ibid.*, Vol. XXXIII, p. 97.
19.  Francisco García, *Vida y Maritirio del Venerable Padre Diego Luis de Sanvitores* (Madrid, 1683; translated by Margaret Higgins in the *Guam Recorder*, September 1936 to July 1939), April 1937, p. 21.
20.  Blair and Robertson, *op. cit.*, Vol. VI, p. 138.
21.  *Ibid.*, Vol. VI. pp. 141–42.
22.  *Ibid.*, Vol. X, p. 262.
23.  Safford, *The Useful Plants of the Island of Guam*, p. 104.
24.  García, *op. cit.*, April 1937, pp. 36, 38.
25.  Blair and Robertson, *op. cit.*, Vol. II, p. 110.
26.  Laura Thompson, "The Native Culture of the Marianas Islands," (Bulletin No. 185, Bernice P. Bishop Museum, Honolulu, 1945), p. 10.
27.  García, *op. cit.*, July 1938, p. 39.
28.  Thompson, "The Native Culture of the Marianas Islands," p. 10.
29.  García, *op. cit.*, April 1937, p. 36.
30.  Thompson, "The Native Culture of the Marianas Islands," p. 13.
31.  *ibid.*, p. 14.
32.  García, *op. cit.*, April 1937, p. 38.
33.  Laura Thompson, "Archeology of the Marianas Islands" (Bulletin No. 100, Bernice P. Bishop Museum, Honolulu, 1932), p. 49.
34.  Blair and Robertson, *op. cit.*, Vol. VI, pp. 140–41.
35.  García, *op. cit.*, May 1937, p. 19.
36.  Thompson, "The Native Culture of the Marianas Islands," p. 22.
37.  García, *op. cit.*, May 1937, pp. 19–20.
38.  *Ibid.*, April 1937, p. 21.
39.  Laura Thompson, "The Function of Latte in the Marianas," *Journal of the Polynesian Society*, Vol. XLIX (Polynesian Society, Wellington, 1940), pp. 447–65.
40.  Blair and Robertson, *op. cit.*, Vol. XXXIII, p. 99.
41.  Hans G. Hornbostel worked in the Marianas Islands for several years during the 1920's as a collector for the Bishop Museum. His wife Gertrude, a German born in the Marianas, was his assistant. Her knowledge of the Chamorro language was a great asset in their work.
42.  Thompson, "The Native Culture of the Marianas Islands," p. 38.
43.  Otto von Kotzebue, *A Voyage of Discovery into the South Sea and Bering's Straits* (translated by H. E. Lloyd; Longman, Hurst, Rees, Orme, and Brown; London, 1821), Vol. III, pp. 81–82.
44.  Thompson, "The Native Culture of the Marianas Islands," p. 41.
45.  *Ibid.*, p. 42.
46.  Blair and Robertson, *op. cit.*, Vol. XXXIII, p. 97.
47.  Thompson, "The Native Culture of the Marianas Islands," p. 40.
48.  *ibid.*, pp. 39–40.

## CHAPTER TWO

# DISCOVERY AND OBSCURITY

THE HISTORY of Guam has been determined largely by events and movements that occurred in other parts of the world. Although seemingly isolated, Guam was influenced by the Renaissance, the Crusades, and the discoveries of early European navigators. The Renaissance stirred men's minds. It prompted them to learn more about strange, faraway lands. Moreover, it recreated in them a desire to enjoy Oriental luxuries, about which they had first heard from Marco Polo and the Crusaders. These desires led to the world's greatest period of geographical discoveries and, incidentally, to the discovery of Guam in 1521.

After Magellan's visit to the Marianas Islands, Guam remained in relative obscurity for a century and a half. The peace of the island was broken only by the occasional visits of Spanish and Dutch explorers and English pirate ships. Among them were García Jofre de Loaisa, Miguel López de Legazpi, Sir Francis Drake, Thomas Cavendish, Oliver Van Noort, Joris Spilbergen and Jacob L'Heremite. Although most of the visitors remained only a few days, they profoundly affected the lives of the Chamorros. For the first time the natives were able to secure iron with which to make tools and weapons. Moreover, their brief contacts with the fair-skinned strangers enabled them to establish a basis for trade and commerce. Some of the visitors, they soon learned, could hurt them with new and frightening weapons. Without their knowledge the Guamanians' island became a minor pawn in a power struggle among faraway nations. Because of its location and its importance

33

as a source of fresh water and food, Guam became a regular stopping place for the Manila galleons. All of these influences and contacts with the outside world eventually made the island an integral part of the Spanish colonial system.

## EVENTS AND MOVEMENTS LEADING TO THE DISCOVERY OF GUAM

The Renaissance or "rebirth" is that period in European history which follows the period commonly called the Middle Ages. During the Middle Ages, the centuries between A.D. 500 and 1300, life in western Europe was marked by constant violence and strife. After the fall of the Roman Empire, barbarians from the north swept down over Europe, murdering and pillaging as they went. For centuries the countries of Europe knew no peace. Life was so difficult and dangerous that men had to join together in fortified villages, towns, and castles for their protection. Under such conditions, individual freedom and independence became impossible. Man feared his fellow men. Life was hard and drab with little joy in it. Education, for the common man, was difficult if not impossible to attain. War and religion became man's chief occupations. If a man did not like to fight, but one other life was open to him; that was in the church. It is no wonder, therefore, that many of the noblest and best turned their backs on fighting and bloodshed and entered the service of the church. Fortunately for western civilization, the church kept the light of knowledge burning through the long, dreary "Dark Ages" and thus, by about 1400, permitted Europe to begin a new way of life, a rebirth of learning, a Renaissance.

With the advent of the Renaissance, many changes took place in Europe. In political affairs, nationalism replaced feudalism. Nations, as we know them today, made their appearance. The invention of the printing press in 1456 made it possible to turn out more and better books at greatly reduced cost. Education and learning became more widespread, and man, because of his increased knowledge, desired to learn more about the community, the nation, and world in which he lived. Through the efforts of

34

crafts and guilds, commerce and industry flourished. Cities and nations became wealthy and powerful. The desire for even greater wealth and power brought about the development of international trade. This, perhaps more than any other single factor, paved the way for new and thrilling geographical discoveries. Among the first to pave the way to international trade, notably with the Indies, was Marco Polo.

MARCO POLO'S TRAVELS: Marco Polo was one of the first European travelers to return to Europe with tales about the fabulous riches of the East. Soon after Marco's birth in Venice in 1254, his father Niccolò Polo and his uncle Matteo set out on a trading expedition to the East. After a long journey across seas and deserts, they finally reached the court of the great Kublai Khan in Cathay, or China. The Great Khan was so pleased with the Venetian brothers, having seen no other Europeans before them,[1] that he sent them on a mission to the pope, asking the Holy Father to send missionaries who might convert his people to Christianity. Failing in their mission,* the Polo brothers, taking seventeen-year-old Marco with them, set out once more for Cathay.

After twenty-five years of exciting adventure in Cathay and the islands of the Indies, the Polos returned to Venice in 1295. The stories that they told about the marvels and riches of the East spread throughout Europe, and the later writings of Marco Polo were eagerly read by priests, seafarers, scholars, and kings. In one of his stories about Cipangu (Japan) Marco Polo wrote:

> I can tell you a wonderful thing about the palace of the lord of this island. You must know that he hath a great palace which is entirely roofed with fine gold, insomuch that it would be scarcely possible to estimate its value. Moreover, all the pavement of the palace and the floors of its apartments are entirely of gold, in plates like slabs of stone, and good two fingers thick; and the windows also are of gold, so that altogether the richness of this place is past all bounds and all belief.

* When the Polo brothers returned from their first trip to Cathay in 1269, they learned that Pope Clement IV had died the previous year and no new pope had been elected. When, by the middle of 1271, the papal throne was still vacant, they returned to Cathay without the missionaries.

They also have pearls in abundance, which are of rose color, fine, big, and round, and they have quantities of other precious stones also.[2]

The written tales of Marco Polo's adventures became one of the most widely read books of the Middle Ages. People everywhere were overwhelmed by his descriptions of the lavish wealth of Cathay, Cipangu, and the Spice Islands (Moluccas). It is no wonder, therefore, that brave men risked the terrors of the unknown seas in their quest for the riches of the East.

THE CRUSADES: It will perhaps come as a surprise to the reader to learn that the history of Guam has been influenced by events that occurred during the Crusades (1096–1273). It might appear impossible because the Crusades took place such a long time ago and because Guam is so far from Europe. But the Crusades and Guam are, nevertheless, bound together by the thread of history.

For a period of two hundred years, that is during the whole of the 12th and the 13th centuries, all of the truly important events of European history were influenced by the Crusades. The Crusades, or wars of the Cross, were undertaken by the nations of western Europe in order to recover the Holy Land of Palestine from the Saracens and Turks. It had become a custom, from an early period in the history of Christianity, for believers from all parts of the Christian world to make pilgrimages to the Holy Land. There they would visit the holy places and worship at the Holy Sepulcher, the tomb of Our Lord. As long as the Saracens had control of Palestine they protected the pilgrims and even encouraged them to visit the Holy Land because they profited from their trade. But when the Seljuk Turks,* who captured the Holy City of Jerusalem about the year 1076, became masters of Palestine, they subjected the Christians to very harsh and cruel treatment. Many of the Christians were killed by the Infidels, as the Mohammedans were called, and the holy places of Palestine were closed to the pilgrims.

---

* The Seljuks lived originally on the northern plains of Asia. They had been converted to Islam by contact with the Mohammedans of Baghdad.

News of the cruel treatment that the Christians were receiving at the hands of the Infidels aroused intense anger in Europe. This created a strong desire to recover the Holy Land from the Turks. Accordingly, at the Council of Clermont in 1095, Pope Urban II proclaimed the First Crusade.

The armies of the First Crusade (1096–99), after suffering the loss of tens of thousands of men at the hands of the Infidels, succeeded in recapturing the Holy City in July 1099. For a period of half a century the Christians maintained their control over Palestine. In 1187, however, they were driven out once more by the greatest of the Mohammedan leaders, Saladin. Although nine vast armies or crusades were directed against the Infidels, the Christian knights of Europe never succeeded in regaining permanent control of the Holy Land.

The Crusades utterly failed in their immediate objective, the recovery of the Holy Land from the Mohammedans. Still, the effects of these remarkable expeditions were very important. As a result of their journeys, the crusaders learned to enjoy Eastern luxuries. On returning home to their own countries, they spread the demand for Oriental goods in all sections of western Europe. Because of this demand Venice, Genoa, and other Italian states established trading depots on the shores of the eastern Mediterranean. Through these depots spices, silks, jewels, tapestries, porcelains, perfumes, precious stones, and other luxury items found their way into Europe. The Italian merchants made great profits from this trade. Their success created, in all parts of Europe, intense interest in trade with the Orient.

TRADE ROUTES TO THE EAST: Until the discovery of ocean routes to the East, goods from India and the Spice Islands came to Europe by three routes. One was overland, across the center of Asia to the Black Sea, and then either by water to Genoa or Venice, or up the Danube River to Cologne and other distributing centers. A second route from India, controlled by Venetian merchants, was by sea to the Persian Gulf, up the Euphrates or the Tigris River to Asia Minor, and thence by sea to the West. The southernmost route was almost entirely by sea. It stretched from Malacca (the distributing center for goods of China, Japan, and the East Indies) westward across the Indian Ocean to southern India. From there it continued on to the Red Sea, up the Red Sea and across the Sinai Peninsula to Cairo and Alexandria, and thence to Venice, Genoa, and the cities of Europe.

The capture of Constantinople by the Ottoman Turks in 1453 had serious effects on trade between the East and the West. In the beginning, the Turks did not close the trade routes completely. They found them to be exceedingly profitable. They were willing to let goods pass through upon the payment of fees. This, however, was not an entirely satisfactory arrangement for the West. The Turks, if they wished to do so, could close the trade routes at any time. To make the situation even worse, they sometimes granted a monopoly of this trade to one of the nations of western Europe. Other nations of western Europe were thus excluded from direct and easy access to the wealth of the Orient. As a result, Europeans became intensely interested in finding new routes to Asia. This search for new routes to the East led to Europe's greatest period of geographical discoveries.

CHRISTOPHER COLUMBUS: The enormous value of the commerce with India and the East during the latter half of the 15th century drove many adventurers to risk the terrors of the unknown seas in the quest for a short and safe route to the Indies. One of these was Christopher Columbus. He proposed the bold plan of reaching the East by sailing west. Columbus believed that by sailing three or four thousand miles westward from Spain he would reach the Indies. He, of course, did not know the true size of the earth. Moreover, he was completely unaware of the fact that an enormous, unknown continent filled the ocean seas between Europe and Asia. Thus his ignorance of the facts fed his hopes and drew him on to his greatest achievement—the discovery of the New World in 1492.

VASCO DA GAMA: By the year 1486, Portuguese navigators, in their search for an ocean route to the Indies, had reached the southern point of Africa, the Cape of Good Hope. A little later, just six years after the voyage of Columbus, Vasco da Gama, a Portuguese admiral, sailed around the cape, crossed the Indian Ocean, and reached Calicut on the Malabar coast of India in 1498. His discovery of an unbroken water route to India brought about important changes in the world's trade routes. Furthermore, his feat raised Portugal to the position of one of the most powerful nations of Europe. Almost a quarter of a century later, da Gama's important discoveries influenced and made possible the circumnavigation of the globe by Ferdinand Magellan.

FERDINAND MAGELLAN: In the hearts and minds of the Guamanian people, Ferdinand Magellan is an outstanding hero. This is amply demonstrated by the importance that has sometimes been attached to Magellan Day, March 6. During the years before World War II, this day was observed in the island's schools and communities with civic addresses, plays, pageants, and other appropriate events. A more meaningful indication of the esteem in which Magellan is held, however, is revealed by the fact that practically all Guamanians possess some knowledge concerning Magellan's life and his supposed role in the history of Guam. Despite the fact that historians do not agree entirely that Magellan discovered Guam, the Guamanian people, now and traditionally, firmly believe that he did.

Fernão de Magalhães, more commonly known as Ferdinand Magellan, has won an honored place in history as the leader of the first expedition to circumnavigate the globe. Magellan was a Portuguese by birth. Although the exact date and place of his birth are uncertain, it is believed that he was born about the year 1480.[3] It is also known that his family was *hidalgo*—that is, of the nobility. As a young man, Magellan won the admiration and respect of his countrymen through his bravery in battle against the Turks and in India. At the same time, because of his extensive travels, he acquired considerable skill in practical seamanship. Accordingly, he was recognized as one of the foremost navigators of his day.

In view of his reputation as a navigator, Magellan made an offer of his services to his king, Dom Manoel. He proposed that he be made leader of an expedition that would attempt to reach the Indies by sailing westward, as Columbus had tried to do. He assured his king that such an expedition would bring great wealth and glory to Portugal. The king, however, says Gaspar, "did not choose to hear it, nor to give it any confidence, but dismissed him with a frown and singular disgrace, very different from what was due to the proposal of Magalhães, and the reputation he had acquired for his valour."[4] The king's scorn for him so angered Magellan that he renounced his Portuguese citizenship, fled from Portugal, and offered his services to Charles I, king of Spain.

Magellan arrived at the court of Charles I in October 1517. There his proposals were listened to with attention and great respect. When the King of Portugal learned that the negotiations were taking place, he became very angry. He did everything in his power to discredit Magellan. His attacks were so bitter and sustained that he almost succeeded in dissuading Charles I from employing Magellan. The Spanish nobles, however, persuaded their king not to lose such an opportunity for increasing the Spanish empire. Accordingly, Charles I ordered ships to be provided for Magellan by means of which he might discover a new way to the East.

On September 20, 1519, Magellan's fleet set sail from the port of San Lucar de Barrameda. His little squadron, bearing 237 men, was composed of the *Concepción*, a vessel of 90 tons; the *Victoria*, 85 tons; the *San Antonio*, 120 tons; the *Trinidad*, 110 tons; and the *Santiago*, 75 tons. Sailing south and west from Spain, the fleet stopped at the Canary Islands and points along the eastern coast of South America. After the *Santiago* was lost in a storm at Port St. Julian, Magellan continued his voyage. On October 21, 1520, he arrived at the Cape of the Virgins, entrance to the famous straits that now bear his name. During passage through the straits, the crew of the *San Antonio*, fearing that they were being led to their destruction, took prisoner the captain of their ship and returned to Spain. On November 28, 1520, Magellan's little fleet completed its passage through the straits and entered the waters of the vast Pacific Ocean. One year, two months, and eight days had elapsed since their departure from San Lucar.

Upon entering the open waters of the vast Pacific, Magellan's little fleet, now reduced to three small vessels, was subjected to the most grueling rigors of the entire voyage. Antonio Pigafetta, Magellan's historian, has described the ordeals of the passage as follows:

We were three months and twenty days without getting any kind of fresh food. We ate biscuit, which was no longer biscuit, but powder of biscuits swarming with worms, for they had eaten the good. It stank strongly of the urine of rats. We drank yellow water that had been putrid for many days. We also ate some ox hides that covered the top of the mainyard to prevent the yard from chafing the shrouds, and which had become exceedingly hard because of the sun, rain, and wind. We left them in the sea for four or five days, and then placed them for a few moments on top of the embers, and so ate them; and often we ate sawdust from boards. Rats were sold for one-half *ducado* apiece, and even then we could not get them. But above all the other misfortunes the following was the worst. The gums of both the lower and upper teeth of some of our men swelled, so that they could not eat under any circumstances and therefore died.

Continuing his narrative, Pigafetta says:

We sailed about four thousand *leguas* during those three months and twenty days through an open stretch in that Pacific Sea. In truth it is very pacific, for during that time we did not suffer any storm.... Had not God and His blessed mother given us so good weather we would all have died of hunger in that exceeding vast sea.[5]

Suffering from scurvy and in a starving condition, Magellan's pitiful crews sighted the island of Guam, according to tradition, on March 6, 1521. According to Guillemard, "it is not absolutely certain which island or islands Magellan first sighted and visited, but there is not much doubt about the matter.* In all probability the high peak of Rota was the first land to show itself above the horizon. Steering for this, Guam must have come into view on

* There is doubt about the island that Magellan visited. In his work *A Voyage Around the World in the Years 1740–44*, Lord Anson conjectures that the two islands which Magellan first fell in with were probably "those of Saipan and Tinian."

their port bow, and discovering it to be the larger of the two, Magellan altered course to S.W., in order to approach its shores."[6] Amid scenes of laughter and rejoicing they replenished their water supply, stocked their ships with fresh fruits and other foods, and generally refreshed themselves. During the course of their brief stay, Magellan accused the natives of stealing one of his ship's boats. He went ashore at the head of a landing party of forty armed men, burned forty or fifty houses and several boats, and killed seven men of the island. He then returned to his ship and on March 9, 1521, set sail, continuing his course to the westward. As a result of his unpleasant experience with the "Indians," Magellan named the island Isla de los Ladrones (Island of Thieves).*

Leaving the Marianas, Magellan sailed westward for a period of ten days and discovered the Philippine Islands. There, on April 27, 1521, he was killed in a battle with the natives of the island of Mactan. Shortly thereafter the *Concepción* was burned, and the *Trinidad* was lost while trying to find its way back across the Pacific. The *Victoria*, under the command of Juan Sebastian Elcano, continued on around the Cape of Good Hope, bound for Spain. On September 6, 1522, the *Victoria*, carrying only 18 men out of the original company of 237 who had set sail almost three full years before, returned to San Lucar. Thus was completed the first circumnavigation of the globe.

## A CENTURY AND A HALF OF OBSCURITY: 1521–1668

The beginning of the 16th century saw an increase of rivalry between Spain and Portugal over the possession of newly discovered lands in the New World and the Indies. Through Magellan's discovery of the Marianas and the Philippines and a new way to the Spice Islands, Spain became engaged in a long and bitter dispute with Portugal. In spite of the Line of Demarcation** estab-

* Some writers remark that Magellan gave to these islands the name of Las Islas de las Velas Latinas, on account of the many vessels with triangular sails which he observed there. But they continued to be commonly called Ladrones; later they took the name of Marianas in honor of Queen Mariana de Austria, widow of Philip IV of Spain.
** In 1493 Pope Alexander VI divided all newly discovered lands between Spain and Portugal. Lands to the west of a meridian 100 leagues west of the Azores and

lished after the discovery of the West Indies by Columbus, both nations claimed the Spice Islands. Portugal, however, denied to Spain all rights to the Spice Islands and the Philippines as well. As a result, there began in the Far East a conflict that lasted nearly a century. In view of this conflict, Charles V of Spain became interested in both the larger and the smaller lands of recent discovery and sent out expeditions for the purpose of investigating them.

FRAY GARCIA JOFRE DE LOAISA: To reap the fruits of Magellan's discoveries, on July 24, 1525, Spain sent out another expedition under the command of Fray García Jofre de Loaisa. The captain of one of the vessels was Juan Sebastian Elcano, who had completed the voyage of Magellan. On his ship sailed Andrés de Urdaneta, who later became an Augustinian friar and piloted the expedition of Legazpi that finally claimed Guam for Spain. After suffering many hardships and losses, the fleet passed the Straits of Magellan and, on September 4, 1526, reached the Ladrones. Urdaneta, describing the natives of the islands, wrote:

> The Indians of these islands go about naked, wearing no garments. They are well-built men; they wear their hair long, and their beards full. They possess no iron tools, performing their work with stones. They have no other weapons than spears—some with points hardened with fire, and some having heads made from the shinbones of dead men or from fish bones. In these islands we took eleven Indians to work the pump, because of the great number of sick men in the ship.[7]

After a stay of four days, during which they took on fresh water and food, the Loaisa expedition departed from Guam and continued on to the Moluccas. There they were taken prisoner by the Portuguese. It was not until 1536, almost eleven years from the time they began their voyage, that the survivors of the expedition returned to Spain.

MIGUEL LÓPEZ DE LEGAZPI: When Legazpi began his voyage on

the Cape Verde Islands should belong to Spain. A year later Spain and Portugal agreed to shift the line to the meridian 370 leagues west of the Cape Verde Islands. This line, continued on around the globe, resulted in giving India and Malaysia to Portugal and all the New World, except Brazil, to Spain. Because of the lack of exact geographical knowledge, both nations claimed the Spice Islands.

November 21, 1564, his expedition sailed from the port of Natividad, Mexico, rather than from Spain. By this time, the conquest and subjugation of Mexico by the great Hernando Cortes
had been completed. New Spain, as Mexico and the Americas
were now called, was ruled in the name of the Spanish sovereigns
by the viceroy, who lived in Mexico City. Thus it was that in 1559
Luis de Velasco, viceroy of New Spain and president of the Royal
Audiencia,* received orders from Philip II of Spain to send out
two ships for the purpose of exploring the western islands toward
the Moluccas. In compliance with the orders of the king, Velasco
began the task of outfitting the expedition. Five years passed, however, before ships and equipment were completed. Miguel López
de Legazpi, member of an old and noble family, and a man of
great wisdom, was appointed leader of the expedition. Andrés de
Urdaneta, who years before had sailed in the expedition of Loaisa,
was asked by the king to accompany the expedition as a pilot and
director. Urdaneta, after his return from the previous expedition,
had renounced military life and had become an Augustinian friar.
He was wise and discreet and was known to be one of the best
cosmographers of his day.

On January 22, 1565, just two months and one day from the
time they left Natividad, Legazpi's expedition reached Guam. At
first some of the other pilots thought they had reached the Philippines. Fray Urdaneta, however, convinced them that they were in
the Ladrones. This he proved to be the case from the lateen sails
of the native boats, "which the inhabitants of the Filipinas do not
make." Even before the ships were anchored, they were surrounded by native canoes. The natives brought them many kinds of food,
but in very small quantity. They would not climb aboard the
vessels, although they were asked to do so by Legazpi. Perhaps
they had heard tales about the eleven islanders who had been
carried away by Loiasa and did not wish to place themselves in
danger. From the safety of their canoes, they traded their food

---

* This was a body of men noble in rank and learned in the law, sent out from
Spain to form a colonial court in each country. In the absence of the viceroy or
governor, the *audiencia* assumed his duties.

for such things as playing cards, beads, and little bits of colored cloth. "The father prior talked to them, using the few words of their language that he remembered, especially counting up to ten, whereat they manifested great pleasure; and one of them mentioned the name Gonzalo,* which, as the father prior said, was the name of a Spaniard who had been found in one of those islands, which was called Goam." The natives signed to them to enter their villages, where they would find food in abundance. "And all the canoes, and those in them, had their arms, which consisted of shields, bundles of throwing-sticks, slings, and egg-shaped stones. ...They are tall, robust, well built, and apparently of great strength. The women, too, are very tall. . . . Both men and women wear their hair, which is of a yellowish color, loose and long, gathering it up behind the head."[8] Legazpi, "who showed them much love and affection, and looked upon them as friends," described his experiences with the antives of Guam, in part, as follows:

On Monday, January 21, we came in sight of land, which afterwards proved to be one of the Ladrones Islands, called Gua.** We directed our bows to that island, but we were no more than two leagues from it when fifty or sixty praus*** under sail surrounded the fleet. These praus were furnished with lateen sails of palm mats and were as light as the wind. ...In each canoe were from six to eight Indians, altogether naked. ... At break of day we coasted the island and the next morning we cast anchor in a very good port. The day had scarcely begun when a great number of those praus appeared about us. There were so many of them that some of our men who counted them affirm that there were more than four or five hundred of them around the ships. All that they had to sell us were articles of food, namely, potatoes, rice, yams, cocoanuts, sugar cane, excellent bananas, and several other kinds of fruit. They also brought ginger, which grows in this island in so great quantity that it is a thing to wonder over; and they do not till or cultivate it,

* Gonzalo de Vigo, a Spaniard, was found on Guam by the Loaisa expedition. He is said to have sailed in the fleet of Magellan and to have deserted from the *Trinidad* when it stopped at one of the islands north of Guam as it tried to return to New Spain from the Moluccas.
** At various times the island has been called Goam, Gua, Guan, Guahan, and Boan.
*** In some manuscripts the word is written *praos* or *ptoas*.

but it comes up and grows of itself in the open fields, just as any other herb. The natives shouted at us, each one inviting us to buy of him. ...In these transactions many jests were played. Afterward our men began to give them nails, which the Indians liked so well that they desired nothing else after that. They would smell them before taking them. For each nail they gave measures of rice containing about half a fenega,* more or less.

After the rice was drawn up into the boat by means of a rope, because the Indians would not trade outside of their canoes, and the packages were opened, it was found that only the top layer was rice and the rest straw and stones. The Indian who had practiced this jest would clap his hands in glee, and laugh long and loud, and go from that vessel to another, to play the same trick.[9]

On January 26, 1565, Legazpi went ashore for the purpose of performing the formal ceremony that was to make Guam a possession of Spain. He was accompanied by Padre Urdaneta; Hernando Riquel, chief recorder of the armada; Mateo del Sanz, the purser; General Andrés de Ybarra; and other priests and gentlemen of the expedition. After selecting a spot in a group of palm trees near the shore, Legazpi ordered an altar to be built. When the task was completed, he drew his sword and cut some branches from the trees. From the branches a cross was hastily made and raised above the altar. Then, taking his sword in his hand and raising it in salute to the cross, Legazpi proclaimed in a loud, clear voice: "I, Miguel López de Legazpi, Governor and Captain-General, by His Majesty, of the people and armada that goes in His Royal service on discovery of the islands of the West, in the name of His Royal Majesty the King, Don Felipe Our Lord, take and apprehend as an actual property and as a Royal possession, this land and all the lands subject to it."[10] Having completed the formal ceremony of possession, Legazpi and his companions gathered around the altar. There Padre Urdaneta, assisted by the other priests of the Order of San Augustine, celebrated Holy Mass.

For several days all was well between the Spaniards and the Indians. The peaceful relations were soon broken, however. One day, as the vessels' crews were refilling their water butts in a small

* A Spanish dry measure varying from one to two bushels.

cove, the natives showed hostility by discharging showers of stones at them. Later, finding a ship's boy asleep in a palm grove, where he had gone while the water butts were being filled, the natives killed him in a barbarous manner. Legazpi was so angered by this brutal act that he sent 100 men ashore to punish the natives. Four of them were captured and three were hanged at the same place where the boy had been killed. The fourth, who was to be hanged also, was saved by the timely intervention of Padre Urdaneta. In spite of the efforts of the priests to restrain them, the soldiers continued their acts of reprisal. They wounded many natives and burned many houses. This was done "so that when Spaniards, vassals of his majesty, anchor there another time, the natives shall give them a better reception."[11]

On February 3, 1565, after a sojourn of eleven days in Guam, Legazpi's expedition continued on its way to the Philippines, where Legazpi died on August 20, 1572. During the seven years that he served there as *adelantado* and governor, he proved himself to be an able administrator as well as a great *conquistador*. As a result of his voyage, Guam was brought under Spanish sovereignty. For a period of over 300 years it was to know the compelling influences of Spanish law and culture.

Another significant result of Legazpi's voyage is that concerned with the discovery of the northern return route across the Pacific. The captain of one of Legazpi's ships, desiring reward and honor for himself, started at once upon the return voyage. Unlike preceding captains, who had tried to return to New Spain by sailing eastward against the wind and the ocean currents, this captain sailed northward beyond the trades into the more favorable westerly winds. He found his way back to the coast of North America at California and followed it southward to Acapulco. A short time later, Legazpi sent the *San Pablo*, carrying about 200 men, including Padre Urdaneta, on the return voyage to New Spain. This vessel also followed the northern route across the Pacific and thus helped to establish it as a regular route.

ENGLISH EXPLORERS VISIT GUAM: Guam's long period of relative obscurity (1521–1668) was broken intermittently by the appearance of foreign vessels in or near the waters surrounding the Marianas. Most of these vessels belonged to Spain. In 1579, however, the *Golden Hind*, under the command of the great English sea captain, freebooter, and naval hero, Francis Drake, approached the shores of Guam. At this time, Spain and England, while not actually at war, were rapidly approaching the hostilities which made them, for centuries, traditional enemies. While the two countries pretended to be at peace, swift English vessels were quietly putting to sea for the purpose of crippling the Spanish power. The most famous of these English freebooters was Sir Francis Drake.

In 1577 Drake sailed from England in a ship later named the *Golden Hind*. His purpose was to destroy Spanish shipping wherever he might find it. He passed through the Straits of Magellan and sailed up the western coast of South America, capturing and destroying Spanish ships as he went. After amassing a fabulous treasure, Drake, fearing to return by the way he had come, struck out across the Pacific bound for England by way of the Cape of Good Hope. In late September or early October 1579 he arrived at an island that he called the "Island of Thieves." This might or might not have been Guam.[12] After a delay of only one day, Drake continued his voyage. In September 1580 he returned to England. By the successful completion of his voyage, he was the first Englishman to circumnavigate the globe.

By the year 1586 Spain and England were engaged in a full-scale war. It was now lawful to despoil Spanish shipping. Consequently, Thomas Cavendish, an English gentleman who had spent most of his wealth at court, set out to rebuild his fortune as the leader of a privateering voyage to the South Sea. With a fleet of three vessels, he left Plymouth, England, on July 21, 1586. He sailed through the Straits of Magellan and, like Drake before him, ravaged shipping and Spanish settlements on the western coast of South America. Then he sailed across the Pacific to the Moluccas. Leaving the California coast, he sailed in a southwesterly direction until he reached the latitude between 12 degrees and 13 degrees north. Keeping nearly in that parallel, he sailed to the west without meeting any land until he arrived at the Ladrone Islands.[13] On January 3, 1588, "they came in sight of the Ladrones, and passed near the Island Guahan, from whence canoes went to them, carrying fruit and vegetables, which they exchanged for pieces of iron. Some of these islanders followed the ship longer than was agreeable to the General, and their behaviour was troublesome, wherefore, to get rid of their company, he ordered muskets to be fired at them."[14]

Continuing on to the Philippines, Cavendish sent a letter to the Spanish governor at Manila. In his letter he boasted of his capture of a galleon. He then sailed for the Cape of Good Hope and home.

DUTCH EXPLORERS VISIT GUAM: With the defeat of the Spanish Armada* in 1588, pre-eminence on the seas passed from the Spanish and Portuguese to the English and Dutch. The Dutch, who in 1579 had rebelled against Spain and established an independent republic, sent their first expedition to the Indies in 1595. They were not interested in establishing colonies or in converting the natives to Christianity. They were interested solely in trade.

In 1598 Olivier Van Noort, a native of Utrecht, was appointed general or admiral** of a fleet that was fitted out by a company of Dutch merchants. The instructions of the commander directed him to sail through the Straits of Magellan into the South Sea. He was then to cruise on the coasts of Chile and Peru, pass over to the Moluccas to trade, and in returning to his native country complete the circumnavigation of the globe.[15] Van Noort carried out his instructions faithfully. On September 15, 1600, "they made the Ladrone Islands, and stopped two days near one of them, supposed to be the Island Guahan, from which above 200 canoes came to the ships, bringing fish, fruits, rice, fowls, and water in gourds, to exchange for iron."

On August 26, 1601, Van Noort, aboard his ship the *Mauritius*,

* A fleet of 130 ships sent by Philip II of Spain to invade England. It was almost completely destroyed by the English.
** In the accounts of this voyage, the commander of the fleet is sometimes called general and sometimes admiral.

returned to Holland. This was the first ship of the Netherlands to circumnavigate the globe.

In the first decade of the 17th century, Spain signed a peace treaty with England and agreed to a twelve-year truce with Holland. In this way she hoped to be able to pacify the two nations whose enmity was most dangerous to her foreign possessions. The truce with Holland, however, was not followed by a peace treaty. Outside of Europe it was hardly observed at all. The Dutch continued to extend their power and influence in the Spice Islands, and, as a result, rivalry between Spain and Holland became increasingly bitter. During the height of this rivalry, the Dutch sent a fleet of six ships to the Indies under the command of Admiral Joris Spilbergen for the purpose of engaging in trade. Going by way of the Straits of Magellan, the fleet reached the Ladrone Islands on January 23, 1616. There they stopped for two days to trade with the islanders for provisions of fruit, fowl, and fish. On the afternoon of the 26th they sailed from the Ladrones bound for the Philippines.

Admiral Spilbergen did not discover new lands on his voyage through the South Sea. He was, however, extremely successful in extending Dutch trading interests in the Moluccas at the expense of Spain and Portugal.

On April 29, 1623, a fleet of seven vessels, under the command of Admiral Jacob L'Heremite,* sailed from Holland for the purpose of raiding Spanish and Portuguese settlements along the west coast of South America. The Dutch were not seeking plunder alone. They were also attempting to seize permanent control of large and valuable territories in the New World. Because of ineffective leadership and dissension among the ships' commanders, the fleet failed in its objective. It was then decided to cruise near the port of Acapulco in hopes of capturing the Manila galleon. That scheme also failed. The fleet then left the American coast and sailed westward to the East Indies.

---

* In view of the fact that L'Heremite died before the completion of the voyage, this expedition has generally been called the Voyage of the Nassau Fleet in honor of Prince Maurice of Nassau, a principal promoter of the expedition.

On January 25, 1625, fifty-seven days after leaving the coast of New Spain, the Nassau fleet arrived at Guam. It anchored on the west side of the island at a distance of a cannon shot and a half from the shore. From the time of its discovery until the period of American occupation, this was one of the most formidable armed fleets ever to anchor in Guamanian waters. At a review which the admiral made before sending boats ashore, the number of men mustered amounted to 1,260.

While at Guam, the fleet took on fresh water and, in exchange for iron, procured rice, fowls, coconuts, yams, potatoes, and bananas from the natives. An account of the voyage relates that "cocoa-nuts were here in inexhaustible quantities; rice was cultivated in many places and the natives sold it by weight, in bales of between 70 to 80 lbs. each; but not one bale was found which had not been increased in weight by the addition of sand and stones."[16]

On February 11, after a stay of seventeen days, the Nassau fleet sailed from Guam bound for the Moluccas.

## THE GALLEON TRADE

From the time of discovery, 1521, until the first attempt at colonization by the Spaniards in 1668, Guam was not only visited by explorers and adventurers but also became a regular stopping place for the Spanish galleons bound from Acapulco to Manila.

Efforts of the Spaniards to find a safe route back across the Pacific from the Indies began with their first expedition into that sea. How to reach the Indies was a serious problem, but how to get back was even more serious. In 1522 the *Trinidad*, one of Magellan's ships, left the Moluccas and tried to sail back across the Pacific to the Isthmus of Panama. She got far out into the ocean sea, but the devastating effects of storms, scurvy, and starvation forced her to turn back. Each succeeding Spanish expedition tried to accomplish the same task, but each in turn failed.

After the Spaniards had subjugated the Philippines and had established trading relations with many nations of the East, Manila became the foremost city of the Eastern Indies. It became the capital of a great commercial empire that extended to China, Japan, Java, Malacca, and the kingdoms of Indo-China. From these far-flung regions came silks, satins, tapestries, Oriental rugs and carpets, gold, diamonds, silver, spices, and drugs destined for the markets of New Spain and of Europe. All these different commodities were collected at Manila, thence to be transported annually in one or more ships to the port of Acapulco, in the kingdom of Mexico.[17] Through this trade, Manila became the emporium of the East.

The establishment of the galleon trade was the culminating act in the long drama of bravery and daring that marked the efforts of explorers and adventurers to gain the wealth and riches of the East. The galleons, loaded with the pick of all the rich stores that came to Manila, left the Philippines in July. They sailed northeastward to about the 38th or 40th degree of latitude. There the westerly winds carried them nearly straight across the ocean to Cape Mendocina on the northern California coast. From there they sailed down the coast, a distance of nearly 3,000 miles, to the port of Acapulco. Because of the storms encountered in the higher latitudes and also in order to avoid English and Dutch pirates who lurked along the American west coast, the Spanish authorities later shifted the route much farther south. Here the vessels encountered less favorable winds and, as a result, often required five months or more to reach Acapulco.

Upon arrival at Acapulco, the galleon would discharge her cargo and begin preparations for the return trip to the Philippines. Silver from the sale of the goods from Manila made up the most important single item of the cargo. Besides silver and articles of necessity, the galleons also carried regular mail, official correspondence, missionaries, troops, arms, and royal officials going out to their posts in the insular governments. Insofar as Guam was concerned, an important item in the cargo consisted of funds sent out for the maintenance of the government in the Marianas. These funds, which amounted to 34,000 pesos a year, were sent from Mexico as the *situado* and *socorro*, or subsidy and relief. Of this, the governor drew 3,000 pesos.

Missionaries, especially, traveled on the galleons in large numbers. Fifteen Dominicans were aboard the Acapulco galleon of 1587. As many as one hundred priests crossed on the *Begona* at a later date. The eagerness with which the missionaries sought royal permission to labor in the islands might be explained, in part, by the fact that persecutions in China and Japan had closed mission fields in those areas.

Not all the passengers were voluntary travelers. Many were social or political outcasts from Mexico and Spain who were being sent into exile in the Philippines. Others were the wild sons of good families sent to the islands to reform. Nor could the soldiers, mostly conscripts, be called voluntary travelers. Their reluctance to serve in the islands is clearly revealed by the mutiny of a body of conscripts from Mexico who nearly gained control of the *Concepción* in 1667 while she was anchored at Guam.

## THE SPANISH COLONIAL SYSTEM

From the moment that Guam became a possession of Spain, it became part of the Spanish colonial system and was subject to the body of laws which was developed for the government of the Indies. These laws served as the foundation for the great administrative machinery that controlled the affairs of the colonies throughout the New World and the Eastern Indies. From the time that Legazpi claimed Guam for Spain until the transfer of the island to the United States of America (1565–1898)—a period of 333 years—the destinies of Guam were directly or indirectly determined by the Laws of the Indies. For that reason, some understanding concerning the important parts of the Spanish colonial system is essential.

In accordance with tradition, papal donation, and the Laws of the Indies, all newly discovered lands belonged to the crown, and the people who lived there were subjects of the king. Whatever was done in those lands was done in the name of the sovereign and, theoretically at least, was in accord with the royal will. In view of the fact that Madrid, the seat of the sovereign authority, was thousands of miles away from many of the overseas possessions, the royal will was expressed through the viceroy, who ruled in the name of the king.

At the pleasure of the king and through the authority delegated by him, all affairs in the Spanish possessions were controlled by the Council of the Indies.[18] Founded in 1511, this board originally possessed all financial, military, ecclesiastical, and commercial authority and at the same time served as a high court of appeal. New laws could be enacted only by a majority of at least two-thirds of its members. The members, appointed by the king, were usually men who had served with great distinction in the Indies. This council was required to remain near the court at all times.

At first the viceroys possessed the entire royal authority. The honors and obedience due them were the same as those due to the king himself. In the course of time, however, their authority was restricted, and possessions lying at a distance from the seat of the viceregal government were set up as separate districts under the control of captains-general. Guam was subject to the rule of the viceroy of Mexico, who, by royal decree in 1681, defined the political status of the Chamorros by granting them legal equality with other Spanish subjects.[19]

Very early the Spanish crown, in order to protect its own authority, found it necessary to place further checks on the power of ambitious viceroys and governors. This was done by means of the royal *audiencia*. The *audiencia*, which acted as a supreme court, was a body of men of noble rank sent out from Spain to form a colonial court in each country. The *audiencia* had administrative as well as judicial powers and, in the absence of the viceroy or governor, assumed his duties.

The *residencia* was one of the most important features of the Spanish colonial system. It was instituted in order to prevent abuses of power by high officials in the colonies, especially the viceroys and governors. After the termination of their appointments, these high officials were required to remain in their districts for at least six months. During that time their successors, or prominent jurists appointed by the Council of the Indies, would listen to and record charges and complaints of every kind against the outgoing officials. Any person, regardless of rank, could appear before the *residencia* to voice his complaints. The justice of these charges was then decided in Spain. Until he successfully met this test, no official could receive another appointment in the service of the crown.

Through the campaigns of the great *conquistadores*, Spain gained control of vast overseas possessions. In order to govern a region and to better protect the natives, who had suffered terribly at the hands of the invaders during the period of conquest, the crown established the system of *encomiendas*. Under this system the king entrusted vast tracts of land to the care of discoverers, military leaders, and others who had rendered valuable service to him. The land, however, did not become the outright possession of the *encomendero* or trustee. He ruled it and derived income from it as long as he fulfilled the original purpose of the *encomiendas*—namely, to give military protection to the natives, to aid in civilizing them, and to convert them to Christianity. Whoever failed to do these things lost his *encomienda*. In order to protect the natives from abuses of power by the *encomenderos*, stringent rules were established. The *encomendero* was forbidden to own a house in his *encomienda*, to allow his relatives to enter it, or to maintain any industrial establishment there. The natives, being free men, were required to pay taxes either to the royal treasury or to the *encomendero*. Since the *encomiendas* were not permanent grants, this system of provincial government was gradually changed so that eventully the *encomenderos* were replaced by *alcaldes-mayor*.

In accordance with the Laws of the Indies, all natives living in Spanish possessions were, in theory at least, entitled to justice under law and to human treatment. With regard to such treatment, both by church and by civil authorities, Roscher relates:

> On the whole the treatment of the Indians was as humane, perhaps, as was practicable, considering that they were regarded as minors and in view of what was necessary to secure the Spanish sovereignty. No Indian was to carry arms or learn the manufacture of them. . . . If they were obliged to live in villages and forbidden to change their dwelling-

place without the permission of the authorities, yet we can find in this only a salutary police regulation by which a relapse to the barbarism of a hunter's life might be prevented. As a matter of fact, the Indian is extraordinarily inclined to such relapses. The prohibition of the whites, mulattoes, etc., from settling among the Indians, and of the merchants from remaining longer than three days among them, was designed to protect them from ruthless exploitation by those of superior abilities. Every Indian village had a native cazique, whose office was often hereditary. The government restricted his authority only to the extent of preventing him from abusing his subjects by means of white corregidores, or protectors, who were entrusted at the same time with the collection of the revenue. Offences against an Indian were to be avenged more severely than if they affected a Spaniard. . . .

The church treated the Indians with very exceptional mildness. The Inquisition never had to do with the Indians. Any heresies were to be tried before the bishops' courts, but there were never really any prosecutions. . . . As for confession, church penances, feast-days, the hearing of mass, and fasts, in short almost every church requirement, they were treated with an indulgence which would have been quite impossible towards the Spaniards themselves.[20]

The Roman Catholic Church, perhaps more than any other single factor, was the dominating influence not only in establishing but also in maintaining Spanish colonies in the overseas possessions. This influence was due primarily to the closeness of the relationship that existed between the state and the church. Concerning this relationship, Roscher wrote as follows:

What supported the crown in its policy toward the Indians more than anything else was the influence of the church, which in Spanish America was not less important than in the motherland. . . .

We must remember the close union which existed in the motherland between the throne and the altar. Because no monarch of the world was esteemed so Catholic as the Spanish, so none had such a power over his country's church with the permission of the pope. Absolutism in Spain rested preferably upon spiritual foundations; upon the right of patronage of the king over bishops; upon his grand-mastership of the religious orders of knights; and finally upon the Inquisition.[21]

The *alcaldes-mayor* were governors of subdivisions of provinces, called *partidos*. These officers were magistrates who exercised almost complete control over all governmental functions in the areas which they governed. They exercised police, military, and judicial powers and, in a word, were charged with the responsibility for instituting all measures that might contribute to order and the public good. The highest official in Guam, in accordance with Spanish law and custom, was the governor, who in some jurisdictions was called the *alcalde-mayor*. The governor, whose term of office was generally for six years, was appointed by the royal court at Madrid. The governor-general of the Philippines, however, was his immediate superior.

Among the Spanish officials in Guam, the second in rank was the *sargento-mayor*. He was the commandant of troops and was responsible for the military affairs of the island. His responsibility was, however, subordinate to that of the governor, in whom superior military power resided. Besides taking care of his military duties, the *sargento-mayor*, on occasion, served as acting governor. Both the governor and the *sargento-mayor* lived in Agana.

Because of its concentrated population and its long history as the political and cultural center of Guam, a system of district organization was developed in Agana that was quite different from that which prevailed in other parts of the island. This was the *barrio* (under the bells) system. The barrio usually consisted of a group of households which surrounded a church or chapel. Families living in the area were, in earlier times at least, obliged to contribute to the support of the church and were under the spiritual jurisdiction of its priests. Each *barrio* or district observed certain religious rites and festivals that were connected with its patron saint. The *barrio* of San Ignacio, the oldest and most centrally located district, was inhabited by the families of highest rank.

After the subjugation of the Chamorros by the Spaniards, these families gradually attained dominant positions in the social, political, and economic life of Guam. Concerning them, Thompson wrote:

> In Agana, especially, were found survivals of the ancient Chamorro
> class system. After the Spanish conquest there arose a property-owning

class composed mainly of the descendants of the Chamorro nobility who had united with Spaniards. The members of this group were called "high people" (manak kilo). They refused to mix with the remainder of the population, who were considered "low people" (manak papa). By the end of the Spanish regime the "high people" consisted of about a dozen intermarrying Spanish-Chamorro families who formed a wealthy and powerful group cultivating a Spanish Catholic tradition. Each family controlled a relatively large amount of land, the largest of which, however, was probably not more than 1,500 hectares. They lived in Spanish adobe houses with tiled roofs and did not engage in any sort of manual work but hired laborers and servants to cultivate their lands. They were firm supporters of the Catholic Church and [were] on intimate terms with the padres. They held the official positions and mingled with the Spanish administrators. They kept aloof from the common people, and some would not even allow their children to attend school but had them taught by private tutors. The young people of the "high class" were raised very strictly, and their marriages were usually arranged for them within the group.[22]

At the time of the destruction of the city during World War II, the *barrios* of Agana were named Anigua, Julale, Santa Cruz, Belibic, San Ignacio, Togae, San Nicolas, San Ramon, San Antonio, and Padre Palomo.

In order to facilitate the affairs of the government outside of Agana, the Spanish authorities divided Guam into municipalities. Each municipality, which might consist of several villages or hamlets, was in charge of a native magistrate called the *gobernadorcillo* or "little governor." The *gobernadorcillo*, with the consent of the governor, had complete executive powers within his district. He was also responsible for the collection of taxes and the assignment of work on public projects. His term of office was for two years.

Besides the *gobernadorcillo*, each municipality also had a native police commissioner who was called the *teniente de justicia*. The commissioner was assisted by two judges who looked after all legal matters related to land problems and salaries. Public law and order were maintained by *alguaciles* or police officers, two of whom were statinoed in each municipality. Each day the *alguacil* supervised the work of men who were designated by the *gober-*

58

*nadorcillo* to perform services for the municipality or the church. Each municipality also had an officer called the zelator, whose duty it was to enforce the religious regulations made by the padres.

The municipalities of Guam were composed of villages or pueblos, each of which was headed by a native leader called the *principale del pueblo*. The pueblos were in turn divided into subdisricts called *barangays*. A *barangay* usually consisted of about fifty village families. The head of the *barangay*, known as the *cabeza de barangay*, took the census, collected taxes, distributed public funds, and was responsible for supervising the public labor of his group.

With Corte as a reference, Thompson has given the following description of the selection of municipal officials in Guam:

> ... the gobernadorcillos, tenientes and judges received their appointments for a two-year term of office as follows. Before the term of those in office had expired, the governor called together a municipal electorate of thirteen, composed of the incumbent of the office of gobernadorcillo, six cabezas de barangay and six principales del pueblo. The twelve chiefs of the barangays and pueblos were selected theoretically by lot from a group of all of the functioning cabezas and principales who had held the office of cabeza, principale or gobernadorcillo for more than twenty-five years. The municipal electorate of thirteen voted by ballot for the ministers of justice, each of whom, in order to qualify for office, had to be present or past cabezas de barangay. For gobernadorcillo they elected by a majority of votes two candidates who, with the current gobernadorcillo, formed a group of three for whom the governor, acting in place of the governor-general, selected one to hold office. He was forced to name the candidate who had received the largest number of votes, however, or to explain his choice. For each of the other offices, the electorate chose one approved subsequently by the governor-general, who made all of the appointments.
>
> Once appointed, the gobernadorcillo had full executive powers with the approval of the governor. He did not consult the principales or cabezas of the municipalities, except regarding unusual problems when together they formed a municipal court representing the people.[23]

SUMMARY: For unknown generations the ancient Chamorros were the only inhabitants of Guam. With the advent of Magellan, however, their island became known to the people of the Western world. From that time on, Guam was visited by an ever-increasing number of outsiders. These contacts, quite naturally, produced changes in the Chamorros' way of life. Because of its location, the island became a regular stopping place for the Manila galleons. Consequently, it acquired new value as an important link in the Spanish economic and political system.

## NOTES

1. L. F. Benedetto, *The Travels of Marco Polo* (translated by Aldo Ricci, The Viking Press, Inc., New York, 1931), p. 5.
2. *Ibid.*, p. 271.
3. Francis H. H. Guillemard, *The Life of Ferdinand Magellan* (George Philip and Son, London, 1890), p. 18.
4. Gaspar de San Agustin, *Conquista de las Filipinas* (Madrid, 1698)
5. Blair and Robertson, *op. cit.*, Vol. XXXIII, pp. 87–89.
6. Guillemard, *op. cit.*, pp. 223–24.
7. Blair and Robertson, *op. cit.*, Vol. II, p. 35.
8. *Ibid.*, pp. 109–10. For the sake of giving the reader clearer insight into Guam's historical past, the quotations contained herein will be longer than those ordinarily found in a book of this kind.
9. *Ibid.*, pp. 197–99.
10. *Colección de Documentos Inéditos Relativos al Descubrimiento, Conquista, y Organización de las Antiguas Posesiones Españolas de Ultramar* (Madrid, 1887), Segunda Serie, Tomo Num. III, pp. 79–81.
11. Blair and Robertson, *op. cit.*, Vol. II, p. 112.
12. Henry R. Wagner, *Sir Francis Drake's Voyage around the World* (John Howell, San Francisco, 1926), p. 170. Wagner says that on the Molyneux globe Drake's route is shown as passing just south of the southernmost islands of the Ladrones, and a stop seems to be indicated.
13. James Burney, *A Chronological History of the Voyages and Discoveries in the South Sea or Pacific Ocean* (London, 1806), Vol. II, p. 90.
14. *Ibid.*, p. 90.   15. *Ibid.*, p. 206.   16. *Ibid.*, Vol. III, p. 34.
17. Richard Walter, *Anson's Voyage Round the World* (Martin Hopkinson, Ltd., London, 1928), p. 224.
18. Wilhelm Roscher, *The Spanish Colonial System* (translated by Edward G. Bourne, Henry Holt and Company, New York, 1904), p. 25.
19. Thompson, *Guam and Its People*, p. 58.
20. Roscher, *op. cit.*, pp. 6–7.
21. *Ibid.*, pp. 10–11.
22. Thompson, *Guam and Its People*, pp. 54–56.
23. *Ibid.*, pp. 62–63.

*CHAPTER THREE*

# THE CROSS AND THE SWORD

FROM THE TIME of discovery until 1668, the Marianas were used by the Spaniards for one reason only. That was to provide replenishment of supplies for the galleon that annually made the trip from Acapulco to the Philippines. This was done cheaply and almost without difficulty insofar as the Spaniards were concerned. Such a situation might have continued indefinitely, except for the fact that the spirit of the times was one of religious zeal and missionary activity.

Activities of the missionaries were spurred on not only by their zeal for the salvation of souls but also at the urgings of the sovereigns of Europe. These sovereigns, in accordance with the wishes of the pope, were required to do all in their power to spread the Christian religion. In his Bull of Partition, Pope Alexander VI addressed himself equally to the secular as well as to the spiritual sons of the church. He stated that "the Catholic faith and the Christian religion should be exalted and everywhere be spread, and the salvation of souls be obtained and barbarous nations be subdued and brought to the faith" and that "the people living in islands and lands of this sort, you will and ought to bring to the Christian religion; nor let perils nor labours at any time deter you."[1] Thus, it might be said that the colonization of the Marianas was due, primarily, to two important factors: (1) the location of the islands, which made them convenient for commerce between New Spain and the Indies and (2) the desire to spread the Christian religion.

## PADRE DIEGO LUIS DE SANVITORES

THE FIRST MISSIONARIES: In the year 1662, the galleon *San Damian*, bound with Jesuit missionaries from Acapulco to the Philippines, stopped at Guam for water. Among the missionaries was Father Diego Luis de Sanvitores. He was born November 12, 1627, in Burgos, Spain, and was a priest of the Society of Jesus. Father Sanvitores, who appears to have been a man of great piety and benevolence, was greatly impressed by the natives in the canoes that surrounded his ship. He decided then to dedicate himself to their conversion to Christianity. As a result, upon his arrival at Manila, he appealed to the governor of the Philippines for assistance in establishing a mission in Guam. The governor, however, gave him neither assistance nor encouragement. Being thus rebuffed, he decided to send an appeal directly to King Philip IV of Spain. Accordingly, Father Sanvitores wrote an ardent and persuasive letter to the king. In his letter he begged for the king's approval of his plan to establish a mission in Guam. He even went so far as to refresh the king's memory of his duties by reminding him of the counsel formerly given by St. Francis Xavier to the King of Portugal "that every day the king ought to devote one quarter of an hour to meditate on the admirable admonitory text of St. Matthew, *What is a man profited, if he shall gain the whole world, and lose his own soul?*, that by such meditation he may be prepared against the time when the King of Kings shall call him to judgment, and say to him, *Render an account of your administration.*"[2] In his letter he asked especially for authority that would enable him to guard the natives against cruel treatment by the Spaniards. At the same time he wrote also to the queen, Philip's consort Mariana de Austria, begging her assistance. His proposals were received with such great favor at court that the king had orders sent to the governor of the Philippines to furnish him with whatever he needed for establishing his mission in Guam. Long before the orders could be carried out, however, Philip IV died.

Mariana of Austria, widow of Philip IV, became Queen Regent of Spain upon the death of her husband. It was in honor of this queen that the Marianas were named. Mariana was as interested in

62

spreading the Christian faith as her husband had been. Consequently, she approved and forwarded the orders which the king had given regarding the establishment of a mission in Guam.

Queen Mariana is an important figure in the history of Guam. Without her approval Father Sanvitores could not have established his mission. Moreover, money and supplies which she sent him made it possible for him to continue his work. Her decision to help Sanvitores was probably influenced by Father Everard Nithard, her confessor. He was a German Jesuit who was hated by some Spaniards. Nevertheless, the queen made no decisions without first consulting him. It is believed that Nithard saw in the plan of Sanvitores a means to extend Jesuit power and influence. Interested, as she surely was, in winning souls for Christ, she was also interested in gaining money for her treasury. Evidence suggests that she considered Guam to be a good business deal. She expected to get much more out of it than she put into it. In this she was sadly disappointed.

Mariana was the daughter of the emperor of Austria. In 1646, at the age of fourteen, she was engaged to Prince Baltasar of Spain. Baltasar, son of Philip IV, was seventeen at the time. Two months after the engagement was announced, the young prince died of smallpox. For strictly political reasons, Philip himself became engaged to the girl who had been destined to be his daughter-in-law. Philip was forty-seven. When they were married, "Mariana was just fifteen, a strong, passionate, full-blooded girl with a hard heart."[3] Of the seven children born to their marriage, only two reached adulthood. One, a boy, became King Charles II when Philip died. Until Charles was old enough to ascend the throne, Mariana ruled for eleven years in his name. It was during this period that she approved the establishment of the first mission in Guam. At the age of fifteen, Charles ascended the throne as the rightful ruler of Spain. Since he was almost an idiot, Mariana ruled as the power behind the throne. She made many enemies, among whom were those who convinced Charles that his own safety depended on the banishment of his mother. Consequently, in 1677, he ordered her to be imprisoned. She died in 1696, still a captive.

Communication between Madrid and Manila was by way of New Spain and thus was slow and subject to many delays. Getting from Manila to Guam was even slower because ships rarely sailed directly from the Philippines to the Marianas. At long last, however, the king's order reached the governor of the Philippines. After much opposition from that official, a mission was appointed for the Ladrone Islands. Father Sanvitores was named superior of the mission. The mission, however, was under the spiritual jurisdiction of the Bishop of Nombre de Dios in Cebu, Philippine Islands. In August 1667 Father Sanvitores sailed from Manila in a ship that had to go first to New Spain and then all the way back across the ocean to Guam. While in Mexico, Sanvitores met with more opposition from the viceroy. This official refused to give him necessary funds. Even these last troubles were overcome, however, and after a long and difficult passage, the mission arrived at Guam.

On June 15, 1688, the Sanvitores mission stepped ashore on the island of Guam.* The mission consisted of Father Sanvitores, four other priests of the Jesuit order, a lay brother, and some lay assistants. Most of the assistants were natives of the Philippine Islands who had volunteered to serve as cathechists. Besides these, there was a garrison force consisting of a captain and thirty-two soldiers. This force was made up of Spaniards and Filipinos. Captain Juan de Santa Cruz was the commander of the military garrison.

The first object of the missionaries was to acquire the good will of the natives. This they were able to do with little difficulty, and in a short time they began the more serious work of the mission.

In many missionary endeavors, inability of the missionaries to speak the language of the people among whom they work creates a somewhat difficult situation. In Guam, however, the situation was not as bad as it might seem to have been at first glance. First of all, the language of the islanders and the general forms of their

---

* This was the first permanent mission established in the Marianas. In 1596, seventy-two years earlier, a religious of the order of St. Francis, along with a sailor, had disembarked from the Spanish ship *San Pablo* and had worked among the people of the Marianas for a year. (Letter of Francisco Tello, governor of the Philippines, to the King of Spain in 1598. Blair and Robertson, *op. cit.*, Vol. X, p. 262.)

society had some resemblance to those of a people of the Philippines called Tagalos.[4] Secondly, the Spaniards had learned a good deal about the language and customs of the islanders from the frequent stopping of their ships at Guam. This advantage, added to the obviously good intentions of the Jesuit fathers, made for friendship and understanding.

The first missionaries in Guam received a friendly welcome from the islanders. This was due in large measure to the fact that these were the first Europeans who treated them with kindness. The kindness of the missionaries was returned by the natives. This was especially true of a *chamorri* or chief named Quipuha, who, as long as he lived, remained a staunch friend of the missionaries. For some time the chiefs among the islanders tried to outdo each other in their kindness to the missionaries. As a sign of his friendship, Quipuha alloted the mission a piece of land in Hagatna,* the principal village of the island, for building a church. Father Sanvitores was deeply touched by these demonstrations of kindness. Feeling that the name Ladrones was unjust, he changed the name of the islands to the Marianas in honor of the queen regent, who was regarded as the patroness of the mission.

The Spaniards were surprised to learn that there were non-natives living in Guam. Two of these had been members of the crew of the Spanish ship *Concepción,* wrecked in the Marianas in 1638.** One of them, a native of Malabar, was named Pedro. This man was very useful to the missionaries as a cathechist and interpreter. The other, a native of India also, came from Macassar. He had been a Christian at one time but during his long sojourn in Guam had reverted to paganism. Besides these two there was a third man, a native of China named Choco (or Chaco, as some accounts give it). This man exercised considerable influence over the islanders. He had been shipwrecked on the island in 1648.

---

* Agana. Hagatna is still used by the Guamanians when talking in Chamorro about the city of Agana.

** The *Concepción* was wrecked on either Tinian or Saipan. Twenty-eight survivors went from island to island until they reached Guam. From there, six of them, accompanied by two friendly natives, set out in canoes and eventually returned to the Philippines.

THE MISSION: The first year after its establishment in Guam was the most successful in the history of the mission. During that time the padres baptized 13,000 islanders and gave religious instruction to 20,000 catechumens.* In spite of its initial success, however, the mission was confronted by a slowly developing air of hostility on the part of the natives. After making inquiries, Father Sanvitores learned that Choco, the native of China, being jealous of the growing influence of the missionaries, was turning the natives against them. Father Sanvitores went to see Choco at his dwelling, which was at a place called Paa at the southernmost end of the island. His purpose was to convert Choco to Christianity. This he succeeded in doing, but Choco, being weak in the faith, reverted to paganism. As the year progressed, the hostility of the natives became more apparent. This resulted from the fact that the liberty-loving islanders came slowly to realize that the new religion, which was based on love, mercy, and humility, was, as administered by the zealous priests, a strict code of living. It deprived them of the freedom they were accustomed to and threatened to change their customs, their habits, and even their manner of dress. The disaffection that Choco had started spread slowly through Guam. Moreover, it spread even to the northern islands and continued to cause ever-increasing opposition.

One of the first disagreements that arose between the missionaries and their converts was related to the deeply entrenched class society that prevailed among the Chamorros. The native society was divided into three distinct classes. As mentioned previously, they were the *chamorris* and their families or *matua*, who were the chiefs and the principal landowners; a middle class, sometimes called *atchaot*, consisting mostly of the younger branches of the *matua*; and an inferior class, called the *manachang*. The chiefs and members of the upper classes asked the padres to stop baptizing people of the inferior class. They felt that such people were too low and common to be entitled to so great a benefit.[5] The missionaries, however, continued the practice.

* These figures were contained in a report submitted to Queen Mariana by Father Sanvitores in April 1669.

Relations between the missionaries and the islanders went from bad to worse. In their zeal, the missionaries often baptized children in spite of the threats of the fathers and the tears and prayers of the mothers. These people had been convinced by Choco that the water used in baptism was poisonous. Moreover, the missionaries angered the *makahna* or wise men. They tried to destroy their influence over the people by declaring them to be impostors and priests of a false religion. Furthermore, they assailed the liberty of the *urritaos* or bachelors. This was done through their efforts to abolish the "great houses" in which the men lived with unmarried women. They tried also to change the marriage custom whereby parents received presents from the bridegrooms for their daughters. And lastly, they tried to put an end to the invocation of the *aniti* or spirits and taught that it was wrong to worship the relics of ancestors.[6] Being consistent with the teachings of the new religion, the missionaries could not have acted otherwise. The natives, however, became increasingly bitter toward the mission.

About the middle of the year 1668 Father Sanvitores, in order to expand the work of the mission, sent Father Morales and several assistants to the island of Tinian. There they were welcomed by the natives, and while this good feeling lasted many of the inhabitants were baptized.

Before the end of October 1668, Father Morales fled from Tinian and returned to Guam. The inhabitants of Tinian, for reasons that are unknown, suddenly attacked the mission. During the violence that followed, Father Morales was seriously wounded. Two soldiers, Sergeant Lorenzo, a Castillian, and Gabriel de la Cruz, a native of the Philippines, were drowned in the sea. It is not known whether they perished while trying to escape or were killed and thrown into the sea by the natives. When he had recovered from his wounds, Father Morales, accompanied by Father Sanvitores, returned to Tinian. After he had succeeded in quieting the natives and reconciling them to the mission, Father Sanvitores returned to Guam. Father Morales then started on a trip of exploration to the northern islands.

By the beginning of the year 1669, the first church in Guam, situated in Agana, was nearing completion. Funds for the church, amounting to 3,000 pesos, were provided by Queen Mariana. She also provided the sum of 21,000 pesos to maintain the mission, besides 3,000 pesos for the establishment of a school. The church, named Dulce Nombre de María, was built of stone and lime and was formally opened on February 2, 1669. The school, begun about the same time as the church, was built of the same material and received the name Royal College of San Juan de Letran.

Quipuha, the staunch friend of the missionaries, died shortly after the dedication of the church. He was the first Chamorro to be baptized. In view of his loyalty to the mission, his passing was a loss felt by all. Because of Quipuha's rank as one of the principal chiefs, Father Sanvitores thought this was a good opportunity to strike a blow against the burial customs of the natives. He therefore insisted that Quipuha's body be brought into the church for Christian services and burial in consecrated ground. Quipuha's kinsmen, however, were opposed to the padre's plan. They insisted that the body of their chief should be laid in the cave where the remains of his ancestors had been deposited. Father Sanvitores' wishes prevailed, nevertheless, and the funeral service was performed in the church. It was conducted with all the solemnity and respect due a person of great distinction and rank. The islanders, however, had more fuel to add to the fires of their discontent.

After the return of Father Morales from the northern islands, a consultation was held to consider his report. As a result of this report, it was decided to divide among the padres the care of the different islands. Before that was done, however, Father Sanvitores wished to visit the islands himself. Accordingly, in July 1669 he left Agana bound for the northern islands. He was accompanied by Pedro, one of the survivors of the ill-fated *Concepción*. At Saipan he found the natives ill-disposed towards the missionaries. At Asomsom and Maug, however, the inhabitants welcomed him, and many of them were baptized. On his return trip from the north, he stopped at Anatahan. There he sent Pedro to seek converts at some of the villages while he visited others. While he was engaged in this task, some of the islanders, enraged because a baby had died shortly after being baptized, attacked Pedro and killed him with their lances. Thus, after thirty-one years in the Marianas, ended the life of the interpreter and friend of the missionaries. Continuing his return trip to the south, Father Sanvitores stopped at Tinian. Finding the natives there divided by bitter quarrels, he tried to pacify them and prevent bloodshed by placing himself between the wrangling parties. Both sides, however, resenting his interference, threw stones at him and forced him to leave. Angered by such treatment at the hands of the natives, Father Sanvitores returned to Guam. There he gathered together a force that consisted of several missionaries, their assistants, and ten natives of the Philippines under the command of Captain Juan de Santa Cruz. With this armed force he returned to Tinian and succeeded in pacifying the natives. As a result of his travels in the northern islands, Father Sanvitores estimated the population of Guam alone to be 50,000 and "of other islands 40,000, and less on others."[7]

After Tinian had become peaceful once more, Father Sanvitores returned to Guam. He devoted all his efforts to the work of the mission and the maintenance of friendly relations with the natives. The mission did not, however, increase in favor with the islanders. In January 1670 one of the padres of the mission, Father Luis de Medina, was sent to Saipan. Shortly after his arrival there, he was killed by the natives. Hipólito de la Cruz, a catechist who accompanied him, was killed at the same time. Father Medina was thirty-two years old at the time of his death. He was the first priest of the mission to die for the Christian faith in the Marianas.

OPEN REBELLION: On July 23, 1670, the islanders rose in open rebellion against the Spaniards. This came about as the result of the death of a native convert named José Peralta. Peralta was found murdered in the woods, where he had gone to cut wood for making crosses. The sergeant major of the garrison, Juan de Santiago, arrested several of the inhabitants of Agana. They were accused of the crime and were put in prison. Upon examination, however, it was found that there was no proof against them, and they were released. The islanders, nevertheless, were aroused to intense anger by this exercise of authority. A short time later, while an attempt was being made to arrest another native who was suspected of being involved in the murder, a fight started. During the fight one of the Spanish soldiers killed a *chamorri* named Chafae. This was more than the natives could endure. They gathered their weapons together and marshaled their forces. The Spaniards, meanwhile, retreated to the mission buildings, where they erected stockades and barriers and set up two fieldpieces for their defense. When they were ready, the natives attacked the mission with a force of almost 2,000 men. Father Sanvitores tried in vain to make peace. He held up a crucifix, but the islanders fired volleys of stones and lances at the image and charged the defenses. Because of their superior arms, the Spaniards repulsed the attack. The islanders, however, as they retreated, threw burning lances and stones wrapped in inflammable material against the thatched roof of the church. They then laid siege to the mission, and the fighting continued intermittently for forty days. Near the end of that time, the Spaniards rushed from the mission in a surprise attack. They drove the islanders back in headlong retreat and killed large numbers of them. Throughout all the fighting, not one Spaniard was killed. The natives, seeing that further resistance was useless, made peace in October 1670.

In June 1671 the mission was reinforced by the arrival of four padres from New Spain. The new priests were Francisco Solano, Alonzo López, Diego Noriega, and Francisco Esquerra. One of them, Father López, later visited all of the islands of the Marianas. From his own examinations he made one of the first detailed maps of the islands. The aid that came to the mission at this time was sorely needed. It was appropriate that the ship which brought the aid and reinforcements was named *Nuestra Señora de Buen Socorro* (Our Lady of Good Help).

With the strength that was added by the arrival of the new padres, it was decided once more to reorganize and expand the work of the mission. Accordingly, the padres and their assistants again spread themselves among the northern islands. Father Esquerra was assigned to Rota and Father López to Tinian, where no missionary had been since the death of Father Medina. Father Solano was assigned to Agana together with Father Noriega, who was ill. Guam, having the most people and being the seat of the mission, was divided by Father Sanvitores into four districts. A church was built in each district. The districts were so organized that each church had jurisdiction over forty villages. When the reorganization was completed, the missionaries renewed their work with increased vigor. The peace that prevailed was, however, an uneasy one, and violence threatened to break out at any time.

DEATH OF FATHER SANVITORES: On the thirty-first day of March 1672, an incident occurred that upset the uneasy peace and brought violence to the island once more. At that time a young catechist named Diego Bazan, a Mexican who was not more than eighteen years old, decided to seek converts among the islanders who lived in the region of Mt. Chochugu.* The people who lived there were known to be extremely unfriendly to strangers. Bazan visited them, nevertheless, and was killed for his intrusion. As if this act were a prelude to general revolt, four other persons attached to the mission were killed on the same day.

At that time, Father Sanvitores was at Nisichan, a village on the east side of the island. When he heard of the death of Bazan and the renewal of violence, he started out immediately to return to Agana. He was accompanied by a young catechist, Pedro Casor, a native of the Philippines. Early in the morning of April 2, 1672, they arrived at the village of Tumhum (sometimes spelled Tomhom and now commonly called Tumon), on the shores of Tumon Bay. The chief of the village, a *chamorri* named Matapang, had an infant daughter whom Sanvitores wished to baptize. "This Matapang," says Gobien, "had been instructed and baptized by Padre de Sanvitores himself after having been cured of a mortal wound by the efficacy of the Padre's prayers; but Matapang was ungrateful, and fell from his duty. Padre Sanvitores endeavored to reclaim him, and demanded to be allowed to baptize the infant.

* According to Father López' map, this would seem to be the area between the present villages of Toto and Sinajana. The valley behind Toto is still called Chochugu by the modern Guamanians.

Matapang replied by threatening to kill him if he did not immediately depart."[8] Father Sanvitores, however, was not frightened by the chief's threat. When Matapang left his house a short time later, Father Sanvitores went in and baptized the child. He had barely finished when Matapang returned. The chief was so loud in his angry threats against the priest that Hirao, another *chamorri*, and other people of the village quickly gathered at the scene. Led by Matapang and Hirao, the crowd attacked the missionaries. Both Father Sanvitores and his assistant were killed. Thus, at the age of forty-five, fell the great "Apostle of the Marianas," the venerable Padre Diego Luis de Sanvitores.*

Although they did not know it at the time, the death of Father Sanvitores deprived the Chamorros of their best friend. He alone had stood between them and the excesses of the military. When his restraining influence was no longer present, the military set out to wreak vengeance on the natives. It was said of him that "the name of Father Sanvitores ought to be as dear to the inhabitants of this archipelago, as that of Las Casas** has been to the savage hordes of America. He alone dared to check the cruelties of the military; and such was the disposition of the conquerors of the fifteenth century, that what they would have regarded as an unpardonable presumption in a soldier, they were afraid to check in a minister of religion.

"At the very time when the torch of discord burnt with a dreadful glare over all the island of Guam, Father Sanvitores, with the boldness of a martyr, traversed the country under no other protection than the standard of Christ; by words of peace and gentleness and the insinuating tone of persuasion, he won the hearts of the inhabitants, and thus diminished the horror they entertained of the Spanish name."[9]

MATAPANG: In their struggles against the Spaniards, the Chamorros were led by strong and courageous leaders. The manner in which

---

* Some accounts indicate that Father Sanvitores was waylaid in the jungle near Tumon by Matapang and Hirao and was struck down with clubs, lances, or machetes.
** Bartolomé de Las Casas, priest and historian, was the friend and defender of the Indians in the New World.

they organized their attacks and the ferocity with which they resisted the prolonged assaults of the Spaniards indicate that their leaders were both intelligent and persuasive. Matapang was one of the greatest of these early leaders. He was "one of those extraordinary men, produced in every country to be the leaders of other men; intrepid from instinct, ferocious from calculation, forgetful of past, and insensible to future miseries; one of those men, in short, whose existence never goes beyond the present. . . . He murmured at the praises bestowed on Sanvitores, and in the conduct and insinuations of this Catholic hero, saw only an additional perfidy. Matapang was the name of this dangerous man; he had left his children to the care of his wife; and she, influenced by the virtue and moderation of Sanvitores, had entrusted them to him in order to make them Christians. Nothing more was necessary to induce Matapang to resolve internally on taking an atrocious revenge. . . . He assembled his comrades, addressed them with all the fire of indignation long suppressed, kindled in their minds the sentiment of vengeance, and artfully gave them to understand that their own future safety and the flight of the Spaniards depended solely from that time forward on the death of Sanvitores. His discourse revived the courage of the most timid; everyone determined to lay a snare for the zealous missionary, and to destroy him in one of those journeys, which he repeated perhaps with too much imprudence. Nor was it long before an opportunity was offered."[10]

## THE SPANISH-CHAMORRO WARS

On the death of Father Sanvitores, Father Francisco Solano became the superior of the mission, and Captain Juan de Santiago assumed command of the military garrison. Father Solano, a priest who thought very much like Father Sanvitores, tried to quiet the islanders and restore peace. Captain Santiago, on the other hand, insisted on the necessity for arresting and punishing those responsible for the death of Father Sanvitores.

On May 2, 1672, Captain Santiago, in command of a detachment from the galleon *San Diego*, which had arrived a few days

73

earlier with supplies and reinforcements for the mission, marched to Tumhum to arrest Sanvitores' murderers. Upon arrival there, they found that Matapang and Hirao had fled. After a fruitless search, they burned Matapang's house and several other houses and canoes and started to return to Agana. In the meantime, the natives had gathered in their rear and had obstructed the road so as to force them to march along the beach, which they had blocked with bushes and logs. In order to get around the barrier, Captain Santiago marched his men out on the reef. In some places they were in water waist deep. This was exactly as the natives had planned. While the soldiers were stumbling over coral boulders and struggling in the water, a fleet of canoes, commanded by Matapang himself, attacked them on their seaward flank. From the cover of the barrier, meanwhile, other islanders attacked them with slingstones and lances tipped with human bones. The soldiers kept up a running fight around Saupon Point (sometimes referred to as Satpon Point). They finally gained the road to Agana, but the captain and several of his men were severely wounded. They succeeded in getting back to the safety of the fort in Agana, but they did so with the bitter knowledge that they had failed in their mission. The fighting continued, however, until November 1673, when it seemed that the natives had once more become peaceful.

The apparent state of peace that existed during the latter part of 1673 and the early part of 1674 was suddenly broken by an act of extreme violence. On February 2, 1674, as Father Esquerra and six companions were on the road between Ati and Funa (between Umatac and Agat), they were ambushed by a large group of natives. The padre and five of his companions were brutally murdered. This act brought about a renewal of violence and warfare throughout the island.

DON DAMIAN DE ESPLAÑA: On June 16, 1674, Captain Damian de Esplaña arrived in Guam to take command of the military garrison. He was the last of the Spaniards to hold the title of military commander. This extraordinary man, a courageous fighter, played an outstanding role in the Spanish-Chamorro wars. Not only was

74

he the last of the military commanders, but he also served twice as governor of Guam. Each time he returned to Guam, he did so with higher rank. When he first came to the island, he held the rank of captain. During his first term as governor he was a major, and during his second term he held the rank of lieutenant general.

Upon assuming the office of military commander, Captain España, whose forces had been strengthened by the arrival of thirty soldiers, set out to subdue the rebellious islanders. He met and defeated them on several occasions and burned the towns of Chochogo, Pepura, Tumon, Sidia-Aty, Sagua, Nagan, and Ninca, as well as many isolated houses and ranches. He was especially brutal in his treatment of the people of Chochogo and Ritidian. His campaign was so successful and his punishments so severe that the fighting ceased temporarily. The peace which followed this campaign was marked by increased activity on the part of the mission. Churches were built at Ritidian, Tarague, and Tepungan (East Piti). The College of San Juan de Letran was reopened, and a school for girls was built at Agana. When Padre Boreus, the new superior of the mission, arrived on the ship *San Telmo* in June 1675, schools were established in several villages, and the children were taught Spanish and religion. Outbreaks of violence continued, however, and in December 1675 the church, rectory, and school at Ritidian were burned by the villagers. Moreover, Brother Pedro Díaz and two of his companions were cut to pieces with machetes. As punishment, Captain España burned the village and killed most of the inhabitants. Thus, while his term as military commander was enhanced by the building of churches and schools, in the minds of the natives Captain España was to be long remembered as a brutal oppressor.

FIRST GOVERNOR OF GUAM: On June 10, 1676, Captain España was relieved by Captain Francisco de Irrisarri y Viñar. Captain Irrisarri, who arrived on the galleon *Acapulco* accompanied by five priests and seventy-four soldiers, held the title of governor. He was the first administrator of Guam to hold that title. With the new title went powers that changed the relationships that had existed for so long between the padres and the military. Where heretofore the superior of the mission, in theory at least, had exercised principal authority, the governor now became the chief administrator.

Governor Irrisarri began his administration by instituting a reign of terror against the islanders. He attacked many villages and burned many houses. His purpose was to frighten them and keep them under control by a strong show of force. At the same time he encouraged the building of more schools and roads. During his administration, Christian rites of marriage were introduced for the first time. The first wedding, which was celebrated in the town of Orote, led to an outbreak of violence that proved to be one of the most serious yet encountered. The wedding was to unite a Spanish soldier and native girl of Orote. The girl's father, being strongly opposed to the marriage, stirred up trouble that resulted in the death of a Spaniard. Governor Irrisarri ordered that the father of the girl should be hanged. The governor's order was so resented by the natives that they attacked Father Sebastian Monroy and six soldiers who were stationed in Sumay. The priest and the soldiers might have escaped had it not been for the treachery of a native named Cheref. Cheref, pretending to be friendly, decoyed them into his boat. When out in the bay, he overturned them. He and other natives then made quick work of the Spaniards by killing them with spears and machetes. At the same time that this was happening, 500 natives attacked Agana. They succeeded in driving the Spaniards into the church and several stone houses and besieged them. From time to time the Spanish soldiers rushed from the safety of the buildings to attack the besiegers. Because of their superior arms, the Spaniards killed many natives and finally succeeded in defeating them. Many of their leaders were now rounded up and killed; others, however, escaped to the safety of Rota.

The outstanding native leader of this revolt was a *chamorri* named Aguarin. Gobien says of him that he was "of an elevated and mischievous genius, who in all their assemblies endeavoured to make his countrymen distrustful of the Spaniards, saying of them that they never pardoned injuries when they had opportunity of taking vengeance; and who was constantly exorting them to exert themselves for their deliverance from the tyranny and from the yoke the Spaniards had imposed upon them."[11] Aguarin was one of those who escaped to Rota.

On June 21, 1678, Captain Juan de Salas arrived in Guam as the new governor. He brought thirty soldiers as well as arms and supplies with him. His first act was to attack and burn the villages of Punton, Tipalao, Orote, Sumay, and Taleyfac, along with other smaller towns and many ranches. One of the Jesuit fathers said of the warfare that "our handful of men was opposed by multitudes. Although our arms were superior, we had to meet them in the defiles of the mountains, where they were at home. We fought adversaries who never presented a battle front, but preferred the cover of ambuscades, attacking with lances and stones, which they hurled upon our heads in clouds."[12] In spite of the courageous efforts of the natives, the Spaniards inflicted terrible punishment on them and forced their submission in the latter part of 1679. For a short time afterwards, there was comparative peace, and the missionaries were allowed to carry on their work unmolested.

DON JOSÉ DE QUIROGA, THE TYRANT: The year 1680 saw the arrival on Guam of a new governor, whose name will live in infamy. He was Captain José de Quiroga. Quiroga had received a military education and had distinguished himself as a soldier in wars on the continent of Europe, especially in Flanders. When he grew tired of fighting, he became a hermit and lived alone near the town of Salamanca, Spain. Padre Thyrsus González, who later was elected general of the Society of Jesus, was his friend and advisor. It was Father González who first told him about the martyrdom of Father Sanvitores and suggested that a man of his piety and military experience could do much to aid the natives of the Marianas and thus serve the cause of God. Little did the advisor know how wrong he was. Quiroga, it was said, "was quick, hasty, and impetuous, unacquainted with those sentiments of generosity which are more effectual than arms in gaining the mind and conquering the heart. Equally severe to himself as to his soldiers, he exposed himself to the same dangers, and submitted to the same privations. He visited timidity with disgrace, and repressed murmurs by cruel punishments. The resistance of the natives was regarded as an outrage by his arrogant soul; the slaughter that he made of them opened the country to him in all directions."[13]

Immediately after his arrival in Guam, Governor Quiroga set out systematically to attack and punish the natives of the island. To punish the crime of one person, he would burn an entire village. When the natives fled from their villages to the mountains, his soldiers followed them. The mountains and poor weapons were no defense against Quiroga's highly trained military force. When he captured chiefs, he had them hanged as criminals. He seemed determined to convince the entire native population that their survival depended on complete surrender to him. They, however, saw an alternative in flight, and many of them escaped to Rota.

After Guam had been secured, Quiroga led an expedition to Rota. There he engaged in fierce battles in which many natives were killed and others captured. Among those who died in battle were Matapang and Hirao. Gobien says of Matapang that "this miserable wretch defended himself with so much obstinacy to the last that they were necessitated to give him many wounds with a lance, whereof he died in the way." Aguarin, however, was not so fortunate. He was captured by the merciless governor, taken back to Guam as a prisoner, and there "brought to trial and executed with all the apparatus that would inspire terror into the barbarians."

By the beginning of 1681 so many natives had been killed* or had deserted Guam that Quiroga found it necessary to make an expedition to the northern islands for the purpose of rounding up the fugitives. Guam's population had so declined that there were not enough people left to cultivate the soil and supply the Span-

* Gobien relates that at the "first trial of the Spanish arms" the inhabitants of the Marianas numbered more than 40,000 and that at the end of two years only 5,000 remained.

iards with the food necessary for their own needs and the needs of the galleons. Accordingly, Quiroga brought back to Guam all the natives that he could lay his hands on. He furthermore destroyed the smaller villages and forced the people to live in a few large villages where it was easier to control them. Roads were now built throughout the island, and churches were erected in Jinapsan, Umatac, Pago, Agat, and Inarajan. All went smoothly for a time until one day the government house and church at Jinapsan were attacked and burned. The natives responsible for the act escaped to Rota. Quiroga followed them, killing many and capturing others.

From the outset of Quiroga's administration, reports concerning the slaughter in the islands began to reach the court of Madrid. The king, Charles II, the son of Queen Mariana, was upset by these reports. He was concerned too with the high cost of the war, since the necessary funds had to come from the royal treasury. Accordingly, he appointed a governor-general over "the Marianas and the lands adjacent" with powers entirely independent of the viceroy of Mexico and of the governor of the Philippines. He instructed his governor-general to do whatever was necessary to bring peace to the islands.

DON ANTONIO DE SARAVIA: The man appointed to be governor-general of the Marianas was Captain Antonio de Saravia. He arrived at Guam in August 1681, while Quiroga was still fighting on Rota. When Quiroga returned, he learned that he had been relieved of his duties by order of the king.

Rather than setting out to punish the islanders, as so many of his predecessors had done, Governor Saravia's first act was to call all the leaders of the people together. When they had gathered, he proposed to them that they take an oath of allegiance to the King of Spain and acknowledge him to be the lord and sovereign of all their islands. This they agreed to do, and on September 8, 1681, the oath of allegiance was administered to them. The text of the oath was as follows:

> We, the governors and other chiefs of places and towns of this island of St. John, called Guahan, the capital and principal of these Marianas

islands, gathered in this church of the Society of Jesus, called the Most Holy Name of Mary, in the hands of the Reverend Emmanuel Solorzano, Vice-Provincial and Superior of the Mission, freely and spontaneously promise before the Most Holy Trinity, Father, Son, and Holy Ghost and before the Most Blessed Virgin Mary and swear with all possible solemnity upon the four gospels to remain faithful subjects of our King and legitimate ruler, Don Carlos the Second, Monarch of Spain and of the Indies, and to obey the laws to which his Majesty decides to obligate us.

By this act it was intended that the islanders should have equality with the other subjects of the king. On this occasion the governor entertained the chiefs with a great feast and distributed presents among the people. He was, indeed, "a man of wisdom and virtue, and if he had been of a stronger constitution, a more accomplished governor could not have been chosen."

The governor now set out to bring about other reforms. He placed the police of the towns and villages under the control of their own chiefs. He even appointed a *chamorri*, Antonio Ayhi, to be lieutenant general of Guam. The islanders now began to take the manners of the Spaniards and to adopt their customs. Craftsmen were sent to the different villages to teach handicrafts, manufacturing of linen, and other useful arts. The children were taught to read and write. During this administration, there was an extraordinary change in all the island. The people became docile and received religious instruction with a willingness not before known. New churches were built, and missionaries were sent once more to the northern islands.

This good and capable governor was permitted to serve Guam but little more than two years. While on a trip to observe progress of the work in the northern islands, he suffered exposure to a violent storm and died in November 1683.

On the death of Saravia, the government of the Marianas fell once more into the hands of the former Captain Esplaña, who now held the rank of major. He was the same leader who, as the last military commander, had acquired a reputation for severity and brutality. Both Esplaña and Quiroga happened to be in Guam at this time, and Esplaña, being the senior officer, became the successor to Governor Saravia.

# Isle de Guahan
## ou Isle S<sup>t</sup>. Jean

Inapsam · Tarragia
Rindiam
Apolo
Ayram
Tuham
Ipao
Apurguam
Agadna · Mapaz · Hamon
Cap Ardulug · Anuguag
Tupungenu · Azan
I. Sienne · Agofan
Opagat · Pagat
Tuparao · Nisiham
Orote · Sumai
I. Punna · Agat · Mapupun · Paga
L. Taraifag
I. Sagua · Pupuro · Jrig
Taragrichon
Sydia
Aty · Tanistofo
L. Dana · Umatag
Morico · Piypug
Habudian
Paa · Asiga
Nargan

1. Map of Guam drawn by Bellin in 1752

2. Harbor of San Lucar. (Photo of copper engraving in T. de Bry's Travel Book, 1594.)

3. Ships in the Ladrones. (Photo of copper engraving in T. de Bry's Travel Book, 1620.)

4. Inhabitants of the Ladrones Islands. (Photo of illustration in T. de Bry's *Peregrinationes*, 1602.)

5. Ancient inhabitants of the Mariana Islands. (Photo of an old print.)

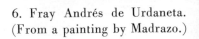

7. Francis Drake. (From an 18th century copper engraving.)

6. Fray Andrés de Urdaneta. (From a painting by Madrazo.)

8. Ferdinand Magellan. (From an old painting.)

9. Magellan's ship "Victoria." (From a cut in Henry
Steven's *Johann Schöner*, 1888.)

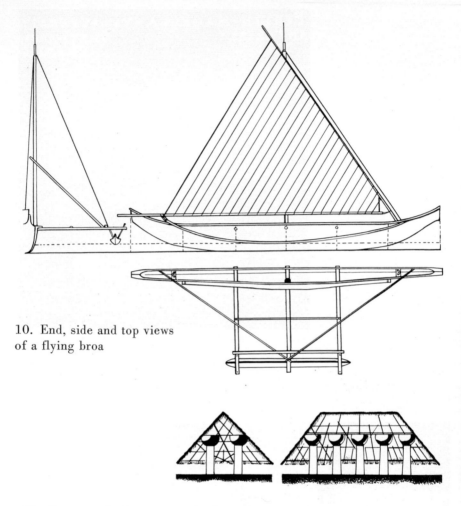

10. End, side and top views
of a flying broa

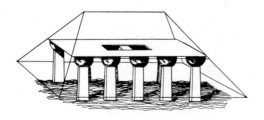

11. Framework of an ancient chief-
tain's dwelling.

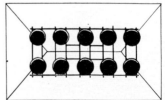

Governor Esplaña now decided to attempt a final conquest of the northern islands. Accordingly, on March 22, 1684, he sent Captain Quiroga, in command of a frigate and a fleet of twenty canoes, to attack the island of Tinian. Striking just at daybreak and taking the inhabitants by surprise, Quiroga forced a quick surrender. Those who offered the slightest opposition were shot. Continuing his campaign of murder and pillage, Quiroga conquered the rest of the northern islands and then built a fort at Saipan. While these things were happening, however, revolt broke out once more in Guam. There the natives, says Gobien, had long regarded "the duties of the Christian life as an insupportable yoke, and they sighed for their ancient liberty without daring to explain themselves. The bad success of former insurrections, the punishment of the seditious, and above all the sad fate of Aguarin, the chief of the last revolt, rendered them timid and circumspect, and they restrained themselves to sigh in secret and lament the loss of their liberty, and to wait with patience till some favorable occasion should offer for them to show their hatred and resentment. They were in this disposition when D. Damian de Esplaña and D. José de Quiroga determined upon the conquest of the Northern Isles."[14]

By sending Quiroga and a large number of soldiers to the north, Governor Esplaña left his position in Guam weak and insecure. The Chamorros were quick to take advantage of this weakness and rose up in open rebellion. The leader of this revolt was a *chamorri* whose native name was Yura but who had received the Christian name of Antonio and thus was called Don Antonio Yura.

On Sunday, July 23, 1684, Yura and about thirty of his countrymen attacked the unsuspecting Spaniards as they were coming from mass. Governor Esplaña was wounded and left for dead on the plaza. At the same time, other natives attacked the fort and the missionary house. The priests and several soldiers fled from the house and managed to reach the College of San Juan de Letran, which stood to the east of the plaza. While the fighting was in progress, the chief of Ritidian sent for help from the natives of Rota. Shortly thereafter more than seventy canoes arrived at Guam to assist the insurgents. In the fighting that followed, Yura was

81

killed. The islanders, being without a leader, fell back to positions where they laid siege to the fort. The Spaniards still held the fort, but at fearful cost. Two of the missionary fathers, several of their assistants, and nearly fifty soldiers had lost their lives. Governor Esplaña, on the other hand, was found to be only wounded, and not seriously.

When knowledge of the revolt on Guam reached the other islands, there was a general uprising against the Spaniards. Quiroga and his soldiers were attacked in their fort on Saipan. After a hard fight they succeeded in beating off their attackers and returned to Guam in the nick of time to reinforce the garrison there. In the face of this increased strength, the natives abandoned their siege and fled to the mountains or to other islands. Both sides were now too weak to continue fighting on a large scale, and a stalemate ensued.

During this stalemate in the wars between the Spaniards and the Chamorros, an English buccaneer ship, commanded by John Eaton, stopped at Guam. On board the ship was William Cowley, who later wrote an account of the voyage. The following extract from this account presents an example of unparalleled barbarity.

Sunday the 15th [March 1685]. We, lying at anchor at Guahan, went on shore and got some cocoa-nuts, and had a free trade with the Indians, till the morning of the 17th, when our men going to the low island which lieth on the west side of Guahan, the Indians fell upon our boat with stones and lances. Upon which we made some shots at them, and killed and wounded some; but our men got no harm. Two days after, the Governor [Esplaña] of the Island, being a Spaniard, came down to a point of land not far from the ship, and sent his boat with a letter written in Spanish, French, and Dutch, demanding what we were and whence we came. Our answer was written in French, that we were employed by some gentlemen of France upon discovery of the unknown parts of the world. The messenger was sent on board again immediately to desire our Captain to come to the shore side, which our Commander did. We quickly came to a right understanding with one another, and satisfied the Governor that we had killed some of the Indians in our own defence; and he gave us toleration to kill them all if we would. These Indians, before we came, revolted from the Spaniards, and seeing us at first did take us for the great ship from Acapulco, which ship in her out-ward-bound voyage seldom carries less than 1,500 souls, her sailing crew being 400, and strikes a great dread upon these Indians. We took four of these infidels prisoners, and brought them on board, binding their hands behind them; but they had not been long there, when three of them leaped overboard into the sea, swimming away from the ship with their hands tied behind them. However, we sent the boat after them, and the boat coming up with them, our carpenter being a strong man, thought with his sword to cut off the head of one of them, but he struck two blows before he could fetch blood; one of them had received, in my judgment, 40 shots in his body before he died; and the last of the three that was killed had swam a good English mile first, not only with his hands behind him, as before, but also with his arms pinioned. But to return to the Spanish Governor's kindness, he sent us 30 hogs, greens and rice, as a present; and our Captain presented him with six small guns. Whilst we were watering our ship, two Indians who were born at Manila came to us, and they told us, that the major part of the Indians were run away to another island 10 leagues off.[15]

Just a little over a year after the visit of John Eaton, William Dampier, a seaman aboard an English privateer, under the command of Captain Swan, stopped at Guam on May 21, 1686.

Captain Swan's ship, after ravaging Spanish shipping and settlements on the west coast of Mexico and South America, struck out across the Pacific for the Marianas. Fifty-one days later, carrying a starving and mutinous crew, she arrived at Guam. The arrival was timely because the last bit of food was about used up. Dampier, who kept a journal of the voyage, learned later that the crew had planned to kill Captain Swan and eat him and, after him, all those who were in any way responsible for the voyage. "This," relates Dampier, "made Captain Swan say to me after our arrival at Guam, 'Ah! Dampier, you would have made them but a poor meal,' for I was as lean as the Captain was lusty and fleshy."

The English ship dropped anchor near the middle of the island on the west side, a mile from the shore. A prao, carrying a priest and three islanders, came out to greet them. Believing them to be Spaniards, the visitors came aboard and were immediately made prisoners. Captain Swan assured the priest that he came not in any hostile manner but wished only to secure provisions. While the priest was held as a hostage, one of the Indians was sent to Governor Esplaña with a letter demanding provisions for the ship. In accordance with the demands, the governor sent Captain Swan six hogs, twelve muskmelons, and twelve watermelons. He also ordered the people living in the village nearest the ship to bake, every day, as much breadfruit as the crew could eat and to assist them in gathering as many coconuts as they desired. When Captain Swan was ready to leave the island, he released the priest and gave him a brass clock, an astrolabe, and a large telescope. In return the priest gave him six hogs, three or four bushels of potatoes, and fifty pounds of Manila tobacco.

With regard to the wars between the Spaniards and the Chamorros, Dampier relates that "not long before we arrived here, the natives rose on the Spaniards to destroy them, and did kill many. But the governor with his soldiers at length prevailed, and drove them out of the fort. So when they found themselves disappointed of their intent, they destroyed the plantations and stock, and then went away to other islands. There were then three or 400 Indians on this island;* but now there are not above 100; for all that were in this conspiracy went away. As for these who yet remain, if they were not actually concerned in that broil, yet their hearts also are bent against the Spaniards, for they offered to carry us to the fort and assist us in the conquest of the island, but Captain Swan was not for molesting the Spaniards here."[16]

In 1688 Major Esplaña, after having served five years as governor of Guam, retired to the Philippines. He left the government in the hands of Captain Quiroga. From the moment that he assumed command, Quiroga was confronted with serious difficulties. The soldiers of the garrison, being unoccupied as a result of the comparative peace that prevailed, had become demoralized and were living in a wild and unrestrained manner. In an attempt to restore order, Quiroga tried to re-establish some semblance of military discipline. The soldiers, however, having grown fond of

---

* "The figure of only three or four hundred natives may be a mistake for 3,000 or 4,000, which would sound more likely; however, many of the Chamorros of Guam might previously have already judiciously removed themselves to the other southern Marianas." (Erik K. Reed, *Report on the Archeology and History of Guam* [Washington, 1952], pp. 49–50.)

the freedom that was now theirs, seized the acting governor and put him in jail. A short time later, the priests succeeded in getting him released. When his authority was once more respected, some of the soldiers were severely punished and others were sent to prison in the Philippines. Quiroga now resumed the task of rebuilding some of the churches that had been destroyed during the last rebellion. At the same time he despatched an expedition to find and establish relations with the Caroline Islands. A *chamorri*, Don Alonzo Soon, accompanied the expedition. After a long and arduous trip, the expedition returned without having found the islands.

In June 1690 Esplaña, now a lieutenant general, returned to Guam and resumed his duties as governor of Guam for the second term. At about the same time, a ship from New Spain, carrying twenty Franciscan fathers, some soldiers, and a large number of convicts, was wrecked on the shores of Guam. The priests and soldiers were rescued, and the convicts were confined in prison. The convicts, seeing the weakened condition of the island government, plotted to kill the governor and the missionaries and make themselves masters of the island. One of their number having turned informer, however, the plot was detected and brutally suppressed. By the order of Governor Esplaña, twenty of the convicts were executed in Agana, and three others suffered the same fate in Umatac. Having failed to regain his health in the Philippines, Damian de Esplaña died in August 1694.

THE FINAL CONQUEST: On the death of Esplaña, Major Quiroga, on August 16, 1694, became governor once more. Being determined to complete the conquest of the Marianas, he led a force to Rota, where the natives quickly submitted to him. On landing at Tinian in July 1695, he found that the inhabitants had retired to the little island of Aguigan that was close by. Here many of the rebellious natives had gathered for a last stand. A short but fierce battle resulted in the surrender of the natives on the terms that they return to Guam and become peaceful subjects of the king. This battle marked the final conquest of the islands.

RESULTS OF THE SPANISH-CHAMORRO WARS: The most obvious result of the Spanish-Chamorro wars was the decimation of the native population. From an estimated 50,000 to 100,000 before the conquest, they were now reduced to less than 5,000. While the reduction of the population was due primarily to the intermittent warfare that continued for a period of twenty-five years, typhoons in 1671 and 1693 and smallpox epidemics, especially that of 1688, contributed to the tragic loss of life.

At the end of the period of conquest, Christianity, which was to play a major role in the history of Guam, was firmly established as the religion of the people.

As a result of the policies of the various commanders and governors who administered the affairs of the island during the wars, Spanish law and the Spanish pattern of government became an integral part of the life of Guam. Such influences were to prevail until 1898 and even after.

SUMMARY: The period from 1668 to 1695 was a momentous one in the history of Guam. During that time permanent changes, for better or for worse, were wrought in the lives of the people of Guam and the other islands of the Marianas. Among the important changes were the following:

1. The Spaniards established the first permanent white settlement, which survived and remained under their jurisdiction until 1898.

2. The religion of the ancient Chamorros, a religion based primarily on myths, superstitions, and ancestor worship, was supplanted by Christianity.

3. The Chamorros, strong and numerous before the advent of the white man, were so weak and reduced in numbers that they could offer no further resistance to the Spaniards.

4. The almost complete annihilation of the Chamorros marked the beginning of the growth of a new people in Guam, the present-day Guamanians.

The next chapter will deal with developments in Guam during the eighteenth century, a period when Guam, as well as the rest of the Marianas islands, languished as a half-forgotten colony in Spain's far-flung overseas dominions.

## NOTES

1. Burney, *op. cit.*, Vol. III, pp. 271–72.
2. *Ibid.*, p. 274.
3. Martin Hume, *Queens of Old Spain* (McClure, Phillips, and Co., New York, 1906), p. 366.
4. *Ibid.*, p. 281.
5. Burney, *op. cit.*, Vol. III, p. 283.
6. Safford, *The Useful Plants of the Island of Guam*, p. 15.
7. García, *op. cit.*, April 1937, pp. 20–21.
8. Charles Le Gobien, *Histoire des isles Marianes, nouvellement converties à la religion Chrestienne, et de la mort glorïeuse des premiers missionaires qui y ont prêché la foy* (Paris, 1700). Partial translation contained in Burney, *op. cit.*, Vol. III, p. 295.
9. Louis de Freycinet, *Narrative of a Voyage Round the World* (London, 1823), p. 38.
10. *Ibid.*, pp. 39–40.
11. Burney, *op. cit.*, Vol. III, p. 297.
12. Cox, *op. cit.*, p. 29.
13. Freycinet, *op. cit.*, p. 37.
14. Burney, *op. cit.*, Vol. III, p. 303.
15. *Ibid.*, pp. 305–6.
16. William Dampier, *A New Voyage Round the World* (London, 1729), pp. 300–1.

## CHAPTER FOUR

# SPANISH OUTPOST

DURING MOST of the 18th century Guam languished as a quiet outpost of the Spanish-American dominion of New Spain. The battle of Aguigan in 1695, which marked the end of the Spanish-Chamorro wars, ushered in an era of disintegration and decline. It did not end until 1771, when the great Don Mariano Tobias became governor of Guam. For almost three quarters of a century the quiet that prevailed on the island was broken only by the annual visits of the Manila galleons and the intrusions of pirate ships and other foreign visitors. This period was also marked by the expulsion of the Jesuits, an event that had far-reaching effects on the lives of the Chamorro people. In order to provide some insight into the history of Guam during this period, the present chapter is devoted to accounts concerned with the visits of Woodes Rogers, John Clipperton, the Caroline Islanders, George Anson, and the Crozet and Malaspina expeditions, as well as the expulsion of the Jesuits and the administration of Governor Mariano Tobias.

## BRITISH PRIVATEERS VISIT GUAM

Captain Woodes Rogers, in command of the British privateers *Duke* and *Duchess*, left Bristol, England, in the year 1708. He sailed for the purpose of preying on Spanish shipping. After rounding Cape Horn, at the southernmost tip of South America, his fleet stopped at the island of Juan Fernández. There he picked up "Robinson Crusoe," whose real name was Alexander Selkirk and who had lived alone on the island for more than four years. From there the fleet sailed as far north as Cape San Lucas on the California coast and then across the Pacific, in fifty-eight days, to Guam. Arriving there on March 11, 1710, Captain Rogers sent the following letter to the governor, Lieutenant General Juan Antonio Pimentel: "We, being servants of Her Majesty of Great Britain, stopping at these islands on our way to the East Indies, will not molest the settlement provided you deal friendly with us, being willing to pay for whatever provisions you can spare. But, if after this civil request, you do not act like a man of honor, and deny us our request, you may immediately expect such military treatment as we are with ease able to give you."[1]

This letter appears to have acted like a charm on Governor Pimentel. He answered at once "with a present of four bullocks, and limes, oranges, and cocoa nuts." In return for the governor's kindness, Rogers invited him and four of his officers aboard ship. There they were dined and entertained by the ship's crew. Later, Rogers and his officers went to the palace in Agana, where they were cordially received by the governor. After partaking of "sixty dishes of various sorts," Rogers gave the governor "two negro boys dress'd in liveries together with scarlet clothe serge and six pieces of cambric." During his week's stay at Guam, Rogers bought "15 small lean cattle, two cows and calves, 60 hogs, 100 fowls, with Indian corn, rice, yams, and cocoa nuts." He was so impressed by the workmanship and speed of the natives' canoes, of which he says, "by what I saw, I believe may run twenty miles an hour for they passed our ships like a bird flying," that he took one of them with him back to London.[2]

On May 13, 1721, the British privateer *Success*, under the command of Captain John Clipperton, stopped at Guam. It dropped anchor near the outer banks of the harbor of San Luis de Apra. A lieutenant and several seamen, carrying a flag of truce, were sent to the nearest village to bargain for provisions. The natives, however, refused to trade, saying that they could not do so without the governor's permission. Accordingly, Mr. Godfrey, the ship's agent, was sent to Agana to see the governor. Three days later he returned with a message that the governor, Don Luis Antonio Sánchez de

Tagle, granted permission to trade. The next six days were spent in provisioning the ship.

The Marquis de Villa Roche, president of the Spanish possessions at Panama, was a prisoner aboard the *Success*. He, with his wife and young daughter, had been a passenger on the Spanish ship *Prince Eugene*, which Clipperton had captured off the coast of Peru. During the time that the *Success* was being provisioned, the marquis asked for permission to go to Agana to make arrangements for his ransom. Permission being granted, he went to Agana. He was accompanied by Mr. Godfrey and another officer, Mr. Pritty. Several days later, Governor Sánchez sent Captain Clipperton a letter "wherein the governor demands the marquis' jewels, some consecrated plate, and two Negroes, being Christians and subjects to the King of Spain: as also a certificate under the captain and officers hands that peace was proclaimed; detaining Mr. Godfrey and Mr. Pritty 'til all this is performed."[3] Hereupon Clipperton sent an immediate reply to the governor. He told Sánchez that the *Soledad*, the last prize ship captured by the English off the coast of Chile, had informed him that there was peace between England and Spain. He stated further that, whether there was peace or not, if the governor did not release his two officers within twenty-four hours and send the ransom for the marquis, he would destroy all the houses along the shore and would burn a Spanish ship that was in the inner harbor.

Three days after sending his letter to Governor Sánchez, having received no reply, Clipperton moved in to the attack. Being unfamiliar with the banks and shoals in the harbor, he quickly ran aground. The *Success* was now in a dangerous position. As related in a journal of the voyage, "at six afternoon, in making up to the ship, we run aground, they having carry'd her into shoal water: so that now we sustain two fires together, one from the battery over our heads, and another from the ship. At nine we got foul of the rocks where we cut away two of our anchors indeavouring to get the ship off; during which time the enemy fired so warmly with stones and shot from a new battery erected on a hill, that we suffer'd extremely in our hull and rigging. Thus the Success is forced to lye in a miserable condition exposed to the continual fire of the enemy."[4] After dumping some heavy guns and cargo, the ship was floated off the reef and started a hasty retreat from the harbor. Ten minutes later it ran aground once more. While some of the crew worked to free the ship, others kept up a fierce battle with the batteries on the shore. "Just as we got afloat," relates the journal, "the enemy fired so smartly from the new battery that their shot raked us through between wind and water, killing one of our people, and wounding two others. Thus have we lost both our bower anchors and cables, the stream and kedge anchors, four hawsers, four of our lower deck guns, nineteen barrels of powder, two men kill'd and six wounded: having stood these fifty hours, a fair mark for the enemy to fire at: and if we had not got clear, I do believe they could have sunk us before morning."[5] After gaining the open sea, Clipperton set his course for China, leaving his two officers behind. An entry in the journal relates that "we are ll very sorry for Mr. Godfrey and Mr. Pritty, not knowing how the governor may use them ashore."[6]

## CAROLINE ISLANDERS ON GUAM

On June 19, 1721, just about a month after John Clipperton's hasty departure from the island, a large canoe bearing natives of the Caroline Islands landed at a deserted spot on the east coast of Guam. The Caroline Islands are scattered over a vast area that lies between Guam on the north and the equator on the south, and between the Philippines on the west and 160 degrees east longitude. European explorers had discovered islands in the above area as early as 1526.* It was not until 1686, however, that Don Francisco Lazeano discovered, southward of Guam, a large island which he named La Carolina in honor of Charles II of Spain. Later all the islands in the area came to be designated collectively under the name of Las Carolinas. These were the same islands that the Chamorro, Don Alonzo Soon, had sought and failed to reach in 1688.

* In that year Diogo da Rocha, a Portuguese, discovered islands eastward of Mindanao in latitude 9 degrees or 10 degrees north and named them Ilhas de Sequeira. These are believed to have been the Palau Islands.

The first group of Carolinians who came to Guam at this time consisted of eleven men, seven women, and six children. The canoe that brought them to the island was similar in construction to those of the Guamanians, but it was much larger. As they came over the barrier reef and approached the shore, "they were perceived by a native of the island who was fishing, and saw them land, which they did in terror, gliding under the palm trees for concealment and to supply themselves with coconuts. He went and gave information to Padre Muscati, who was in that district, and the Padre immediately went with some of the Marian Islanders to succour the strangers. The women among them were terrified and made lamentable cries, but one of the men, more courageous than the rest, jumped on shore from the canoe, and advanced to the Father Missionary, to whom he offered some things of his island. The Father received his present, and embraced him, and this dissipated all terror."[7]

Two days after the arrival of the first group of Carolinians, a second strange canoe, in which there were four men, one woman, and a child, landed on the west side of Guam. Having been granted a friendly reception, they were taken to Governor Sánchez, who was residing in Umatac. The people who landed from the first canoe were sent for, to see if they were from the same islands. When they arrived, it was learned that the two canoes, in company with four others, had departed from the island of Faraulep, intending to go to the island of Ulithi. A violent storm, however, separated them, and for twenty days they had been cast about upon the open sea without knowing where they were.

After the Carolinians had been at Guam about four months and had succeeded in collecting a number of hatchets, nails, and other instruments of iron, which they considered to be of great value, they wished to return to their own islands. Governor Sánchez, however, had dreams of extending the Spanish dominions to include the Carolines. He decided, therefore, to hold the leaders of the Carolinians as hostages and to send the others back. In this way he hoped to be able to establish regular trade between the Marianas and the Caroline Islands. The governor furthermore asked Father Juan Antonio Cantova to go to the Carolines for the purpose of spreading the Christian religion. Father Cantova was willing to do so, but the superior of the Jesuits at Manila would not give his consent. As a result, most of the Carolinians were permitted to leave Guam. Father Cantova was compelled, temporarily, to suspend his plans for visiting the Carolines.

After many delays Father Cantova was granted permission to attempt the establishment of a mission in the Carolines. On February 2, 1731, accompanied by Father Victor Uvaldec and a number of Guamanians and Spaniards, he departed from Guam. About a month later they landed on a small island not far from Yap and established their mission. Because they were in need of supplies, Father Victor embarked for a return trip to Guam. Father Cantova and fourteen of his companions were left behind. Instead of returning to Guam, however, Father Victor was forced by contrary winds to go to the Philippines. He was obliged to remain there a whole year before he could return to the islands with supplies. When he finally returned, he learned that during his absence Father Cantova and all his companions had been killed. Reasons for the natives' attack on Father Cantova and his companions are unknown. It would seem, however, that the Carolinians had learned about the brutality of the Spaniards from the Chamorros who sought refuge on their islands during the period of the Spanish-Chamorro Wars. As a result, they took action calculated to prevent their own destruction by the Spaniards.

## The Anson Expedition

On September 18, 1740, a fleet of eight vessels, under the command of Commodore George Anson, sailed from England. Their purpose was to attack Spanish shipping and settlements in the New World and in the South Seas. By such attacks the British hoped to be able to cut Spain off from her overseas possessions and to deprive her of her principal source of wealth. With that goal in mind, Anson's fleet, carrying almost 1,000 men, sailed around Cape Horn into the Pacific Ocean. This large complement of men was carried in two men-of-war, the *Centurion* and the *Gloucester*,

94

and six small auxiliary vessels. After sacking and burning Spanish towns along the coasts of Chile and Peru, the fleet sailed northward toward Acapulco. There the English hoped to be able to capture the Manila galleon. From Spanish prisoners taken during his raids along the coast, Anson learned that the galleon, loaded with supplies and treasure, was scheduled to depart from the harbor of Acapulco on March 3, 1742. It was bound for Guam and the Philippines. In an attempt to intercept her, Anson deployed his ships in a fanlike formation, fifteen leagues outside the harbor, and waited for the galleon to come sailing into the trap. For twenty days the English ships maintained their stations, out of sight of land, but the galleon never left the harbor. In spite of all their precautions, the scheme of the British squadron had become known to the Spaniards. They postponed the sailing of the treasure ship until the following year. Being thus thwarted in his desire to gain such a rich prize, Anson's fleet, consisting now of only the two men-of-war, left the Mexican coast bound for the Philippines.

Leaving the Acapulco region on May 6, 1742, the *Centurion* and the *Gloucester* stood to the southwest until they arrived at about 13 degrees north latitude. This was the parallel at which most ships fell in with the trade winds and thus were usually assured a quick and safe passage across the Pacific. Because of unfavorable winds, however, it was seven weeks before Anson's ships fell in with the true trade winds. This delay, besides unduly prolonging the trip, was accompanied by the reappearance of scurvy among the ships' crews. So many men were stricken by the disease that the ships, for lack of hands, were barely able to navigate.

It was not until August 23, one hundred and nine days after leaving the Mexican coast, that he sighted Anatahan and Sariguan in the northern Marianas. During the passage the *Gloucester*, having been badly damaged in a storm, was set on fire and destroyed. Her officers and crew, added to those on the *Centurion*, increased the distress of all hands. "Our deaths," relates Anson, "were now extremely alarming, no day passing in which we did not bury eight or ten, and sometimes twelve of our men; and those who had hitherto continued healthy began to fall down apace."[8] The wretched condition of the crew made it absolutely necessary for them to land and refresh themselves. They found, however, that Anatahan afforded no place for a ship to anchor. As a result, they were compelled to turn southward, seeking other islands. On the morning of the 27th of August they sighted three islands: Saipan, Tinian, and Aguigan.

The following excerpt from Anson's journal presents a detailed and interesting account of his arrival and reception at Tinian:

It was the 26th of August 1742, in the morning, when we lost sight of Anatahan. The next morning we discovered three other Islands to the eastward, which were from ten to fourteen leagues from us. These were, as we afterwards learnt, the Islands of Saypan, Tinian, and Aguigan. We immediately steered towards Tinian, which was the middlemost of the three, but had so much of calms and light airs, that tho' we were helped forwards by the currents, yet next day, at day-break, we were at least five leagues distant from it. However, we kept on our course, and about ten in the morning we perceived a proa under sail to the southward, between Tinian and Aguigan. As we imagined from hence that these Islands were inhabited, and knew that the Spaniards had always a force at Guam, we took the necessary precautions for our own security, and for preventing the enemy from taking advantage of our present wretched circumstances, of which they would be sufficiently informed by the manner of our working the ship; we therefore mustered all of our hands, who were capable of standing to their arms, and loaded our upper and quarter-deck guns with grape-shot; and that we might the more readily procure some intelligence of the state of these Islands, we showed Spanish colors, and hoisted a red flag at the fore top-mast-head to give our ship the appearance of the Manila Galeon, hoping thereby to decoy some of the inhabitants on board us. Thus preparing ourselves, and standing towards the land, we were near enough, at three in the afternoon, to send the cutter in shore, to find out a proper berth for the ship; and we soon perceived that a proa came off the shore to meet the cutter, fully persuaded, as we afterwards found, that we were the Manila ship. As we saw the cutter returning back with the proa in tow, we immediately sent the pinnace to receive the proa and the prisoners, and to bring them on board, that the cutter might proceed on her errand. The pinnace came back with a Spaniard and four Indians, which were the people taken in the proa. The Spaniard was immediately examined as to the produce and circumstances of this Island of Tinian, and his account of it surpassed even our most sanguine hopes; for he informed us that it was uninhabited, which, in our present defenceless condition, was an advantage not to be despised, especially as it wanted but few of the conveniences that could be expected in the most cultivated country; for he assured us, that there was great plenty of very good water and that there were an incredible number of cattle, hogs, and poultry running wild on the Island, all of them excellent in their kind; that the woods produced sweet and sour oranges, limes, lemons and coco-nuts in great plenty besides a fruit peculiar to these Islands (called by Dampier, Breadfruit); that from the quantity and goodness of the provisions produced here, the Spaniards at Guam made use of it as a store for supplying the garrison; that he himself was a Sergeant of that garrison, and was sent here with twenty-two Indians to jerk beef, which he was to load for Guam on board a small bark of about fifteen ton, which lay at anchor near the shore.[9]

Immediately after landing at Tinian, Anson and all members of the crew who were able to stand up began making preparations to care for the sick. Near the shore they found many huts that had been inhabited at one time. One of these huts, which the detachment from Guam was using as a storehouse, was unusually large. After clearing out some bales of jerked beef, which were found there, they converted it into a hospital for the sick. When all was in readiness, 128 patients were brought ashore. "Numbers of these," according to the account of Anson's voyage, "were so very helpless, that we were obliged to carry them from the boats to the hospital upon our shoulders, in which humane employment the Commodore himself, and every one of his officers, were engaged without distinction; and, notwithstanding the great debility and the dying aspects of the greatest part of our sick, it is almost incredible how soon they began to feel the salutary influence of the land; for, though we buried twenty-one men on this and the preceding day, yet we did not lose above ten more men during our whole two months' stay here; and in general, our diseased received so much benefit from the fruits of the Island, particularly the fruits of the acid kind, that, in a week's time, there were but few who were not so far recovered as to be able to move about without help."[10]

When his men were well on the way to regaining their health, Anson began to explore the island. He was at once completely

97

overwhelmed by the numbers of cattle, pigs, and poultry that he saw everywhere, roaming in a wild state. When he asked his Guamanian prisoners why there were no people living in Tinian to care for the animals, he was told that less than fifty years earlier the Spaniards had forced the people to move to Guam. Being left untended, the cattle, pigs, and poultry had run wild. The following account, from Anson's journal, is interesting not only because it describes the situation that prevailed in Tinian at that time, but also because it presents a vivid picture of similar conditions that prevailed in Guam and other islands of the Marianas as well:

> The fortunate animals too, which for the greatest part of the year are the sole lords of this happy soil, partake in some measure of the romantic cast of the Island, and are no small addition to its wonderful scenery; for the cattle, of which it is not uncommon to see herds of some thousands feeding together in a large meadow, are certainly the most remarkable in the world; for they are all of them milk-white, except their ears, which are generally black. And though there are no inhabitants here, yet the clamour and frequent parading of domestic poultry, which range the woods in great numbers, perpetually excite the ideas of the neighbourhood of farms and villages, and greatly contribute to the cheerfulness and beauty of the place. The cattle on the Island we computed were at least ten thousand; and we had no difficulty in getting near them, as they were not shy of us. Our first method of killing them was shooting them; but at last, when ... we were obliged to husband our ammunition, our men ran them down with ease. Their flesh was extremely well tasted, and was believed by us to be much more easily digested, than any we had ever met with. The fowls too were exceeding good, and were like-- wise run down with little trouble; for they could scarce fly further than an hundred yards at a flight, and even that fatigued them so much, that they could not readily rise again; so that, aided by the openness of the woods, we could at all times furnish ourselves with whatever number we wanted. Besides the cattle and the poultry, we found here abundance of wild hogs. These were most excellent food; but as they were a very fierce animal, we were obliged either to shoot them, or to hunt them with large dogs, which we found upon the place at our landing, and which belonged to the detachment which was then upon the Island amassing provisions for the garrison of Guam. As these dogs had been purposely trained to the killing of the wild hogs, they followed us very readily, and hunted for us; but though they were a large bold breed, the hogs fought with so much fury, that they frequently destroyed them, so that we by degrees lost the greatest part of them.[11]

Anson was greatly impressed by the many *latte* sites which he found scattered over the island. These structures, monuments to the ancient Chamorro culture, were grim reminders of the large numbers of people that had formerly lived on Tinian. In view of the numerous *latte* on the island, Anson estimated that Tinian alone must have had a pre-Spanish population of at least 30,000. His thinking in this regard is revealed by the following passage in his journal:

> It may perhaps be doubted, if the number of the inhabitants of Tinian, who were banished to Guam, and who died there pining for their native home, was so great, as what we have related above; but, not to mention the concurrent assertion of our prisoners, and the commodiousness of the Island, and its great fertility, there are still remains to be met with on the place, which evince it to have been once extremely populous: For there are, in all parts of the Island, a great number of ruins of a very particular kind; they usually consist of two rows of square pyramidal pillars, each pillar being about six feet from the next, and the distance between the rows being about twelve feet; the pillars themselves are about five feet square at the base, and about thirteen feet high; and on the top of each of them there is a semi-globe with the flat part upwards; the whole of the pillars and semi-globe is solid, being composed of sand and stone cemented together, and plaistered over.... If the account our prisoners gave us of these structures was true, the Island must indeed have been extremely populous; for they assured us, that they were the foundations of particular buildings set apart for those Indians only, who had engaged in some religious vow; and monastic institutions are often to be met with in many Pagan nations. However, if these ruins were originally the basis of the common dwelling-houses of the natives, their numbers must have been considerable; for in many parts of the Island they are extremely thick planted, and sufficiently evince the great plenty of former inhabitants.[12]

On September 18, while Anson and most of his crew were on shore, a sudden violent storm tore the *Centurion* from its anchors and drove it out to sea. Mr. Saumárez, a lieutenant who was on board, took command of the ship and ordered all preparations necessary for riding out the storm. By the time the storm was over, the ship had been driven so far away that it could not be seen from the island. Anson and his crew on shore, amounting in all to 113 men, believed that the ship was sunk. They were stranded and felt that they would never leave the island again. After they had recovered from their original shock, Anson set everybody to work building a large boat which he hoped would be able to carry them to Macao on the coast of China. Eighteen days later, however, the *Centurion*, which had survived the storm, returned to the island.

Throughout his stay at Tinian, Anson was plagued by the fear that the Spaniards on Guam would learn of his presence in the islands. Scurvy and the effects of the storm had so weakened his crew that he felt it would be impossible to resist a strong attack by the Spaniards. During the time, especially, that the *Centurion* was out at sea, Anson's fears had increased, for he and his men, states the journal, "had reason to expect, that the Governor of Guam, when he should be informed of their situation, might send a force sufficient to overpower them, and to remove them to that Island; and then, the most favorable treatment they could hope for would be to be detained prisoners for life; since, from the known policy and cruelty of the Spaniards in their distant settlements, it was rather to be expected, that the Governor, if he once had them in his power, would make their want of commissions (all of them being on board the Centurion) a pretext for treating them as pirates, and for depriving them of their lives with infamy."[13]

Anson's fears arose primarily as a result of the extreme weakness of his crew. His knowledge concerning the Spanish establishment in Guam, however, should have quieted his fears. The following excerpt from the account of his voyage reveals that he knew all about the fortifications and strength of the garrison at Guam:

As this is a post of some consequence, on account of the refreshment it yields to the Manila ship, there are two castles on the sea-shore; one is the castle of St. Angelo, which lies near the road, where the Manila ship usually anchors, and is but an insignificant fortress, mounting only five guns eight pounders; the other is the castle of St. Lewis, which is N.E. from St. Angelo, and four leagues distant, and is intended to protect a road where a small vessel anchors, which arrives here every other year from Manila. This fort mounts the same number of guns as the former: And besides these forts, there is a battery of five pieces of cannon on an eminence near the sea-shore. The Spanish troops employed on this Island, consist of three companies of foot, from forty to fifty men each;

and this is the principal strength the Governor has to depend on; for he cannot rely on any assistance from the Indian inhabitants, being generally upon ill terms with them, and so apprehensive of them, that he has debarred them the use of firearms or lances.[14]

On October 21, 1742, after thoroughly stocking the *Centurion* with fresh water and supplies, Anson sailed from the Marianas, setting his course for Macao. Reaching Macao, a Portuguese settlement on the Canton River in China, Anson remained there about five months, refreshing his crew and repairing his ship.

## THE SOCIETY OF JESUS IN GUAM

The venerable Father Sanvitores, who brought Spanish culture and the Christian religion to Guam, was a Jesuit, a member of the Society of Jesus. The Society of Jesus, founded by St. Ignatius of Loyola, was established as a religious order of the Roman Catholic Church on September 27, 1540. Its principal purpose was to counteract the influences of the Protestant Reformation and to stem the growing respect shown for the natural law as opposed to the laws of God. Because of the missionary zeal of its members, the society grew rapidly. The Jesuits gained wealth and power, not only in Europe but also in many other parts of the world.

By the close of the 18th century, many of the governments of Europe were inspired with jealousy and suspicious hatred of the Jesuits. The society, organized primarily for missionary labor, had gradually taken on much of a secular character. The Jesuits were not only missionaries and teachers, but they were also scientists, geographers, financiers, and powerful and almost independent administrators in their missionary fields. What was most exasperating to their enemies, however, was the growing political influence of the Jesuits. Because of their jealousy and fears, the monarchs of Europe set out to destroy the Jesuit order.

In 1759 the Jesuits were expelled from Portugal, in 1764 from France, and on February 27, 1767, the decree of confiscation and banishment from Spain and all Spanish possessions was issued by Charles III. The orders which the Spanish king sent to the civil and military authorities in all his dominions were enclosed in double envelopes and sealed with three seals. On the inner cover appeared the ominous words: "Under pain of death this package is not to be opened until April 2, 1767, at the setting sun." The letter read as follows:

> I invest you with all my authority and all my royal power to descend immediately with arms on the Jesuit establishments in your district; to seize the occupants and lead them as prisoners to the port indicated inside of 24 hours. At the moment of seizure, you will seal the archives of the house and all private papers and permit no one to carry anything but his prayer book and the linen strictly necessary for the voyage. If after your embarkation there is left behind a single Jesuit either sick or dying in your department, you shall be punished with death.[15]

Under the terms of the banishment decree, all the property and possessions of the Society of Jesus were either to be confiscated by the crown or turned over to religious orders or agencies designated by the crown. While the possessions of the Jesuits in Guam did not represent great wealth, they were, nevertheless, quite extensive. The major holdings consisted of all the churches and rectories in Guam and Rota, the College of San Juan de Letran, with all that pertained to it, a drug store, and several ranches. The ranches were well cared for and were in flourishing condition. San Ignacio de Tachogna, the finest of the ranches, was eleven leagues in circumference and was situated in the interior of Guam, between Agana and Pago. On this ranch the Jesuits had a large herd of cattle and a number of horses. Besides this stock, they also had in their possession a good supply of garden implements called *fosinos*, new machetes for clearing the forest, steel, iron, blacksmith's tools, tanbark and vats for tanning, carpenter's tools, paints, stones for grinding pigments, *metates* and *manos* (used for grinding maize), and material and instruments for making ornaments for the churches and altars. Each of the fathers also owned clothing, papers, books, and other personal effects.

In view of the fact that ships stopped at the island so infrequently, more than two years passed between the time of the issuance of the banishment decree and the actual removal of the Jesuits from Guam. Eventually, however, a small vessel arrived at the island. The officer in charge, who brought the order of expulsion, had been instructed to take away in his vessel all the Jesuits together with their personal belongings. Knowing that this would be impossible, he made a statement in writing to Governor Enrique de Olavide y Michelena. He stated that his little vessel could not accomplish the task; that it would require several vessels much larger than his own to take away all the belongings of the fathers. At the time that the banishment decree was proclaimed, Father Xavier Stengel, the superior of the mission, was on the island of Rota. He had gone there to hear confessions and administer the annual communion. A canoe was sent to bring him back to Guam. Since one of the fathers had died sometime before the arrival of the decree, it was necessary to take back a certified statement of his death to account for his not sailing with the others. When all was in readiness, on November 2, 1769, the schooner *Nuestra Señora de Guadalupe* sailed from Guam carrying the Jesuit fathers together with some of their personal effects. Because of the smallness of the vessel, however, most of their belongings were left behind.

The removal of the Jesuits from the Marianas was a sad occasion, not only for the fathers but for the Guamanian people as well. "The Jesuits had been in the islands for a century, and whatever may have been the harsh means by which they were established there, they had won the love and confidence of the natives, and were kind and just in their dealings with them, protecting them when necessary against acts of cruelty, injustice, and oppression on the part of the military authorities, and never exacting service from them without due compensation."[16] They had taught not only the Christian doctrine and the elements of learning but many useful arts as well. Through their contacts with missions of their order in other parts of the world, they had brought new ideas, products, and plants to Guam. After their departure their farms were neglected, and their cattle, now the property of the crown, were permitted to run wild. The spiritual administration of the Marianas was turned over to the friars of the Order of Saint Augustine, who had come as passengers on the vessel bringing the decree of banishment. The Augustinian fathers remained in Guam until its seizure by the United States in 1898.

## DECLINE AND RECONSTRUCTION

As a result of the Spanish-Chamorro wars, the Chamorro people were unable to offer further resistance to the Spaniards. Diseases too, introduced by Europeans, had wrought havoc with the native population. From an original total estimated by Sanvitores to be between 50,000 and 100,000, they were, as related by Lord Anson, reduced to approximately 4,000 by 1742.

Anson's account of the Marianas, where he landed in 1742, runs in part as follows:

> They were formerly most of them well inhabited, and, even not sixty years ago, the three principal islands Guam, Rota, and Tinian together, are said to have contained above fifty thousand people. But since that time Tinian hath been entirely depopulated, and only two or three hundred Indians have been left at Rota, to cultivate for the island of Guam; so that now no more than Guam can properly be said to be inhabited. This island of Guam is the only settlement of the Spaniards; here they keep a Governor and garrison, and here the Manila ship generally touches for refreshment in her passage from Acapulco to the Philippines. It is esteemed to be about thirty leagues in circumference, and contains, by the Spanish accounts, near four thousand inhabitants, of which a thousand are said to live in the city of San Ignacio de Agana, where the Governor generally resides, and where the houses are represented as considerable, being built with stone and timber, and covered with tiles, a very uncommon fabric for these warm climates and savage countries. Besides this city, there are upon the Island thirteen or fourteen villages.[17]

The Chamorro population, after 1742, continued to decline. This was due primarily to the fact that a great majority of the men had been killed during the Spanish-Chamorro Wars. The remaining women refused to bear children for fear of having them treated as slaves. Accordingly, by 1783, the native population had been reduced in number to approximately 1,500. The Abbé Raynal has described the unfortunate situation of the Chamorros as follows:

> ... Such savages could not resist the European arms and troops. Nevertheless, most of them suffered themselves to be put to death rather than they would submit. A great number of them were the victims of the disgraceful maladies which their inhuman conquerors had introduced among them.... The population decreased, throughout the whole Archi-

pelago, to such a degree, that it became necessary, five and twenty or thirty years ago, to unite the feeble remains of them in the single island of Guam. . . . In this chief place of the colony [Agana], and in twenty-one small hamlets scattered around the island, fifteen hundred inhabitants are distributed, the unfortunate remains of a population formerly numerous.[18]

The pattern of population decline that prevailed in Guam and the Marianas was established during the early stages of contact with the whites and other non-natives. It was repeated later in other parts of the Pacific region. With regard to this matter, Keesing has said: "Everywhere, apparently, the early stages of contact were marked by a decline in numbers. In some instances this involved the extinction of whole communities, tribes, or even minor ethnic groups."[19] Because of the accumulated effects of such early contacts, the Chamorros, especially, were rapidly brought to a point of almost complete extinction. Had it not been for inter-marriage between the Chamorros and non-natives, the Marianas might eventually have been depopulated. As a result of such inter-marriage, however, the present-day Guamanian people came into being, and the original Chamorro stock has almost completely disappeared. Keesing has described the decline of the Chamorros and the rise of a new population as follows:

> The American island of Guam offers a situation unique in Micronesia and indeed in the Oceanic region as a whole. Here quite intensive contact goes back to the sixteenth century. The island was a regular port of call for Spanish ships, and besides having white residents and visitors, it was a place of exile for lawbreakers and political prisoners from the Philippines. Later came Japanese merchants and then the Americans. The original Chamorro population was first decimated by vain struggles against Spanish troops, and then intermarried extensively with Filipino, white, and, to some extent, Japanese strains. . . . Obviously, all local family lines are by now woven in complex fashion out of the Chamorro, Filipino, and other strains. This, indeed, represents the extreme instance within the South Seas of how, out of a mixing process, a neo-native population is compounded.[20]

Thus it can be seen that, because of the ravaging effects of wars and disease, the ancient Chamorros became morally and physically exhausted. Consequently, they were brought to the verge of ex-

105

tinction. It was during this period of decline, when the Chamorro people had reached the lowest ebb in their disintegration and defeat, that a new governor came to Guam and started the long and difficult process of reconstruction.

Guam's period of reconstruction began with the arrival on the island of Governor Don Mariano Tobias on September 15, 1771. Governor Tobias was exactly the kind of man that Guam needed in her darkest hour to lift her people from the depths of despair and lead them to a fuller and more fruitful way of life. "This unexpected revolution," says Raynal, "hath been brought about by M. Tobias. . . . If the Spaniards, from the beginning, had been inspired with the reasonable views of the prudent Tobias, the Marianne Islands would have been civilized and cultivated."[21] He, "an active, humane, and enlightened man, hath at length understood that population would not be restored but that it would even still continue decreasing, unless he could succeed in introducing agriculture into his island. Stimulated by his example, the natives of the country have cleared those lands, the property of which he had promised them. . . . Their enjoyments have increased with their occupations; and they have at length experienced happiness in one of the finest countries in the world: so true it is that everything may be accomplished by mildness and benevolence, since these virtues are capable of extinguishing resentment even in the mind of a savage."[22]

Governor Tobias was convinced that the best means for rebuilding Guam's population and for restoring some measure of economic security lay in the establishment of a sound agricultural economy. Accordingly, he set about instituting widespread reforms. One of his first official acts was to make land available to the islanders for agricultural purposes. In order to set a good example and to stimulate interest in agriculture, he himself laid out some very extensive gardens. Being a man who was not afraid to get his hands dirty, when freedom from official duties permitted, he worked in the fields and assisted with the cultivation of the crops. For a period of many years before his arrival in Guam, the islanders had ceased to occupy themselves with any sort of cultivation on

106

a large scale. The galleons brought food and supplies for the missionaries and the garrison, and the islanders lived on fish, breadfruit, and other native foods. Because there was no need for them to work too hard, life for the islanders had become lazy and indolent. Governor Tobias, because of his philosophy of work and his vigorous actions, quickly changed the situation. His reforms applied not only to the natives but to the Spaniards as well. Fortunately, his program met with the wholehearted approval and support of the church fathers.[23]

During the early years of the mission, the Jesuit fathers had brought new plants and methods of farming to Guam. The long years of war, however, and the disruption that followed, resulted in the almost complete stoppage of farming activities. To remedy the situation, Governor Tobias allotted a certain portion of land to every family. With his encouragement and under his guidance, the land was quickly divided into gardens, orchards, and ploughed or spade-worked fields. Every variety of European vegetables and fruits was introduced to the island. Plants introduced in earlier times were cultivated once more. The cultivation of rice, maize, indigo, cotton, cacao, and sugar cane became widespread and flourished in many parts of the island. Maize, one of the principal crops, was found especially to give wonderful results. With regard to this crop, Crozet wrote: "It is common to find on the maize fields, plants twelve feet high, with eight to ten cobs, nine to ten inches long, well stocked with good nourishing grain. The Indian reduces the maize to flour and makes bread of it."[24]

In the orchards limes, lemons, oranges, pineapples, and mangoes grew abundantly. The mangoes, which were brought from Manila and were of superior quality, thrived in the soil of Guam.

At the same time that he was fostering the rebirth of agriculture, Governor Tobias encouraged the development of cattle raising and animal husbandry. One of his first acts, in this regard, was to set crews of men to work clearing the grazing lands. Because of neglect, they had become covered with small trees and shrubs. Crozet relates that "long ago the Spaniards cleared spaces of land for pastoral purposes. No other nation possessing colonies in the tropics appears to have laid themselves out like the Spaniards for the formation of savannahs. The whole art of this rural operation consists in making small clearings, which are only separated from each other by bushes and clumps of trees, simply cleared and cleaned of every variety of underwood. The Spaniards sow the clearings with varieties of grass seeds suitable for pasturage."[25] These savannahs, shaded on all sides, retained their freshness and sheltered the cattle against the sun and heat.

As rapidly as the savannah lands were cleared, herds of cattle were rounded up, tamed, and driven to the grasslands for controlled grazing. Wild cattle roamed the island in large numbers. "The cattle formerly transported from America to the savannahs of Guam and the other Ladrone Islands," says Crozet, "have multiplied without end. These animals have run wild, and now, when one wishes to eat them, one has either to shoot them or take them by lassoing. I noticed that the Guam cattle are generally white, with black ears, without any variety of color, but with big frames and well nourished, and their flesh is very good to eat."[26]

In order to make farming easier and more efficient, Governor Tobias imported horses from Manila and donkeys and mules from Acapulco. The natives were taught how to break cattle in and to use them for riding and pulling wagons and carts. They found that the cattle were easily broken and made very fine teams. Almost every family had several cattle which they saddled and used for riding. They guided them by means of cords which passed through holes pierced in the nostrils of the animals.

The forests were also full of goats, pigs, and poultry which the Jesuits and other Spaniards had brought over in earlier times. They were running wild and could be had for the taking. Governor Tobias encouraged his people to trap and domesticate them. He also imported deer from the Philippines. These thrived in Guam and multipled so rapidly that they soon became a threat to the crops.

Governor Tobias established cotton mills and salt pans on the island and brought in craftsmen to teach the arts of the blacksmith, the wheelwright, and the carpenter. The natives quickly learned all these trades and practiced them with great skill. They also learned to make lime and bricks, and some of them became expert masons.

Because of his interest in education, the governor established two free public schools where the children were taught reading, writing, and arithmetic, as well as vocal and instrumental music. The schools were separate: one for boys and one for girls.

Shortly after he assumed office in 1771, Governor Tobias established the first Guam militia. The militiamen, two hundred strong, wore special uniforms and were well paid. They were under the command of four Spanish captains. Other officers were islanders of mixed blood and Filipinos. Because the governor strongly believed that indolence was one of the greatest evils in life, the militiamen were not permitted to become fat and lazy. Besides their daily military duties, they were required to cultivate certain portions of land assigned to them by the governor. "The soldiers," relates Crozet, "thus plough, sow, and harvest the lands, the produce of which serves to nourish them, and being thus always occupied, they are happy and well contented with the rice, or the bread made from the maize, which they have themselves cultivated and harvested."[27]

## THE CROZET EXPEDITION

On September 27, 1772, just about one year after Tobias became governor, the *Mascarin,* commanded by Captain Crozet, dropped anchor in Apra Harbor. The Crozet expedition was sent out by the French for the purpose of discovering new lands in the South Seas. When Marion du Fresne, the original leader of the expedition, was killed and eaten by cannibals in New Zealand, Crozet was appointed commander of the *Mascarin.* In his journal, Crozet wrote the following description of Apra Harbor:

> The harbour is situated on the western side, and almost in the middle of the island. It is bounded on the south by a tongue of land [Orote Peninsula] running two leagues out into the sea, and on the north by a reef of similar length which almost surrounds it. The entrance is very narrow, and protected by a brick battery, which the Spaniards call St. Luis, mounted with eight bronze twelve-pounders of an old pattern. The

harbour is capable of holding four vessels, sheltered from all winds except those from the south-east, which never blow but feebly in these parts. It is dangerous to enter without pilots, because of the numerous rocks and coral reefs.[28]

When Crozet and several of his officers arrived at Agana, they were received in a very friendly manner by Governor Tobias. When they explained to him that members of their crew were suffering from scurvy, he responded quickly and generously by sending on board large quantities of fresh meat, vegetables, and fruits, especially oranges and limes. He also provided quarters for them in the College of San Juan de Letran and insisted that they have their meals at his own table. Crozet was so pleased with his reception in Guam that he wrote in his journal: "In the whole extent of these seas there is no other harbour where weary navigators can re-establish their health more quickly or where they can obtain better or more abundant refreshment. The island of Guam appeared a terrestrial paradise to us; the air was excellent, the water was very good, the vegetables and fruits perfect, the mobs of cattle as well as those of goats and pigs innumerable, while there was no end to the quantity of poultry."[29]

Crozet, a competent and highly respected officer, spent his first few days in Guam arranging for the proper care of his crew. The scurvy-stricken seamen were brought on shore and lodged in the former Jesuits' college, where, with the generous help provided by Governor Tobias, the sailors quickly recovered. Afterwards Crozet and his men traveled to many parts of the island, observing its sights. From his observations, Crozet wrote the following description of Agana as it appeared in 1772:

> The chief settlement, which the Spaniards call the town of Agana, is situated four leagues to the north of the harbour on the sea-coast, at the foot of some low mountains, in a beautiful country full of springs, and watered by a small, very clear, and good brook. The Commandant* of the island lives there. The streets of the town are laid out in straight lines, the private houses are for the most part built solidly of wood, raised on piles, about three feet above the level of the ground, and most

---

* While in Guam, Governor Tobias held the rank of major in the Spanish army. Later he was promoted to lieutenant colonel.

of them are roofed with shingles, or with tiles, the rest with palm leaves. There is a beautiful church highly decorated according to Spanish custom. The Commandant's house is spacious and well built. The former residence of the Jesuits, now occupied by the St. Augustine brotherhood, is spacious and convenient; but the former Jesuits' college, built for the education of the Indians, is not inhabited, their successors, the St. Augustines, having removed the college to a building near their convent. There is a barracks capable of lodging a garrison of five hundred men, and there is the King's fine large magazine. All these public buildings are built of brick and tile. The island of Guam is the only island in the vast extent of the South Sea, sprinkled as it is with innumerable islands, which has a European built town, a church, fortifications, and a civilized population. [30]

During the seven and one-half weeks that Crozet remained in Guam, he had many opportunities to observe the habits of the people and to study their way of life. Nothing was too small or insignificant to escape his attention. With regard to the natives, he estimated that they were about fifteen hundred in number. Besides those living in Agana, they lived in twenty-one small settlements, all on the seacoast. Such settlements were usually composed of five or six families, who made their living by fishing and by growing grain crops and vegetables.

Crozet was unusually impressed by the breadfruit tree, which he saw growing in large numbers all over the island. He thought it to be one of the most useful plants that nature had given to man and thought it strange that such a tree should be found only in the islands of the South Seas. Its fruit, said Crozet, "tastes exactly like bread, has the same nutritive properties, supplies its place in every respect, and has a fragrant and delicious odour which our cleverest bakers will never be able to impart to our bread. . . . The fruit can be eaten when it has attained its full size, but though it be still green. In this stage the islanders cook it before eating; they take off its knotty rind and cut it in slices like pieces of bread. When they wish to preserve it, they cut it in round slices, and in this very thin sea-biscuit form, they dry it in the sun or in the oven. This natural biscuit preserves its quality for years, and very much better than does our ships' biscuit. Our sailors ate it green, slightly grilled; they also made their soup of it; they had no other bread, and we attributed the quick recovery of those suffering from scurvy to the breadfruit diet."[31] When Crozet left Guam, he took many breadfruit plants with him. He planned to take them to some of the French colonies, where he thought their cultivation might be beneficial to the natives. His plan did not succeed, however. All but two of the plants died before the completion of the voyage.

During their convalescence, some of the sailors in Crozet's crew amused themselves by fishing. They caught eels, mullet, goby, carp, and other kinds of fish. Most of these were fresh-water fish and proved to be excellent eating. The sailors noticed, however, that the natives would not eat them. They preferred salt-water fish, which in general seemed to be of inferior quality to the fresh-water ones. With regard to poisonous fish, Crozet relates:

> Among those which are caught on the coast of Guam, as in all the Marianas Islands, there are some which are very unwholesome, for they nourish themselves on the little polypes, which form the coral. It appears that these sea-insects, like the sea-galleys and sea-nettles, have some caustic property which is imparted to the fishes, and the fishes have a coralline taste which betrays their poisonous properties. The Indians know which are unwholesome, but it is better not to eat any sea-fish at all. This, however, does not hold good with the sea-turtles which are caught on the coasts of Guam. They are very good and as big as those of the island of Ascension, but the Spaniards and Indians do not eat them. I collected sufficient to form a good supply during our journey to the Philippines.[32]

At the time of the visit of Crozet in 1772, the Guam mission was under the spiritual jurisdiction of the Augustinian fathers, who had replaced the Jesuits. At that time there were five priests attached to the mission. One of them was appointed to the parish of Agana. Three others served different parishes in various parts of the island. The fifth was assigned to the island of Saipan, where a small native population had been located. Crozet noticed that the islanders were passionately fond of cockfighting and that on Sundays and holidays they assembled, after mass, near the doors of the church. There they conducted their cockfights. In discussing the relationships that existed between the priests and the governor, Crozet wrote: "These good monks thoroughly second the views of

M. Tobias for the welfare of his beloved Indians. I cannot repeat too often, in praise of this excellent man, that he has no other ambition than that of making his islanders happy. . . . The Indians look upon him and love him as a father."[33]

When Crozet's expedition landed at Guam, more than two hundred sick men had been taken ashore. All had completely recovered, however, and were ready to sail once more. After having filled their water butts, they took on abundant supplies of beef, pigs, goats, poultry, vegetables, and fruit of every description. They paid for the beef, but the governor would not let them pay for any other provisions. On November 19, 1772, the Crozet expedition sailed from Guam, bound for the Philippines.

## GOVERNOR TOBIAS REMOVED

In June 1774, after having served less than three years as governor of Guam, Mariano Tobias was transferred to Manila. His untimely removal was a severe blow to the program of reconstruction that he had started. Reasons for his removal are not definitely known. It would seem, however, that jealousy at the Spanish court was one of the principal reasons. Because of the manner in which he administered the reconstruction program in Guam, Tobias had become a well-known personality. This was due primarily to the accounts written about him by the Abbé Raynal, whose books were read throughout Europe.

In Manila, where he served as a lieutenant colonel with the garrison forces, Tobias became unhappy and embittered. This might have been due to the fact that he wanted to return to Guam, where, according to contemporary accounts, he wished to spend the remainder of his days. His despair was heightened by domestic difficulties with his wife, who, for unknown reasons, wished to be separated from him. La Pérouse, who was in Manila from February 28 to April 9, 1787, wrote concerning Tobias:

I saw at Manila that honest and virtuous governor of the Mariannes, M. Tobias, too celebrated for his own repose by the praises of the Abbé Raynal. . . . She [his wife] instituted a suit of divorce against him, and demanded a separation, on pretense of not being obliged to live with

113

an impious man, a resolution that was highly applauded by all the fanatics. M. Tobias is lieutenant colonel of the regiment which forms the garrison of Manila; he is acknowledged to be the best officer in the country; the governor has, nevertheless, ordered that his appointments, which are very considerable, should be left in possession of his pious wife, and that he should receive no more than twenty-six piasters a month for the subsistence of himself and sons. This brave soldier, reduced to despair, was waiting for an opportunity of escaping from this colony to go and demand justice.[34]

A sad state, indeed, for a good and capable man who, because of his deeds, has earned the right to be called one of Guam's greatest governors.

## RETURN OF THE CAROLINIANS

In 1788 a large number of canoes bearing Caroline Islanders landed near Talofofo Bay. They were met by Don Luis de Torres, the vice-governor. He treated them kindly and persuaded the governor, Lieutenant Colonel Don José Arlegue y León, to let them remain for a short time and engage in trade. "They told Torres that they had previously had a commercial intercourse with the inhabitants of this island, and only given it up on hearing of the settlement of the white men, and having themselves been witnesses of their cruelty. In 1788, after a long time had elapsed, they undertook this expedition to barter for iron. Torres asked them how they had found their way here, as the distance from Ulle to Guahon is above three hundred miles; they answered, that the description of the way was preserved by them in their songs, and after this their pilots had found it. It is really very remarkable that they did not miss an inconsiderable island like Guahon, when the stars and the songs were their only guides, in a voyage of three hundred miles."[35]

After securing iron and other trade goods, the Carolinians left Guam, promising to return the following year. They kept their word, but on their trip back to the Carolines in 1789 they were lost in a storm. Thus, trade between the islands was discontinued for fifteen years. "Torres," Kotzebue relates, "waited fifteen years in vain for his friends, to whom he had become attached on account

114

of their gentle dispositions. In the year 1804 the American ship Maria, from Boston, took in provisions at Guahon; the captain of it, Samuel William Bell, undertook, with the super-cargo, Thomas Borman, a voyage to the Carolinas, where he intended to make the attempt to catch bêches de mer,* and de Torres embraced this opportunity of visiting his friends, as the captain promised to bring him back to Guahon. The Maria sailed in July, and the first group at which she touched was Ulle. Torres found here several of his old acquaintances, who piloted the ship into the group. . . ."[36]

Torres asked his friends among the Carolinians why they had not returned to Guam after 1789. He was told in reply that since the fleet which had gone there fifteen years earlier had not returned, they had concluded that their countrymen had all been murdered by the Guamanians. Torres assured them, however, that no harm had been done to their countrymen in Guam. He told them that a severe storm had come up the day after they left and that in all probability they were all drowned. The Carolinians agreed with him. They were glad to learn that no murder had been done, as they had imagined. Moreover, they promised to resume their trade with Guam the following year. They kept their promise, and, beginning in 1804, trading voyages were made regularly each year by the Carolinians. The Chamorros, who by this time had lost their skill at canoe-making, gave them iron in exchange for canoes. Later, groups of Carolinians settled in Guam, Saipan, and Tinian. They, however, remained apart from the Chamorros and retained their own language and customs. The following excerpt from Kotzebue's journal presents some interesting insights into the trade between Guam and the Caroline Islands:

> Since this time [1804], eighteen canoes assemble every year at the island-group of Lamureck, thence they sail to Fojo (a desert island, according to the description, lying to the north of Lamureck) which they reach in two days, rest there, and then the fleet sails in three days to Guahon. The whole voyage is therefore concluded in five days. They visit Guahon in April, and commence their voyage home in May, or at the latest in June, as, after that, the S.W. monsoon becomes dangerous.

* A species of large snail without a shell. It is found in warm climates, usually near coral reefs.

115

Their boats are of such a kind, that they upset with the least carelessness, which happens several times a day in such a voyage; but as they are expert swimmers and divers, it has no other consequence than that they have a hearty laugh. On such an occasion they all immediately leap into the water, right their canoe, and swim along with it till they have baled out the water with their hands. It is much worse when the outrigger breaks, for then they are not able to preserve the equilibrium of their canoe on account of their narrow construction. There, however, does not pass a voyage but this accident happens, and they repair it while swimming, which requires several hours. A European would hardly be able to hold out in a voyage of five days, constantly washed by the waves. The Carolinians are often even fourteen days in this situation, without any food except a few cocoa-nuts, as their canoes cannot carry a cargo; and sea water for their drink, as much as they please. They have, when there is a whole fleet, generally two pilots, who are only of the lower class, but far exceed the higher in sagacity, and are often elevated to the rank of nobility for their merit.

Some years ago, a fleet, which was only a day's voyage from Guahon, was overtaken by a violent storm, and driven far out of its course. When the storm abated, the two pilots disputed; the one affirmed that Guahon still lay to the west, and the other thought the contrary, as the S.E. storm had driven them so far, that the island must lie to the E. of them. Both had always possessed the confidence of the islanders; they were now at a loss whose advice to pursue, and, in the end, the fleet divided into two parties. The party sailing to the W. probably found its grave in the waves, as nothing was afterwards heard of them; the other, after it had laboured several days to gain the wind to the E., happily reached the island, and the pilot, as a reward for his services, was made a tamon [noble].[37]

## THE MALASPINA EXPEDITION

In February 1792, Guam was visited by Don Alejandro Malaspina, in command of the corvettes *Atrevida* and *Descubierta*. They had been sent out by Charles IV, king of Spain, on a voyage of scientific investigation. This was the first of four scientific groups that were to stop at Guam between 1792 and 1828. Scientists accompanying this expedition included two of the outstanding naturalists of Europe: Thaddaeus Haenke and Luis Nee. They were the first to make systematic studies and collections of plants on the island. Haenke, a brilliant scientist and an extremely determined

116

man, did not arrive in time to join the expedition when it sailed from Cádiz. Because of his misfortune, he was to suffer shipwreck and trudge on foot across a continent before he could join the expedition. Safford relates the following story of Haenke's adventures:

> Haenke was a Bohemian by birth. He received his botanical education from Jacquin, who for a time was professor of chemistry and botany in Vienna, and upon his recommendation was appointed botanist of the expedition by the King of Spain. Although he set out for Cadiz immediately on receiving his appointment, he reached that port only to find that the two corvettes had just set sail (July 30, 1789). Following them in the first vessel bound for Montevideo, he suffered shipwreck on one of the numerous shoals at the mouth of the Rio de la Plata, losing nearly all his books, papers, and effects. He succeeded in reaching shore, however, with his Linnaeus* and a collecting outfit, but he found that the expedition had already sailed. Knowing that it was to stop on the coast of Chile, he set out at once on foot, crossing the Pampas of Argentina and the Chilean cordillera of the Andes, collecting and drying plants on the way. On reaching Santiago, Chile, to his great joy he found there Malaspina and a number of his officers, who had left their ships at anchor in the harbor of Valparaiso to pay an official visit to the capital. He immediately reported for duty and was assigned to the Descubierta.[38]

After Haenke joined the group, the expedition sailed northward along the west coast of South America, Mexico, and North America to as far as Port Mulgrave in southern Alaska. While there, they engaged in scientific explorations and applied the name of their leader to a glacier, the Malaspina Glacier. Upon the completion of their work, they sailed southward to Acapulco. Leaving Acapulco on December 21, 1791, the expedition sailed for Guam. It came to anchor on February 12, 1792, in Umatac Bay. Concerning their arrival at Umatac and the work of the expedition's members while in Guam, Safford writes:

> Many of the crew were suffering from an epidemic caught at Acapulco. Haenke proceeded to Agana and the northern part of the island, Nee to to the hills near Umatac, each making collections of plants. Don Antonio Pineda, who shortly afterwards lost his life in the Philippines, occupied

---

* This pertains to a method of plant classification proposed in 1735 by the Swedish naturalist, Karl von Linne.

117

himself with the geology and zoology of the island. The governor, Lieut. Col. Don José Arlegue, offered them every facility for carrying on their work. Don Juan Ravenet made sketches of a couple of the natives and of a native of the Caroline Islands, between which group and Guam a regular traffic had existed since 1788. The expedition set sail at daylight on the morning of February 24. A few plants were collected on Tinian, one of the northern islands, but the bulk of the collection from the Mariannes was made on the island of Guam.[39]

Leaving Guam on February 24, after a stay of twelve days, the Malaspina expedition continued its botanical studies in the Philippines and the Society Islands. "Malaspina," relates Safford, "shortly after his return to Spain was thrown into prison, suspected of revolutionary designs. The Spanish Government refused to publish his narrative, and when a map appeared embodying the results of his explorations his name was not allowed to appear upon it. . . . The narrative, much abridged, finally appeared in 1885, seventy-six years after the death of the brave and unfortunate navigator. For the most part it consists of bare statements of facts, resembling a log book, and has few descriptions and little detailed information concerning the countries visited."[40]

SUMMARY: During the first quarter of the 18th century the pirates Woodes Rogers and John Clipperton stopped at Guam. By means of threats, Rogers was able to remain on the island for one week. Moreover, he was able to wrest food and supplies from Governor Pimentel. Clipperton, on the other hand, got an entirely different reception. When he threatened to destroy houses and burn a Spanish ship, Governor Sánchez ordered the batteries at Apra Harbor to fire on him. The Spaniards, surprisingly, put up such a good fight that Clipperton was forced to flee in utter defeat. During the remainder of the century, Guam was free from visits by English pirates.

Groups of Caroline Islanders arrived at Guam in 1721. They were given a friendly reception. Because of the interest aroused by their visit, Governor Sánchez tried to establish a mission in the Carolines. The attempt was unsuccessful. Moreover, it resulted in the massacre of Father Cantova and fourteen companions.

## SUMMARY

In 1769 the Jesuits were expelled from Guam. Their departure wrecked the island's economy and added to the general decline that had set in after the Spanish-Chamorro wars. Upon the arrival of Governor Tobias in 1771, the situation was greatly improved but only temporarily. When Tobias was removed, the island quickly settled back into its accustomed rut. Except for the visits of Crozet and Malaspina and the re-establishment of trade with the Carolines, the remainder of the 18th century was quiet and uneventful.

## NOTES

1. Robert C. Leslie, *Life Aboard a British Privateer in the Time of Queen Anne, Being the Journal of Woodes Rogers, Master Mariner* (Chapman and Hall, Ltd., London, 1889), pp. 113–14.

2. *Ibid.*, p. 115.

3. William Betagh, *A Voyage Round the World, Being an Account of a Remarkable Enterprize, Begun in the Year 1719, Chiefly to Cruise on the Spaniards in the Great South Ocean* (London, 1728), p. 153.

4. *Ibid.*, pp. 154–55.

5. *Ibid.*, pp. 156–57.

6. *Ibid.*, p .157.

7. Burney, *op. cit.*, Vol. V, p. 19.

8. Walter, *op. cit.*, p. 283.

9. *Ibid.*, pp. 286–87.

10. *Ibid.*, p. 289.

11. *Ibid.*, pp. 290–91.

12. *Ibid.*, pp. 293–94.

13. *Ibid.*, p. 303.

14. *Ibid.*, p. 320.

15. Thomas Campbell, *The Jesuits, 1534–1921* (The Encyclopedia Press, New York, 1921), p. 514.

16. Safford, *The Useful Plants of the Island of Guam*, p. 21.

17. Walter, *op. cit.*, pp. 319–20.

18. Abbé Raynal, *A Philosophical and Political History of the Settlements and Trade of the Europeans in the East and West Indies* (translated by J. O. Justamond, London, 1783), Vol. III, pp. 387–88.

19. Felix M. Keesing, *The South Seas in the Modern World* (The John Day Co., New York, 1945), pp. 43–46.

20. *Ibid.*, p. 53.

21. Raynal. *op. cit.*, p. 389.

22. *Ibid.*, pp. 388–89.

23. A. M. de Rochon, *Crozet's Voyage to Tasmania, New Zealand, the Ladrone Islands, and the Philippines in the Years 1771–1772* (translated from the French by H. Ling Roth, London, 1891), p. 84.

24. *Ibid.*, p. 92.

25. *Ibid.*, p. 85.

26. *Loc. cit.*

27. Rochon, *op cit.*, pp. 93–94.

28. *Ibid.*, pp. 80–81.

29. *Ibid.*, p. 82.

30. *Ibid.*, p. 81.

31. *Ibid.*, pp. 87–88.

32. *Ibid.*, p. 91.

33. *Ibid.*, p. 98.

34. Jean François Galaup de La Pérouse, *A Voyage Round the World in the Years 1785, 1786, 1787, and 1788* (London, 1798), Vol. II, pp. 311–12.

35. Kotzebue, *op. cit.*, Vol. II, pp. 240–41.

36. *Ibid.*, pp. 241–42.

37. *Ibid.*, pp. 242–44.

38. Safford, *The Useful Plants of the Island of Guam*, p. 25.

39. *Ibid.*, p. 26.

40. *Ibid.*, pp. 27–28.

## CHAPTER FIVE

# FINAL CENTURY OF SPANISH RULE

THE NINETEENTH CENTURY was the final century of Spanish rule in Guam. It saw the end of the long period of colonial administration that had its beginnings in 1565. During the century, ships of many nations visited the island. Among them were American, Russian, French, English, and Spanish vessels. The arrival of the American ship *Lydia* in 1802 seemed to be an omen of things to come at the end of the century.

Between 1817 and 1828 three scientific expeditions visited Guam. They explored the island, studying its plant and animal life. Their journals are almost the only source of much of the historical information concerning this period.

During the 19th century, as well as throughout most of its history, Guam was plagued by a shortage of natural resources. Consequently, the island was never able to become self-supporting. Under normal conditions the land could produce enough food to support a limited population. After epidemics, earthquakes, and typhoons, however, the people were brought to the verge of starvation. Because of this fact, problems affecting Guam's economy have always been a matter of real concern to the island's administrators. During the 19th century three Spanish governors stand out from the rest as having made serious attempts to strengthen the island's economy. In spite of their efforts, however, conditions became worse. They did not begin to improve until after the island had been acquired by the United States in 1898.

## AMERICAN SHIPS VISIT GUAM

By the beginning of the 19th century American ships were stopping, although infrequently, in the Marianas Islands. The Americans, engaged primarily in sealing and whaling, were seeking bases in the northern Marianas where they could refresh their crews and provision their ships. One of the first accounts concerning the visit of an American vessel to the island was written by William Haswell, first officer of the *Lydia,* out of Boston. Early in March 1801 the *Lydia* sailed from Boston, bound for Manila and Canton. At Manila the ship was chartered to take Don Vicente Blanco, new governor of the Marianas, to Guam. Leaving the Philippines on October 20, 1801, the *Lydia* reached Guam seventy-one days later. The great length of the voyage was due to the adverse winds and ocean currents which prevail at that time of year.

Aboard the *Lydia* when she left the Philippines were twenty-four passengers. These included Governor Blanco, his wife, their three children, two servant girls, and twelve menservants; a priest and his servant; and a judge and two servants. Throughout the trip the passengers caused a great deal of trouble. When their baggage came on board, it could not be distinguished from the rest of the cargo and was stowed in the hold. As a result, whenever the governor or members of his party wanted articles from their baggage, sailors had to be sent below to search for the desired items.

On January 6, 1802, the *Lydia* sailed into Apra Harbor. As she did so, a gun was fired from Fort Santa Cruz. The ship's anchor was dropped immediately. Shortly thereafter several men came out in a small boat to inquire who they were. As soon as they were told that Governor Blanco was aboard, they set out at once to carry the information to Don Manuel Muro, the retiring governor. About midnight an officer bearing a letter from Don Manuel came on board. He informed the new governor that boats would be sent out in the morning to take him and his party ashore. Accordingly, early the next morning three boats were sent out. One, a handsome

122

barge with a uniformed crew, was for the governor and his family. As Governor Blanco left the *Lydia,* he was given a salute of nine guns as well as three cheers from the crew.

Shortly after Governor Blanco went ashore, a British ship arrived in the harbor. Her captain told Haswell that he and his crew had captured the ship from the Spaniards off the coast of Peru. They were trying to return to England by way of the Cape of Good Hope. Their ship was leaking so badly that they were compelled to stop at Guam. They knew that the island was Spanish territory but hoped, nevertheless, that they would not be detained. In this, however, they were mistaken; most of them were imprisoned.

While the *Lydia* was being provisioned for the return trip to the Philippines, Haswell spent several days in Agana. He was impressed by what he saw and wrote the following description of the palace and other principal buildings of the capital:

> The Buildings of the Governors and Chief Officers are built with stone and are good houses. The Palace is two story and situated in a very Pleasant part of the Town with a large Plantation of Bread fruit trees before it and a Road from it to the Landing Place. It is a Large Building and in the Old Spanish stile. The first Story is stores, the Second is high, the Audience Chamber is near a 100 feet long and 40 Broad and 20 high and well ornamented with Lamps, Paintings, etc. At each end of it is private Apartments. In the Front is a large Balcony which reaches from one end of the house to the other. Behind the Palace is the Baracks and Guard Room. It is a large building and capable of containing 500 Men with ease. To the Northward stands the Church built like one of our Barns at home. It has a Low Steeple for the Bells. On the inside it is well adorned with Pictures, Images, etc. On the S.E. and near the Church is the Free School which has a spire and here the Alarm Bell is hung, also the School Bell. The Scholars never leave the house but to go to Church.
>
> The Houses of the Officers are near the Palace in the Main Street and are all two story high; but they make no other use of the lower Apartments than to Keep Cattle in them. They are Roomy, high and airy.[1]

At the time of Haswell's visit to Guam, functions of government were exercised by the governor and, to a limited degree, by the church as well. This sometimes led to conflicts between the church and the civil authorities. All officers accused of crimes were tried by the governor and other officers of the army. They had the power to inflict any punishment deemed proper, except death. If a man was sentenced to die, it was necessary to send him to Manila to be condemned. Afterwards, he was brought back to the island to be executed.

All inhabitants were required to pay a yearly rent for their houses and land. Their cattle too were the property of the crown and could be taken from them at any time. If a Guamanian wanted to kill a cow, he had first to get permission from the governor or the priests. Only very old cattle could be killed.

> They are called free Men [said Haswell], but I think contrary. If the Governor wants a Road cut he calls on all the Men and sets them about it and only finds them Rice till it is done. The same with any other work for Government. The Old governor carried it too far and was call'd a great Tyrant. He made them Build two Forts and a Bridge and cut a Road through a high Rock, build a School House and some other things and never allow'd them to be Idle. But for want of a Supply from Manila the Poor were near Starving, as he did not give them time to Cultivate the land his fears of the English was so great. The Church also has its modes of Tryal. They have a kind of Inquisition or tryal by Tortures Established, but I never heard of their punishing any person. The Poor Indians Respect the Fryars highly, but the governor will not let them meddle with the Affairs of government, as they often want to do. They were at variance about a Man that had committed Murder and fled to the Church for Protection. One of the Officers took him from the Church under the Altar. The Priests Resented, but were forced to hold their Tongues. They sat on Tryals before, but now they are excluded and sent to mend things Spiritual and the Governor takes care of things Temporal. But we carried out a Judge with us to Examine his behaviour and to hear the Complaints of the Poor and to see them Redressed.[2]

In 1802 Guam's defenses were quite extensive. Several good batteries were strategically placed so as to defend the island against attackers, especially the English. Two batteries were located in Agana. One, at the landing place on the shore, consisted of four guns. The other, on the cliff above the town, consisted of seven guns. Apra Harbor was defended by two forts: Santa Cruz, with six guns, and the Fortress of Orota, on Orote Peninsula, with four guns. Umatac Bay was defended by the Castle of San Angelo, a fort with six guns. Besides these, two guns were placed to defend a pass in the mountains.

Troops under arms numbered ninety-three men. About half of them were Filipinos; the rest were Guamanians. They were nicely uniformed and presented a good appearance. They had well-oiled arms and a good military band. There was also a native militia of about one thousand men. They carried old guns that were so rusty they could not be fired.

Money paid to the soldiers was the only cash in circulation on the island. Once a month, they received their pay from the governor's secretary. As soon as they had been paid, they spent most of the money at the island's only store, owned by the governor. In this way, the money never really left the governor's hands. Some governors, upon retiring, left the island with eighty or ninety thousand dollars.[3]

The *Lydia* departed from Guam on February 16, 1802, and returned to Manila. In his journal, Haswell estimated the population of the entire island to be about 11,000.* At least one other American ship, commanded by Samuel Williams, stopped at Guam early in the century. Concerning early attempts of the Americans to establish limited colonies in the northern Marianas, Kotzebue wrote:

> The trade of this ocean makes it desirable for the navigators who possess it, to have similar settlements on the more eastern islands. Their connection with the Sandwich islands [Hawaiian Islands] renders the stealing of people easy there; and the island of Agrigan, one of the most northern of the Marianas, seemed to be particularly adapted for such a settlement, though it is mountainous, unfit for cultivation, and cannot even feed oxen; and affords no protected anchoring-place.
>
> Captain Brown, with the ship Derby, from Boston, was in Atooi in the year 1809 or 1810. On this island, he was joined by Mr. Johnson, ship-builder to the king, who had fallen into disgrace, on account of an accident which had happened to a ship. They weighed anchor during the night, and carried off fifteen women who were on board. They ap-

---

* This would seem to be an overestimation. Governor Medinilla's census, "made with the greatest accuracy and minuteness," listed the total population of Guam, Rota, and Tinian as being 5,389 in 1816.

proached the island of Oneeheow. A boat brought refreshments from shore. It was expected: seven men who were in it were taken on board, the boat was then hoisted up, and they directed their course to Agrigan. They missed the island; it was to the north: not to lose time in contending against the wind, they attempted to land on a southern island. They did so at Tinian, where they remained in two parties. One party, consisting of Johnson, with four men, and the Sandwich islanders, were to build a boat to sail to Agrigan; the other party, composed of the second mate of the ship, with three men, who had been discharged, intended to convert a long-boat, which they had bought of the captain, into a ship, for the purpose of carrying on commercial speculations on these seas. The Sandwich boat was left behind: both parties went over to Saypan, which island afforded better timber, and there carried on their work. But the Sandwich islanders remembered their liberty, vengeance, and their country. When the mate had finished his vessel, which they intended to make use of to return home, they took advantage, when the party was dispersed and unarmed, to fall upon them; the mate and one white were killed: war raged.

It was, in the mean time, made known in Guahon, that there were strangers in Saypan and Tinian; the Governor, D. Alexandro Parreño, sent thither, and it was in the course of these bloody combats, that, in June, 1810, Johnson, with four whites, two negroes, the seven Sandwich islanders, and the fifteen women, were brought to Guahon, where he himself still remains.

In May, 1815, by command of the captain-general of the Philippines, D. Gose Gardoque, a settlement on Agrigan was broken up, and nearly forty men, of whom one was an American, three Englishmen, and the rest Sandwich islanders, brought to Guahon.[4]

Nine years after the first group of intruders was removed from Agrigan, many of the Hawaiians were still on Guam. In 1819, when a French scientific expedition under the command of Captain de Freycinet stopped at the island, J. Arago, reporter and historian of the expedition, wrote:

> ...A brig from Manila accidentally touched at the island, and carried the intelligence to the Governor of the Marianas, of these individuals residing in a country under his jurisdiction. M. Medinilla gave orders to the Captain of his vessel to go in search of the persons shipwrecked, and convey them to Guam. The natives of the Sandwich Islands were made slaves of, under the ridiculous pretext, that the crew of the vessel, on board of which they were, had mutinied....

126

All these unfortunate persons are now before us; they are going to perform some of the dances of their own country, and are waiting with the greatest impatience for the signal to begin. . . .

Every individual of the colony appears to arrogate to himself the same rights over them as a barbarian slave-master, and has no more scruple in beating a Sandwich islander, than a Turk has in empaling a Christian.[5]

In his report, Arago did not mention the Americans and Englishmen who were taken prisoner with the Hawaiians. Because of the limited means of escape, however, it is quite probable that they too were still on the island.

As early as 1817, it would seem, the Spaniards ceased in their efforts to prevent the intrusions of Americans and other foreigners into the northern Marianas. "It is well known, from authentic information," relates Kotzebue's journal, "that there is already a new settlement on Agrigan. In pursuance of the present order of the captain-general, no obstacle is to be thrown in the way of the settlement; the settlers are only to acknowledge the supremacy of Spain; and a Spaniard is to be sent as chief magistrate. Nobody has, however, yet been sent."[6]

## OTTO VON KOTZEBUE

On November 24, 1817, the ship *Rurik*, commanded by Otto von Kotzebue, a lieutenant in the Russian navy, approached the shores of Guam from the north, looking for a place to anchor. The *Rurik*, fitted out at the expense of Count Romanzoff, chancellor of the Russian empire, was bound on a voyage of scientific exploration in the South Seas. Scientists aboard the ship included the botanist Adelbert von Chamisso, the naturalist Johann Friedrich Eschscholtz, and the expedition's artist, Ludwig Choris.

"As soon as the morning dawned," wrote Kotzebue, "I again directed my course to the northern part of the island, along the west coast of which I intended to proceed to the south, till we discovered the town of Agana. The northern part of the island of Guahon rises perpendicularly from the sea, to a moderate height, and runs to the south in a straight line, as far as the eye can reach: a beautiful forest of variegated green covers the upper part

127

of the island, and affords a very pleasing view to the mariner. The wind blew so high that we were obliged to take in the top-gallant sails. At eleven o'clock we had the northern point of Guahon behind us, and were under the lee of the island where the monsoon, checked by the height of the land, died away to almost a perfect calm. A breeze now and then, which put the ship a little in motion, wafted to us the most aromatic odours from the shore, to which we were near. The seaman who has long been deprived of land, knows, particularly, how to prize these pleasing sensations."[7]

As the ship moved southward along the coast, Kotzebue was impressed by the fact that not one native canoe sailed out to meet them. "Could I have transported myself back to the time when Magellan discovered these islands," relates Kotzebue, "the Rurik would long since have been surrounded by many canoes, with happy islanders. This was not the case now; the introduction of the Christian religion has not diffused here its benign blessings; for, since that time, the whole race of the natives of the Landrones has been extirpated. We looked in vain for a canoe, or a man on the shore; and it almost seemed as if we were off an uninhabited island. The sight of this lovely country deeply affected me. Formerly these fertile vallies were the abode of a nation, who passed their days in tranquil happiness; now only the beautiful palm-groves remained to overshadow their graves; a deathlike silence every where prevailed."[8] A short time later, however, a native was seen on the shore; but he ran hastily into the woods when he saw the ship. Shortly afterwards, a large boat of European make rowed out to meet them. Kotzebue's journal contains a lengthy account of his landing at Guam. It runs, in part, as follows:

> A young Englishman, of the name of Robert Wilson, who held the place of pilot in Agana, had been sent by the Governor to conduct us to a safe harbour, if we intended to stay at Guahon. While he steered S.W. along the coast, we could, without interruption, continue the survey. We soon saw the town of Agana, in the south, which is pleasantly situated on the shore; and, on the west, leans against a tolerably high hill, which forms a cape (here called the Devil's Cape) ; on the summit is a fortress, in which, while still at a distance, you see a small white house. I expressed to Wilson my wish rather to anchor before the town

128

of Agana than in Umatac Bay, where, as is well known, Malaspina, some years ago, had so very bad a berth, and was answered, that it was only in former times, when the present harbour was unknown, that ships anchored at Umatac or Agana, where the situation was in several respects so bad, that many ships have perished there. At twelve o'clock when the town already lay S.E. of us, we saw a canoe under sail coming up to us, in which Wilson, through a telescope, recognized a deputy of the Governor. I immediately lay-to, and we soon had the pleasure of seeing on board, Don Ignacio Martínez, lieutenant of artillery, who, as he did not know our flag, asked to what nation we belonged. He was much astonished to see Russians before him, but still more so when he heard that we were making a voyage of discovery, and showed even double the politeness natural to the Spaniards. After he had written down the name of the ship, and mine, he took his leave, and hastened to communicate this important news to the Governor.... We now hastened to get into the harbour: a long narrow tongue of land, called Orote, on the western point of Guahon, before which lies a small rocky island, forms the entrance.... The harbour is protected, towards the north, by a small low island, called Appapa [now known as Cabras Island]; it...appears, on sailing from the north, to be connected with the continent. From this island there runs, to the west, a coral reef, the uttermost point of which, with the cape of St. Carlos de Orote, forms the entrance of the harbour, which is a mile and a quarter broad; but in the middle of it there is a shoal,* which is, however, not dangerous for small ships; but I would advise large ones not to keep in the middle of the passage, but rather to the south of the bank, and as near as possible to St. Carlos de Orote, where the water is deep enough for the largest vessels. At two o'clock in the afternoon, we entered the harbour by the northern passage; its depth was five fathoms and a half, the bottom consisted of coral, and we were in a basin of water as smooth as a mirror, where ships can also lie at anchor; but as the depth is considerable, and the bottom not good, they generally go to the inner harbour, which is one of the safest in the world. An east wind obliged us to tack to the entrance of the inner harbour, an attempt which Wilson thought dangerous, on account of the many coral banks, and which no ship had hitherto ventured. He advised me rather to cast anchor here till the wind had veered to the west, which it usually does in the morning; but as this would have taken me too much time ... we resolved rather to attempt to work through directly. According to the old

* Kotzebue was told that a short time before his arrival a Spanish galleon, richly laden and bound for Manila, had been wrecked on this shoal and the whole cargo sent to the bottom.

custom, a sailor was obliged to be on the mast-head, another on the bowsprit, and the mate in the shrouds. We were timely warned of every danger, and tacking, to the great terror of Wilson, who had already protested against all responsibility, fortunately entered in safety the inner harbour. As the entrance is so very narrow the Rurik was obliged to be warped in: all hands were put in motion; and, at five o'clock, we were inside of the harbour La Caldera de Apra. We here found a deputy from the Governor of Agana, who, in a very polite letter, invited me and all my gentlemen into the town, and had already sent us some mules, which waited for us on the opposite shore of the island Appapa, near the village of Piti. I accepted the invitation with pleasure; left Lieutenant Schischmareff to anchor near the fortress of St. Cruz, which lies on a small island in the harbour, and went on shore, accompanied by our scientific gentlemen, and Mr. Wilson.[9]

The sun was nearly setting when Kotzebue and his companions reached Piti. There the other members of his party mounted mules, while he rode a horse, the only one on the island, which the governor had sent especially for him. As they passed through small villages on their way to Agana, the half-naked villagers greeted them in a quiet but friendly manner. "The inhabitants of Guahon," wrote Kotzebue, "are called by the Spaniards los Indios. They are all Christians; and are partly descended from natives; but most of them from people brought hither by the Spaniards from Mexico and the Philippines, after the original race was extirpated."[10]

At about eight o'clock in the evening, Kotzebue's party arrived at Agana. Going first to Wilson's house, they washed themselves and put on clean clothes; then they presented themselves at the palace to pay their respects to the governor, Don José de Medinilla y Pineda. Concerning his first meeting with Governor Medinilla, Kotzebue wrote:

> After I had acquainted him with the object of my voyage, and told him that I landed here with hope of obtaining fresh provisions, he promised, with the greatest readiness, to provide me with every thing the season of the year produced, and regretted that it was not now the time of fruit, which was there in abundance. He immediately gave me a proof of his desire to serve me, by ordering his aide-de-camp to send to the Rurick, at break of day, fresh meat, fruit, and vegetables, and daily to supply the crew with them. The governor is, in fact, the only real Spaniard; the other officers, and even the priests, are natives either

of Manila or Mexico, and descendants from Spaniards. He is about forty years old, and, notwithstanding his bad health, an agreeable companion, and a particularly polite host. He must know how to make himself useful to the government, as his administration had been prolonged for three years longer, though, according to the law, the Governor of a Spanish possession can only fill his office for three years. I had little difficulty in conversing with him by Wilson's assistance, but I tried in vain to turn the conversation on the Marianas, respecting which, I wished to learn many things; but, mysterious as all the Spanish governors are in this quarter of the globe, he always contrived to give the conversation another turn. But he took the more care to please our palate. After he had several times offered us tea and chocolate, he conducted us to a table, richly laid out with fruits, confectionary, and the choicest wines. We enjoyed ourselves very well, as we thought this was to be our supper. Scarcely had an hour elapsed, when we were shown into the dining-room, where the table, covered with the richest dishes, awaited us. We did not know whether it was the custom here to eat without intermission, or whether they gave only the Russian stomach credit for such powers of digestion, but we soon observed that they all ate with an excellent appetite. At table I met the vice-governor, as he is called here, Don Luis de Torres; and this amiable man particularly interested us, as he had visited the Carolinas.... He related to us a great deal about them, and promised to give us, in writing, the observations he had made there.[11]

After dinner, Kotzebue and Chamisso were invited to spend the night at the palace. The other gentlemen in his party spent the night in the houses of minor government officials. After breakfast the next morning, Kotzebue, having expressed a wish to see the town, was accompanied by Governor Medinilla on a tour of inspection. His description of the town is as follows:

The town of Agana, which should properly be called a village, is situated on a beautiful plain, some hundred paces from the shore; to the right and left are fine palm groves: in the south, a high mountain forms the back-ground; from its summit, hang large spreading trees, which overshade a part of the town, and give it a picturesque appearance. An inconsiderable stream, which flows through the town, supplies the inhabitants with water. The houses, which are constructed in the same manner as in the villages, form several regular streets. Only seven or eight houses are built of coral stone, which belong either to the government, as that of the Governor, or to the civil officers.

On the eastern part of the town is a considerably large church, and a convent; the whole clergy consists of two priests, who are natives of Manila, and descendants from the Malays. It is said that, always after a certain time, generally every twenty years, a violent storm rises in the S.W., which causes the sea to run so high that the town is overflowed, and the inhabitants obliged to fly to the mountains. Only the stone houses are able to resist the fury of the water; the bamboo cages are all destroyed. Two fortresses of coral stone defend the town; one of them lies on the shore, but has not yet any guns; the other lies to the west, behind the town, on an eminence; has a few guns, and seems to be built chiefly to restore tranquillity in case of a riot; but as they have no powder, as I was informed by the Governor, I do not see the use of the two fortresses. The town has two hundred houses, and contains 1,500 inhabitants, who, as I have already said, derive their origin from Mexico and the Philippines. There is only a man and his wife on the whole island, of the original branch. With the death of these two people the race of the old Ladrones will be entirely extinguished. The Governor had the kindness to show them to me, and our painter took their portraits. The military consists of militia, and appears to be in good condition: the officers are natives. The soldiers, who are obliged to provide their own clothing, looked very neat.... On my walk, the Governor showed me several canoes, which he had purchased from the Carolinians; and told me, on this occasion, of the great dexterity of these people in swimming and diving. When the galleon, already mentioned, perished, some Carolinians, who were here at the time, fetched the barrels filled with piasters out of the cabin of the ship, which was lying several fathoms under water...."[12]

Early in the afternoon, Kotzebue and Dr. Eschscholtz, the naturalist, mounted their animals and started back to the ship in Apra Harbor. Along the way, they stopped at the villages of Tepungan and Asan. Wherever they stopped, the people brought them fresh water and fruits. "The sportive, cheerful disposition of the South Sea islanders," wrote Kotzebue, "is no longer found among these people; they have been too long oppressed, and all their actions are indicative only of subjection. They are entirely under the command of the Governor; and though the government demands no taxes, their condition is but poor. The present Governor is a good man, who treats the poor half-savage Christians like his children; the former one (Don Alexandro Parreno) was a tyrant, whom they never approached without trembling; and, perhaps, on this account, they are still distrustful.

"Tobacco is universally prized; men, women, and children constantly smoke cigars; they have also betel in their mouths, which gives a disagreeable red dye to the teeth and lips. In all the Spanish settlements the government has the sole right of planting tobacco; but every body is allowed to do it in Guahon."[13]

At about five o'clock in the afternoon they reached the ship, which was anchored in the inner harbor, near fort Santa Cruz.

The next day, November 26, Captain Taitano, commandant of the fortress of Orota,* visited the ship and invited Kotzebue and several of his officers to his house in Agat. After giving members of his crew permission to go on shore to pick oranges, Kotzebue and his party started for Agat. "A narrow footpath," relates Kotzebue, "led us across the tongue of land through thick bushes, and we soon saw the sea, and were in a large bay, in which lie the three small islands laid down on my chart. We went then through an avenue of palm-trees, into the adjoining village of Agat, two miles behind which we saw a round mountain, the highest in the whole island. Taitano received us very politely, and the romantic scenery with which his house is surrounded made an agreeable impression on us, and we all returned to the ship, where the crew had already arrived, as highly delighted with their walk as with their oranges. The sailors saw in the forest a stag, and several lizards five feet long. Besides cats and dogs, stags are the only quadrupeds we have seen. There are no poisonous reptiles, or snakes."[14]

On November 28 Kotzebue and his officers returned to the *Rurik* from Agana, where they had gone to pay their respects to Governor Medinilla and to bid him goodbye. Kotzebue wrote in his journal that he was accompanied to the ship by Don Luis de Torres "with all the officers; and the Governor, who intended to give me some dispatches to Manila, promised to follow, and to remain on board during the night. We spent a pleasant evening in the society of the

---

* The fortress of Orota, situated at the tip of Orote Peninsula, once guarded the entrance to the outer harbor. Fort Santa Cruz, a mile to the east, guarded the entrance to the inner harbor. Both, at this time, were neglected and in decay.

Spanish officers, who all remained on board during the night; the governor had been detained, and did not come till the morning of the 29th. The ship was abundantly supplied with fresh provisions, among which there was even a live ox. We parted with grateful hearts: when the Governor got into his boat, we fired a salute of five guns, and the crew gave three cheers. At eight o'clock we were already out of the harbour."[15]

## THE FREYCINET EXPEDITION

A little more than a year after Kotzebue's visit, on March 17, 1819, the French corvette *Uranie*, under the command of Captain Louis de Freycinet, arrived at Guam. Important members of the Freycinet expedition, sent out for the purpose of engaging in scientific studies in the South Seas, were the botanist Charles Gaudichaud-Beaupré, the zoologists Quoy and Gaimard, and the artist-reporter Arago. A stay of several months allowed the naturalists to make extensive collections and observations not only on Guam but on the islands of Tinian and Rota as well. In 1823 Arago wrote a book in which he described his experiences with the Freycinet expedition. His account of the expedition's stay at Guam, although extremely critical of the Spaniards, presents detailed information about the island in the time of Governor Medinilla.

After sailing along the west coast of Guam for half a day, the *Uranie*, on March 17, dropped anchor in Umatac Bay, about a cable's length from a Spanish ship that had arrived from Manila the day before. The ship, *La Paz*, had brought Governor Medinilla to Umatac. On the following day, the governor went on board the *Uranie* to pay his compliments to Captain Freycinet. "The ceremony of saluting," wrote Arago, "occasioned a very serious accident to two soldiers of the garrison, who, little accustomed, no doubt, to the management of cannon, were burnt in such a way, as to excite apprehensions for their lives; but their good constitutions, and the care of our surgeons, preserved them from what was considered almost the certainty of death."[16] Later, Arago described Umatac as being a small village of thirty hovels, built on piles and constructed of the ribs of palm leaves.

In Umatac, Freycinet and his crew came into close contact with leprosy for the first time. Arago relates that the dread disease was quite prevalent among the people of Umatac and that both men and women were "covered with a disgusting and active leprosy, that leaves on the body black and livid marks even when it disappears, and is a continual subject of dread to the Europeans who have to deal with them."[17] Concerning the prevalence of leprosy in Anigua, a *barrio* of Agana which he visited later, Arago wrote:

A few hundred yards from Anigua are several solitary houses, in which are kept lepers of both sexes, whose disease is so virulent that it commonly deprives them of the tongue or some of their limbs, and is said to become a contagious distemper. I have delineated two of these unfortunate creatures, exhibiting to the eye the most hideous aspect of human misery. One shudders with horror on approaching these houses of desolation and despair. I am persuaded, that by enlarging these paltry buildings, collecting in them all the persons in the island severely attacked by the leprosy, and prohibiting all communication with them from without, they might expel from the country this frightful disease. . . .[18]

Arago was not overly impressed by what he saw in Guam. He obviously felt that previous visitors to the island had, in their journals, exaggerated the beauties of the place. Concerning the palace in Agana, the environs of the city, and the general way of life of the people, he wrote:

The governor received us in his palace, which is built of stone and wood. It is newly whitewashed, and cleaned in such a manner as to lead us to suspect that these embellishments have been executed solely on our account. Eight pieces of artillery defend the gate. At its side is a very neat and spacious guardhouse. . . .

At the back of the palace is a pretty large piece of ground, which is called the garden, but in which probably nothing was ever sown. How then can the inhabitants be expected to cultivate their possessions, while their chiefs set the example of neglect? The square [Plaza de España] in front of this edifice is the only one in the city: it is tolerably large, but irregular. . . .

The country round the town is not more cultivated than that at a distance from it. You may see, indeed, humble huts, round which a few yards of rice, Indian corn, and tobacco are cultivated: but how much ground is lost! what culpable indolence prevails! I should have guessed that the country belonged to the Spaniards, from the sacrilegious state of neglect in which it is left. . . .

The arrival of a ship at the settlement is a remarkable event. As soon as one is descried, the people quit their ranchos, and proceed toward the capital. The most active prepare the articles they have to barter; and interest, for once at least, rouses them from their apathy. The streets are peopled, and we perceive a little motion in a country that might have been taken the day before for the realm of sleep.

The governor, in paying his compliments, observed, that he considered this as a happy year. Two Russian frigates, the Kamtschatka and the Kutusow, anchored here; the former on the 7th December, 1818; the latter, on the 14th of January, 1819. They were engaged separately on voyages of discovery, undertaken by order of their government. The brig Rurik, which we met with at the Cape of Good Hope, had also staid a week here. . . .

At Agana there are a royal college and several secondary schools. . . . The principal of the college has six dollars a month, or a shirt, and his allowance of provisions. The master of a secondary school, who implicitly follows the precepts of his superior, has only two dollars. . . .

The common people are very superstitious at Agana, and yet more so in the country; for superstition is the daughter of ignorance. Since our arrival, we have had four shocks of an earthquake, which have been attributed to the dissolute morals of the settlement. If we were to believe the inhabitants, God pays no attention to any country but theirs. No event takes place, however trifling, in which they do not discern a great cause.

There is no country in the world where sons pay more respect to their fathers. Age does not free them from obedience; and I have seen men of forty tremble at a mere reprimand from their father. They never mention their name without the prefix of señor, and a slight inclination of the head.

Males here may marry at fourteen, and females at twelve; but such precocious matches are very rare.

The number of children in a family is commonly from three to five. I have seen an old man, who had twenty-seven, all living, and consoling him in his infirmities. . . .

There is a woman in the settlement, the number of whose progeny amounts to a hundred and thirty-seven. To mention such instances is to prove their rarity.[19]

During the time that Freycinet and his crew were in Guam, the birthday of the king of Spain was celebrated as a festive occasion.

The beginning of the festivities was announced by the firing of cannon and the ringing of church bells. Four soldiers, accompanied by a drummer, went through the streets on a tour of inspection, making certain that the streets, as well as houses and yards, were clean. The front of the palace was draped with flags. On the balcony was a large portrait of the king, to which all the people respectfully took off their hats. In the evening, public dances were held in the Plaza de España.

The dances that were performed indicate that, as early as 1819, the music and dances of the ancient Chamorros had been replaced by importations from Spain, Mexico, and the Philippines. Only one dance, called the dance of the ancients, was believed to be representative of the Chamorro culture of pre-Spanish times. Arago, one of the interested spectators, was completely unimpressed by it. "Formed in a circle," he wrote, "the performers took hold of each other by the hand, and turned round, humming a monotonous tune; they repeated unceasingly the same figure, and vainly fatigued themselves in endeavouring to amuse us."[20]

The dance of the ancients was followed by a comedy in fifteen or sixteen acts in which two persons, grotesquely dressed and carrying three little pigs, appeared by turns on the stage. Their actions brought roars of laughter from the audience. The evening's entertainment was concluded by an interesting ballet called the *Dance of Montezuma*, brought from America. Even the costumes came from America. According to Arago,

> They ... are magnificent, and their antiquity has not tarnished their lustre. The silk of which they are woven is extremely fine; the flowers, and the various colours with which they are covered, are well arranged, and the fringes round the borders still brilliant. Certainly nothing so handsome had before been seen at Guam; and these mantles, with the embroidery, would give every nation a high idea of the industry of the people who made them.[21]

Arago was impressed by the fact that the native Guamanians, in spite of their difficult lives, did a great deal of singing. "Music is one of the most agreeable amusements of the inhabitants of the Marianas," he wrote. "They sing the moment they awake, they sing during the hours of rest, and they fall asleep singing.... Almost everybody has some taste, and plays tolerably well; but their voice is nasal, and accords better with their native airs than with those of Spain, which are more varied. The national couplets are always composed in honour of some saint of Paradise, or to celebrate some great event, such as the arrival of a ship. Our coming awoke the slumbering muse of the poet of the place; and we often heard songs, the burthen of which related to our voyage, and to some persons of the expedition; and which, if they did not indicate talents, were at least an evidence of a turn for satire."[22]

From the moment of their arrival in Guam, Freycinet and his men were overwhelmed by the friendliness and generosity of the inhabitants. They soon learned, however, that the generous giving of gifts was an ancient custom that imposed certain obligations upon the receivers. Concerning this practice, Arago wrote:

> The inhabitants of the Marianas are in general mild, and confiding in their behavior towards foreigners; but they like to be treated familiarly. You cannot give them a greater pleasure than by addressing them in the easy language of friendship. . . . [If you accept a gift] gratitude requires you to acquit yourself of the obligation; and, according to the custom of the country, you must offer something of at least double the value of the object which you have received.
>
> Before we were acquainted with this singular practice, we were astonished at the generosity of these poor people: but when you are informed of the custom, buy, and never accept any thing; if you do, you are certain to be plundered. If you make a present of a pocket-hankerchief to-day, to-morrow you will be asked for a shirt, and in a few days after for a sheet.
>
> At Agana, the inhabitants are so given to this custom, that if you at any time neglect to make presents in return for what you have received, you will soon hear the generous donor remind you of his gift, talk to you of it at every hour of the day, and finally desire to have it back, without a blush. This is general; and from the highest officer at Guam (I except the Governor, whose real generosity we have had opportunity of appreciating, and Don Luis de Torres), to the most wretched peasant of Toupoungan, every body is mindful not to derogate from this ancient law: a curious example of it happened from my having one day, out of compassion, given an old shirt to a sick man at Agana. As we were about to depart, his daughter brought it back, telling me in a tone of regret, truly affecting, that her father could not reward me for my present. In a

138

moment of generosity I offered her another; moreover gave a parting kiss to the young messenger, and exonerated her family from every species of obligation.[23]

## DUMONT D'URVILLE

Dumont d'Urville made two visits to Guam. On the first of these, in May 1828, he was in command of the *Astrolabe*, which had been sent out on a voyage of scientific exploration.* With him were the zoologists Quoy and Gaimard, who had accompanied the Freycinet expedition to Guam nine years earlier.

The Astrolabe [wrote Safford] anchored at Umatac and was boarded by José Flores, alcalde of the village. He told the captain that he had seen the ships of Malaspina, who visited Guam in 1792, thirty-six years before. In the roadstead d'Urville saw two ships which had been captured by the Spaniards from the independents of Mexico and were now being taken to Manila. Three years before this there had been a mutiny on board some Spanish vessels lying at anchor in the roadstead of Umatac. The squadron was commanded by Don Andrés García Camba, Caballero de Santiago, afterwards governor of the Philippines. General Camba had served in South America against the revolutionists and had been captured at the battle of Ayacucho, December 9, 1824, in which the South American colonies won their final victory over Spain. On the 1st of January, 1825, he sailed in command of a squadron composed of the ship Asia and the brigantines Aquiles and Constante, bound for the Philippines. The water of the squadron becoming scarce, they anchored in the roadstead of Umatac and filled their casks. On the night of March 10, while weighing anchor, the crews suddenly rose, set fire to one of the vessels, maltreated the commanding officer, and drove him ashore, together with his officers and 100 loyal men. Ganga Herrero, the governor of Guam, went on board and tried to restore discipline, but they put him ashore, hoisted the flag of the insurgent republics of America, and set sail for Peru to join the independents. The general, accompanied by his officers and loyal men, proceeded in a whaling vessel to Manila, where they arrived April 4, and were received with great hospitality by all classes of people.[24]

## DISSATISFACTION WITH SPANISH RULE

After returning to Europe upon the completion of his first voyage

---

* His second visit was in January 1839, when, commanding the *Astrolabe* and the *Zélée*, he stopped briefly at Guam.

to Guam, d'Urville wrote an interesting account of the expedition's adventures. He stated that Governor Don José Ganga Herrero, who administered the affairs of the island from May 1823 to August 1826, was very popular with the Guamanians. He permitted them to trade freely with any ships that stopped at the island. His successor Medinilla, who returned for a second term as governor in 1826, was, on the other hand, intensely disliked by the people.

> He [relates Safford] forbade all traffic with visiting vessels, monopolizing it for himself. Among the officials visiting the ship was the captain of the port, a Scotchman named John Anderson, who had come to the island with Freycinet. He had served temporarily on the Uranie as chief quartermaster, and was allowed to remain in Guam at his own request. D'Urville describes him as a fine-looking man, well-behaved, and speaking French pretty well. Anderson knew Quoy and Gaimard, having been shipments with them on the Uranie. He came to investigate the sickness on board, fearing that some contagious disease might be introduced into the island. He gave d'Urville information regarding the hydrography of the region. As an illustration of the conditions in Guam, he said that Medinilla, the governor, on his return from Manila had brought back more than 60,000 pesos worth of all kinds of goods to sell to the natives of Guam, and that he conducted a very profitable business, since he permitted no competitors in trade.[25]

Rapid decline in the affairs of Guam following the removal of Governor Tobias, and the lack of enterprise and progress since that time, were due in large measure to the manner in which many of the governors monopolized Guam's trade. Governor Medinilla was especially guilty of the restrictive practice. "How should industry flourish?" asked d'Urville. "The governor is the sole trader. He receives annually money for the salaries of the officers, which he sends back, giving them instead inferior goods at prices fixed by himself."[26]

During the first half of the 19th century, the Guamanian people became increasingly dissatisfied with the restrictive trade practices of the Spaniards and with the methods employed by them to compel the islanders to work. Their complaints eventually became a matter of real concern to the governors. This resulted in the exchange of numerous communications with the captain-general of the Philippines for the purpose of seeking solutions to Guam's problems.

> At Agana, the capital of Guam [wrote Safford], there are a number of letter books containing copies of the official communications of the governors of the Marianas to their immediate superior, the captain-general of the Philippines [these documents were destroyed during the American reoccupation of Guam in 1944]. In these letters various questions are discussed at length regarding the policy which should be pursued to make the Marianas Islands self-supporting and profitable to Spain, and to make the natives prosperous and happy. Arguments are advanced in favor both of protection and of free trade with visiting vessels. Attempts were made to compel the natives to till the ground, and inducements were offered by tempting their self-interest. Causes of the failure of the population to increase were sought in the destruction of the crops by hurricanes and pests, in the use of unwholesome or injurious food, and in the disinclination of the natives to work more than was necessary for their daily needs. Some of the governors greedily monopolized all trade, forcing the natives and the soldiers of the barracks to buy goods from them at prices arbitrarily fixed by themselves, and forbidding the natives to sell their products to the whalers who flocked to the islands. Others gave the natives free license to trade and entered into their daily life by cultivating farms of their own after the native fashion. Efforts were made to benefit the islands by decrees of the captains-general of the Philippines, to whose ears came stories of dishonesty and oppression on the part of the governors, and confidential subordinates were sent to the islands to see what could be done for their good.[27]

One of the men sent to Guam to investigate the deplorable conditions that prevailed there was Francisco Ramón de Villalobos. In the following pages we will study his policies and those of Don Pablo Pérez and Don Felipe María de la Corte: governors who, during the 19th century, stand out from the rest as having worked hard and well for the benefit of Guam.

From the time of the expulsion of the Jesuits down to 1898, the history of the Guamanian people was one of unrelenting struggle for survival. While it is true that there was little actual starvation, the islanders were increasingly plagued by diseases and constant shortages of food. Such shortages were caused not only by neglect of the island's economy by the Spanish government but also by the greed of various governors. The priests too, being unwilling or unable to provide adequate leadership, neglected the economic welfare of the people. Their zeal for the salvation of souls was not, as in earlier times, balanced by concern for the welfare of bodies.

By royal decree, the Jesuits were banished from Spanish possessions, and their place was taken by the Augustinians. This change may or may not have affected the religious life and welfare of the Chamorros— probably not. . . . But it wrought a mighty change in the routine and welfare of the Chamorro's stomach. The Jesuits have always worked with their hands as well as their heads, and have shown remarkable aptitude for getting work out of others, and particularly out of the uncertainly converted. Under Jesuit leadership the Chamorros had learned a very fair amount of husbandry, and the island was well cultivated. Cattle had been a crown monopoly, cared for by corvee on crown lands. The natives had added many fruits and vegetables to their diet since the Spaniards came, and had learned to eat meat. The Jesuits left, and their successors, zealous for souls, paid no attention to bodies. The "parocco" no longer inspected the crop and demanded news of the harvest. No energetic overseer in black cassock superintended the ploughing and seeding or saw to it that the cattle were regularly salted. And the Chamorros, with their newly-acquired appetite for the fleshpots of the conquering whites, not only reverted, but slumped, to ancestral type. There began an era of semi-hunger that has continued ever since.[28]

By 1828, conditions in Guam had become so bad that Don Mariano Ricafort, captain-general of the Philippines, sent Don Francisco Ramón de Villalobos to the island to conduct an investigation.

Villalobos' investigation confirmed what was already well-known: that Guam's economy, due to mismanagement and neglect, was in a deplorable state. This sad state of affairs could be traced back to the period immediately following the Spanish conquest.

After the conquest the surviving islanders, who by this time had been concentrated into villages, continued to live off their lands. Since so many people had died during the conquest, there was plenty of land for all. This was true in spite of the fact that the Spaniards had taken over large tracts of land, called royal estates, for government use. At various times, attempts were made to increase food production. For this purpose, "there were established in suitable localities ranches where, under the direction of Spaniards or natives, the ground was tilled and cattle raised, all these products being handled by the Governor who apportioned them as a patriarch would, there being enough beef, hogs, and chickens, corn and other products for the maintenance of the Governor and the garrison and their families, while horses, asses and mules were also raised for use in traveling."[29]

A further drain on Guam's limited food supplies occurred when the island's garrison was increased to 150 men. Both officials and troops received their salaries from the treasury of Mexico. Since they were the only persons on the island with money, they were able to secure the best food and living conditions for themselves. Funds for the support of the government were brought to Guam each year by the Manila galleon. Its arrival "was announced as soon as the ship was sighted, with the boom of cannon which echoing from hill to hill set the whole colony in motion; soldiers and missionaries left Agana for Umatac where the officers, the crew and the passengers landed to have some recreation, gambling and amusing themselves in a manner which brought no small profits to the natives."[30]

Money acquired from the soldiers of the garrison and from passengers on the galleons made it possible for a few industrious islanders to attain considerable wealth. However, since the governor controlled all trade on the island, they were unable to use their money profitably. Various governors, wrote de la Corte, "thought of nothing else than to improve their own opportunity to exploit commerce as it was customary in all the Indies, and in Guam, like elsewhere, the chances were not lacking for the committing of abuses, which brought about the consequent complaints, disagreements and judicial proceedings."[31] Thus, during this period, the people of Guam lived off the soil as far as food was concerned and off the government as far as other needs were concerned. The people raised just enough food to care for their needs. Commerce was almost nonexistent, and "everybody lived in quiet contentment both of body and mind, the only event which ever stirred the quietness being the petit jealousies and intrigues which are the only incentives of life in small, isolated communities."[32]

## CHANGE OF CONTROL

In 1808 Spain was defeated in war by the armies of Napoleon. This was the signal of revolt for all of Spain's colonies on the American mainland. By December 1824 all the rebellious colonies had won their independence. Liberation of the Spanish colonies in America had profound effects on the economy of the Marianas. Control of Guam and the rest of the Marianas was shifted from Mexico to the Philippines. Moreover, the annual grant for supporting the insular government was reduced from about 20,000 to 8,000 pesos. Later, this too was discontinued.

When the change of control occurred, Spaniards on the island consisted of the governor, the *sargento-mayor*, other minor officials and their families, and a garrison force composed of three companies of fifty men each. The native inhabitants, numbering about 5,920, lived in Agana (called a city), Umatac (called a villa), and in the towns of Agat, Inarajan, Merizo, and Pago. All of these towns were large enough to support churches. The island had no industry or commerce, and the entire population, 3,000 of whom lived in Agana, lived off the products of the soil.

With the shifting of administrative control from Mexico to the Philippines, the Spanish government decided to reorganize the government of Guam. On December 17, 1828, an organic statute was decreed and placed in effect. By the terms of the statute, great power was concentrated in the hands of the island's treasurer. He was given charge of the collection and distribution of funds, the nomination of government employees, control over public works, regulation of politics, and the distribution of land. Moreover, the royal estates were divided among the natives. To encourage the growth of industry, the governors were forbidden to engage in trade. Commerce was declared open to the islanders, and free ports were established. This law, however, did not greatly change economic conditions on the island. According to de la Corte, it "did not give the Islands any chance for development, because as long as expenses continued to be paid from outside sources, the means providing for the needs of the Islanders continued, although in

144

smaller scale, and as the latter were few in number, they made not the least effort to improve their condition."[33]

After 1828 commerce in the Marianas was, in theory at least, free and uncontrolled. In reality, however, control merely passed from the governor to the treasurer. The two officials then worked together to maintain the government monopoly. Since a vessel had to be chartered each year to bring funds from Manila, it was thought advisable to bring in goods and supplies at the same time. These goods, bought by the treasurer with government funds, were sold to the people through the government store. In this way the treasurer became a business agent for the governor. Since all goods brought to the island came in government-chartered ships, no private individuals could secure goods with which to compete with the government store. Thus the development of trade and industry was retarded and the government monopoly was maintained.

## WHALERS VISIT GUAM

Beginning about the year 1823, whalers, mostly British, began to stop at Guam. These ships, most of which made the long trip around the Cape of Good Hope, interrupted their cruise by stopping at the island. At that time Guam was the only island in the North Pacific where the whalers could give their men some rest, get fresh provisions, and prepare for a new cruise. For whale hunting, the year was usually divided into two cruises. One, beginning in April and ending in September, was confined to the North Pacific region. The other, between November and March, took place in the South Pacific.

At the end of each cruise, the whalers rested for a month or more at Apra Harbor and Umatac. While in port, they took on water, wood, and provisions. Crew members bought, regardless of price, all the articles they could lay their hands on. Since their voyages lasted from two to four years, they had few opportunities for spending their money. Visits by British whalers, in the opinion of de la Corte, "made annually by 30 ships or more for a period of over 30 years, should have created a new life in the Marianas, but as their population was made up of Government employees ignor-

145

ant of what real commerce is and of poor natives who were satisfied with the simple joys of their everyday life, without ever giving a thought to the future, the first were satisfied with increasing the price of the articles imported from Manila for the needs of the natives, and the latter with transferring all the money they made so easily to the hands of the cheap and narrow-minded speculators, which, with the exception of a not-small share of it which went to the padres, particularly to those of the city who collected a goodly share of it for saying high and low masses, and for celebrating wedding ceremonies and funerals, which were, so to speak, the only articles of luxury known to the Islands."[34]

Shortly after the whaling trade began, American whalers entered the Pacific to compete with the British. Since sailing distances were much shorter for the Americans, they were able to make more trips than their competitors. Soon whale oil prices went down, and the trade began to decline. This decline had serious adverse effects on Guam's economy. At about the same time, the whaling traffic began to be diverted to the Hawaiian Islands, which lay outside the monsoon belt. This further depressed Guam's trade. After a time, however, the price of whale oil went up once more, and the Pacific whaling fleet was increased to nearly 300 ships. Since the Hawaiian Islands and the Marianas had the only ports where whaling ships could be provisioned, Guam regained a large share of the whaling traffic. The whalers usually sailed from the Hawaiian Islands between September and December and worked south of the equator until February or March of the following year. They sailed northward as far as Guam, where they rested and took on supplies for the return trip to Hawaii.

> They were thus forced to stop here [wrote de la Corte], in order to give rest to their crews, and take aboard water, wood, pigs, and fresh stores six months or more, spending an amount which could be estimated at an average of 600 pesos per vessel, and as there were at least 60 of these, the annual income would be estimated at 40,000 pesos.
> This traffic, which was based on the bare necessities of the ships and their crews, could have easily been extended so as to include articles for comfort and even luxury, if any intelligent person had started here a store to provide these ships with money, naval supplies and canned

goods, thus increasing the business to hundreds of thousands of dollars; but in the Islands, there was no one who understood this and when a Manila business house thought of it, it was too late; but even then that house would have reaped a good harvest, and might perchance have created a change in the Islands, had it not been because on account of private reasons of some of the members of the firm, the idea had to be given up entirely.[35]

Since neither the government nor private individuals were willing or able to take full advantage of the whaling trade, Guam received only limited profits from an industry that could have greatly improved the island's economy.

## GOVERNOR FRANCISCO RAMÓN DE VILLALOBOS

As a result of the investigation conducted by Villalobos in 1828, the captain-general of the Philippines relieved Governor Medinilla of his duties and appointed Villalobos in his place. Villalobos, an artillery captain, became governor of Guam on September 26, 1831.

Governor Villalobos, an energetic man, began his administration with a determined attack on Guam's poverty. He stimulated the growth of agriculture and industry in an attempt to make the island self-supporting. Since he believed that the true wealth of a country was measured by the amount of money it had in its treasury, he tried to control trade with visiting whalers in such a way as to prevent money from leaving the island. Concerning this matter, he wrote to the captain-general:

> The lack of circulation of coin is the cause of the very small interior and exterior trade of the territory, which consists almost entirely in bartering certain goods for others, with the countless difficulties arising therefrom which caused the establishment of money by our remote ancestors. This same cause has prevented the natives from dedicating themselves exclusively to one branch of industry or trade, each family finding itself obliged to engage in all occupations according to its needs, with the consequent imperfections and scarcity resulting therefrom, and, finally, as it is not possible for a single person or family to procure for itself as many articles and resources as are necessary for its nourishment, clothing, and conveniences, these natives have lacked the advan-

147

tages enjoyed by other countries, in which free circulation of money secures for them everything needful.

It is evident, then, in order that the Marianas Islands may issue from so sad a plight, it is indispensable that there should be in them an abundance of money, and as long as this is not the case, whether, as in the former system little comes in and soon goes out, or whether great sums come in and go out immediately, as will happen in the present system, the evil will always be the same or nearly the same.

At present there are in the Marianas Islands no articles of export to attract the attention of the foreigner but some edibles or beverages made from the coconut palm. Freedom of trade once established, it would introduce many articles, and the few things produced by the country would not suffice to pay for them, so that the difference would have to be made good in money. From this it would follow that money paid for salaries would remain here only temporarily; the country would be merely a channel through which the money from the royal treasury would flow to foreign parts with no hope of its return. The Marianas would be deprived of the spirit of agriculture and industry, which I think ought, in a certain degree, to come before commerce, and the islands would be no less poverty-stricken than they have been up to the present time.[36]

Governor Villalobos was completely dedicated to the task of improving economic conditions in Guam. To bring about the desired results, he started numerous projects. Some were successful; others failed. In his correspondence with the captain-general, he suggested many ways in which the island's wealth could be increased. Since he knew that his garrison forces were too small to prevent the landing of foreigners on the island, he proposed that they be made to pay port fees. Moreover, since the island was lacking in exports, he believed that the islanders should be compelled to produce exportable articles. Dyewood, indigo, cotton, tortoise shell, mother-of-pearl, arrowroot and bêches de mer, he felt, were especially desirable. He recommended improvements in animal husbandry, more extensive cultivation of land, and the production of wines, brandies, sugar, and other articles. To keep money on the island, he favored a plan whereby foreign visitors could trade with the islanders only in terms of barter. He also suggested that proceeds from the port fees be used, in part, as premiums to persons who excelled in some branch of agriculture or industry.

"By these methods," said Villalobos, "sustained with constancy and intelligence and favored by the docility and good disposition which I observe in the inhabitants of these islands, I believe that the day will really come in which the Marianas will have much money, many goods; that they may without difficulty be self-supporting, like other provinces; that ships will concur and that all amplitude desired will be given to trade."[37]

Villalobos did much to benefit the people of Guam. He established a hospital for lepers and provided for their care and comfort. He also appointed hunters to supply the hospital with fresh meat by killing wild hogs and cattle. Through his efforts, vaccination against smallpox was administered to the islanders. The Guam Militia was reorganized. Coffee cultivation, "which article may be the wealth of this country," was promoted; and the large swamp east of Agana was prepared for rice cultivation. Moreover, he encouraged the growing of sweet potatoes to supply visiting ships, and of plantains, bananas, taro, and yams for native comsumption instead of corn, which was attacked by rats and weevils. "The six years of his incumbency were a busy six years for Guam. He systematized the affairs of the treasury, especially the schedule of port fees; he personally superintended the building of roads and bridges; with his own money he built a pottery; he opened the Atantano Valley for the culture of rice; he studied agricultural conditions and taught the planters how to better their crops. History gives but a bald view of men and events, but we get a clear picture of this man from his recorded actions, and can easily imagine him, nervous, vigorous, hurrying from one task to another, driving his workmen and himself as well to the point of exhaustion, and yet beloved by them; very much the aristocrat, but wandering alone over the island and stopping to talk crops with the poorest ranchero."[38]

As a result of frequent mutinies which occurred among the crews of foreign ships in the harbor, England decided to establish a consulate in Guam or in the Bonin Islands. When Governor Villalobos learned about the plan, he was strongly opposed to it. He was afraid that an English consul at Guam would quickly learn how weak the island's defenses were and, in consequence, the English would take over the island. On the other hand, if the consulate was established in the Bonins, the whaling fleet would assemble there, and the Guamanians would be deprived of their trade with the vessels. Villalobos therefore "proposed that an arrangement be made whereby the British Government would authorize the governor of the Marianas to act in settling cases of mutiny and the like. He also recommended the establishment of a store of marine supplies by either one of the two governments and called attention to the presence of many ships at Guam with liberty to trade with the islanders, the governor being prohibited from engaging in trade of any kind. Orders having been issued to collect import duties from the ships coming to Guam, Villalobos informed the captain-general that it would be practically impossible to carry out the provisions of the decree. He stated that if guards were placed on board the ships, the cost of maintaining them would exceed the amount received for duties. If no guards were stationed, the duties would only be imaginary, on account of the bad faith of those who sold, and their 'lack of delicacy.' Moreover, if it should come to light that a sale had been secretly made and the corresponding duties on the same be extracted from a foreign captain, his pride and insolence would be apt to compromise the dignity of the authorities beyond all bearable limits or bring about disagreable consequences resembling perhaps an unhappy affair between the ex-governor Ganga-Herrero and an English captain, Mr. Stavers, who, in 1824, died from injuries received while resisting arrest. In view of these difficulties Villalobos on his own authority ventured to grant free trade between the visiting ships and the islanders."[39]

In 1837 Don Francisco Villalobos, after having served six years as governor of Guam, returned to the Philippines. In the long list of Spanish gentlemen who served as governors of Guam, Villalobos' name stands out as that of one who was dedicated to improving the lot of the Guamanian people.

## DON PABLO PEREZ

For a period of about ten years after Villalobos' departure from Guam, affairs on the island were administered by various governors whose administrations were routine and undistinguished. In April 1848 Governor Gregorio Santa María died while in office and was succeeded by the island's treasurer, Don Felix Calvo. Calvo served as acting governor until September 8, 1848. At that time Don Pablo Pérez, a lieutenant colonel in the Spanish Army, arrived from Manila to take over the governorship.

On August 10, 1848, about a month before Governor Pérez' arrival, Guam was struck by a devastating typhoon. About five months later, on January 25, 1849, the island was rocked by a severe earthquake. Many churches and several government buildings were badly damaged. A short time later, a group of Caroline Islanders, in two large ocean-going canoes, arrived at Guam. They said that the earthquake which shook Guam was accompanied by a tidal wave which swamped their island and destroyed their homes. Governor Pérez granted them permission to settle in Guam with other Carolinians already living on the island.

Among the first reports forwarded by Governor Pérez to the captain-general in Manila were figures regarding the population of the Marianas. He also sent a list of ships anchoring at Guam, a report on the recent typhoon and earthquake damage, and a list of the useful woods of the island. He mentioned the fact that a shortage of laborers existed in Guam, especially of men skilled in mechanical trades, and begged the captain-general to send convicts to the island to remedy the situation. At that time Guam's few skilled craftsmen consisted of former convicts who were permitted to remain on the island after their prison terms had expired. In his reports, Pérez criticized the Guamanians' method of cultivating the soil with the *fosino* or thrust hoe. Because of this, he believed, "their harvests are small which might be large." As a result of the recent typhoon and earthquake, he found roads and bridges badly damaged. He reported, moreover, that there was a

151

lack of suitable tools for carrying on public works and of iron for making such tools.

Perez' reports, it would seem, were given a great deal of publicity in Manila. In response to them, the captain-general sent supplies of rice, corn, and other foods to the island. Furthermore, young ladies and gentlemen of Manila, members of prominent families, put on shows and other forms of entertainment to raise a relief fund for the sufferers in Guam. Governor Pérez, a scholarly man as well as a good administrator, was overwhelmed by the kindness of the citizens of Manila. Expressing his thanks and the thanks of the Guamanian people, he wrote:

> The governor of the Marianas Islands in the name of the inhabitants, who do not cease giving thanks to the Almighty for not having succumbed to a desolating epidemic and the most horrible of earthquakes, which still continue, saw themselves threatened anew by a devouring famine which threatened to put an end to their miserable existence. But Providence, which incessantly watches over those peoples who implore its aid, willed that the beneficent hand of our Superior Government, ever benevolent and philanthropic, should put a happy end to so much misfortune and unhappiness so great.
>
> What joy was ours on the 3rd day of September 1849, when there arrived at this port the frigate Union, bearer of most bounteous supplies of rice, maize, and other grains, at prices more moderate than have ever before been known in these possessions! It is impossible to describe the joy and animation of the people of this community, whose misery and poverty were increased by a plague of worms which consumed as much rice, maize, and other seed as were sown in the months of July, August, and September; so that if succor had not arrived so opportunely the ruined crops could not have been replaced for lack of seed. Such was the scarcity that on the 29th of August, four days before the arrival of the said ship, the only remaining five cabanes of rice were put at auction and sold at 5 pesos a caban. From this alone may be formed an idea of the great if not the total lack which was suffered here. Like one who suddenly recovers from a mortal illness to perfect health, so was the air of contentment and rejoicing which seized upon all souls in their most sincere gratitude to the author of so many and such great benefits. Nor was our gratitude less to those gentlemen who contributed the subscription in money of $674.45, which was distributed among the poor of these islands on this the birthday of our adored Queen, Doña

Isabella II (whom God Save), in accordance with the directions of the Superior Government.

Without elements, means, or resources whatever for manifesting our gratitude, I directed that on the 9th of the same month of September a Mass of Thanksgiving be celebrated by three priests, something very rarely seen in this city, with a sermon preached eloquently and eruditely, as is his custom, by Padre Fray Manuel Encarnación, the parish priest of the village of Agat, who, in speaking of the calamities suffered by these islands, made his hearers understand and exhorted them to the gratitude due our Government, which so prodigally relieved our necessities, finishing the function with a solemn Te Deum, and displaying the Most Holy Sacrament. All the people, bowing down like those of Israel before His Divine Majesty, breathed forth their prayers and vows for the happiness of their benefactors.

In order to give another proof of the sentiments of gratitude which filled us and to carry out in a certain way the beneficent ideas of our Government, which especially distinguish it, as is seen by the sublime acts which illustrate the pages of the history of our colonies, I decided to act as godfather to the first girl baby which might be born, and I gave to it the name of Isabella, in memory of our August Queen; and the lieutenant-governor acted in the same capacity for the first boy baby, which he called Narcissus, in memory of His Excellency our Captain-General, Count of Manila, who so justly rules these remote regions, each one of us giving to his godchild 50 pesos and an outfit of decent clothing, which event took place at 9 o'clock on the morning of the 16th of September, with the assistance of the authorities and of nearly all the population, so that these children may be living testimony of the remembrances of the generosity of our Sovereign and of Your Excellency, who knows so well how to act as the instrument of so many and such great acts, which history will record for the honor and the glory of the great Spanish Nation.[40]

In August 1851, the captain-general responded to Governor Pérez' request for laborers by sending sixty-five Filipino convicts to the island. They arrived on the ship *Calavelino*. On their way over, two of the convicts had died, and the rest were suffering from scurvy, ulcers, and skin diseases. No medicine was available for treating them. However, an Irish doctor named William George, who had served as a druggist on a whaler and had been permitted to settle in Guam, attempted to care for their needs. Since his private supply of medicines was soon exhausted, the lepers' hospital provided assistance by furnishing lint, bandages, and drugs. Within a short time, all but six of the convicts were able to work. In view of the fact that all of them were farm laborers, the governor assigned them to work on the ranches of some of the island's most successful farmers. Father Manuel Encarnación, the priest of Agat, was assigned eighteen of the convicts. The ranchers were required to feed and care for the prisoners in accordance with regulations established by the governor.[41]

As long as there were no ships in Apra Harbor, the governor had no fear that the prisoners would escape. During the seasons when the whalers visited the island, he planned to divide the prisoners into gangs, place them under guard, and put them to work at places as far away from the harbor as possible. When the whaling fleet was in, as many as 15 or 20 ships were in the harbor at one time. Since most of them were usually short-handed, there was great danger of their smuggling prisoners on board just before the ships sailed.

About a month after the convicts arrived at Guam, Governor Pérez learned that they were secretly conspiring to overpower the authorities and take over the entire island. Before they could act, however, they were surprised by the guards, who fired upon them and charged them with bayonets. One was killed, two wounded, and their leader, Fortunato de los Angeles, was captured. The rest scattered into the hills and jungles. Before a week had passed, all were captured. In his report to the captain-general concerning the incident, Pérez wrote: "I acknowledge that I was mistaken. Believing that men whom Your Excellency had pardoned from the punishment of death by your decree of the 11th of last January would live grateful of such a boon, I never dreamed that they would rise against the authorities and attempt to make us the victims of their ferocity."[42]

The prisoners were sent back to Manila in the same ship that brought them to Guam. Thus ended the attempt of Governor Pérez to introduce convict labor into the island. Later attempts were more successful. In May 1855 Pérez relinquished the governorship and returned to the Philippines.

## FELIPE DE LA CORTE

Felipe María de la Corte y Ruano Calderón, a captain of engineers with the rank of lieutenant colonel, relieved Don Pablo Pérez as governor of Guam on May 16, 1855. The chief aim of his administration was to alleviate the dire poverty of the Guamanian people, which, in spite of the efforts of previous governors, had become worse instead of better. In one of his first reports to the captain-general in Manila, he described the pitiful hand-to-mouth existence of the islanders. He reported that during good and bad years alike, they starved for some part of the year. His first plan, therefore, was to build granaries in which surplus crops might be stored until needed. "His ideas and methods," wrote McIntosh, "would have raised a community of his native Aragonese to comfort and even wealth—but the Chamorro stolidly planted enough to eat for one year, and if that crop failed he did not eat until next seed-time. He saw no reason for working hard merely to fill the governor's granaries. If the government paid him for his crop, he might be induced to grow as much as five bushels extra for cigar money, but the community-storage idea passed over his head."[43] For lack of understanding and cooperation, de la Corte's plan was doomed to failure. Nevertheless, during the eleven years that he served as governor of Guam, de la Corte worked unceasingly to improve the island's economic conditions. When one scheme failed, he tried another. His reports and his later writings reveal that he was an educated man who understood political and economic theories and principles.

During de la Corte's first year as governor, the Spanish government discontinued its annual supply of funds for the support of the government of Guam. When her colonies in North and South America won their independence, Spain was deprived of a source of great wealth. As a result, her remaining colonies could not be given financial assistance. Therefore they were required, insofar as possible, to become self-supporting. For this reason, de la Corte was asked to make a complete report on conditions in the Marianas. Concerning the economic situation at that time, he wrote:

155

The Marianas ... find themselves in a state of complete stagnation, commercially and socially; because if an analysis be made of the character of the natives, it will be rather a heterogeneous mass of people who, for the greater part, work isolated by themselves and for themselves.

The employees of the different branches of the Government live on their salaries, lacking the most necessary articles required in any half-civilized country, and spend twice as much as in any of those countries which are not civilized.

The Marianas have no stores, and there are no carpenters, blacksmiths, tailors, shoemakers, or even a house servant who is really a house servant. Every man is everything and no man is anything. The natives, which form the mass of the population, live isolated in their own houses; each one plants whatever he is going to eat, brings from the country what he needs, makes his own house and clothing, raises his own animals or hunts and fishes those he needs; and if one of them begs for it as a favor he pays for it more dearly than if he had bought it, no matter whether the favor be done by his own father or brother. . . . Every imaginable effort is made not to buy that which in some way can be procured at home or in the Island; although the labor spent in getting it may be worth more than what the article would cost in money. This custom is so deeply rooted that from the highest to the lowest in the land everybody acts alike, because everybody thinks that money is only intended to buy finery or to pay for masses, and that he who uses it to buy foodstuffs is lazy, no matter whether he works hard all day long in order to get a salary to pay for it.

The consequence is that no one cares to earn such a salary, nor does anyone prefer to do any work which brings payment in coin, if it prevents him from providing for the needs of his family. . . .

These habits have created a sort of savage independence full of caprice. no one has the ambition to earn money if he has to do constant work and eat the same food. . . . They are a sort of obstinate children, without any present needs, and without any accumulated wealth, since they scarcely own any animals, furniture or objects of value; and in the midst of this apparent poverty, they pay with the greatest indifference 10 pesos for a funeral, 50 for an ox which they do not use, 8 for a skirt, 30 for the image of a saint or for a poor necklace or for any similar trinket, so that in the midst of a poor community, it may be said, comparatively speaking, that individual wealth exists. . . .[44]

Besides numerous foreigners who visited Guam in whaling ships, by 1855 there were several foreigners residing on the island. One, Captain Samuel J. Masters, was the United States consul at Guam.

156

Masters, a former police magistrate in the Hawaiian Islands, represented the United States in all negotiations with the Spaniards and protected the rights of American citizens aboard the whalers. Another American, a doctor, was a staff member of the hospital in Agana. At the same time, there were four other foreign residents, all Englishmen. Before being permitted to remain on the island, all foreigners were required to secure permission to do so from the captain-general.[45]

In 1856, about a year after de la Corte became governor, Guam was stricken by an epidemic of smallpox. The disease, it was believed, was brought to the island by a passenger from the American schooner *Frost*, which anchored at Apra Harbor in March. Father José Palomo believed that the disease was introduced from the Philippines. "This fatal epidemic," he wrote, "perhaps might have been avoided, had a strict quarantine been enforced on a sailing vessel coming from Manila, which vessel just one day before entering San Luis de Apra had thrown overboard the body of a passenger who had died of smallpox; but instead of doing that, the passengers in whom the incubation of the disease had already begun were allowed to land and from them the smallpox spread until almost every inhabitant of the Island had it."[46] Regardless of its origin, for nine months the disease afflicted the people of the island. Lack of vaccines and adequate medical care resulted in death for 3,644 Guamanians.[47] To replace the loss, Carolinians and, later, Japanese were permitted to settle in the Marianas in fairly large numbers.

In his report, de la Corte concluded that Guam's principal problem was poverty. Such poverty, he believed, was due to the limited resources of the island and the refusal of the people to work and accumulate wealth. "It is not necessary," he wrote at some length,

"to tire oneself in seeking other causes of that poverty, which is the only thing that retards the progress of the population of the Marianas Islands. Other things to which it has been attributed are accidents. The use of hurtful food, poor clothing, and other things, far from being considered a cause, are in reality the effects of that poverty and the direct means through which it works for the speedy destruction of this

157

unhappy portion of the human race. This poverty, the general and sole cause, has not, however, been perceived by many, because they could not believe that it could occur in the midst of a soil which produces abundant and varied fruits, in spite even of those plagues, and because they have confounded with wealth the occurrence here at all times of fruits growing spontaneously which the natives use for food during the periods when more wholesome kinds are lacking. . . . The prosperity of a country depends, instead of upon the abundance of its spontaneous products, rather upon the wealth accumulated in it, and here precisely is the great defect and the origin of the evil in the Marianas Islands. In them, most excellent Señor, nobody possesses anything, with very few exceptions. Here all live absolutely for the day, and domestic utensils, tools of laborers, lodgings, and everything—absolutely everything—is so mean, so little durable, and so incapable of constituting wealth that all, or nearly all, could with solemnity declare at all hours that they are poor. . . . To correct the evils upon which I here have touched, and to ameliorate the condition of these islanders, my predecessors, with laudable zeal, have reproduced without ceasing, exhortations, orders, and decrees that they should plant and harvest wholesome and abundant fruits. But who would believe it? With fat harvests, of which the grain has sometimes even been burned for lack of consumers, poverty has continued and reached even to us; for not having sought the means of accumulating that wealth then superfluous, to fill out the dearth later in worse seasons, all has perished at the moment, and without object. And what is still worse, it has created in these natives the idea in good years as well as in bad, of large crops as well as of small, that they cannot hope for a beneficial change. They have logically figured that it is futile to work for superfluous harvests which may have to be burned, consequently not relieving them in the periods of scarcity which are sure to come later; that it is better to work little than to work without result. On account of this they have been accused of possessing a lazy disposition, which they are far from manifesting on occasions in which they clearly see the good results from their work."[48]

The eleven years of de la Corte's administration were a series of agricultural and economic experiments. While many of them were failures, they served to prove what could or could not be grown or produced on the island. In spite of his failures, his administration was one of real value to the people of Guam. By his efforts, he created new interest in agriculture and encouraged the development of new skills and trades. He left the islanders poor, perhaps as poor as he found them, but he had taught many of them the value of work and thrift. In January 1866, at his own request, he was relieved by Francisco Moscoso y Lara. De la Corte, wrote Father Palomo, "who was His Majesty's Special Commissioner, ruled the Marianas as already stated, from 1855 to 1866, with honest purpose and working assiduously to develop the country, but he accomplished nothing of moment, because no one can fight against nature, making a flourishing colony out of a country with nothing but a handful of inhabitants."[49]

## FINAL YEARS OF SPANISH RULE

Guam's history during the second half of the 19th century was influenced by the administrations of a large number of Spanish governors who came and went in rapid succession. Most concerned themselves with the problems of Guam's economy, which was growing steadily worse.

Governor Moscoso, de la Corte's successor, concentrated on the development of agriculture. To stimulate interest in farming, he organized a society called Sociedad Agrícola. Its members consisted of the governor, other government officials, and leading citizens of the island. With the assistance of the society, Moscoso planned to send vegetables and other farm products to markets in Manila. Like numerous governors before him, however, he found that the islanders would not produce more than was necessary for their own needs. In an attempt to remedy the situation, he imported farm laborers from Japan. Some of the Japanese died, however, and the rest returned to their homeland. Of over a hundred imported, only one remained in Guam. Failing in his agricultural program, Moscoso, in 1869, established a biennial mail service between Guam and Manila. This time he planned to send native handicrafts as well as some farm products to the Philippines. Although the mail service lasted over twenty years, "it did very little toward the development of this unlucky country," wrote Father Palomo, "for the reason that wages in the Philippines being lower than in the Marianas, the cost of production in the latter is necessarily higher than in the former, and consequently there is little incentive for the Chamorros to work in order to produce articles which, when sold in Manila, would bring them very little returns."[50]

During the administration of Don Luis de Ybáñez, who succeeded Moscoso in 1871, nineteen Filipinos, including eight priests, were sent as prisoners to Guam. They were leaders of an unsuccessful revolt against the Spaniards at Cavite, Philippine Islands. About two years later, while Don Eduardo Beaumont was governor, the "misruled Republic of Spain deported to the Marianas several hundred Spaniards who were nothing more than a band of thieves, the very scum of Spain, ninety per cent of whom could neither read nor write. [Thus did they] deport to an archipelago nine thousand miles away, against the Spanish constitution, wretches who only were good to corrupt the morals of the natives."[51]

Beaumont was relieved as governor in 1875 by Don Manuel Brabo. The latter was succeeded in turn by Francisco Brochero in 1880. Although they tried, neither of them was able to bring about lasting improvements in Guam.

In March 1884, Brochero was succeeded by Don Ángel de Pazos. A few days after he took office, Governor de Pazos was assassinated by a soldier. His death was part of a plot by a group of forty soldiers to seize control of the island. According to Palomo, "Don Antonio Borreda, who became Governor ad interim, endeavored to profit by this murder, trying to win promotion by making it appear that the private act of an individual was the result of an insurrection, and to accomplish this he had several people imprisoned who, under torture, were made to testify; by so doing he finally succeeded in having four soldiers sentenced to death and executed, while a good many other soldiers were sent to presidio."[52] The four soldiers who were executed were shot on the beach at Agana on April 10, 1885.

Governor Borreda's administration was followed by that of Don Francisco Olive, who was governor for nearly three years. He in turn was succeeded by Don Enrique Solano in July 1885. Solano was followed in rapid succession by Governors Joaquín Vara de Rey, Luis Santos, and Vicente Gómez, each of whom held office for about one year. The next governor, Emilio Galisteo, served for about two years.

On December 24, 1895, a lieutenant colonel of infantry, Jacobo Marina, assumed the governorship. Don Jacobo's term of office was marked by serious difficulties with Filipino prisoners. "The Spanish for many years used Guam as a place of confinement for prisoners from the Philippines. Early in December, 1896, the steamship Venus, one of the mail steamers that in those days plied between Manila, the Caroline Islands, and the Marianas, left in Guam about 120 prisoners who had been sent over from Manila. The prisoners were confined at night in the buildings. . . occupied as the marine barracks, Agana. On Christmas Eve one of the Filipino soldiers in the insular artillery reported to the commanding officer and governor that he had overheard the details of a conspiracy that had been entered into by the prisoners to revolt that evening, kill their guards, assassinate the governor, and take charge of the island until they could arrange for means of escape. The details having been verified, the guards were ordered to exercise extraordinary precautions and the force on watch was doubled. One of the guards, having detected some movements which he thought were the beginning of the revolt, opened fire on the prisoners and the fire was immediately taken up by the whole guard of soldiers. Before the firing ceased 40 prisoners had been killed and nearly all of the remainder were wounded. The survivors were returned to Manila by the same vessel that brought them over."[53]

Don Juan Marina, brother of Don Jacobo, became governor in April 1897, two months after his brother left the island. Don Juan was the last Spanish governor of Guam. In 1898 he, together with the rest of the Spanish garrison on the island, was captured by American forces during the Spanish-American War. With his surrender, Spanish rule was ended on the island of Guam.

In his account of Spanish rule in the Marianas, Father José Palomo (first Guamanian priest and later a monsignor) felt called upon to defend Spain's administration of the islands as follows:

Before finishing this historical sketch, I wish to do justice to Spain, who, as it is clearly seen, did not send her sons to the Marianas to ex-

161

ploit them, but on the contrary to civilize their inhabitants and teach them the true faith; and if the Mariana archipelago was not developed by the Spanish Government [governors] as Australia and New Zealand were developed by other nations, it must be attributed to the fact that these Islands lack the requisite elements for their development. A country like this, so small, with so small a number of inhabitants, somewhat far from all markets, cannot do much by itself, nor can it attract the attention of enterprising men or large capital, when there are larger and richer colonies where they can work to better advantage and profit; and if this is true concerning these points, it is also undeniable that nature has made man so that he will not burden himself with work, unless his needs or his interests compel him, nor will he work hard, unless necessity forces him to do it; and he is not given to ponder long over it, unless in the background there be glory, honor or the shining gold. Therefore [although] the Chamorros have not done much work, it must be said in their defense that their needs were few and that they did not expect their endeavors would have brought them any profits in their own country.[54]

## Spanish Military Commanders and Governors of Guam

The following list contains the names and dates of accession to office of the Spanish military commanders and governors of Guam.[55]

### Military commanders

| | |
|---|---|
| Captain Juan de Santa Cruz | June 16, 1668 |
| Captain Juan de Santiago | May 2, 1672 |
| Captain Damian de Esplaña | June 16, 1674 |

### Governors

| | |
|---|---|
| Captain Francisco de Irrisarri y Viñar | June 10, 1676 |
| Captain Juan Antonio de Salas | June 21, 1678 |
| Captain José de Quiroga | June 5, 1680 |
| Captain Antonio Saravia | August, 1681 |
| Major Damian de Esplaña | November 3, 1683 |
| Major José de Quiroga | ?    1688 |
| Lieutenant General Damian de Esplaña | June  ? 1690 |

| | |
|---|---|
| Major José de Quiroga | August 16, 1694 |
| General José Madraso | August 1, 1696 |
| Major Francisco Madraso y Asiam | September 15, 1700 |
| Major Antonio Villamor y Vadillo | September 1, 1704 |
| Lieutenant General Juan Antonio Pimentel | September 1, 1709 |
| Captain Luis Antonio Sánchez de Tagle | November 21, 1720 |
| Captain Juan de Ojeda | April 4, 1725 |
| General Manuel Arguelles Valda | September 28, 1725 |
| Major Pedro Laso de la Vega | February 12, 1730 |
| General of the Fleet Francisco Cárdenas Pacheco | |
| | August 21, 1734 |
| Major Miguel Fernando de Cárdenas | April 2, 1740 |
| Captain Domingo Gómez de la Sierra | September 21, 1746 |
| Lieutenant (Navy) Enrique de Olavide y Michelena | |
| | September 8, 1749 |
| General Andrés del Barrio y Rabago | November 6, 1756 |
| Lieutenant (Navy) José de Soroa | November 20, 1759 |
| Lieutenant (Navy) Enrique de Olavide y Michelena | |
| | June 9, 1768 |
| Major Mariano Tobias | September 15, 1771 |
| Major Antonio Apodaca | June 15, 1774 |
| Captain Felipe de Cera | June 6, 1776 |
| Lieutenant Colonel José Arlegue y León | August 21, 1786 |
| Lieutenant Colonel Manuel Muro | September 2, 1794 |
| Captain Vicente Blanco | January 12, 1802 |
| Captain Alejandro Parreño | October 18, 1806 |
| Lieutenant José de Medinilla y Pineda | July 26, 1812 |
| Captain José Montilla | August 15, 1822 |
| Captain José Ganga Herrero | May 15, 1823 |
| Lieutenant Colonel José de Medinilla y Pineda | August 1, 1826 |
| Captain Francisco Ramón de Villalobos | September 26, 1831 |
| Lieutenant Colonel José Casillas Salazar | October 1, 1837 |
| Major Gregorio Santa María | October 1, 1843 |
| Treasurer Felix Calvo (acting governor) | April 7, 1848 |
| Lieutenant Colonel Pablo Pérez | September 8, 1848 |
| Lieutenant Colonel Felipe María de la Corte | May 16, 1855 |

Lieutenant Colonel Francisco Moscoso y Lara
                                        January 28, 1866
Colonel Luis de Ybáñez y García          August 17, 1871
Lieutenant Colonel Eduardo Beaumont y Calafat
                                        March 24, 1873
Lieutenant Colonel Manuel Brabo y Barrera  January 15, 1875
Lieutenant Colonel Francisco Brochero y Parreño
                                        August 15, 1880
Colonel Angel de Pazos Vela-Hidalgo      March 14, 1884
Captain Antonio Borreda                  August 4, 1884
Lieutenant Colonel Francisco Olive y García
                                        November ? 1884
Lieutenant Colonel Enrique Solano        July 17, 1885
Lieutenant Colonel Joaquín Vara de Rey   April 20, 1890
Lieutenant Colonel Luis Santos           August 14, 1891
Lieutenant Colonel Vicente Gómez Hernández
                                        August 23, 1892
Lieutenant of Infantry Juan Godoy (acting governor)
                                        September 1, 1893
Lieutenant Colonel Emilio Galisteo Brunenque
                                        October 26, 1893
Lieutenant Colonel Jacobo Marina         December 24, 1895
Lieutenant of Infantry Ángel Nieto (acting governor)
                                        February 15, 1897
Lieutenant Colonel Juan Marina           April 17, 1897

SUMMARY: The last century of Spanish rule in Guam opened and closed with the arrival of American ships. In 1802, the first American ship on record called at Guam, bringing a new Spanish governor. Before the end of the century, another American ship steamed into Apra Harbor, captured the island for the United States, and sailed away with the last of the Spanish governors.

The century saw a number of scientists, voyagers, whalers, and ships of many nations visit the island. Among the many vessels were those belonging to Americans, Russians, French, and English, as well as Spaniards. Between 1817 and 1828 the island was visited by no fewer than three scientific expeditions, which included such leading scientists of their day as Kotzebue, a Russian; Freycinet, a Frenchman; and d'Urville, another Frenchman. Aside from the scientific reports which these visitors made, the writings on their visits to the islands provided the few written accounts of life on Guam during the early part of this century.

The administration of Guam changed hands during the century. First its source of administration was shifted from the viceroy of Mexico to the governor-general of the Philippines. With the change in administrative jurisdiction came the island's first organic legislation. The Spanish governors continued with their attempts to make Guam a more productive island, but none succeeded very well. During this century, three Spanish governors stood out above the others in their efforts to improve the island. They were Blanco, Villalobos, and de la Corte.

The big change came for Guam, however, with the capture of the island by the United States in 1898, thus ending Spanish rule, which began in 1668 when Father Diego Luis de Sanvitores waded ashore to begin the Christianization process of the island and its people.

The three hundred and some odd years of Spanish rule had its many ups and downs. Guam and the western world were introduced one to another. While Spain brought countless benefits to the island, two matters of the greatest significance stood out among them: Christianity and Western traditions, culture, and heritage. These provided Guam with the basis for the many substantial gains in politics, economics, education, and other facets of modern living that were to come during the next half-century.

## NOTES

1. William Haswell, *Remarks on a Voyage in 1801 to the Island of Guam* (Historical Collections of the Essex Institute, Salem, Massachusetts, Vol. LIII, No. 3, July, 1917), p. 206.
2. *Ibid.*, pp. 209–10.
3. *Ibid.*, pp. 212.
4. Kotzebue, *op. cit.*, Vol. III, pp. 86–88.
5. Jacques Etienne Victor Arago, *Narrative of a Voyage Round the World in the Uranie and Physicienne Corvettes, Commanded by Captain Freycinet* (Treuttel and Wurtz, London, 1823), Part II, pp. 26–27.
6. Kotzebue, *op. cit.*, Vol. III, p. 88.
7. *Ibid.*, Vol. II, p. 230.
8. *Ibid.*, p. 231.
9. *Ibid.*, pp. 232–36.
10. *Ibid.*, p. 237.
11. *Ibid.*, pp. 238–40.
12. *Ibid.*, pp. 245–47.
13. *Ibid.*, pp. 248–49.
14. *Ibid.*, p. 251.
15. *Ibid.*, p. 252.
16. Arago, *op. cit.*, Part I, p. 239.
17. *Ibid.*, p. 240.
18. *Ibid.*, p. 243.
19. *Ibid.*, pp. 245–58.
20. *Ibid.*, Part II, p. 6.
21. *Ibid.*, pp. 32–34.
22. *Ibid.*, pp. 49–50.
23. *Ibid.*, pp. 45–46.
24. Safford, *The Useful Plants of the Island of Guam*, pp. 30–31.
25. *Ibid.*, p. 31.
26. *Loc. cit.*
27. *Loc. cit.*
28. K. C. McIntosh, "War Provisions for Guam," *United States Naval Institute Proceedings*, Vol. XLII, No. 2 (March-April, 1916), pp. 471–72.
29. Felipe de la Corte y Ruano Calderón, *A History of the Marianas Islands from the Time of the Arrival of the Spaniards to the 5th of May 1870, with Continuation by Padre José Palomo* (translated by Gertrude Hornbostel, manuscript, Bishop Museum, Honolulu), p. 41.
30. *Ibid.*, p. 40.
31. *Ibid.*, p. 39.

32. *Ibid.*, p. 41.
33. *Ibid.*, p. 42.
34. *Ibid.*, pp. 44–45.
35. *Ibid.*, pp. 45–46.
36. Safford, *The Useful Plants of the Island of Guam*, p. 33.
37. *Ibid.*, p. 34.
38. Cox, *op. cit.*, p. 32.
39. Safford, *The Useful Plants of the Island of Guam*, pp. 35–36.
40. *Ibid.*, pp. 36–37.
41. *Ibid.*, pp. 37–38.
42. *Ibid.*, p. 38.
43. McIntosh, *op. cit.*, p. 473.
44. Corte and Palomo, *op. cit.*, pp. 46–47.
45. Reed, *op. cit.*, p. 61.
46. Corte and Palomo, *op. cit.*, p. 49.
47. Reed, *op. cit.*, p. 79.
48. Safford, *The Useful Plants of the Island of Guam*, pp. 39–40.
49. Corte and Palomo, *op. cit.*, pp. 49–50.
50. *Ibid.*, p. 50.
51. *Loc. cit.*
52. *Loc. cit.*
53. Cox, *op. cit.*, p. 33.
54. Corte and Palomo, *op. cit.*, p. 51.
55. Cox, *op. cit.*, pp. 33–34.

*CHAPTER SIX*

# GUAM BECOMES AN AMERICAN POSSESSION

DURING THE comparatively peaceful period between the American Civil War (1861–65) and the Spanish-American War (1898) the United States furthered its process of westward expansion by acquiring numerous possessions in the Pacific region. After the Civil War the American people were so engrossed with domestic problems that they had little time or concern for matters outside their own country. Indeed, isolationist sentiment was so strong that opposition to further expansion became widespread. In spite of such feelings, however, the need for overseas bases became increasingly important. Continued Spanish occupation of Cuba and Puerto Rico and increased activity by the Germans and the British in the Pacific islands aroused the fears of the American government. As a result, American expansion in the Pacific progressed steadily throughout the latter half of the 19th century. In a period of less than fifty years, the United States formally acquired Jarvis and Baker islands (1857); Howland (1858); Midway (1867); Hawaii (1898); and American Samoa, Wake, Guam, and the Philippines (1899).

### THE SPANISH-AMERICAN WAR AND THE CAPTURE OF GUAM

In 1895 the people of Cuba rose in open rebellion against their Spanish masters. They sought to free themselves from Spanish rule, which they had endured for almost four hundred years. They were "determined to unfurl triumphantly, even over ruin and ashes, the flag of the republic of Cuba." In her attempts to suppress the rebellion, Spain resorted to harsh and sometimes brutal measures. Most of the Cubans were concentrated into militarized camps and villages. All remaining outside the concentration camps were treated as rebels. Lack of food and sanitary facilities resulted in death for thousands of them. Exaggerated newspaper accounts of Spanish brutalities so aroused the American people that they demanded intervention on the side of the Cubans. President Grover Cleveland, however, resisted the demands as long as possible. He tried to persuade the Spaniards to grant Cuba home rule. For interventionists like Senator Henry Cabot Lodge, Captain A. T. Mahan, USN, and Theodore Roosevelt, Assistant Secretary of the Navy, this was not enough. They demanded outright intervention. Their purpose was to acquire for the United States strategical command of the approaches from both oceans leading to a future canal that might be built across the isthmus of Panama.[1] Lodge and Roosevelt, furthermore, desired distant bases in the Pacific, especially in the Philippines, from which to carry on American trade with the Orient. By late 1897, when William McKinley was elected president, demands for American intervention in the Cuban revolution had become so great that they could no longer be resisted. The slightest incident could plunge the United States into war. That incident was provided on February 15, 1898, when the American battleship *Maine* blew up in Havana harbor with a tragic loss of 260 men. After brief but fruitless negotiations, Congress, on April 25, 1898, declared that a state of war existed between Spain and the United States.

The Spanish-American War lasted but three months. As a result of the brief warfare, however, Spain's fleet was almost completely destroyed, and remants of her overseas possessions were lost. At the beginning of the war, a small Spanish squadron was based in the Philippines. On May 1, 1898, in the Battle of Manila Bay, this fleet was quickly destroyed by a superior American force commanded by Commodore George Dewey. A short time later, the USS *Charleston* and three troop transports, the *City of Pekin,*

*City of Sydney*, and *Australia*, were dispatched from San Francisco
to Manila to join Dewey's forces. The *Charleston* was commanded
by Captain Henry Glass, USN. Lieutenant William Braunersreuther
was the navigator. Another officer on board was Lieutenant Junior
Grade Robert E. Coontz, who later served as governor of Guam.

> At Honolulu [wrote Coontz] we received sealed orders. . . . Twenty-
> four hours out from Honolulu, on our way to join Commodore Dewey,
> Captain Glass mustered all hands on the quarter deck, ripped off the seal
> and read his orders. They were, in effect, to proceed to the Island of
> Guam, capture it in the name of the United States, take the necessary
> steps regarding its fighting population, and then proceed on to Manila.
> Very few of us had even heard of Guam, except in a vague way. Some
> had an idea where the island was located, and some remembered that
> in the early days some American traders cleared for Guam. . . . We had
> coaled to capacity, and the current was with us. Our course was about
> west by south, but our speed, on account of our convoys, was not great.
> We spent days drilling our recruits, and had the convoy do the same.
> Once, on the way, the captain left the ship in his gig and inspected the
> transports. By the time we crossed the 180th meridian, we felt that we
> were ready for the enemy.[2]

On June 20, 1898, the *Charleston* and her convoy arrived at
Guam. Because of the remoteness and isolation of the island, the
people of Guam did not know that Spain and the United States
were at war. The last mail steamer to visit the island, almost two
months before, had brought news to the effect that the trouble
between the two countries was being settled peaceably. It was,
therefore, with some degree of curiosity but with no feeling of fear
that the Spaniards watched the approach of the American vessels
on the morning of June 20.

Arriving off Apra Harbor at 8:30 a.m., Captain Glass, having
ordered the transports to stay a safe distance outside and await
instructions, sailed directly into the bay aboard the *Charleston*.
"We did not know," related Coontz, "that the old Orote fort [Fort
Santiago] had been abandoned, and that Fort Santa Cruz was
unmanned. As we neared the harbor we saw several vessels anchored, and we anticipated some Spanish capture, but they turned

out to be Japanese recently arrived from Yokohama. With all hands at general quarters and guns loaded we steamed in under Point Orote.

"Had there been soldiers at the fort they could have fired on us and done serious damage before we could have got by, but there was no one there. As we neared Fort Santa Cruz, Slocum, who had the forward battery, fired ten shots, but the only thing that happened was that a couple of men in a canoe quickly paddled away, double time, for the beach! They proved to be fishermen."[3] Thus, finding the harbor completely undefended, the *Charleston* came to in a position to control the surrounding terrain and dropped anchor.

Immediately after anchoring, Captain Glass sent one of his officers to the Japanese vessel in the harbor to obtain information about conditions on the island. At about the same time a small boat, flying the Spanish flag, put off from the landing place at Piti and approached the *Charleston*. In the boat were Lieutenant Commander Don Francisco García Gutiérrez, captain of the port; Don José Romero Aguilar, a surgeon of the Spanish army; and Francisco Portusach, the only American citizen living on the island. Portusach had recognized the ships as American and accompanied the Spaniards in order to act as interpreter. These men boarded the warship. In answer to questions from Captain Glass, they told him that they did not know that war had been declared between the United States and Spain. The captain informed them that war existed and seized them as prisoners. When they told him that no resistance could be made by the Spanish forces on the island, Captain Glass released them on parole for the day. He directed them to return to Agana and ask the governor, Lieutenant Colonel Don Juan Marina, to come on board the *Charleston* at once. While Captain Glass awaited the return of the Spanish officers, an examination was made of the harbor, and dangerous shoals were marked. During the afternoon the *City of Pekin* and the *Australia* entered the bay. The *City of Sydney* remained outside until the following morning.

About 5 p.m. the governor's secretary, Don Pedro Duarte

Anducar, boarded the *Charleston* and presented the following letter to Captain Glass:

Private

Government "P.M." of the
Marianne Islands, Agana
June 20, 1898

Mr. Henry Glass,
Captain of the North American Cruiser Charleston:

By the captain of the port on which you have cast anchor I have been courteously requested, as a soldier and, above all, as a gentleman, to hold a conference with you, adding that you have advised him that war has been declared between our respective nations, and that you have come for the purpose of occupying these Spanish islands.

It would give me great pleasure to comply with his request and see you personally, but, as the military laws of my country prohibit me from going on board a foreign vessel, I regret to have to decline this honor and to ask that you will kindly come on shore, where I await you to accede to your wishes as far as possible, and to agree as to our mutual situations.

Asking your pardon for the trouble I cause you, I guarantee your safe return to your ship.

Very respectfully,
Juan Marina[4]

As it was then too late to send a landing party ashore, Captain Glass sent the secretary back to Agana. He was instructed to tell Governor Marina that a letter would be sent to him early the next morning. Meanwhile, the captain and General Anderson, who was in command of the troops on board the transports, completed plans for capturing the island. Lieutenant Braunersreuther was ordered to take command of a landing party composed of marines from the *Charleston* and the *City of Pekin* and two companies of Oregon Volunteers from the *Australia*. Early the next day he was to proceed to Agana for the purpose of capturing the governor, other officials, and any armed force found there. After destroying military supplies and the defenses of Agana, he was to convey his prisoners to the *Charleston*. The lieutenant was specifically ordered to respect, insofar as possible, all private property. Moreover, he was to prevent marauding by the troops under his command. Since Captain Glass wished to proceed to Manila as quickly as possible,

173

he ordered the landing party to complete its mission in one day's time. The men were equipped in light marching order and supplied with rations for only one day.[5]

The next morning, June 21, Lieutenant Braunersreuther and Ensign Waldo Evans proceeded in a whaleboat to Piti, under a flag of truce. They were accompanied by an interpreter and two correspondents. The boat was manned by four armed sailors. At Piti they were met by the governor and his staff. After formal introductions had been exchanged, Braunersreuther presented the following letter to the governor:

> USS Charleston
> San Luis d'Apra
> Guam Island
> June 20, 1898

Sir:

In reply to your communication of this date, I have now, in compliance with the orders of my Government, to demand the immediate surrender of the defenses of the island of Guam, with arms of all kinds, all officials and persons in the military service of Spain now in this island.

This communication will be handed you to-morrow morning by an officer who is ordered to wait not over one-half hour for your reply.

> Very respectfully,
> Henry Glass
> Captain, U.S. Navy,
> Commanding[6]

Calling the governor's attention to the fact that it was then 10:15 a.m., Braunersreuther reminded him that he had only half an hour in which to prepare his reply. At the same time he informed the governor that three transports and a formidable warship loaded with troops were in the harbor and ready for action. Thanking the lieutenant, Marina and his staff retired to a nearby building. Exactly twenty-nine minutes later the governor reappeared and, handing Braunersreuther a sealed envelope addressed to Captain Glass, informed him that that was his reply. Over the governor's protest, the lieutenant broke the seal and read the letter, which ran as follows:

174

Government "P.M." of
the Marianne Islands
Piti (Agana)
June 21, 1898

Sir:

I am in receipt of your communication of yesterday, demanding the surrender of this place.

Being without defenses of any kind and without means for meeting the present situation, I am under the sad necessity of being unable to resist such superior forces and regretfully accede to your demands, at the same time protesting against this act of violence, when I have received no information from my Government to the effect that Spain is at war with your Nation.

God be with you.

Very respectfully,
Juan Marina
The Governor "P.M."[7]

After the letter had been read, the Spaniards were informed that they were prisoners of war and, as such, were to be taken aboard the *Charleston* immediately. The governor, after a short consultation with his advisers, protested against being made a prisoner, saying that Braunersreuther had come on shore under a flag of truce for an exchange of ideas on the condition of affairs and that he now found himself and his officers prisoners. Braunersreuther replied that he had come on shore with orders from Captain Glass, his commanding officer, to deliver a letter to the governor. All during this brief argument, Braunersreuther had in his possession the governor's reply to Captain Glass's letter, "making a complete surrender of the entire place under his command. This alone, if it meant anything," Braunersreuther wrote later, "permitted me to make any demands I desired and deemed proper to make." Braunersheuther gave Governor Marina ten minutes in which to write an order to his military authority in Agana, directing him "to have at the landing at Piti at 4 p.m. the fifty-four Spanish soldiers with their arms, accouterments, and all ammunition, together with all the Spanish flags in the place (four in all), the two lieutenants of the companies to march the soldiers down." Marina wrote the letter, which was read by Braunersreuther and sent to Agana. A general demur was made at the hour fixed upon, but the American lieutenant insisted that it must be done.[8] The Spaniards were then given an opportunity to write letters to their families. Shortly after noon they were sent out to the *Charleston* as prisoners. The party of Spaniards consisted of Governor Marina, Lieutenant Commander Gutiérrez, Surgeon Romero, and Pedro Duarte. In addition to being the governor's secretary, Duarte was a captain of naval infantry. On his return trip with the prisoners, Braunersreuther met the two divisions of the landing party on their way in to the shore. He directed them to return to their ships. The formal surrender of Guam had already been completed.

Shortly after two o'clock on the same day, Captain Glass and his executive officer, Lieutenant Commander Gottfried Blocklinger, were pulled across the harbor to Fort Santa Cruz. Three correspondents accompanied them. There, at 2:45 p.m. on June 21, 1898, the American flag was formally raised over Guam for the first time. The flag raising was accompanied by a salute of twenty-one guns from the *Charleston* and the playing of "The Star-Spangled Banner" by the bands of the transports. That evening the captain sent a color guard to lower and bring back the flag.

In the middle of the afternoon, after the flag raising, Lieutenant Braunersreuther went ashore to accept the surrender of the armed forces on the island. He headed a party consisting of Lieutenant John T. Myers, Ensign Evans, Passed Assistant Surgeon Ammen Farenholt, forty marines, and a number of sailors. They proceeded to Piti in four boats. There they disarmed the garrison troops, who had marched from Agana to the harbor. This force consisted of two companies, one of Spaniards and one of Guamanians. The Spaniards, fifty-four in number, were taken aboard the *City of Sidney*. Their officers, Lieutenants José Barruesco and Marcelino Ramos, along with the other Spanish officers who had been taken aboard the *Charleston* in the morning, were given staterooms on the *Sydney*. The *Charleston* lacked accommodations for so many extra passengers. The Guamanian troops, about sixty in number, were also disarmed but were permitted to return to their homes.

Before sailing from Guam, Captain Glass engaged in a limited

12. Early Spanish church at Umatac

13. The Royal College of San Juan de Letran as it appeared in 1818. It is believed to have been built by the Jesuits around 1669. No trace of the building remains nor do any of the oldest inhabitants have any recollection of its existence.

14. A fishing party in the Mariana Islands in 1818. (From a drawing by Jacques Arago made at that time.)

15. View of harbor and roadstead, Umatac, 1818

*(Note: Because of their significance, the sketches on these two pages are included in spite of their poor reproduction. The plates used were produced from positive prints*

16. Convento or monastery of Umatac, 1818

17. Spanish Governor's summer residence, Umatac, 1818

*made from enlarged dull-surfaced negative prints made in turn from microfilm of original drawings that appeared in an old volume.)*

18. Native bake oven and distillery, 1818

19.  Dulce Nombre de Maria cathedral in Agana, 1925

20. 1925 photo of the old Spanish bridge south of Agat on the way to Umatac, one of Guam's few old historical landmarks remaining today.

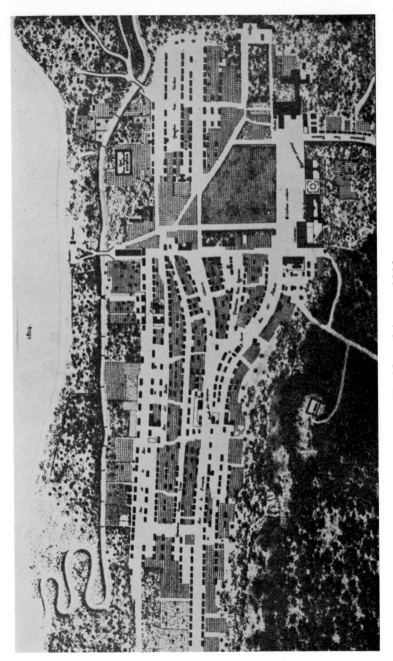

1819

21. Map of Agana, 1819

tour of inspection. Later, in his official report, he stated that no coal was found on the island and that, during the previous eighteen months, no Spanish war vessel had visited Guam. The forts at Agana, Apra Harbor, and Umatac, he reported, were of no value. Only four small cast-iron guns were left on the island. They were formerly used for saluting but at the time were condemned as unsafe even for that purpose. From a personal examination of Fort Santa Cruz, the captain concluded that the fort was entirely useless for defensive purposes and that it was not necessary to expend any mines in blowing it up. On June 22, the *Charleston* and convoy sailed for Manila. No American or Spanish military personnel were left on the newly captured island.

## THE FOUR ACTING GOVERNORS

When Governor Marina and the Spanish troops were removed from Guam, the island was left without responsible government leaders. Two men claimed the right to act as governor. Francisco Portusach, an American citizen, was the first to claim the governorship. He stated that he had had a meeting with Captain Glass aboard the *Charleston*. During the meeting, he said, the captain had directed him to look after the affairs of the island until an American governor could be sent out. His claim was later confirmed by Douglas White, one of the correspondents with the convoy. Since, however, his commission was not in writing, his claim was contested by José Sisto, the only Spanish official permitted to remain on the island. Sisto, the island treasurer, claimed that his status as the senior civilian official gave him the right to act as governor. He thereupon assumed charge of the administration. Because Captain Glass, in his proclamation of siege, had failed to include the rest of the Marianas, Sisto appointed himself provisional governor of all the islands. As governor, he paid himself a large salary in advance from the island treasury.

For a period of about six months, a bitter dispute raged between Portusach and Sisto. The two leaders, with their respective following, were on the point of resorting to force to settle the dispute when, on January 1, 1899, the collier *Brutus* arrived at the island.

On the same day the officer in command of the ship, Lieutenant Vincendon L. Cottman, was visited by Portusach and Padre Palomo. They told him that Sisto had illegally assumed control of the government. Moreover, they said, Sisto had divided the funds in the treasury among himself and other government employees. The next day Sisto came on board the ship. He confirmed what had been reported and stated that he was ready to turn over control of the government to Cottman. For lack of authority, however, Cottman refused the offer. After heated and prolonged discussions with Sisto, Portusach, and Padre Palomo, Cottman decided that Sisto was the legitimate governor. He, however, was to remain as governor only until the status of Guam should be finally decided between Spain and the United States.

On August 12, 1898, about three months after the Spanish-American War started, Spain sued for peace. By the terms of the armistice, Spain relinquished her claim to Cuba and agreed to cede to the United States Puerto Rico and one island in the Marianas. The status of the Philippines was to be decided later at a peace conference to be held in Paris. Before the peace conference convened, Germany, on September 10, 1898, entered into a secret agreement with Spain for the purchase of the Caroline Islands. This was followed by a treaty whereby Spain sold the Carolines, the Palaus, and all the Marianas, except Guam, to Germany for $5,000,000. When the American peace commission went to Paris, it was instructed by President McKinley to demand of Spain that she cede the island of Luzon, in the Philippines, to the United States. Later, the President changed his mind and demanded the cession of all the Philippines. At first, the Spanish delegates resisted the American demands. When, however, the Americans offered a compensation of $20,000,000, Spain quickly accepted the offer. By the terms of the Treaty of Paris, signed December 10, 1898, the United States secured from Spain a protectorate over Cuba and outright possession of the Philippines, Puerto Rico, and Guam.

With the matter of the ownership of Guam finally settled, Commander Edward D. Taussig, commanding officer of the USS

*Bennington,* was dispatched to the island. The *Bennington* arrived at Apra Harbor on January 23, 1899. Two days later, Taussig and other officers from his ship paid a visit to Agana. They called on Governor Sisto and inspected the government buildings. Unlike other naval officers who visited the island, Taussig went beyond his orders. He began to administer the island's affairs. On January 28 he issued Order No. 1:

1. All laws and regulations of the former Government will remain in force until otherwise directed.

2. Passed Assistant Paymaster Barron P. DuBois, U.S. Navy, to collect and disburse all revenues of the island from and after February 1st, 1899.

3. The inhabitants are informed that subjects of Spain may elect to remain on the island as subjects of Spain and that they will receive the protection of the United States Government while conducting themselves in an orderly and law-abiding manner.

4. All inhabitants electing to remain subjects of Spain are directed to make their declaration to the Local of their district. All officials and employees of the island government will be continued until further notice.

On the same day Taussig directed Sisto to turn over to Paymaster DuBois all government records and money. Two days later he issued Order No. 2. Dated January 30, 1899, this order declared that all former Spanish government lands bordering on Apra Harbor were now the property of the United States Navy. On the morning of February 1, a battalion of marines and a volunteer band were landed from the *Bennington* and marched from Piti to Agana, where they took part in impressive ceremonies in the Plaza de España. There, at 10 a.m., the American flag was raised over the palace. At the same time a flag was also raised at Fort Santa Cruz. With the playing of "The Star-Spangled Banner" and a salute of 21 guns from the *Bennington,* formal ceremonies were completed, and Guam was a possession of the United States.

Shortly after the ceremonies of possession were completed, Commander Taussig started an investigation of the island's affairs. He was especially concerned about the impoverished state of the treasury. Through his investigation he learned that Governor Sisto had paid himself eighteen months' salary in advance. Five treasury employees had been given a year's advance pay. Immediate steps were taken to recover the money. The five treasury employees returned all they had been given, except for a small sum. Sisto returned nothing. With the money that was returned, funds in the treasury amounted to $2,969.33. The matter of the refund from Sisto was left unsettled. Treasury funds were derived from a poll tax of $1.50 a year upon each male between eighteen and sixty years of age. Other sources of revenue were from taxes upon slaughtering cattle, branding livestock, and cockfights. Taxes on real estate, industries, and sums paid for exemptions from forced labor added to treasury funds. The tax for exemption from forced labor was payable in advance. Revenues produced $600 a month while the expenses amounted to $725. Money in the treasury was of many kinds. It consisted of Chilean, other South American, Mexican, and Philippine coin. The South American coins were badly worn and were greatly reduced in value. Every trading vessel imported more and more of the cheap South American coins. Meanwhile, Mexican and Spanish money was being exported by the local merchants to pay for imported goods. The bad money was driving out the good. To remedy the situation Commander Taussig ordered all taxes to be paid in Mexican or Spanish money. South American money was accepted only at certain discounts. American money was accepted at twice the value of Mexican money. Treasury funds were used mainly to pay the salaries of government officers, members of the re-established native militia, and treasury employees.

Before Taussig left the island, he prepared a report for the Secretary of the Navy in which he recommended that certain officials be sent to Guam. Among these were a governor, a tax collector, a registrar of land titles, and a doctor. Since the people seemed friendly toward the United States, he suggested that a lieutenant's guard would be a large enough garrison force. He recommended that $3,000 be provided to repair the palace and buy needed furniture. (Most of the furniture had been removed by the Spanish officials.) He also suggested that household effects, a small vehicle and two horses, two or three cows, and plenty of vegetable seeds should be sent to the island. On February 15, after a stay of twenty-three days, Commander Taussig left Guam for the Philippines. Before departing he ordered Governor Sisto to turn over control of the island to a Guamanian, Don Joaquín Pérez. Pérez was the *gobernadorcillo* of Agana. Don Vicente Herrero, another Guamanian, was appointed island treasurer. Taussig also asked Lieutenant Cottman, who had left the island shortly after Taussig's arrival, to prepare and submit a report to Washington on conditions in Guam. Cottman's report, dated February 20, 1899, said in part:

If the Government intends to make Guam a self-supporting island and a creditable colony it will be necessary to commence immediately and use heroic measures. The following are suggested as some of the necessary means to this end.

1. First of all send the Spanish priests to Spain or to one of the Spanish Islands and the native priest to one of the other islands, I believe he claims some of them. These priests are the moral lepers of the place and are a great drawback and detriment; they have considerable political influence. As the people are all Roman Catholics send here four American priests, judiciously selected for their suitability. Priests similar to the Catholic Chaplains in the Navy would be suitable.

2. Having gotten rid of the moral lepers send four government doctors whose first duty will be to examine all the natives in the island and corral all the lepers and send them out of the island, the leper settlement at Molokai [Hawaii] is suggested as rendezvous. There are about six lepers now in the island. Next let the doctors establish a hospital with sufficient surrounding ground for a ranch and collect all the syphilitics in the island and start a colony that will be self supporting, say at Merizo. If any of the cases can be cured by treatment let such be released from settlement when cured. Let the doctors look into the sanitary requirements. All the towns need sewers.

3. Establish a government pharmacy and have compulsory examination of all natives and for the present free treatment.

4. Send all the Filipino convicts back to Manila.

5. Compel all males above 18 to do a day's work six days in the week, until they become accustomed to work; this will prevent their laying around the homes idle and drinking La Tuba. Make them build a good carriage road all around the island.

6. Establish Public Schools and compel all children to go to school

and teach them English, having male teachers for the boys and women teachers for the girls.

7. Establish an Industrial School.

8. Make American the business as well as the official language.

9. Establish a government experimental agricultural station and stock farm in one, send out all kinds of vegetable seed, grain seed, fruit seed and grazing grass seed that is suitable for the tropics; have a fair amount to distribute free under supervision of the Agriculturist of the Experimental Station. Send out half a dozen good milk cows and a bull or two, Texas horses, ducks, partridges and quail, also agricultural implements and some axes and saws.[9]

Upon Taussig's departure, Acting Governor Pérez administered the affairs of the island. He was assisted by a council composed of four laymen and a priest. The council had also been appointed by Taussig. Members of the council were Padre Palomo, Don Juan Torres, Don Vicente Roberto, Don Luis Torres, and Don Antonio Martínez. This group governed the island with little difficulty until after the arrival of Lieutenant Louis A. Kaiser on March 24, 1899. Kaiser was the commanding officer of the collier *Nanshan*. Immediately after his arrival he began to take part in government affairs. He discussed problems with government leaders, inspected public buildings, and took steps to improve sanitation. On April 2, as a result of trouble with Filipino ex-convicts on the island, he forbade persons without passes to be on the streets from 9 p.m. to 5 a.m. A short time later he issued an order forbidding native soldiers to take part in religious celebrations. This order was resented by Governor Pérez and members of the council.

On May 9 Colonel Eugenio Blanco, the Spanish governor of the northern Marianas, arrived in port on board the SS *Elcano*. He asked Kaiser to turn over to him certain arms, munitions, and medical supplies which had belonged to the former Spanish government of Guam. By the terms of the Treaty of Paris, these items were to be returned to the Spaniards. Because he had no copy of the treaty, Kaiser refused to turn over the material. The Spanish governor departed for Saipan empty-handed. On June 16 a letter arrived from General Elwell S. Otis, the American general in command in the Philippines. He suggested to Kaiser that the arms be delivered to the Spaniards. Since Otis did not have jurisdiction over Guam, Kaiser was in doubt as to what to do. He finally decided not to heed the general's suggestion. Shortly thereafter the Spanish ship *Esmeralda* entered the harbor. The officer in charge was the representative of the governor of Saipan. He requested delivery of the arms, and Governor Pérez gave him the keys to the arsenal. When Kaiser heard of this, he gave Pérez a written order to the effect that the governor of Saipan could not have the arms. Pérez protested, but Kaiser demanded and secured the return of the keys. Pérez then called a meeting of the council, which was held on July 11. The council approved Pérez' action and declared that he had acted within his authority as governor. Kaiser, however, insisted as the senior officer present that he was in charge of the government. Pérez thereupon suggested that the lieutenant act as governor. This Kaiser refused to do. The next day, while walking near the arsenal, Kaiser saw arms being loaded into carts. He demanded that Pérez convene the council. When Pérez refused, Kaiser ordered his removal from office. He then appointed William Coe, a half-caste Samoan who had arrived on the island shortly before its seizure by the *Charleston,* to the post of acting governor. Kaiser's attempt to manage affairs through acting governors, whose authority he infringed upon whenever he chose, was not too successful. A short time later, upon the establishment of naval rule and the appointment of an American governor, this troubled period came to an end.

## The Establishment of Naval Government

After Guam had been ceded to the United States, the problem of governing the island became a matter of real concern to officials in Washington. In view of the island's distance from the mainland and its possible use as a coaling station, President McKinley decided to make the Department of the Navy responsible for the government of Guam. Accordingly he issued the following Executive Order, under which the island was administered until August 1, 1950.

183

Executive Mansion
Washington, D.C.
December 23, 1898

The Island of Guam in the Ladrones is hereby placed under the control of the Department of the Navy. The Secretary of the Navy will take such steps as may be necessary to establish the authority of the United States and to give it the necessary protection and Government.

[Signed] William McKinley

On January 12, 1899, President McKinley, on the recommendation of the Secretary of the Navy, John D. Long, appointed Captain Richard P. Leary, USN, to be the first American governor of Guam. Governor Leary was directed to proceed to the island as quickly as possible and establish therein "the Naval Government of Guam." He was, however, not issued detailed orders concerning the manner in which he should administer the affairs of the island. The following statement from Secretary Long's instruction to the new governor embodies the ideas on which the naval government of Guam was to be established.

It should be the earnest and paramount aim of the Naval Administration to win the confidence, respect, and affection of the inhabitants of the Island of Guam, by securing them in every possible way that full measure of individual rights and liberty which is the inheritance of all free peoples, and by proving to them that the mission of the United States is one of benevolent assimilation, substituting the mild sway of justice and right for arbitrary rule.

Among other things, the instructions informed the island's commandant that certain of the old Spanish laws were to remain in effect in the newly acquired territory. Such laws were to be enforced "within the absolute domain of Naval authority which necessarily is and must remain supreme in the ceded territory until legislation of the United States shall otherwise provide."[10]

Thus Guam was placed under "temporary" naval rule until such time as the Congress of the United States should determine its legal status. Since the Congress was slow to act, naval rule continued, with the exception of the period of Japanese occupation, until passage of the Organic Act in 1950.

In order to carry out the Navy's mission in Guam, the entire

184

island was designated as a naval station. Naval officers were regularly assigned to serve as heads of the naval government of Guam. At the same time such officers assumed additional duties as commandant of the United States Naval Station, Guam. The island's governors were appointed by the Secretary of the Navy and commissioned by the President. Since the naval governors held two jobs—those of governor and commandant—their authority extended to all phases of island life. In view of the fact that Congress failed to act, the governors were compelled to use their own judgment in deciding what should be done in Guam. Thus all real power was concentrated in the hands of one man. In this regard, naval government was similar to that which prevailed under the Spanish governors. From the very beginning, naval governors, of necessity, ruled by means of executive orders, verbal orders, and proclamations. Consequently, naval government was highly centralized and based on personal authority. It remained so throughout most of the period of naval rule.

As naval rule developed, all the activities of the island government (the local name given to the naval government) came gradually to be exercised by various departments. By 1923, twenty-five years after the beginning of American rule, the naval government of Guam was organized into ten departments.[11] Although the number of departments changed from time to time, they remained basically pretty much the same throughout the entire period of naval rule. In most instances the heads of departments were naval officers who were assigned to their positions by the governor. They, like the governor, performed official duties for both the naval station and the Island Government. Whenever possible, qualified Guamanians were assigned duties in lower ranking positions in the various departments.

In his dual role the naval governor was the supreme authority on the island. His actions could be checked only by the President and by his superiors in the Navy Department. Major matters of concern to him as governor were those of economics, agriculture, commerce, construction of buildings and roads, education, finance, public health, population, law, and politics. As commandant, he was interested chiefly in the maintenance and development of the naval station. During the half century of naval rule, these matters constantly occupied the attention of most of the naval governors. Governor Leary was the first American governor to be confronted with these problems.*

## RICHARD P. LEARY

Captain Richard P. Leary began exercising his duties as the first American governor of Guam on August 7, 1899. The naval government of the island dates from the following proclamation, which he issued three days later:

PROCLAMATION TO THE INHABITANTS OF GUAM AND TO WHO IT MAY CONCERN:

Pursuant to the provisions of a Treaty of Peace between the United States and Spain, concluded by their respective Plenipotentiaries at Paris, France, the Tenth Day of December, Eighteen Hundred and Ninety-Eight, the future control, disposition and government of the Island of Guam are ceded to the United States.

Now therefore, by virtue of the authority vested in me by his Excellency, The President of the United States, I, Richard P. Leary, Captain, United States Navy, and Governor of the Island of Guam, do hereby announce and publicly proclaim my actual occupation and administration of this Island, in the fulfillment of the Rights of Sovereignty thus acquired and the responsible obligations of government thus assumed.

That, you, the Inhabitants of Guam, are hereby informed that in establishing a new Political Power, the authority of the United States will be exerted for the security of the persons and property of the people of the island and for the confirmation of all your private rights and relations.

That, all political rights heretofore exercised by the Clergy in dominating the people of the Island, are hereby abolished, and everyone is

* Governor Leary was sent to Guam aboard the USS *Yosemite*, which was fitted out as a station ship for the island. On May 1, 1899, President McKinley himself visited and inspected the ship and crew before its departure from the New York Navy Yard. After an uneventful voyage across the Atlantic and stops at Gibraltar, Port Said, Colombo, Singapore, and Manila, the *Yosemite* reached Guam on August 7, 1899, just over three months after leaving the United States. About a week later, Lieutenant William Edwin Safford, USN, Guam's first American "lieutenant governor," arrived aboard the USS *Brutus*. Because of diseases and lack of adequate housing, Governor Leary chose to live aboard the *Yosemite* rather than in the palace at Agana. As a result, Lieutenant Safford was given the greater part of the responsibility for carrying out the naval mission in Guam.

guaranteed absolute freedom of worship and full protection in the lawful pursuits of life, so long as that protection is deserved by actual submission to and compliance with the requirements of the Government of the United States.

That, all public lands and property and all rights and privileges, on shore or in the contiguous waters of the Island, that belonged to Spain at the time of the surrender, now belong to the United States, and all persons are warned against attempting to purchase, appropriate or dispose of any of the aforesaid properties, rights or privileges without the consent of the United States Government.

That, for the present preservation of law and order, the existing laws not conflicting with the provisions of this proclamation will continue in force until modified or annulled by competent authority, and all persons are enjoined to render prompt and cheerful obedience to the same in order that the blessings of good government, with the benefits of civilization and freedom, coupled with happiness and prosperity for the greatest good of the greatest number, may be the heritage of all residents of the Island, as Worthy Citizens of the Island of Guam, under the Free Flag of the United States.

In Witness whereof, I have hereunto set my hands and caused the Seal of the United States Naval Station, Isle of Guam, to be affixed.

Done at Agana, Isle of Guam, this 10 day of August in the year of our Lord one thousand eight hundred and ninety-nine, and of the independence of the United States of America, the one hundred and twenty-third.

Richard P. Leary
Captain, United States Navy
Governor of Guam

Upon arrival, the officers and men of the *Yosemite* were very much surprised at the conditions they found existing in Guam. Since the American knew almost nothing about the island, many of them expected to find it inhabited by savage "South Sea Islanders." They soon learned, however, that the Guamanians were civilized people who possessed a long established Spanish-Catholic tradition and that a number of them could even speak English. The Guamanians, on the other hand, were just as surprised at the Americans, who they had been led to believe were barbarians and heretics. They found that, in general, the newcomers sought only to befriend and help them. On both sides, however, a certain amount of suspicion and distrust prevailed.

After the Spanish-American War the United States became a colonial power for the first time in its history. Because of the lack of experience in dealing with dependent peoples, early American governors experienced real difficulties in administering the affairs of newly acquired colonies. Perhaps nowhere else did the colonial governors find so much labor before them as in Guam. Years of neglect on the part of Spanish governors had left their mark on the Guamanian people. Illiteracy, unsanitary conditions, and new and frightening diseases were but a few of the problems that confronted Governor Leary and other early American governors. Added to these were problems created by the Americans themselves. Since American troops were new to conquest and familiar with only one race other than their own, they needed a great deal of control and correction in matters unofficial and nonmilitary. In many cases they were lawless and turbulent. The marine battalion which accompanied Governor Leary to Guam consisted of one major, two captains, three lieutenants, eight sergeants, eight corporals, four musicians, and ninety-nine privates.

For more than three months after his arrival on the island, Governor Leary lived on board the *Yosemite*. After needed repairs had been made on the palace, he moved to Agana on November 26, 1899. His entrance into the capital city was an impressive sight. He rode in an imported carriage drawn by white stallions imported from the Philippines. The horses were handled by a Filipino coachman. In the procession were the *Yosemite's* band and the governor's Japanese steward and house servants. Following the grand entrance, he established himself in the palace, which had been furnished with equipment, furniture, and supplies brought from the United States.

During the time that the governor remained on the *Yosemite*, government affairs in Agana were handled by this aide, Lieutenant William Edwin Safford. Safford was thirty-nine years old, a graduate of the Naval Academy, and a native of Chillicothe, Ohio. He was a studious man who had spent a great deal of time studying the plants and peoples of the tropics. Moreover, he spoke Spanish with ease. After his arrival on August 13, Safford moved into

188

quarters over the public treasury. Among his possessions was a library of more than 200 valuable books. Two days after his arrival, Safford relieved the acting governor, William Coe. From Governor Leary he received instructions to do whatever he thought was necessary and to call on the governor only in emergencies. Soon the people "began to bring their troubles to him in his office on the second floor of the Palace or to his home in the evening, and he received them with an unfailing courtesy and understanding that won him the regard of the people of the island. The lieutenant regarded his position as an opportunity to do something for the inhabitants and to ameliorate the conditions under which they lived, and in his dealings with them he asked them to treat him as if he were one of them and not to grant him favors because he was an official. He made an altogether different type of official from the ordinary Spaniard who had come to profit and depart. He formed a close friendship with Padre Palomo, the refined, intelligent, and well-educated native priest, who was the most influential man on the island, and who became the lieutenant's advisor." Lieutenant Safford resigned his commission in the Navy in 1902. At that time he became assistant curator of the Office of Tropical Agriculture in the United States Department of Agriculture. While stationed in Guam he had diligently collected plants and studied the Chamorro language. In 1905 he published a valuable work entitled *The Useful Plants of the Island of Guam*. The book dealt not only with plants but with the island's history as well. To this date, his work is still one of the most valuable sources of information concerning the history of Guam.

Excessive drinking by some marines, especially those stationed in Agana, led to frequent misunderstandings and fights between American troops and some of the islanders. Among these islanders were Guamanians, Filipino ex-convicts, and political prisoners deported from the Philippines. The political prisoners had been deported to Guam because of their resistance to the establishment of American rule in their islands. *Tuba*, a drink made from the juice of the coconut, was the beverage that was the principal cause of the disorders. The situation became so bad that Governor Leary,

189

on August 16, 1899, was compelled to issue General Orders No. 1 and 2. The first of these forbade the sale of liquor to any person who was not a resident of the island before August 7, 1899. The second prohibited the importation of liquor except by special licenses issued by the government. To prevent the marines from getting *tuba* and thus to keep the peace between them and the islanders, the governor issued General Order No. 8 on November 1, 1899. This order, stating that "drunkenness, the chief source of all crime and trouble in this island, must and shall cease," established prohibition on the island. Special licenses could still be obtained from the government to buy liquor for medicinal purposes. These measures did much to help restore order.

Before his departure for Guam, Governor Leary had read the reports sent to the Navy Department by Lieutenant Cottman and Commander Taussig. They apparently had influenced his thinking with regard to the role of the church on the island. In a report to the Navy Department, dated August 28, 1899, he declared his intention to deport the Spanish priests from Guam. He was convinced, he said, that to permit the priests to stay would be "subversive of good government and prosperity, injurious to the interests of the community and incompatible with the moral teachings and principals of civilized society. . . . I have informed those priests that transportation to Manila has been ordered for them in the USS Nanshan, and it is my intention to see that they avail themselves of the opportunity to leave this island."[12] When the governor's intentions became known on the island, the priests, Spanish Augustinian Recollect friars, became greatly disturbed. Father Francisco Resano was ordered by his superiors to move to Saipan. A short time later three of the priests visited Lieutenant Safford. They told him that they wanted to become American citizens and begged to be allowed to remain on the island. Safford, who was powerless in the situation, informed them that in time the governor's order would be carried out. About three days before Leary had sent his report concerning the priests to Washington, he issued General Order No. 4. This order forbade religious processions in the streets and the public celebration of village saints' days. Thereafter, religious feasts were to be celebrated inside the churches, chapels, or private homes. His campaign to separate church matters from civil and political affairs continued when he ordered all couples to marry at once according to law. He also issued a decree making divorce possible. Later, he outlawed cockfighting on Sunday and forbade the ringing of church bells at 4:00 a.m., the hour when most Guamanians arose to begin their day's work. General Order No. 19 was issued some time later to "check the pernicious habit of gambling that prevails among young children and to discourage the habit among adults." Another order directed the *gobernadorcillos* to remove all crucifixes and saints' pictures from school classrooms. It also ordered the teachers to discontinue instructions in the church catechism. The governor, moreover, did not yield in his determination to deport the priests. On September 6, 1899, most of the friars were ordered to board the Japanese ship *Jun-ho-maru* and were deported to Saipan. The priests of Agat and Merizo were sent to Manila aboard the *Nanshan*. Padre Palomo alone was permitted to remain on the island. Needless to say, the governor's action aroused intense anger among the Guamanian people. Moreover, news of his policies reached the United States. There, many newspapers and magazines protested his expulsion of the priests and his other measures concerning religion. Nevertheless, his policies were permitted to stand. About five months later the archbishop of New Orleans, apostolic delegate for the new possessions of the United States, asked to be permitted to stop off at Guam on his way to the Philippines. Governor Leary agreed and extended him an invitation. Later, he withdrew the invitation, and the archbishop was not permitted to visit the island.

Upon the establishment of the naval government, officers of the United States Navy were placed in all important positions of government. Guamanians were appointed to assist them. The governor, like Spanish governors before him, was in complete charge of all government affairs. He exercised all executive, legislative, and judicial authority. He soon came to fill the following positions: inspector of customs, postmaster, judge of the

Supreme Court, and inspector of public schools. Lieutenant Safford also had many jobs. He was the registrar of lands, deeds, and titles; auditor of the treasury; judge of the court of first instance; and judge of the criminal court. By April 15, 1900, the government was so organized that it was possible to publish an official list of the various departments. In addition to Governor Leary and Safford, there were a translator, Atanasio Taitano, and a keeper of records and town crier, Nicolas Lazaro. The captain of the native militia, Lorenzo Fránquez, was placed under the Military Command. This department was headed by the colonel in charge of the marine garrison. The Medical Department was composed of three Navy doctors and a leper hospital attendant, Pedro Namauleg. William Coe was the deputy collector of customs. This office was in the Treasury Department, which also included a receiver and paymaster of island funds, Juan de Torres; a chief clerk, Joaquín Díaz; a clerk, Manuel Untalan; and an Agana city clerk, Demetrio Quitugua. The Post Office Department consisted of the marine colonel as assistant postmaster and a clerk, Atanasio Taitano. The governor was the head of the Department of Justice. Lieutenant Safford was the head of the Land Office. He was assisted by an assistant registrar, Vicente Camacho, and a writer. Operations at Apra Harbor were under the supervision of William Coe, captain of the port, and Henry Millinchamp, the government pilot. Millinchamp had occupied the same post under the Spaniards. The Department of Education was headed by the governor. It included a principal of public schools in Agana, Felipe Cruz; a teacher of English, Mrs. J. M. Rumberg, wife of an American settler on the island; four native teachers in Agana and others at María Cristina, Anigua, Asan, Tepungan, Sinajana, Agat, Umatac, Merizo, Sumay, and Inarajan. The colonel in command of the marine garrison was the head of the Public Works Department. Pedro Duarte, the former Spanish secretary and captain, was the inspector of roads and sanitation. After being carried away in the *Charleston,* he had been released in the Philippines. He then returned to Guam to be with his wife and family. His wife was the daughter of Henry Millinchamp. Besides the colonel and Duarte, the Public Works

192

Department included a Navy lieutenant, one warrant machinist, and a native. The jailer of Agana Prison, Juan del Rosario, along with two assistants, two constables, and a prison recorder, made up the Department of Prisons. The Department of Agriculture consisted of four inspectors of crops and livestock.

At the beginning of American rule, most Guamanians raised their food on tracts of land which they owned. Although most tracts were small, land ownership was a source of great pride. Property lines, in many cases, were poorly drawn. In order to safeguard land ownership, Governor Leary issued General Order No. 3 on August 21, 1899. This order made it necessary to secure government permission before selling or transferring any land. It also ordered the people to register all titles in the office of the registrar of land titles. As registrar, Lieutenant Safford was in charge of the registration books. Soon many people came to him to have their lands registered. During the registering it was found that many persons could not sign their names. Consequently, General Order No. 13 was issued. It required every adult resident of the island to learn to write his or her name before the first of July 1900. It also urged the people to learn to read, write, and speak the English language.

In the fall of 1899 Lieutenant Safford began an examination of land ownership on the island. He found that a few families owned vast tracts of land which they did not cultivate. One of the large landowners was Don Vicente Herrero. He owned a vast tract of land on the east coast, south of the Yigo district. Moreover, between the Ylig and Talofofo rivers he owned another tract that was 16 square miles in area. Safford concluded that owners of large tracts should be compelled to sell land to those who were willing to cultivate it. Accordingly, he drew up a system of land taxation that was proclaimed on January 5, 1900, as General Order No. 10. Under the terms of this order a tax was imposed on all privately owned land. The rate of the tax depended on whether the land was within the limits of a town, was suitable for farming, or was forest or grazing land. The rates declined in amount in this same order. Moreover, districts that were far removed from Agana were given a tax reduction of 20 per cent. This was because of the difficulty which they had in transporting their farm products to market. The tax went into effect immediately and had to be paid at the end of June and the end of December. Not long after the tax became effective, Don Vicente Herrero turned over to the government most of his land in the southern part of the island. He kept only a narrow strip along the shore. Other large landowners, finding the tax too much of a burden, followed Don Vicente's example. The new land policy was expected to open up agricultural lands that had been lying idle. In this regard, the policy was not too successful.

Soon after his arrival, Governor Leary learned that many couples on the island were living together without the benefit of a marriage ceremony. Consequently, on September 15, 1899, he issued General Order No. 5. This order provided for a fine and imprisonment for unlawful cohabitation after November 3, 1899. Until that date the government would issue licenses and perform civil marriage ceremonies free of charge. Shortly thereafter the governor issued a decree providing for divorces, even though they would not be recognized by the Catholic Church. These orders created a great deal of misunderstanding and confusion among the people. They succeeded, however, in abolishing concubinage.

A form of economic slavery or peonage existed on the island at the time of the American occupation. Many persons, on borrowing money or goods, made written agreements to pay off the debt by personal labor. However, by having to work for low wages and by having the debt increased by charges for one thing or another, they were never able to get out of debt.

Benigno Acosta, for instance, borrowed money (16 pesos) from Doña Luisa Quitugua in November 1898 with which to pay the funeral expenses for his mother and then went to work for his creditor. The agreement stipulated that for attending to her farm in the locality called Ipao he was to receive two pesos a month and a third of the foodstuffs; he was to be responsible for unjustified losses of cattle and for damages caused by them; and was to plant daily five coconuts. But the lady kept him from guarding the cattle by sending him on errands and prevented him from getting a share of the crops by having him burn lime all of the time. Considering himself a slave, Benigno presented his case to Safford who solved it by taking the boy into his own employ to clear his ranch above San Ramon at six pesos a month and board and arranging with his creditor the payment of the debt.[13]

In a proclamation dated January 1, 1900, Governor Leary abolished peonage. By his order all contracts for personal labor were annulled. Persons who were bound by such contracts were permitted to work for money and pay off their debts.

In the field of health and sanitation, many reforms were ordered. People were no longer permitted to dump trash outside their houses, nor were dogs allowed to scavenge. Late in August 1899 a dispensary was established in Agana. Free treatment was given to the local population. The sick in the villages of Piti, Sumay, and Agat were treated in a dispensary set up in the harbor area. Despite these efforts a typhoid fever epidemic broke out late in 1899. A number of deaths resulted. In order to provide for the proper keeping of death records, the governor issued General Order No. 17 on April 3, 1900. By this order the *gobernadorcillos* of the districts were required to report all deaths to the governor. Burials could not take place without a written permit from the governor's office. From August 7, 1899, to July 31, 1900, a total of 1,141 persons were given free medical treatment. Some of the diseases for which treatment was given were typhoid fever, dysentery, hookworm, gangosa, and leprosy.

The above-mentioned reforms were but a few of the many changes wrought on the island by Governor Leary. Some of his reforms were readily accepted by the people; others were deeply resented by them. Several of the orders aroused so much resentment that Leary's successor was compelled to change or retract them. This was especially true of the orders concerning religious affairs. Nevertheless, the laws which he decreed during the early months of his administration had profound effects on the lives of the Guamanian people. Moreover, the manner in which he administered the island's affairs established a pattern that was followed by succeeding governors. During the latter part of his administration, which lasted a little less than a year, Governor Leary devoted

195

much of his time to the strict enforcement of his new reforms.

## SEATON SCHROEDER

On July 19, 1900, Governor Leary was relieved by Commander Seaton Schroeder. Governor Schroeder concerned himself with matters of taxes, property laws, education, and health. He was especially concerned about the state of the island's treasury and was determined to prevent the balance on hand from falling below $10,000 (Mexican). A serious and unexpected drain on the treasury occurred, however, when on November 13, 1900, the island was struck by a devastating typhoon. Concerning the typhoon, Schroeder wrote:

It first began to be realized at about four in the morning that something unusual was happening. The barometer was falling rapidly, and the wind was so strong that the storm shutters in Government House had to be closed, barred and supported as well as possible from inside. One shutter after another was crushed in and everything wrecked within. Not long afterwards, a fierce, ripping sound announced that the galvanized roof had begun to go, and in a short time the whole of it had been deposited in greater or smaller sections on the slopes and summit of the high ridge at the back. The occasional downpours of drenching rain added their quota to the terrifying conditions; and as cellars are unknown in Guam, not much refuge was to be found anywhere. At about noon the wind shifted rapidly to the eastward, showing that the storm had passed to the southward and was speeding on its way westward. I made my way out to see if anything could be and was being done to help the townspeople, but I found that several parties of seamen and marines had anticipated me and were at work rescuing those in danger. The fury of the wind made it impossible to stand or even to crawl in exposed places; the only recourse was to lie flat and roll or wriggle to the shelter of some wall or low ruin. I reached a piece of wall and stood behind it for a moment to catch my breath, but soon was driven from there by fragments of it being blown off and down on me; fortunately the fragments did not have far to fall, and, although brought to my knees, I escaped injury beyond a few bruises and a wrenched shoulder. By that time practically everything in the shape of tiles, timbers, roofing, and coconuts that could be blown about had already been blown away and there was less danger from that source. But the sea was slowly rising, sucked up by the diminished atmospheric pressure indicated by

196

the low barometer; and it engulfed all the low parts of the town, finally reaching the plaza in front of the Palace.[14]

During the typhoon the station ship *Yosemite* disappeared from Apra Harbor. She was torn loose from her moorings and driven over the Callahan Bank, which juts out from Cabras Island. If she had been stopped by the reef, she would have gone to pieces, and every man on board might have drowned. As it was, she drifted over it, and the people on board were eventually saved, although the ship herself was doomed. On the morning following the typhoon the collier *Justin* put to sea in search of the missing ship. After a long search the *Yosemite* was found many miles northwest of the island. She was a hopeless wreck. The *Justin* tried to tow her back to port, but the task proved to be impossible. She was sinking rapidly. Her commanding officer and crew were transferred to the *Justin*, taking with them all money and papers. Then "the USS *Yosemite* went down with her colors flying; and after she had taken the final plunge the people on board the *Justin* stood with bared heads while three volleys of musketry gave to her the burial rites of a human."[15]

The typhoon dealt a severe blow to the island. Agana and most of the other towns were laid in ruins. Nearly all houses, except those made of coral masonry, were destroyed. At the southeast end of the island a tidal wave swept over the village of Inarajan, killing or drowning twenty-eight persons. A small trading boat with two men on board was driven out to sea and was never seen again. Other casualties included five seamen aboard the *Yosemite's* steam launch. They were lost when their boat was swamped in Apra Harbor. Besides the loss of life, most of the island's food supplies were destroyed, and the people faced starvation. Governor Schroeder commandeered what provisions were left and rationed them out to the people who were unable to buy. He also sent the slow-moving *Justin* to Manila for fresh supplies. Before the emergency ended, he had spent $9,182 for the purchase of food for the needy. Because of severe injury to the island's coconut trees, it was four years before any copra was again exported.

Schroeder's attempts to build up the island's financial resources were in vain. Besides the financial drain caused by the typhoon, treasury funds were further depleted when $3,000 was transferred to a fund for building a hospital in Agana. This fund was increased by $1,755, which was donated by the people of Agana and officers of the naval station. The cornerstone of the Maria Schroeder Hospital was laid by Mrs. Schroeder on June 10, 1901. It was blessed by the venerable Padre José Palomo who, according to the governor, was a veritable "saint on earth" who guided his people "with a sweet holiness that could not fail to impress all who came in touch with him."[16]

During Schroeder's administration a sanitary slaughterhouse and market was built in Agana. Licenses for slaughtering and rented market stalls were required. Money from licenses and rent was expected to make up for the cost of building the market, "but the main object sought was the securing of clean and healthy meat, and presentation of an object lesson to the townspeople who are thought to be receptive of good influences."[17]

Governor Schroeder devoted much time to winning the loyalty and friendship of the Guamanian people. In spite of mismanagement and neglect by their former Spanish rulers, many Guamanians still felt loyal to Spain. Spanish traditions, instilled in the people over a period of almost 300 years, could not be overturned in a few months' time. Like those of Leary before him, Governor Schroeder's efforts to win the loyalty of the Guamanians was made more difficult by the actions of "carpetbaggers" and marines of the garrison force. At times bad behavior on the part of some Americans so aroused Guamanian leaders that they protested vigorously to the governor. After Schroeder instituted a "get tough" policy, relations between Guamanians and Americans began slowly to improve. Concerning this problem, Governor Schroeder reported to the Navy Department as follows:

> I have had occasion at various times to note and to mention to the Department that many little actions on the part of the natives of the island indicate a friendly feeling for the American government, its flag, and its representatives here. This feeling is quite unmistakable and will, I hope, become well grounded. Among the less thoughtful the feeling of

uneasiness engendered by the detestable spirit of lawlessness displayed by a part of the Marine battalion has undoubtedly checked somewhat this feeling of satisfaction with the new regime; but I am glad to think that the more intelligent persons understand that the present detachment is not truly representative, and the steps taken to restore order tend to reassure them; it is hoped that in time one prime difficulty will be removed, viz. the dread by this peaceable and law-abiding people of complaining and testifying against those who maltreat them.[18]

In April 1902 Governor Schroeder appointed Pedro M. Duarte to the position of auditor for the island government. He was responsible for carrying out a new system of accountability for all government funds. At the same time the governor recommended to the Secretary of the Navy that Mexican dollars used in Guam be replaced by Philippine silver dollars of fixed value. The low value of the Mexican dollar, he reported, would "inure to the injury of this community, and also of the Government in the purchase of supplies from the United States."[19]

A census of the island, taken during Schroeder's first year as governor, showed the population on September 1, 1901, to be as follows:[20]

|  | Males | Females | Total |
|---|---|---|---|
| Citizens of the U.S.A. | 6 | 8 | 14 |
| Citizens of the island of Guam | 4,539 | 5,091 | 9,630 |
| Spaniards | 6 | 8 | 14 |
| Italians | 0 | 2 | 2 |
| Japanese | 12 | 1 | 13 |
| Chinese | 3 | 0 | 3 |
| TOTAL | 4,566 | 5,110 | 9,676 |

During the year 1902 the number of births on the island was 412 and the number of deaths 243. Because of suspicion and fear, large numbers of islanders refused to take advantage of medical care provided by the new government. Many died without having been seen by a medical officer. Others waited so long before applying for treatment that, when they did so, they were already beyond all hope of recovery. Among adults dysentery and tuberculosis were the chief causes of death. Infant mortality, due to unclean methods at birth, accounted for most of the deaths among children.

In an attempt to correct the situation, Governor Schroeder ordered all midwives to be instructed in sanitary methods by the navy medical officer.

Before the United States acquired Guam, the Spaniards, in 1890, had established a leper colony at Pago. The colony was destroyed by a typhoon in 1892, and after this a hospital was established at Asan. In 1900 the Asan hospital also was destroyed by a typhoon. The few lepers confined there had gradually slipped out during the interregnum following the withdrawal of the Spanish government. "In February [1902]," reported Governor Schroeder, "I received the painful report of the discovery of four lepers, living in the midst of a friendly community, where they had been harbored in well-intentioned but ill-advised concealment. A careful search was at once inaugurated with the result that several more were soon located, and others have come in since." He decided to segregate them, and, after examining a number of locations, established a colony on the shore of Tumon Bay, in the northwest part of the island. According to the governor's report, "it took some little time to select the spot, condemn and clear the land, erect the buildings and secure the personnel, but those to be restrained, so far as known, are now all domiciled in the Colony, 24 in number, and July 1st was the date of their enforced reclusion and the application of the laws and regulations drawn up in that connection. Everything possible has been and will be done to mitigate the unhappiness and distress of these unfortunate people."[21]

On September 22, 1902, Guam was shaken by a violent earthquake. Practically every coral masonry building on the island was damaged if not entirely destroyed. The bell tower and one wall of the cathedral in Agana were demolished "after having resisted all nature's assaults during two centuries and a quarter."[22] Property damage ran to many thousands of dollars.

Governor Schroeder was a man of many interests. He gave wholehearted attention to the island's problems at a time when such attention was sorely needed. He built schools, reformed the court system, encouraged agriculture, built roads and bridges, started a topographical survey of the island, and even forwarded to Washington a request for American citizenship made by a small group of Guamanians. Moreover, with regard to the island's name, he wrote:

> I have the honor to recommend that the appellation "Ladrone Islands" frequently appended to the single name Guam, be discarded, and that announcement of the fact be made to the Post Office Department and to the Public. The epithet once carelessly applied to the group in the 16th century was not adopted, and the social conditions which aroused Magellan's wrath having entirely disappeared many years ago, its occasional application now naturally causes some resentment. When this Island came into the possession of the United States, the official name of the group was and had been for over two centuries "Marianas," which has been continued by the German possessors of the other Islands. It is suggested that "Island of Guam" alone is a sufficiently defining name. . . .[23]

After having served on the island for about two and a half years, Seaton Schroeder, on February 6, 1903, was relieved of his duties as governor of Guam. He was succeeded by Commander W. E. Sewell, who held the governorship for less than one year. Sewell, who was sent home because of poor health, died soon after he reached the United States. His duties were taken over by Lieutenant Raymond Stone, who for three months served as acting governor until the arrival of Commander G. L. Dyer.

## G. L. Dyer

Commander Dyer became governor of Guam on May 16, 1904. He found that the economy of the island was primarily agricultural. Most of the people lived in the towns and villages and went daily to their ranches in the country. These ranches consisted of small clearings without fences in which they usually planted corn and sweet potatoes. A small shack of the most primitive kind, where the owner and his family lived for short intervals, was found on most ranches. The people were "poor, ignorant, very dirty in their habits, but gentle and very religious."[24] A few spoke Spanish. All, however, spoke their native Chamorro. Their methods of cultivation were primitive, their wants were few, and their lives were free from ambition or the desire for change or progress. They were

201

"like children, easily controlled and readily influenced by example, good or bad."[25]

Governor Dyer believed that "no American will be willing to live here permanently." Consequently, he felt it was necessary to train Guamanians to take over the jobs being performed by Americans attached to the naval station. Skills needed were those of carpenters, masons, mechanics, plumbers, printers, and clerks. Americans who had had experience with Guamanians were of the opinion that they could not be developed into skilled workmen, or even into laborers who could be relied upon to work steadily. In spite of such opinions, Governor Dyer ordered the establishment of an apprenticeship system that applied to all jobs held by Americans.

In 1904 two-thirds, or about 7,000, of the people of Guam lived in Agana. In the heart of the city was the great church of Dulce Nombre de María, built on the site donated by Chief Quipuha in 1669. It was in badly shattered condtion as the result of a severe earthquake in September 1902. Nevertheless, its great bell tolled every morning at four o'clock, calling the people to matins and to their daily tasks. Spread out from the church, on all sides, were the public buildings and houses of Agana. Sanitary conditions of the worst possible sort prevailed in the town.

Agana, situated on a low plain, had an elevation of from five feet near the beach to about eleven feet at the foot of the cliffs behind the town. A small sluggish stream, the Agana River, flowed through the town and emptied into the ocean just beyond. The river was used for bathing, as a laundry, and as an open sewer. The water, however, was not used for drinking purposes because it was brackish. This was due to the fact that, during unusually violent storms, the town and the river were flooded by the ocean.

For drinking water the people of Agana dug wells in the town, striking fresh water at depths of from three to six feet. Height of water in the wells did not vary much between the rainy and dry seasons. The water did not have its source in springs but rather was merely rain water which sank through the sand and coral into the general water table. The rain water, soaking through the soil, dissolved and carried along a great deal of lime. This made it very "hard" and thus little suited for washing clothes. It was more palatable, however, than the river water and therefore was used for drinking and cooking.

Because the site of the town was so flat and its soil so porous, it had no surface drainage. Waste material from men and animals, deposited all over the town, was moved about by the rain and eventually seeped into the water table below. It was this polluted water that was tapped by the wells. Needless to say, the people of Agana were constantly afflicted by numerous diseases. Lumbricoid worms were a special affliction. Nearly every inhabitant, from three months to eighty years of age, had such parasites in very large numbers. Consequently, the general health level was unusually low.

In his efforts to improve Agana's water supply, Governor Dyer considered many possibilities. He thought of collecting rain water from the roofs of houses and storing it in a large underground reservoir. However, since most houses had thatched roofs, the plan proved unworkable. Next he considered sinking artesian wells because he believed that "the millions of gallons of water falling from the clouds during the year are certainly not carried off by the few small rivers, and there are large areas where the water disappears into the earth with no evident outlet whatever."[26] This plan, too, for lack of funds, was doomed to failure. Finally he called for the building of an extensive reservoir system in the upper valley of the Pago River. Detailed plans for such a system had been made in 1902 by civil engineer L. M. Cox, USN. Estimated cost was approximately $50,000. The United States Congress, however, refused to appropriate funds for the project.

Early in 1904 the building which housed the Maria Schroeder Hospital was the only one on the island suitable for such a purpose. It was owned by the island government's Department of Public Works. Its main floor, in an unfinished condition, was used by the Navy Medical Department as naval sick quarters. The hospital had no operating room, no accommodations for a sick officer, and no quarters for the medical corpsmen. They slept in a corridor. By late 1905, however, the hospital had been greatly improved. Such improvements placed a serious strain on the island's treasury. The building was finished, and a large wing, containing a laboratory, operating room, and dentist's office, was added. Moreover, additional land behind the hospital was acquired for future expansion. Completion of the hospital marked one of the most important advances in the island's progress. The success of its methods and treatments tended gradually to overcome the suspicions of the islanders, who during illness were still inclined to resort to their own methods.

In 1904 the principal road on the island was that from Piti, the landing place at Apra Harbor, to Agana. It was built and maintained at federal expense and was in excellent condition. There was no suitable road, however, from Piti to Sumay and Agat. Thus two of the island's principal villages were cut off from quick and easy contact with the capital. Except for rough trails that were almost impassable, the villages of Umatac, Merizo, and Inarajan were completely isolated from Agana. With a cable station already located at Sumay and the possibility of a large naval base being built there, a road from Piti to Sumay became an absolute necessity. Another road from Piti to the beach on Cabras Island, where coal was stored, was also necessary. Since funds for building such roads were not available in the island treasury, Governor Dyer was compelled to appeal to the Navy Department for federal funds. Some money was made available but always in extremely limited amounts. With the limited funds, however, old roads were maintained and new ones, extending in directions which seemed to have the most traffic, were built. The road from Agana to Yigo, a mere trail, was improved and extended. That leading across the island in the direction of Pago was extended some distance beyond the village of Sinajana. When the governor secured more funds from local revenues, he ordered the construction of a road across Orote Peninsula from Sumay to Agat. Moreover, the road from Piti toward Sumay was extended to the Sasa River, where a substantial bridge was built. However, in spite of the extensive building program, a road between Piti and Sumay was not completed. Consequently, people from the southern villages who had business to transact in Agana or who wished to trade there, were required to travel to the capital by a long and difficult route. From Inarajan, Merizo, or Umatac they sailed in canoes to Agat. From Agat they walked or rode in bullcarts to Sumay. At Sumay they were transported across Apra Harbor to Piti. From there they rode or continued on foot to Agana. By following such a route they avoided a difficult and oftentimes dangerous canoe trip around Orote Point. Later, as funds became available, the entire road system was improved and greatly extended.

As late as 1904 no major improvements had been made at Apra Harbor. In that year, however, Governor Dyer recommended to the Navy Department that dredging operations be started. He suggested that the channel across the reef, from the inner harbor to Piti, and also the channel to Sumay be deepened to allow loaded ships to enter at low tide. Funds were appropriated for the work, but they quickly proved to be insufficient. Nevertheless, as commandant of the naval station, Dyer ordered the work to be continued. By mounting a boiler and steam winch on an old square lighter, makeshift dredging gear was constructed. With such gear, the channels were deepened and widened. For lack of funds, however, major dredging operations could not proceed. Large-scale dredging, in the opinion of both American and Japanese contractors called in to examine the harbor area, would cost approximately $50,000. To protect shipping, buoys were placed at the entrance to the harbor and along dangerous channels and reefs. Lighthouses were recommended for Orote Point and Ritidian, but they were never built.

Establishment of a station of the transpacific cable in Guam made it possible for the Philippine Meteorological Bureau to extend its area of operations to include the Marianas region. At the request of Father José Algue, S.J., director of the Philippine weather bureau, Governor Dyer agreed to send weather information to the Philippines at regular intervals. With such information telegraphed from Guam, Father Algue was able to give the coasts of China and Japan two or three days' advance notice of the approach of typhoons. On April 2, 1905, the cable from Yap was landed at Guam, making telegraphic communication between the two points complete. Later that same month, the cable was extended from Yap to Manado, in the Celebes. There it connected with the telegraphic system spreading throughout the Far East. By means of this extensive system it was possible to warn vast areas of the danger of approaching typhoons.

Guam's first weather station was set up on the station ship *Supply*, anchored in Apra Harbor. At regular intervals, weather data was sent to the manager of the cable station at Sumay. He then telegraphed the information to the Philippines. In emergencies, weathermen on the *Supply* sent their information to the cable station by means of flag signals, However, since flags had to be hoisted seven times for a four word message, this system was used only when absolutely necessary. In June 1905 a regular weather observatory was established at the cable station. Thus the station ship was relieved of a duty that could be better handled by an establishment on shore.

During Dyer's administration, and for a long time afterwards, most of Guam's trade was controlled by Japanese. The absence of a line of freight-carrying vessels between San Francisco, Guam, and Manila made it easy for the Japanese to move in. They established stores and regular schooner service and practically monopolized trade—all at high fixed prices. The tariff on imports, moreover, sent prices even higher. "Under these conditions," wrote Dyer, "living expenses for the natives are cruelly high. Under the present organization the customs duties are necessary for island revenues but they should be abolished on all articles coming from the United States and Manila, and for the present at least, the native merchants should be allowed the privilege of having a certain amount of freight brought out by the Naval Transports."[27]

During the period from the last years of Spanish rule to 1905, no mapor repairs had been made on public buildings in Agana. Consequently, most buildings were sadly in need of repair. This was especially true of the palace or Government House, at it was called by the Americans. Accordingly, during 1905, the lower story of Government House was completely renovated. Cement floors were laid, and useless storerooms were converted into necessary offices. A large sum of money was spent on the building, but more was needed to make it safe in typhoons and earthquakes. Also, according to Governor Dyer, "the remaining rubble walls of the upper story should be taken down and replaced by a strong wooden frame sheathed with boards. All the openings should be filled with typhoon shutters provided with iron bars. The building needs a new roof, guttered throughout, and a suitable cistern and distributing tank. A vast quantity of water now goes to waste."[28] In time, all of the recommended improvements were made.

One of the government's most pressing needs was a storehouse for supplies and equipment. Government stores were scattered about Agana in damp cellars and temporary warehouses. As a result, the annual loss was considerable. In July 1902, plans and estimates for a storehouse had been sent to the Navy Department. A year later, Congress appropriated the necessary funds. However, in spite of repeated requests by cable and letter, by 1905 materials had not been shipped to Guam and construction of the building had not yet commenced.

A suitable post-office building was another pressing need of the naval government in 1905. Since most of Guam's mail was military correspondence, the post office, during late 1904 or early 1905, was set up in a room in one of the government buildings in Agana. There, in cramped and unsuitable quarters, it continued to handle an ever-increasing volume of business. Mail from the United States to Guam left San Francisco in an Army transport on the last day of each month. It usually reached the island about the 21st or 22nd of the following month. Upon arrival at Guam, the transport deposited mail, supplies, and passengers. After picking up mail bound for the mainland, it proceeded to Manila, Japan, and thence, via Honolulu, back to the United States. On the occasions when the Navy transport *Solace* or other naval vessels interrupted their return trip from the Philippines by stopping at the island, it was possible to send mail directly from Guam to the mainland. Since Guam had no bank, the Post Office Department, in 1904, authorized the establishment of an international money-order system in the island's post office. This made trade with the Philippines, Japan, and China, from whence came most of the goods sold to the islanders, much easier.

Governor Dyer was constantly aware of the need for improving the delivery of supplies to the island. On several occasions he recommended to the Navy Department that two freight-carrying steamers be assigned to the route between San Francisco and Manila. Moreover, he asked that such steamers be ordered to make regular stops at Guam. In this way he hoped to be able to speed up delivery of supplies and equipment. "In some cases," he wrote, "important articles have not been received here for more than a year after the requisitions have been approved by the Bureau interested."[29]

Commander Dyer was governor of Guam for only about one and a half years. During that time, however, he wrought many changes. He established and defined the duties of the Department of Public Health and strengthened the compulsory education laws. In 1905 he replaced the island's Supreme Court with a court of appeals. At about the same time he disbanded the insular artillery and established a regular police force. Late in 1905 he was relieved by Lieutenant Luke McNamee, who became acting governor.

## E. J. DORN

Captain E. J. Dorn arrived at Guam on December 28, 1907, and assumed the duties of the office of governor. His term of office lasted almost three years. During that time he instituted numerous reforms affecting sanitation, taxes, commerce, agriculture, and education—which was his special interest. His first *Annual Report,* submitted to the Navy Department just about ten years after the acquisition of Guam by the United States, presented an interesting account of the first decade of American rule.

By 1908 most Guamanians had accepted American rule. Ten years of contacts with fairly large numbers of Americans had wrought important changes in their ideas and attitudes. Acceptance of the American regime was shown by the enthusiasm with which the people of all classes joined in the celebration of America's national holidays. Moreover, respect shown for the authorities and flag and openly expressed confidence in the justice of the American government demonstrated the loyalty of the people to the new regime. Governor Dorn was so pleased with the rapid advance of the Americanization process that he felt that "with the spread of the public school system and the sentiments thereby inculcated in the minds of the younger generation, the United States will have, in Guam, a most loyal and devoted possession."[30]

Acceptance of American rule was made easier by the fact that a great deal of effort had been devoted to improving health conditions on the island. Moreover, throughout most of the first decade of American control, crops had been normal and most of the people were well fed. Taxes were paid promptly and, in general, the people seemed to be law-abiding, contented, and happy. However, in spite of the generally good conditions that prevailed, the island was far from being self-supporting. Agriculture was the chief occupation. Most of the people who lived in the towns and villages went out each day to work on their small ranches. There each family produced just enough food to support itself. Farming methods were primitive and inefficient. When, on rare occasions, surpluses were produced, they could not be sold because means of transportation to markets were lacking. To make the situation even worse, many people gave up farming in order to take better-paying jobs on government projects in the Agana area. Because he believed the islanders should not become too dependent on the government, Governor Dorn took it upon himself to "urge upon the people the necessity of greater attention to the cultivation of the land in more modern and scientific methods, lest, failing the continuation of the liberal appropriations heretofore made by Congress, a time will come when the neglected ranches, having again become jungle, and the ready money now paid for Government labor being no longer available, an era of distress will surely follow."[31] This problem, clearly recognized by Governor Dorn, was a matter of real concern to all succeeding governors and continues even to the present.

The population of Guam on June 30, 1908, was 11,490. This

figure included military personnel and other off-islanders as well as Guamanians. The population distribution was as follows:[32]

### POPULATION OF GUAM, 1908

| | |
|---|---:|
| GUAMANIANS | 11,159 |
| NAVAL STATION PERSONNEL | |
| Officers and families | 23 |
| Naval employees and families | 26 |
| Navy enlisted men | 33 |
| Marines | 90 |
| OTHER OFF-ISLANDERS | |
| Americans | 14 |
| Chinese | 6 |
| Englishmen | 14 |
| Germans | 11 |
| Greeks | 1 |
| Hawaiians | 1 |
| Hollanders | 1 |
| Irishmen | 1 |
| Japanese | 101 |
| Puerto Ricans | 1 |
| Spaniards | 8 |
| TOTAL | 11,490 |

By 1908 the islanders had so adapted to the American health program that they regularly availed themselves of treatment at the dispensaries and clinics. Most, however, were still afraid to remain in the hospitals as patients. The Maria Schroeder and Susanna Hospitals in Agana met the needs of the entire island. Schoeder Hospital cared for the native male population over the age of twelve. At the same time it was the general hospital for the island's military forces. The Susanna Hospital cared for women as well as all children under twelve. It had been established in October 1905 through the efforts of Assistant Surgeon N. T. McLean, USN, and his wife. Funds for its support came from the island government and from an endownment of $10,000 from the Russell Sage Fund. A drugstore, operated by the hospital, also brought in a small amount of money. Fees, intended to cover only actual costs, were charged for treatment. No provisions were made for caring for the insane, who were fortunately few in number. If dangerous,

they were usually confined in the jail. In 1909, however, a small
house for dangerously insane persons was built near the gangosa
colony at Ypao.

Besides the hospitals in Agana, clinics and aid stations were
established in every village. Moreover, colonies for lepers and
gangosa patients were maintained by the island government. By
1908, patients at the Tumon leper colony numbered 88. This was
a considerable increase over the 24 first confined to the colony in
1902. Patients confined to the gangosa colony at Ypao numbered
99. During the latter part of 1908, after thorough examinations by
naval medical officer, 47 patients were released from both the
Tumon and Ypao colonies. They, however, were required to report
to the hospital at regular intervals for examinations and treatment.

During 1908 and 1909 the island's rice crop failed. To aid the
people, Governor Dorn imported rice from Manila. Before new
food shipments arrived, however, many people were compelled to
fall back on the fruit of the federico palm as a source of food.
During the next planting season, larger crops of rice and corn
were planted. Coconuts too were cultivated on a much larger scale.
In order to protect crops and remove the cause of almost endless
quarreling, the governor ordered the ranchers to build fences
around their land. He also issued an order prohibiting the sale of
land to aliens. His order was directed primarily at the growing
influence of the Japanese traders who "still control the major part
of the business of the Island, but their monopoly of certain goods,
notably rice, kerosene, and canned goods has been severely shaken
as a result of the permission granted to the governor by the
Department, to carry, under certain conditions, commercial freight
on the Supply and on colliers coming to Guam. In each case a
reasonable price was fixed for goods thus imported, which had
to be met by the traders, and inured to the benefit of the people."[33]

On July 1, 1909, American money replaced Mexican and
Philippine dollars as the medium of exchange. This made trade
and the keeping of accounts much easier for all concerned. During
that same year the governor began calling meetings of Guamanian
leaders to advise him on proposed changes in laws, especially tax

laws. Such meetings were the forerunners of the Guam Congress, which was established eight years later.

A threatened schism in the church occurred when a newly appointed apostolic prefect, a German Capuchin, arrived on the island. He tried to replace the native and Spanish priests with German priests of his own order. After much agitation and cabling to Rome, serious trouble was averted when the objectionable priests were ordered to the German Marianas. Governor Dorn was very much relieved at their departure because he felt that "the church and the religious customs of the people form so intimate and important a part of their whole life, both private and public, that any serious dissensions therein would be fraught with danger to the peace and content of the whole community."[34]

## ROBERT E. COONTZ

Commander Robert E. Coontz became Guam's eighth American governor on April 30, 1912. Fourteen years earlier, as an officer aboard the *Charleston*, he had participated in the capture of Guam by American forces. At the time of his appointment to the governorship, he was a member of the Naval Board of Inspection and Survey in Washington, D.C. Before reporting for duty in Guam, he talked with ex-governors Dorn and Potts and gathered all the information he could obtain regarding conditions on the island. He was accompanied to the island by Lieutenant Commander A. W. Hinds, who served as head of the Department of Public Works. Hinds later became acting governor.

Upon his arrival in Guam, Coontz relieved Governor G. R. Salisbury, who sailed aboard a collier for Manila. One of his first official acts was to call a mass meeting of the people of Agana. In firm and deliberate tones he told them that he intended to maintain peace and order while he was governor. The islanders, before his arrival, had long been engaged in petty quarrels that had resulted in factional bitterness and acts of violence. "In my first address to the people," he wrote, "I told them that I would be a hanging governor. If the person who committed a crime were insane it would be no harm to hang him, and if he were not crazy, the ends of justice would best be served, by hanging. There were no murders in the island while I was there. My successors were also hanging governors, and after the next murderer was executed in the center of the plaza at the capital of Guam, and the public was invited to witness the hanging, there was little trouble of this character."[35]

Governor Coontz soon found that the government of Guam operated in a peculiar manner. Although the island had been under American rule for almost fifteen years, Spanish law was still in full effect. The governor, however, could issue any orders or decrees he thought necessary, and these superseded the Spanish law. This, according to Coontz, "is an unusual mixture of authority, but it works well."[36] American governors before him had proclaimed 180 new laws. As a result, the islanders reported to Coontz that they were sometimes confused. Accordingly, he announced that during his term of office new laws would be extremely few. They were—he issued only three.

When Governor Coontz arrived at Guam, the island was experiencing one of the driest seasons in its history. Indeed, water was so scarce that the people of Agana lined up at the ice plant and were given a pint of water at a time. Fortunately rain began to fall a short time later, and soon there was an ample supply of water. To insure a permanent water supply, the governor asked for a federal appropriation of $11,000. His request was so ably presented that $25,000 was made available for the project. With the funds a reservoir was built on the cliff above Agana, and water from a spring was piped into it from a distance of several miles. Upon completion of the project, Agana received an increased supply of unpolluted water, and health conditions began to show an immediate improvement.

As governor, Coontz did a great deal of entertaining. He held one public reception each month, and twice a month he sponsored dances for military and native leaders at Dorn Hall. This hall was used first as a school and at night as a movie theater and dance hall. Movies, introduced to Guam during Coontz's administration, were a new and exciting experience for the Guamanians. One of the first

213

movies shown pictured a railroad train moving along at full speed. At one point it seemed to rush straight out at the audience. Its apparent approach was so frightening that a panic resulted. Adults rushed for the doors, and children fled through the windows. Fortunately, the windows were open and low and no injuries occurred. However, it was some time before many members of the audience could be persuaded to return.

In December 1912 Governor Coontz was ordered to transport all lepers in Guam to Culion Island, in the Philippines. Congress had appropriated funds for the care of lepers, and for the sake of economy it was decided that all Guamanian and Filipino lepers should be confined in one colony. Removal of the Guamanians was a heart-rending occasion. On their way from Tumon to the ship the lepers had to pass through Agana. Weeping relatives and friends gathered along the streets to watch them pass. To Governor Coontz the procession looked like a "big funeral. One leper was eighty-eight years old, and whether or not he survived the trip I never learned. The day before their departure two of them escaped. One was a blind man, and the other was a woman who could not walk. The blind man carried the woman on his back, and they went many miles into the fastness of the island, where we eventually recaptured them in a starving condition. We sent them to Culion on the next transport. For several years after that there were only two cases of leprosy on the island."[37]

About four months before the removal of the lepers, Guam was struck by a severe typhoon. A transport was in at the time, and several hundred of her passengers were being entertained by the governor in Agana. As the typhoon approached, the passengers were ordered to return to their ship. Before all could do so, however, the ship's captain removed his vessel from the harbor in order to ride out the storm. Sixty passengers were left on shore. After considerable difficulty and some danger they managed to return to Agana. There they were quartered in the palace and in the houses of other officers. When the typhoon passed they were put on a Navy lighter and taken out to the transport. Kenneth Coontz, son of the governor, boarded the vessel at the same time.

He was on his way to the United States to enter the Naval Academy. Although no lives were lost during the typhoon, crop damage was great, and recovery, even with government help, was slow.

Since Guam was a closed port, no foreign vessels were permitted to enter Apra Harbor without special permission. From time to time, however, ships in distress came in for help. During Coontz's administration, the *Comet,* a German ship, hove to off Orote Point. When an officer was sent out to the ship, her captain reported that he had engine trouble and wanted to enter the harbor to make repairs and send cables. Permission was granted. When the ship was anchored, the captain and one of his officers traveled to Agana by bullcart. There Governor Coontz received them in a friendly manner. By their words and actions, however, the governor suspected that they were German naval officers rather than civilians. While Mrs. Coontz talked to them, the governor slipped into his office and checked an old German naval register. Surely enough, both men were listed as naval officers. Upon returning to the reception room, Coontz demanded to know who they were. When they finally admitted that they were German officers, the governor ordered them to leave the harbor within twenty-four hours. The *Cormoran,* a German cruiser, entered the harbor shortly afterwards. Her captain too claimed to have engine trouble and was given time to make repairs. Later, during World War I, the *Cormoran* was sunk in Apra Harbor.

Shortly after Governor Coontz arrived at Guam he appointed Pancracio Palting to be chief justice of the court of appeals. Palting was a Filipino who had married into a Guamanian family. His salary was ninety-nine dollars a month. The governor felt that "if we paid anyone a salary of a hundred dollars a month he might become arrogant and proud."[38] Coontz found that Palting was loyal to the government and satisfactory to the people. "Old Francis Portusach and Pedro Duarte, whom I had known when we took Guam in 1898," wrote the governor, "were both still living there in 1912. Portusach was a planter and Duarte was postmaster and worked also as a surveyor in the island government."[39]

During the year and a half that Coontz served as governor, he brought about many changes and improvements in Guam. He devoted much of his time to public works, both insular and federal. On September 23, 1913, he was succeeded by Commander A. W. Hinds. Six years later, on October 24, 1919, Coontz was confirmed by the Senate of the United States as a four-star admiral and chief of naval operations.

## WILLIAM J. MAXWELL

Commander Hinds served as acting governor until March 28, 1914, when he was relieved by Captain William J. Maxwell. During the six months that he controlled the affairs of government, Hinds continued the public works projects that had been started by Governor Coontz. When Governor Maxwell arrived, he continued the same projects and started new ones of his own. He established the Bank of Guam and the Insular Patrol. Moreover, since World War I began in Europe about the time he became governor, he had to deal with new and difficult international problems.

The Insular Patrol, established in late 1914 or early 1915, was composed of enlisted men of the Marine Corps. Members were carefully selected by the commanding officer of marines and sworn in as peace officers by the governor. They were stationed in various districts of the island and supervised the construction and repair of roads, bridges, systems of water, and municipal buildings. Since, in reality, they were assistants to the village commissioners, they were responsible for enforcing regulations regarding health and sanitation. They also supervised the planting of trees and crops, stamping out of animal diseases, and marketing of products. In general, they were expected to live among the people, learn their needs, and help them in every way possible. By hard work and good example they sought to make the islanders good and useful members of their communities.

The Insular Patrol was under the direct control of the governor. His authority, however, was exercised through his aide. Beneath the governor's aide, in the scheme of organization, was a Marine Corps officer with the title of Head of Police Department and Chief of Insular Patrol. Other members of the organization, at the time of its establishment, were as follows: one sergeant as assistant chief of police, warden of the civil jail, and sergeant of the Insular Patrol; one corporal as a desk man, one private as chief forester, and seven to ten privates as insular patrolmen. Besides these there were a number of native policemen who served under a Marine Corps sergeant. The native police were used almost entirely to patrol the city of Agana. In the beginning they did not "make good policemen, as they are inclined to favor their friends and discriminate against their enemies."[40] With strict marine supervision, however, they soon became thorough and efficient policemen. Under succeeding governors the Insular Patrol was expanded and became one of the most valuable and respected agencies of the island government.

The Bank of Guam was established by Executive General Order No. 193, issued on December 14, 1915, by Governor Maxwell. As a "branch of the Treasury of the Naval Government of Guam," it was the first banking institution of any kind ever established on the island. It was housed in a small room on the first floor of the palace. In 1919 it was moved to a permanent building of its own. Its capital of $15,000 was provided by a transfer of gold from the island treasury. The bank opened for business on January 3, 1916. The statement of its financial condition on July 10, 1916, was as follows:[41]

Resources

| | |
|---|---|
| Cash on hand | $15,536.75 |
| On deposit in the United States | 15,421.39 |
| Cash in transit to meet exchange | 8,000.00 |
| Loans and discounts | 2,983.08 |
| | $41,941.22 |

Liabilities

| | |
|---|---|
| Capital | $15,000.00 |
| Deposits | 25,503.86 |
| Bills payable | 1.95 |
| Undivided surplus | 620.39 |
| Reserve and operating fund | 8,815.02 |
| | $41,941.22 |

Since it filled a real need in the business life of the island, the bank was an immediate success. During its first year of operation it began to make substantial loans to businessmen. Such loans were for goods and supplies purchased during commercial trips of the station ship *Supply*. The money was loaned on good security, and the bank had a lien on the goods. Loans were handled in such a manner that they soon proved to be a real convenience to merchants as well as a profit to the bank. Returns during the first year for interest depositors, who shared in the profits, averaged 8.8 per cent. Banking relations were quickly established with Manila, Hongkong, Shanghai, Yokohama, Sydney, Honolulu, and San Francisco. Funds could be exchanged by cable with any of these points. By June 1917 the bank had assets amounting to $109,216.98.

During the first five years of operation, the bank's volume of business grew steadily. By 1920 the bank required "more time and attention than can properly be given to it by the Disbursing Officer of the Naval Station."[42] As a result the governor asked the Navy Department to send out a special officer to serve as the bank's cashier. In the same year the guaranteed rate of interest on class B deposits was reduced from 7.2 to 5 per cent. As of July 1, 1921, the rate of interest charged on loans was reduced from 12 to 10 per cent.

The Bank of Guam was managed by a board of directors composed as follows: governor of Guam, chairman; cashier and comptroller, appointed by the governor; auditor of Guam; treasurer of Guam; one representative of the depositors; and the teller of the bank, who also served as recorder.[43] Board meetings were held once each month for the purpose of discussing and outlining general policies.

By 1922 the Guamanian people had become so accustomed to using the bank that its depositors numbered 636. Of this number, 150 were children. Children were encouraged to deposit nickels and dimes in order to become familiar with the bank and to acquire habits of saving and thrift. Efforts to teach native merchants the value of bank credit were so successful that, in 1922, about 80 per cent of the import and export business of the island was financed by the bank. Such business amounted to about $600,000.

By 1923, six years after its opening, the bank's assets had increased from $15,000 to $368,882.36. Because of its influence over all phases of island life, the Bank of Guam, in a few short years, had become "the most valuable institution of the Island Government."[44]

SUMMARY: The years 1898 and 1914 are important milestones in the history of Guam. The former is important because, during that year, the Spanish-American War occurred. The importance of the year 1914 lies in the fact that, in that year, World War I began in Europe. Both events had far-reaching effects on the lives of the Guamanian people.

As a result of the Spanish-American War, Guam became an American possession. The actual capture of Guam by the forces under the command of Captain Glass was neither a violent nor an overly dramatic event. It was important, primarily, because it marked the transference of political control over Guam from an old and declining nation of the Old World to a young and emerging nation of the New World. This, needless to say, completely changed the course of Guamanian history.

For approximately six months after the American capture of Guam, the island was in a state of near civil war. This condition was a result of the removal of the Spanish officials, which left the island without a responsible government and gave rise, on the part of opposing factions, to claims to the governorship. The arrival of Captain Leary, as the first American governor, put an end to the conflict.

Governor Leary's administration established the pattern of government that was to prevail in Guam for almost a half century. The government was one in which specific functions were assigned to various departments created by the governor. Each department was headed by a military man who was directly responsible to the governor. The governor, in turn, was resposible to the Secretary of Navy. However, because of limited communication facilities and the great distance from the mainland, government in Guam was truly a matter of one-man rule. Despite that fact, the naval governors introduced many needed changes and improvements in Guam.

219

This was especially true in the fields of agriculture, public health and sanitation, education, finance and taxation, land management, and public works. By 1914, when World War I began in Europe, Guam was an American possession enjoying many benefits made possible by a firmly established naval government.

The next chapter will deal with happenings and events in Guam during the period between World War I and World War II.

## NOTES

1.   Samuel Flagg Bemis, *A Diplomatic History of the United States* (3rd edition, Henry Holt and Co., New York, 1950), p. 443.

2.   Robert E. Coontz, *From the Mississippi to the Sea* (Dorrance and Co., Philadelphia, 1930), p. 201.

3.   *Ibid.*, pp. 204–5.

4.   Cox, *op. cit.*, p. 77.

5.   *Ibid.*, p. 78.

6.   *Ibid.*, pp. 77–78.

7.   *Ibid.*, p. 78.

8.   *Ibid.*, p. 79.

9.   Henry P. Beers, *American Naval Occupation and Government of Guam, 1898–1902* (Administrative Reference Service Report No. 6, Office of Records Administration, Navy Department, Washington, 1914), p. 14.

10.   Governor of Guam, *Annual Report, 1914* ("Annual Reports of the Governors of Guam, 1901–1941," file microcopies of reports in the National Archives, The National Archives of the United States, Washington, 1950), p. 2.

11.   Governor of Guam, *Annual Report, 1923*, p. 4.

12.   Beers, *op. cit.*, pp. 25–26.

13.   *Ibid.*, p. 29.

14.   Seaton Schroeder, *A Half Century of Naval Service* (D. Appleton and Co., New York, 1922), pp. 255–56.

15.   *Ibid.*, p. 258.

16.   *Ibid.*, p. 242.

17.   Governor of Guam, *Annual Report, 1901*, p. 4.

18.   *Ibid.*, p. 10.

19.   *Ibid.*, p. 265–4.

20.   *Ibid.*, p. 265–4.

21.   *Ibid.*, p. 265–6.

22.   Schroeder, *op. cit.*, p. 266.

23. Governor of Guam, *Annual Report, 1901*, p. 265–13–14.
24. Governor of Guam, *Annual Report, 1904*, p. 2.
25. *Ibid.*, p. 2.
26. Governor of Guam, *Annual Report, 1905*, p. 9.
27. *Ibid.*, p. 47.
28. *Ibid.*, p. 49.
29. *Ibid.*, p. 57.
30. Governor of Guam, *Annual Report, 1908*, p. 1.
31. *Ibid.*, p. 2.
32. *Ibid.*, pp. 2–3.
33. Governor of Guam, *Annual Report, 1909*, p. 2.
34. *Ibid.*, p. 4.
35. Coontz, *op. cit.*, pp. 334–35.
36. *Ibid.*, p. 333.
37. *Ibid.*, pp. 345–46.
38. *Ibid.*, p. 357.
39. *Ibid.*, p. 357.
40. Governor of Guam, *Annual Report, 1916*, p. 11.
41. *Ibid.*, pp. 20–21.
42. Governor of Guam, *Annual Report, 1921*, p. 36.
43. Governor of Guam, *Annual Report, 1923*, p. 39.
44. *Ibid.*, p. 40.

## CHAPTER SEVEN

# THE PERIOD BETWEEN TWO WORLD WARS

THE ASSASSINATION of Austrian Archduke Francis Ferdinand at Serajevo, June 28, 1914, was the spark that started a world-wide conflict called the First World War (1914–18). Within a relatively short time most of the nations of Europe were engaged in a bitter struggle. The great majority of Americans wanted no part of the war, but their sympathies in general lay on the side of Great Britain, France, and the other Allies and against Germany, Austria, and other nations of the Central Powers. Although it tried desperately to stay out of the war, the United States was eventually drawn in on the side of the Allies.

## GUAM IN THE FIRST WORLD WAR

Shortly after the war started, President Woodrow Wilson issued a proclamation of neutrality for the United States. When Governor Maxwell was informed of the President's action, he in turn, on August 11, 1914, issued a proclamation of neutrality for Guam. Six days later the American steamer *Rio Pasig* entered Apra Harbor. It had a cargo of coal for one of the warring nations and carried four passengers whose names were not listed on the ship's papers. After a thorough inspection the governor ordered the ship to be held in port for having violated the neutrality proclamations. In addition, a censorship was placed on the cable station to prevent contacts between the ship's crew and the outside world. Later the vessel was permitted to leave, and the censorship was lifted.

On August 25, 1914, Governor Maxwell was notified by cable that Japan had entered the war on the side of the Allies. Since Germany owned all of the northern Marianas, Japan's entry into the war brought the area of conflict close to Guam. Almost immediately Japanese and German warships began playing hide-and-seek among the islands. In October 1914 a small boat from the German cruiser *Cormoran* entered Apra Harbor. On board were three officers of the Imperial German Navy and four New Guinea natives. They were ordered to leave within twenty-four hours. Failing to do so, the boat and its crew were interned. About five days later the Japanese battleship *Katori* cruised around the island at from three to eight miles off shore. She seemed to be searching for German ships that might be hiding in Guamanian ports. She showed her flag and radioed her call letters only when she approached the three-mile limit. Failing to find what she was looking for, she finally sailed away. A few days later, on November 8, the Japanese merchant ship *Nippon-maru* steamed into the harbor. She did so in spite of the fact that she had been met outside and warned off by a boarding officer. When her captain was unable to give satisfactory reasons for entering the harbor, he was ordered to leave at once, which he did.

On December 14, 1914, a ship that was to cause serious trouble in Guam arrived at the island. She was the German cruiser *Cormoran*. It was from this same ship that three officers had been interned two months earlier. After dropping anchor, the *Cormoran's* captain informed Governor Maxwell that his ship was in need of coal and provisions. A quick check of the ship proved that such was the case. However, since the *Cormoran* was a warship of a warring nation, her presence in the harbor violated the neutrality of the United States. Accordingly, the governor ordered her to leave within twenty-four hours. Since she was truly short of coal and provisions, she was unable to leave within the allotted time. As a result, the ship and her officers and crew were interned. The crew of the *Cormoran* consisted of 33 officers and 340 enlisted men. They greatly outnumbered the marines who were responsible for the defense of the island. Consequently, they were a real threat to the island's security. Moreover, since food supplies were limited, they merely aggravated an already bad situation.

Two days after the *Cormoran* was interned, the Japanese cruiser *Iwate*, flying the flag of Vice Admiral Matsumura, stopped off the harbor entrance, outside the three-mile limit. The Japanese were curious about the status of the *Cormoran*. They apparently were following her in order to engage her in battle. Moreover, they wished to learn whether or not the Americans were violating their own proclamations of neutrality by giving aid and protection to an enemy warship. Before a boat from the *Iwate* could reach shore, it was met outside the harbor by a boarding party sent by Governor Maxwell. There the Japanese were told that the *Cormoran* had been interned and that that would would be her status until the end of the war. Having gained such information, the *Iwate* continued on her way.

While the *Cormoran* was tied up in Apra Harbor, her officers and crew were permitted to spend much of their time on shore. Over a period of many months, the German government tried to secure their release. American authorities insisted that they had been interned in accordance with international law and thus were able to block the German moves. By May 1916, however, it appeared that the *Cormoran* had not been interned in accordance with the full requirements of international law. Accordingly, new articles of internment were drawn up between naval authorities in Guam and the commanding officer of the *Cormoran*. The articles were approved by the Navy Department, and the *Cormoran's* crew continued to be "guests" of the naval government of Guam.

As fighting between the Allies and the Central Powers became increasingly bitter, the United States found it almost impossible to remain neutral. The American people were not at all neutral in their feelings and sympathies. By late 1916 a majority of Americans were demanding that the United States enter the war on the side of England, France, and the other Allies. President Wilson, however, resisted all efforts to push the nation into war. Announcement of a campaign of "unrestricted submarine warfare" on January 31, 1917, forced President Wilson to break off diplomatic relations with Germany. As soon as news of the break reached Guam, all of the *Cormoran's* crew members were required to remain on board their ship. Since it looked as though the United States and Germany might soon be at war, it "did not seem desirable that they should be at large on the Island, as supervision would not have been possible."[1]

After several American ships had been sunk without warning by German U-boats, President Wilson appeared before Congress on April 2, 1917, and asked for a declaration of war. Four days later the Senate and the House of Representatives completed action on a war resolution, and the United States and Germany were at war.

Meanwhile, on May 30, 1916, Captain Roy C. Smith had become governor of Guam. When war was declared, he was immediately notified by cable. Accordingly, in April 1917 he demanded the surrender of the *Cormoran* and her crew. Until this time the crew members had been internees; now they were to become prisoners of war. The *Cormoran's* commanding officer resisted the governor's demand. He agreed to surrender the crew but not the ship. His proposal was refused by the governor. Just after the American boarding party left the ship, the vessel was shaken by a violent explosion. The Germans had decided to send their ship to the bottom rather than let it fall into American hands. Crew members jumped overboard and were rescued by station craft and boats from the *Supply*. Two warrant officers and five enlisted men were drowned. Two others were missing. The bodies that were recovered were buried in the naval cemetery with military honors.

The *Cormoran* sank in 120 feet of water about half a mile from the nearest land. Sometime later it was learned that she was blown up by a charge of high explosives in one of her coal bunkers. The charge had been on board since the arrival of the ship. The captured Germans were confined on shore as prisoners of war. Officers and their servants were imprisoned at Camp Barnett while the enlisted men were held at Asan. The prison camps contained messing, lighting, and toilet arrangements within double barbed wire stockades. The camps were quickly erected by the Public Works Department.

In view of the fact that the German prisoners placed a heavy strain on the island's food supplies, it was decided to send them to the United States. Accordingly, on April 30, 1917, the officers and crew of the *Cormoran* were transferred to the United States aboard the army transport *Thomas*. Four Chinese laundrymen, who were among the prisoners, were released. Twenty-eight New Guinea natives were permitted to remain on the island, since it was feared that they might suffer ill effects if they were sent out of the tropics. They were employed in various ways by the island government and seemed contented and happy.

After removal of the German prisoners of war, the people and the government of Guam prepared to do whatever they could to assist the national war effort. Notice of the first Liberty Loan reached Guam on June 12, 1917. Exactly three days later the governor cabled Washington that naval personnel and civilians on the island had subscribed for bonds to the amount of $70,000. The largest subscriptions came from personnel of the naval station and the USS *Supply*. However, civilians too purchased their share of bonds. In view of the small amount of money on the island, funds collected through the sale of Liberty bonds represented a tremendous effort on the part of the people of Guam. Even more important, however, was the fact that, for the first time, the islanders were given an opportunity to demonstrate their loyalty to the United States. From the beginning to the end of the war, the people of Guam demonstrated that they were beyond all doubt patriotic and loyal Americans.

Although most of the fighting during World War I occurred in Europe, German possession of the northern Marianas made an attack on Guam a distinct possibility. To withstand such an attack, the island could muster a defensive force composed of about 400 marines, 64 sailors, 40 Insular Force natives, and about 900 members of the Guam Militia. Several gun batteries were located on Orote Point and in the harbor area. Because of extremely limited supplies of guns and ammunition, however, the island's defenders, in all probability, could not have resisted a determined German attack. Fortunately for Guam, such an attack never came.

With the beginning of the war, most Guamanian men and boys began to experience some form of military training. As of February 5, 1917, all boys from twelve to sixteen (the limit of school age for boys was extended from twelve to sixteen for this purpose) were required to attend drill for an hour every afternoon except Saturday and Sunday. Later, Wednesday afternoon was omitted. The drill was under the general supervision of the inspector-instructor of military training and was conducted by marines of the Insular Patrol. Training consisted of setting-up exercises and squad and company close-order marching without arms. Within three months, 645 boys were under instruction in Agana and 499 in the rural districts, making a total of 1,144. Besides these, there was in Agana a company of about 100 young men called the Guam Cadets who were given special training in the use of the rifle under marine supervision. Members of the Insular Force, about 40 in number, were young Guamanians who were in the United States government service as Navy personnel. They received instructions in the use of firearms as part of their regular training.

On March 15, 1917, universal military training went into effect on the island, and the Guam Militia was organized. The active militia consisted of all males between sixteen and twenty-three years of age. From the active militia, members passed into a militia reserve in which they served until the age of forty. The militia was governed by the Military Board, which consisted of the commanding officer of marines, the military aide, and an inspector-instructor. The military aide was the chief of the Insular Patrol, and the inspector-instructor was a Marine Corps sergeant. All militia instructors were marines of the Insular Patrol. The number of active militia enrolled on June 30, 1917, was 920.

Members of the militia were organized into companies and, in the beginning, were required to drill for two hours each week. In Agana, officers and noncommissioned officers were drawn from the Guam Cadets. Most of the militiamen trained without arms. The cadets, however, were allowed to drill with reserve rifles, of which there were about 300. Since the men furnished their own khaki uniforms, the organization was of little expense to the government.

228

By June 1917 the governor was able to report to the Navy Department that "the movement will develop in time 2,000 fully drilled and efficient infantry. They are ready and willing to go where ordered."[2] During the war, however, Guamanian militamen were not called upon to serve outside Guam.

## THE GUAM CONGRESS

On February 3, 1917, Governor Roy C. Smith convened the First Guam Congress. The congress was an advisory council consisting of thirty-four island leaders, including village commissioners, deputy commissioners, and other prominent men of the various districts. All were appointed by the governor, held office at his pleasure, and served without pay. Besides Guamanians, the congress included certain naval and Marine Corps officers of the island government who attended the meetings as representatives of the governor. Governor Smith informed the delegates that it was their duty to "consider and recommended measures for the improvement of the Island and the welfare of its inhabitants."[3] Meetings were held on the first Saturday of each month and oftener if necessary. Regarding this early congress, Commander Roy E. James, USNR, wrote:

> The First Guam Congress was not a legislative body. It could initiate discussion on any matter raised by the members, and if so minded, could make recommendations to the governor but the actual legislation was prepared and promulgated by the governor. The Congress functioned as a sort of advisory council on such matters as the governor might care to submit to it for consideration. It had no authority whatever with respect to taxation or the appropriation and expenditure of local tax and customs receipts. It was, indeed, nothing more than a gathering of local personages, selected and appointed by the governor, who met on the first Saturday of each month to discuss matters of local interest. . . .[4]

The governor, in the beginning at least, seemed to be well pleased with the work of the congress. About four months after its establishment he reported that "the idea has been well received by the inhabitants. They meet and discuss with interest all matters affecting the Island and have made some valuable recommendations. It makes them feel that they are taking a part in their own government and stimulates interest in public affairs. It promises to be of value in promoting discussion and spreading knowledge of the needs of the Island and awakening interest in its improvement."[5]

Through discussions with members of the congress, the governor was able to learn the needs and wishes of the people. In general, such discussions dealt with minor village and district problems. In June 1925, however, a matter of the utmost importance was discussed by the congress. At that time eleven members of the United States House of Representatives arrived on the USS *Chaumont*. With the approval of Governor H. B. Price, they were invited to attend a session of the Guam Congress. While there they were addressed by three Guamanian leaders. The native leaders asked for American citizenship for the people of Guam. They expressed the thanks of the people for the benefits that had come to them under American rule, and they "told our visiting Congressmen of the loyalty, fidelity, and good character of their brother Chamorros. They voiced in effective way the great desire and hope of these people for the rights of American citizenship."[6] Although the visiting congressmen listened with great attention and were favorably impressed, American citizenship was denied to the Guamanian people for another twenty-five years.

From 1925 to 1930 the Guam Congress limited its discussions to village problems. In general, it tended to act only on matters pleasing to the governor. Its powers were so limited that during the late 1920's some governors disregarded it entirely. By 1930, when the congress had completely lost its value, Governor Willis W. Bradley decided to dissolve it and establish a new congress.

## MILITARY AVIATION

The first marine aviators ever to serve west of San Francisco were ten pilots and ninety enlisted men of Flight L, 4th Squadron, who arrived in Guam on March 17, 1921.[7] Upon arrival they were quartered at a new air station that was being built on Orote Peninsula. This station, with all its buildings and facilities, was constructed during 1921–22. Both marines and Guamanians were employed on the project up to December 31, 1921. At that time, however, funds ran short, and native labor was dispensed with. Aviation activities were reduced to a minimum, and every available marine was put to work in order to complete the new base.

Construction of the air station resulted in real hardship to a number of Guamanians. In his report for 1922, Governor Ivan C. Wettengel noted that "the Federal Government does not own one foot of the ground on which the Air Station is built. Some of the property is leased by the Marine Corps and part of it by Yards and Docks. When aviation took over the property, six-month leases were effected and the natives, who owned most of the property, vacated immediately, leaving in many cases their houses. It was believed that outright purchases would be made in a short time, but to date this has not been accomplished. The result has been an injustice and hardship to owners who left their homes and have no money to acquire others."[8]

In 1926, personnel of the air station were placed under the command of the commanding officer, marine barracks. Thus they lost the independent status which they had enjoyed since their arrival on the island. During that same year a new administration building was constructed. It housed the squadron offices, sick bay, dental office, aerological office and guardhouse, all under one roof. Built by the marines themselves, it added greatly to the comfort and efficiency of the command.

Early in 1927 a Chinese civil war threatened the lives of foreigners living in Shanghai, Peking, and other Chinese cities. To protect American lives, four regiments of marines were sent from the United States to China. As aviation support for the troops, a headquarters detachment and a fighter squadron were dispatched from San Diego. At the same time, the air squadron at Guam was ordered to China. Accordingly, on April 11, 1927, four officers and ninety-eight enlisted men of the Guam squadron departed from the island. They sailed aboard the USS *Gold Star*. Both the Guam and stateside squadrons reached Shanghai on May 3. They soon learned, however, that arrangements had not been made with the Chinese government for the use of a landing field. As a result, they had to withdraw to the American naval station at Olongapo, Philippine Islands. During the next year and a half they patrolled coastal sections of the Chinese mainland, keeping an eye on the war.

Upon departure of the aviation squadron from Guam, only a handful of men remained behind to staff the air station. They continued to make weather observations and send required reports to Washington. Until the latter part of 1928, however, their principal duty consisted of the upkeep of the station and equipment. On September 23, 1928, Patrol Squadron 3-M was assigned to the island, and the station was revived once more. For the next two years, personnel of the station consisted of about eighty-five enlisted men and from four to six officers. On February 24, 1931, after ten years on the island, the marine aviators were withdrawn, and the station was closed. They returned about thirteen years later, during World War II.

## WILLIS W. BRADLEY

On June 11, 1929, Commander Willis W. Bradley, Jr., assumed office as governor of Guam and commandant of the naval station. His term of office began at about the same time that the United States, as well as the rest of the world, entered upon a period of severe economic depression. In spite of the evil effects of the Great Depression, Governor Bradley's term of office proved to be a truly outstanding one.

From the beginning of American rule, little attention had been paid to the civil rights of the Guamanian people. In 1930, however, Bradley, a democratic-minded governor, took steps to remedy the situation. One of the most urgent problems confronting him was that of determining who might or might not be regarded as citizens of Guam. Many rights and privileges depended upon such determination. For example, bona fide citizens of Guam could enter, live in, and travel within the United States. They could hold title to land in Guam, could leave the island for an extended stay, and could return when they wished to do so. Aliens, on the other hand, were denied such privileges. In view of the pressing need for determining Guam citizenship, Governor Bradley, on March 26, 1930, issued the following proclamation:

> Know ye, that by virtue of the power and authority vested in me as Governor of Guam, I declare the following persons to be citizens of Guam and to be thereby entitled to all the rights and privileges inherent to citizens of Guam and to all rights, privileges, and protection which are extended to citizens of Guam by the Government of the United States of America; provided, that such persons have not by act or deed, since the date of the occurrence which conferred citizenship upon them, pledged allegiance to any foreign prince or power or renounced allegiance to the Government of Guam:
>
> Every person born or naturalized in Guam and subject to the jurisdiction thereof.
>
> Every person residing in Guam on 1 February, 1899, who at that time owed no allegiance to any foreign prince or power other than to the Crown of Spain, and that solely by virtue of allegiance to the Government of Guam.
>
> Every woman who, prior to 22 September 1922, married a citizen of Guam; provided, that such woman might, at the time of her marriage to said citizen of Guam, have been lawfully naturalized in the United States of America.
>
> Every child heretofore born or hereafter born out of the limits and jurisdiction of the Island of Guam, whose father was or may be a citizen of Guam at the time of such birth; provided, that the rights of citizenship shall not descend to a child whose father never resided in Guam.
>
> Every child under the age of twenty-one years at the time of the issue of a certificate of naturalization by the Government of Guam to the father of said child; provided, that the said child takes up actual residence in Guam within a period of two years from the date of naturalization of the father.
>
> In witness whereof, I have hereto set my hand and caused the seal of Guam to be affixed.
>
> Done at the city of Agana this twenty-sixth day of March, in the year of our Lord one thousand nine hundred and thirty, and of the Independence of the United States the one hundred fifty-fourth.[9]

As a result of Bradley's proclamation, the island's courts began at once to bring order out of the citizenship chaos then existing. About ten days after the issuance of his citizenship proclamation, Governor Bradley issued the following order, which officially established the Great Seal of Guam: "Effective this date [April 4,

1930] the official seal of the Naval Government of Guam will be that shown on the plan of the Guam flag approved July 4, 1917, by Governor Roy C. Smith, and now filed in the office of the Auditor-Registar. . . ."[10]

Because of his desire to define and protect the civil rights of the Guamanian people, Governor Bradley decided to proclaim a bill of rights for Guam. "An extended acquaintance with Guam and with its problems [he wrote] leads me to believe that the United States should grant a bill of rights to this island people and that such an act would be justified by the high principles of American government. The residents of Guam are deserving of some basic law or grant not subject to change at the will of the governor, something which will give them the fundamental rights of citizenship now enjoyed by all Americans."[11]

Accordingly, on December 24, 1930, Bradley proclaimed a bill of rights for Guam. The document was modeled after the first ten amendments to the United States Constitution. Unfortunately this bill of rights was not approved by higher authorities in Washington. As a result, it never went into effect. When law codes of the island were revised in 1933, however, many provisions of the bill of rights were incorporated into them.

Governor Bradley was a man of varied interests. His interest in the island's public buildings led him to insist that all such buildings, new or remodeled, should be permanent structures. During his administration one of Guam's finest public buildings was constructed. It was the Coontz Building, named in honor of Robert E. Coontz, the island's eighth American governor. The Coontz Building was a modern two-story reinforced concrete structure. Its interior was finished almost entirely in ifil wood. When construction was commenced, it was expected that the building would house the Bank of Guam and the office of the auditor-registrar on the first floor. The second floor was to be used for living quarters for the comptroller and cashier of the bank. However, because of the poor condition of the quarters which housed the island's courts, Bradley ordered changes that converted the second story into permanent quarters for the judiciary. The building was completed in November 1929, at a cost of nearly $30,000. Completion of the Coontz Building provided the government with excellent quarters for public offices, the Bank of Guam, and the island's courts.

Believing that the names of individuals prominent in the history of Guam should be commemorated, Bradley established a policy of naming public buildings and public places in their honor. In keeping with this policy, most of Guam's schools and other public buildings were named in honor of governors and religious leaders who were prominent in the island's history.

Governor Bradley believed that the government should not compete with local business interests. Government, he felt, should lend a hand only with those projects that were beyond the capacity of private firms on the island. "The government," he wrote, "is seeking to withdraw from all such work and is encouraging the establishment of private enterprise whenever possible."[12]

In 1930 nearly all of the 61 miles of island government roads in service were maintained by prisoners. Paid labor was used only on major road-building jobs. Such labor was performed at a total average cost of $233.00 per mile for the year. Since this system was found to be unsatisfactory, contracts for maintaining most of the roads were awarded to various private firms.

Telephone and electric light services were government monopolies. However, a limited number of private individuals and firms were furnished light and telephone service. Moreover, a certain amount of private enterprise prevailed even in these monopolies. Maintenance of the telephone lines between Agat, Umatac, Merizo, and Inarajan was awarded to private contractors. Poles were erected and lines were repaired by such contractors. The telephone system, according to Bradley, incurred "a rather heavy deficit each year owing to the very limited number of phones on rural lines. . . .The present rural lines are of exceedingly poor construction: ground return, iron wires, and poles of all descriptions."[13]

Private enterprise made slight gains in the towns of Sumay and Agat. There the functions of garbage collection and street cleaning were awarded under contract to private individuals. In the city of Agana, however, garbage was collected by prisoners under police supervision.

The island market, a government-owned establishment, was operated by Mr. Pascual Artero. He was granted a three-year lease by the island government. At the end of fiscal year 1930, however, the government "planned to lease only the slaughtering space for another term of three years, since the contractor has now provided himself with a modern meat market."[14]

While Bradley did many things for Guam, his name is associated more popularly with the Guam Congress than with any other of his varied projects. During the '20's the congress was ignored many times, and by 1930, when it had completely lost its value, Governor Bradley decided to dissolve it and established a new congress. In order to select members for the Second Guam Congress, a general election, the first in Guam's history, was held on March 7, 1931. Since this was an entirely new experience for the islanders, they were given a great deal of preliminary instruction on elections and voting procedures. The election was supervised by the Executive Department and was "carried on without disorder or confusion of any kind. The people of the Island took a great interest in all of the matters pertaining to this first registration and election and demonstrated that they may be depended upon to investigate quite thoroughly the qualifications of candidates and to vote in accordance with their personal convictions."[15]

The Second Guam Congress consisted of two houses: a House of Council with sixteen members, and a House of Assembly with twenty-seven members. In a general way, the House of Council corresponded to the Senate of the United States and the House of Assembly to the House of Representatives. Councilmen held office for four years while assemblymen were elected for two-year terms. The newly elected congress met for the first time in Agana on April 4, 1931. Like the congress before it, the Second Guam Congress had no legislative powers. Although its members were the elected representatives of the people, it was merely an advisory body. According to Governor E. S. Root, it was expected that the congress would "take upon itself most of the burdens of strictly local affairs, legislating upon them, subject to the approval of the Governor, and that in the execution of these functions it will offer an opportunity for its members to gain experience in political economy and parliamentary procedure. These things are most essential if the political development of the Island is to continue and if the people are to be ready to partake actively in the affairs of their own government when the United States sees fit to delegate such responsibility to them."[16]

In order to lend dignity to the new congress, Governor Bradley ordered the construction of two small but substantial buildings to house the body. The buildings, called the Council Hall and the Assembly Hall, were built at Bradley Park. This park, which included an athletic field, covered about 12 acres and was situated on the Agana-Piti highway, just inside the Agana city limits in Anigua. Funds for construction of the buildings were expected to be raised through the sale of stamped paper of the Guam Guard Mail.*

During the first year after its establishment, the Second Guam Congress passed a number of resolutions and sent them to the governor. A few were adopted; most, however, were rejected. Since the congressmen had had little experience in the affairs of government, their ideas and methods oftentimes failed to secure the governor's approval. In an attempt to improve the situation, a system of conferences was inaugurated. Once a month an executive committee of the congress met with the governor. The committee, composed of six members, three from each house, presented the recommendations of the congress to the governor and discussed them with him. Through such conferences "the Governor was able to both advise and educate them as to political matters."[17]

The Second Guam Congress ceased functioning at the time of the Japanese invasion of Guam in 1941. Throughout the occupation and for about two years after the recapture of the island from the Japanese, the congress was unable to meet. It was not until May 1, 1946, that it was able to resume its sessions.

* The Guam Guard Mail was a local mail service established by Governor Bradley on April 8, 1930. It served the outlying districts and was not in any way connected with the United States Post Office Department.

On July 13, 1946, by order of the naval governor of Guam, an election was held for the purpose of selecting members of a new congress. The new congress, consisting of thirteen members of the House of Council, one from each municipality, and thirty-three members of the House of Assembly, one for each one thousand inhabitants of the island, was elected from the various districts. All citizens of the island, male and female, twenty-one years of age and over, were permitted to vote. The new congress, like those before it, could not legislate. It was merely an advisory body, and the governor was free to accept or reject its advice and recommendations. It was not until the passage of the Organic Act in 1950 that the Guam Congress became truly the lawmaking body of Guam.

During his two-year term of office, Governor Bradley proclaimed laws that had far-reaching effects on the lives of the Guamanian people. In the field of civil rights, especially, his acts were of lasting importance. He defined Guamanian citizenship and provided for the naturalization of aliens. Moreover, he proclaimed a bill of rights, reorganized the Guam Congress, and ordered the first general elections ever held in the island's history. One of Guam's ablest naval administrators, he was relieved of his duties on May 15, 1931, by Captain Edmund S. Root.

## GEORGE A. ALEXANDER

Captain Edmund S. Root served as governor of Guam until June 21, 1933. On that date he was relieved by Captain George A. Alexander. Alexander, like Governors Bradley and Root before him, administered the affairs of Guam at a time when the rest of the world was caught in one of the worst economic depressions in recorded history. Surprisingly, however, Guam suffered very slightly in comparison with the rest of the world. Indeed, in spite of reduced federal appropriations, the prosperity of the island was actually increased. This was done by producing more food and cash crops, especially copra, than ever before. New lands were broken for cultivation, and a greater variety of crops was raised. Farming activities reached a peak "not before seen in Guam."[18]

238

# GEORGE A. ALEXANDER

During Governor Alexander's administration, agriculture continued to be the backbone of the island's economy. It was the only
source of income for most of Guam's people. A goodly number,
however, were employed in various government jobs. In 1933 many
ranchers received added income from the sale of surplus farm
products. Some of the surplus was "disposed of in both China and
the Philippines, with the idea of educating the people to seek
foreign markets for their surplus."[19] Most of the surplus, however,
was sold in the Agana public market. During the year, cash sales
in the market amounted to $13,720.92.

Near the end of February 1933 an agricultural and industrial
fair was held in Agana. Many types of vegetables, fruits, and even
forage crops were displayed. Other exhibits, such as furniture,
woven articles, and needlework aroused great interest. So many
articles were sold that it was decided to build a sales booth at the
Piti dock on steamer days for the benefit of people passing through
Guam. Considering all conditions, the fair was a great success. It
"would have compared favorably with any county fair held in the
United States."[20] Such fairs became annual events.

Governor Alexander, like several governors before him, encouraged farmers to grow kapok, "which thrives in Guam and is
of an excellent quality."[21] The government required kapok trees
to be grown on all government-leased land. A cleaning and seeding
machine was purchased in the United States, and kapok was
cleaned by the government, free of charge, for all who brought it
in. Moreover, arrangements were made to buy and export all that
was presented for sale.

In 1934 copra exports amounted to 1,874 tons. This was 100
tons more than was exported the year before. Increased production
was due to the governor's special interest in the matter. Because of
falling copra prices on the world market, Guamanian farmers
received only 80 cents a hundred pounds for their product. This
was 8 cents a hundred pounds less than they had gotten in 1933.
Had it not been for the governor's efforts, the low copra prices
might have resulted in real hardship to the people. To meet the
situation, he urged them not only to produce more copra but to

turn out a better product as well. For a number of years the farmers had allowed the quality of Guam's copra to fall. Unripe nuts had been used, and the copra was not well dried. Frequently the product was allowed to become dirty while being dried. To correct the situation government officials were required and leading farmers were encouraged to build copra driers whose use gave a better, cleaner, and more uniform grade of copra. Thus, in spite of lower prices, production and income were increased. In 1935, more than double the amount of copra was cut than during the previous year. About 3,618,910 pounds, valued at $72,439.71, were exported.

Increased production of rice, the principal food article in the native diet, was given every encouragement. A survey of the rice situation, ordered by Governor Alexander, showed that about 260 acres of rice lands were being cultivated in 1934. Under normal harvest conditions, such lands could be expected to yield about 416,000 pounds of rice each year. During the three years before 1935, there was imported into Guam about 2,335,773 pounds of rice per year. Thus, it was estimated that, in 1936, Guam would have a shortage of about 1,919,773 pounds of rice. To reduce the shortage, plans were made to put an additional 151 acres of rice land under cultivation by the end of the year. Moreover, completion of a reinforced-concrete dam near Inarajan was expected to add another 390 acres to the land available for rice cultivation. A gasoline-driven rice huller and polisher, purchased by the government, made harvesting easier and more efficient. Experimental plantings of so-called upland rice yielded good harvests. Despite all efforts, however, the rice shortage was not greatly reduced. Demand continued to be far greater than the supply, and Guam was never able to produce locally all the rice needed by her people.

## Early Political Development

At the time of Guam's first general election, March 7, 1931, the islanders were intensely interested in political affairs. Just two years later, however, their interest had so declined that the number of registered voters fell to about fifty per cent of the number in

1931. In the election of 1933, moreover, twelve seats in the Guam Congress were left unfilled because of a lack of candidates. The positions were filled later by appointments of the governor. Rapid decline in political interest seems to have been due to dissatisfaction with government policies. At the time of the first general election, the belief was widespread that the Second Guam Congress, then being elected, would have real lawmaking powers. When this proved to be untrue, the people became dissatisfied. At the same time that the Second Guam Congress was elected, moreover, a complete change was made in the method of selecting village commissioners and deputy commissioners. Before that time they had been appointed by the governor. Now they were to be elected by the people. This gave the people some voice in their government, at least at the village level, and was a matter of real satisfaction to them. During the administration of Governor Root, however, the people were deprived of their right to elect the commissioners. It appeared, said Root, that "the scheme of having the Commissioners elected by the people was not a successful one. The Commissioners basically are employees of the Government and are the agencies through which the Governor is able to demand certain things of the people of the districts. Sometimes these things are not in accordance with the personal desires of those concerned and as long as the Commissioners were elected they were inclined to act with the wishes of the people rather than the desires of the Governor. Upon the recommendation of the Second Guam Congress the Governor removed the Commissioners from the elective lists and made them appointive, with the understanding that should any changes in personnel be made, Congress would make recommendations concerning the persons to be appointed."[22] Needless to say, the Guamanian people were displeased with the action of their government.

By 1934 the island's political situation had not shown much improvement. Generally speaking, the people refused to take an active part in political affairs. During the year, three district commissioners were dismissed from their jobs "for neglect of or indifference to the performance of their duty, and more energetic and able men were appointed to replace them."[23] Furthermore, five members of the congress resigned, for one reason or another, and the vacancies were filled by the governor.

Contact between the governor and the congress was maintained through an executive congressional committee. The committee consisted of six members, three from each house. Once each month the committee met in conference with the governor. Reports on the meetings were forwarded by the governor to each house.

At the meeting of the executive congressional committee on July 17, 1936, the governor was told about a petition that had been prepared by the congress. He was informed that both houses of the Guam Congress, sitting in joint session on July 11, 1936, had unanimously passed a resolution petitioning the United States to grant American citizenship to the people of Guam. Moreover, the committee asked that $5,000 be set aside from naval government funds in order to send two Guamanian congressional delegates to Washington, D.C., where they would submit their petition to the Congress of the United States. "The Governor, while expressing sympathy and understanding with the ambitions of the Chamorro people in their desire to become United States citizens, nevertheless declined to accede to the request that local tax funds be set aside for the purpose indicated." In denying the request for funds, he said:

> ... For many years the Federal Government has been furnishing some $35,000 annually to be disbursed for purely local purposes, i.e., care of lepers and insane, education, etc. In view of the fact that the Federal Government is furnishing these funds because the local government is unable to bear the expense of the activities referred to above, the Governor was of the opinion that to make available the funds requested, for the purpose indicated, would be a breach of faith on the part of the Naval Government with the Federal Government.[24]

On October 19, 1936, Guam was visited by United States Senator and Mrs. William Gibbs McAdoo. A demonstration honoring the senator and his wife was staged in the Plaza de España in front of Government House. Members of the Guam Congress, the Guam Militia, Boy and Girl Scout troops, the American Legion, and the civilian population took part in the demonstration. In the course of the demonstration the Honorable Baltazar J. Bordallo, chairman of the House of Council, and the Honorable Eduardo T. Calvo, chairman of the House of Assembly of the Guam Congress, addressed the senator and the assembled people. In their brief addresses they called upon the senator to support the plan of the Guam Congress to secure American citizenship for the Guamanian people. Senator McAdoo replied briefly, "advising that steps looking toward citizenship for the natives of Guam should be conducted through the proper channels."[25]

Following these setbacks, the Guam Congress proceeded to raise the necessary money by popular subscription. On November 17, 1936, the Honorable Baltazar J. Bordallo, delegate from the House of Council, and the Honorable Francisco B. Leon Guerrero, delegate from the House of Assembly, left Guam aboard the USS *Gold Star* for the United States. About three months later, on February 10, 1937, United States Senators Tydings and Gibson introduced S. 1450 (75th Congress, 1st session), "A Bill to Confer United States Citizenship upon Certain Inhabitants of the Island of Guam and Extend the Naturalization Laws Thereto."[26] The bill failed.

## THE GUAM MUSEUM

In order to preserve Guam's material culture, the Guam Museum was established and formally opened on November 1, 1932. Opening exercises were conducted by Mid-Pacific Post Number 1 of the American Legion. Shortly after its establishment the museum's collection began to grow. Relics of the ancient Chamorro civilization, of Spanish times, and even of the early years of American occupation were exhibited. In 1934 the museum was given a display of photographs of all the American governors of Guam.

During the first three years after its establishment, the Guam Museum was operated and controlled by the local post of the American Legion. The Legionnaires spent their own money and much of their time in developing it. In January of 1936, however, "the Naval Government felt that it would be unwarranted in continuing to expect the Legionnaires to expend their personal funds in the upkeep of the Museum. The need for additional funds, availability of the Museum to the public daily and a salaried attendant, had become evident."[27] Accordingly, on February 1, 1936, Governor Benjamin V. McCandlish issued Executive Order No. 37. By the terms of the order, the museum was made a naval government activity. Moreover, a Guam Museum committee was established. The committee immediately began a study of the best means of reorganizing, classifying, and preserving the exhibits. Contact was established with the Bishop Museum in Honolulu and museum authorities in Manila. Much information was obtained to assist the committee in its work. In response to one such request for information, Mr. E. H. Bryan, Jr., curator of the Bishop Museum, spent six weeks in Guam advising and assisting the Guam Museum staff. By the end of 1936 the museum was well on its way to carrying out its mandate, as given in the governor's order, "to insure that the material evidences of earlier civilization on the Island of Guam may be properly preserved and cared for."[28]

From 1937 to 1941 Mrs. Agueda I. Johnston was the museum committee member in charge of the ancient Chamorro collections. Under her leadership many relics were added to the ancient Chamorro exhibits. During 1937, lighted glass cases, a study room, and a relief map of Guam were installed. Two special exhibits, one commemorating the golden jubilee of the ordination of the Very Reverend Monsignor José Torres Palomo and the other honoring Armistice Day, were presented. Within a very short time, the museum became a center of interest to school children, the people of the island, the naval colony, and visitors passing through Guam.

In 1938 Captain Spencer L. Higgins, USN, classified and presented the museum with a large collection of mineral- and fossil-bearing rocks which had been gathered from all parts of the island. Other gifts were made to the museum during the year. They included copies of the books *Historia de las Islas Marianas*, written by Don Felipe María de la Corte, and *The Diary of Padre Aniceto Ibáñez*. Another gift was a certified copy of the baptismal certificate of Father Diego Luis de Sanvitores. An excellent stamp collection was exhibited in August 1938 by Mr. W. G. Johnston and Mr. F. D. Brunton. In 1940 Captain Higgins presented other gifts to the museum. They included four specimens of gold ore and a book entitled *Journal of Paleontology*. The book contained information on the foraminifera of Guam. Former Governor James T. Alexander gave the museum a cattle branding iron believed to have been the first ever used on the island.

The Guam Museum, with all the valuable articles and documents it contained, was completely destroyed during the period of bombardment and invasion in 1944. Many articles were taken as souvenirs.

## PUBLICATIONS

Guam had two prewar publications. The *Guam Recorder*, the more important of these, was founded in March 1924. From the very beginning it "constituted the island's and the Naval Station's most complete and interesting record and has been closely associated with the official life of both the Naval Station and the Naval Government."[29] On October 2, 1933, the naval government purchased the *Recorder* from its owner and editor, Mr. W. W. Rowley. At that time it was decided to devote the magazine more and more to matters of interest to the islanders, who as a rule read only very little. The magazine was a monthly publication that was printed "at no cost to the Naval Government, if there be taken into account the expenses formerly incurred for the publication of official orders, notices, etc."[30] Members of the editorial staff served without pay. Starting in January 1936, the naval government began printing the *Recorder* in its own printing shop. Thus the magazine was placed on a sounder financial footing.

In 1937 the *Recorder* was greatly improved, both in content and in form. A number of articles on scientific matters were contributed by qualified persons. Among them were translations of original Spanish documents made by Mrs. Margaret L. Higgins. Others included articles on the insects, plants, and ancient culture of Guam. Such articles presented scientific knowledge that was vital to the life of the island. Besides these, articles dealing with current island events, vital statistics, and government reports were also published.

In 1938 the editor of the *Recorder* was a U.S. Navy lieutenant. Other members of the staff were a navy printer, four native printers, one native messenger, and a native artist who was employed on a piecework basis. From time to time they were assisted by a few qualified members of the naval colony. Monthly circulation in 1938 was about 800 copies. The subscription price was one dollar a year. Besides subscriptions, the magazine was supported by income from advertising and commercial job printing.

The *Guam Eagle* was the island's only daily newspaper. Published in mimeographed form, primarily for the American colony, it carried local, national, and international news. It was printed in the Naval Communications Office under the direction of the district communications officer. Stencil cutting and mimeographing were done by the office personnel. Daily circulation in 1941 was about 610 copies. The paper was distributed to various parts of the island by the local bus company and two messengers. One of the messengers made deliveries to Marine Corps personnel stationed at Sumay. Complimentary copies were sent to visiting ships in Apra Harbor. The *Eagle* was supported by naval government subsidy and distributed free of charge. Neither the *Guam Eagle* nor the *Guam Recorder* was re-established after World War II.

## COMMERCIAL AVIATION

Until World War II, the history of commercial aviation in Guam was determined almost entirely by Pan American World Airways. In 1934 Juan T. Trippe, president of Pan American, announced that his company was "getting ready to fly the Pacific." His announcement created widespread discussion because, to that date, no major ocean had been spanned by commercial aviation. The longest overwater scheduled flight at that time was between Dakar in French West Africa and Natal in Brazil, a distance of 1,864 miles.[31] It was flown only by mail planes. The transpacific service planned by Pan American involved a route that was 8,746 miles long. Passengers and cargo, as well as mail, were to be carried. Before the new service could begin, however, bases had to be built. Accordingly, early in 1935 the 15,000-ton steamer *North Haven* was outfitted in San Francisco. Her cargo and complement of passengers consisted of food, fuel, supplies and equipment, 44 airline technicians, and 74 construction workers. When all was in readiness, she departed from San Francisco and proceeded to Midway and Wake. At each island, bases were built to receive the planes that were to come a short time later.

The first flight over the transpacific route to Guam was made by the Sikorsky S-42B *Clipper*, the NR823M. Commanded by Captain R. O. D. Sullivan, she was engaged in a survey flight over the proposed route. The *Clipper* left San Francisco on October 5. After stops at Honolulu, Midway, and Wake, she arrived in Guam on October 13, 1935. Three days later she began her return trip and arrived at San Francisco on October 24, 1935.

Upon the completion of necessary survey flights, Pan American was ready to begin transpacific airmail service. Accordingly, on November 22, 1935, the *China Clipper* departed on the first airmail flight across the Pacific. The occasion was of such importance that the governor of California proclaimed the day officially as Pan American Airways Day. Postmaster General James A. Farley came from Washington, D. C., to witness the start of the flight. When the *Clipper* took off from the waters of San Francisco Bay, her departure "was watched by 125,000 people from convenient locations near the Golden Gate. Twenty-four hours later the Clipper was in Honolulu. Six days later it was at anchor in Manila Bay after 59 hours, 48 minutes of flying time. On December 6, the Clipper was back at Alameda and the first round-trip flight over the Pacific was completed in her log book."[32] Thereupon, regular flights were established between San Francisco and Manila. Within a short time, airmail from the United States arrived in Guam on a weekly schedule.

During March 1936 the *North Haven* arrived in Apra Harbor with supplies necessary for building a small hotel at Sumay. The hotel was built in preparation for the arrival of Pan American passengers. About six months later, on October 14, 1936, Pan American's first passenger flight arrived in Guam. The passengers were prominent representatives of the press who were traveling as guests of the company. Twelve days later, on October 26, 1936, the first paid passenger flight, westbound, reached the island. This marked the beginning of regular passenger service between Guam and the mainland. In February, 1937, the first Guamanian passengers, Miss Julia T. Martinez and Mr. Trinidad T. Calvo, took off for Manila, P.I., to attend the 31st International Eucharistic Congress in Manila. In his *Annual Report* for 1938, Governor James T. Alexander noted that "the advent of the transpacific airways service has made itself felt in the affairs of the Island. The postal receipts have trebled in the past year. The people themselves occasionally travel by air. Many Americans prominent in letters, business, national and international affairs, in passing through, take a keen interest in Guam and, in turn, leave their impressions and modern ideas with those who live here. The condition of the people, their mode of life, the effectiveness of government and the affairs of the Island are constantly being viewed at first hand by air travellers in positions of authority or in positions to mold public opinion here and abroad. Air transportation may be said to have removed the most remote of the U.S. Island possessions from behind a vast sea barrier, placing Guam and its interests within 48 flying hours of California's shores."[33]

In April 1940 the Navy Department, for the first time, utilized Pan American transportation to return Navy personnel to the United States. Personnel involved were three officers and their families. Because of the lack of government transportation and the need to reach the United States within an allotted time, they were transported by Pan American.

During the fiscal year ending June 30, 1940, Guam received airmail from San Francisco and Honolulu 49 times; from Navy Yard, Cavite, Philippine Islands, 49 times; from Hongkong 47 times; and from Macao twice. Airmail was dispatched to San Francisco, Honolulu, Manila, and Hongkong 49 times each, and to Macao once. Rapid and efficient mail service strengthened the island's economy and did much to decrease the isolation of Guam from the rest of the world.

On March 27, 1936, after having served almost three years as governor, George A. Alexander was relieved by Commander Benjamin V. McCandlish. Two years later, McCandlish was succeeded by Commander James T. Alexander. He, in turn, was relieved by Captain George J. McMillin.

## GEORGE J. MCMILLIN

Captain George J. McMillin was the last naval officer to serve as governor of Guam prior to World War II. He assumed the duties of his office on April 20, 1940. He could not know that slightly more than a year and a half later his administration would be brought to a sudden and violent end. Nor, of course, could he know that Guam would be occupied by foreign troops, that the Guamanian people would undergo an ordeal by fire, and that he himself would languish in a Japanese prison camp. Although he did not know it at the time, he was to witness the end of an era— the end of a way of life in Guam that would never again be wholly restored. Because of that fact, a careful study of Guam as it was during his administration is in order.

GOVERNMENT ORGANIZATION: Just prior to the Japanese invasion in 1941, the naval government of Guam was organized as follows:

1. Office of the Governor
2. Guam Congress
3. Department of Law (Island Attorney and deputies)
4. Judiciary Department
   a. Police Court
   b. Island Court
   c. Court of Equity (Justice Court)
   d. Court of Appeals
5. Executive Department
   a. Chief Commissioner
   b. Commissioners
6. Department of Education
   a. Public schools (native)
   b. Public schools (American)
   c. Private schools

249

7. Department of Health
   a. Sanitation
   b. Public health
8. Department of Agriculture
   a. Agriculture
   b. School farm
   c. School farm research
   d. Animal husbandry
   e. Fisheries
   f. Forestry
9. Department of Industries
   a. Public works
   b. Public utilities
10. Bank of Guam
11. Police Department
    a. Police
    b. Insular Patrol
    c. Civil Jail
    d. Prison farms
12. Military Department
    a. Military training
    b. Guam Militia
13. Department of Records and Accounts
    a. Fidelity accounting
    b. Property accounting
    c. Cost accounting
    d. Statistical accounting
14. Department of Customs and Immigration

Except for minor changes, organization of the naval government of Guam in 1941 was about the same as it was at the beginning of naval rule.

ECONOMIC CONDITIONS: Until the very beginning of World War II, affairs of the island of Guam continued to be little affected by political, economic, and industrial problems of the world at large. Health, education, and general living standards continued to improve. By 1941, most Guamanian workers were employed. They worked either on their ranches or on federal or island government projects. Added income was derived from the manufacture of *aggag* woven articles. Other articles, including ornamental apparel and women's purses, were made from land shells. The shells, about one-half inch in length and one-quarter inch in thickness, were used to produce such items as belts, bracelets, earrings, buttons, and purses, all of which found a ready market both on the island and in Hawaii and the mainland.

By 1940 soap manufacturing had become an important part of the island's limited economy. In that year three soap factories were in operation. "Their factories," wrote Governor McMillin, "are capable of supplying the entire Navy with salt-water soap of excellent quality. The Naval Government is now trying to obtain the right for local manufacturers to bid on contracts for salt-water soap for the Navy. In the past, these bids were mailed to the manufacturers here in Guam, but the bids arrived after the contracts had been awarded, due to the slow mail service from Washington, via mail steamer."[34] The governor's efforts to aid the soap industry were successful. During 1941 local soap factories supplied 250,000 pounds of salt-water soap to the United States Navy in the Pacific.

HEALTH CONDITIONS: In 1941 work was begun on an isolation ward at the Naval Hospital for the treatment of tuberculosis patients. Except for a mild epidemic of German measles early in the year, general health conditions were very good. Dr. Ramon M. Sablan, M.D., a native of Guam, was engaged in private practice on the island. In addition, as of April 1, 1941, he was employed by the island government to conduct a tuberculosis survey of the entire population. Personnel of the Department of Health at that time included the following:[35]

1. Health officer: commanding officer of the Naval Hospital
2. Assistant health officer and quarantine officer:
   a. Medical officer of staff assigned to this duty

    b. Medical officer of Marine Barracks, Sumay, for Municipalities of Agat and Sumay and quarantine officer of Sumay

3. Hospital corpsman on full-time duty with the assistant health officer
4. Hospital corpsmen on detached duty at outstations
5. Sanitary inspector at Agana
6. Red Cross nurses: three native graduate nurses
7. Midwives: examined and licensed annually

The outpatient department of the Naval Hospital included the dressing room of the officer of the day; an eye, ear, nose and throat clinic; and a clinic for women and babies. In addition there was a dispensary at Marine Barracks, Sumay, in charge of a medical officer. Outlying dressing stations, each under the supervision of a medical corpsman, were located at Agat, Dededo, Inarajan, Merizo, Piti, and Yona. A dressing station in Agana, supported by the Red Cross and cared for by two native nurses, was available to the children of the city.

The following cases of communicable diseases were reported during 1941:[36]

| | |
|---|---|
| Tuberculosis, pulmonary | 103 |
| Tuberculosis, extrapulmonary | 23 |
| Pneumonia, lobar | 22 |
| Pneumonia, broncho | 13 |
| Dysentery, amebic | 25 |
| Dysentery, bacillary | 4 |
| Catarrhal fever, acute | 347 |
| Tonsillitis, acute | 23 |
| Conjunctivitis, acute | 231 |
| Dengue | 4 |
| Meningococcic meningitis | 1 |
| Poliomyelitis | 1 |
| German measles | 135 |
| Chicken pox | 99 |
| Erysipelas | 2 |
| Impetigo | 3 |
| Leprosy | 1 |
| Mumps | 2 |

| | |
|---|---|
| Venereal diseases, all forms | 28 |
| Yaws | 20 |
| Septicemia | 1 |

Tuberculosis, then as now, was the island's principal health problem. "Under the present conditions," wrote McMillin, "no decline in tuberculosis mortality can be expected."[37]

JUDICIARY DEPARTMENT: In 1941 the island's courts consisted of the Police Court, the Justice Court, the Island Court, and the Court of Appeals. In general, the Police Court had jurisdiction over criminal misdemeanor cases in which the penalty was not more than six months' imprisonment or a fine of one hundred dollars. The Justice Court, generally speaking, had jurisdiction over all civil cases involving property valued at seventy-five dollars or less. It also handled cases of criminal misdemeanor in which the penalty was less than a fine of three hundred dollars and imprisonment for less than one year. When the Justice Court heard civil cases that involved twelve dollars or less, it was referred to as the Small Claims Court. No lawyer or other person than the actual litigants could take part in filing, prosecuting, or defending a case in the Small Claims Court. At the beginning of 1941, Captain Terrell J. Crawford, USMC, was judge of the Police Court and the Honorable José C. Manibusan presided over the Justice Court. On June 6, 1941, when Captain Crawford left the island, Judge Manibusan became acting judge of the Police Court as well.

The Island Court was a court of general jurisdiction. It handled most cases that were not specifically assigned by law to other courts. In addition, it heard all cases involving matters of probate, appointment of guardians, trustees and receivers, and all actions for the annulment of marriage and for divorce. This court also served as an appeals court for certain cases that arose in the lower courts. The Honorable José M. Camacho presided over the Island Court. Judge Camacho died on October 27, 1940, after having served the naval government for thirty-eight years.

The Court of Appeals was the highest court in the island's judicial system. It consisted of a presiding justice and four associ-

253

ate justices. During 1940–41, Lieutenant Commander Roger Edison Perry, USN, was the presiding justice. Associate justices were Lieutenant Commander Tilden I. Moe, USN; Lieutenant John F. Castree, USN; the Honorable Vicente P. Camacho; and the Honorable Ramón M. Sablan. In November 1940 Associate Justice Camacho resigned. The Honorable José L. G. Rios was appointed to fill the vacancy.

The Court of Appeals heard all criminal cases sent to it by the Island and Justice Courts, and all civil and special cases appealed from the Island Court. Whenever the Island Court ordered a prison sentence of more than one year, the judgment did not become final until the case was reviewed and approved by the Court of Appeals. Besides these duties, the Court of Appeals had the power to issue writs of mandamus, certiorari, prohibition, and habeas corpus. In addition, it could issue any other writs necessary for the proper exercise of its powers as an appeals court.

DEPARTMENT OF LAW: The legal department of the naval government was administered by the attorney general, who was appointed by the governor. This department dealt with all legal matters in which the government was in any wise interested. It also handled all matters of public prosecution in the courts. As an extra duty, it processed all requests for the transfer of land. Since real property in Guam could not be sold without the approval of the governor, requests for such sales had first to be investigated by the island attorney. The incumbent at this time was Edward C. Duenas, who was beheaded by the Japanese toward the close of World War II.

EXECUTIVE DEPARTMENT: In 1941 the Executive Department consisted of the head of the department, a naval officer; the chief commissioner of Guam, assistant head of the department; and fourteen commissioners of outlying municipalities. The office of deputy commissioner was discontinued on September 30, 1940, as an economy measure. The chief commissioner was also the administrative head of the Chief Commissioner's Office. This office was responsible for seeing to it that court decisions and rulings were enforced. Don Antonio Suarez was prewar Chief Commissioner.

The principal task of the Executive Department was "to encourage the people of Guam in industry and thrift, in order that the Island will be as nearly self-supporting as possible."[38] This goal was to be attained by adhering to the following policies:

A. The native population must be educated concerning the activities of the Naval Government, and the reasons for these activities.
B. Confidence in and cooperation with the Naval Government must be encouraged by personal contacts with all groups of the population, preventing or removing causes of friction, investigation and remedy of minor cases of injustice or apparent discrimination, and by study of the problems of various classes of the population with the view to helping to solve them.
C. Liaison must be maintained with other departments with the end in view of helping them in their work and by encouraging the people to give intelligent cooperation to all agencies of Government. Policies (A) and (B) above are general, based on the fact that no progress can be made with the rural population (by any activity of Government) if the people continue to be ignorant or apathetic concerning plans for their advancement. (C) above is expanded as follows:
  1. The total production of food, meats, grains and vegetables must be greatly increased.
  2. Standards of sanitation, public health, and health education as laid down by the Health Department must be maintained. This department cooperates to the fullest extent, through local Commissioners, with the Health Department.
  3. There are still products, now imported, which may be produced locally and such production is encouraged.
  4. Advice and material assistance, if approved by the Governor, will be tendered private individuals who wish to start new industries in Guam.[39]

Through the commissioners, the Executive Department supervised numerous activities at the village and municipal levels. On March 8, 1941, it supervised the island's general election. The election was held for the purpose of selecting one-half the councilmen and all the assemblymen for the Second Guam Congress.

DEPARTMENT OF AGRICULTURE: The Department of Agriculture

was one of the island government's most important departments. It concerned itself with all phases of the island's agricultural economy. Its principal purpose was to produce enough food to make the island self-sustaining. To carry out this purpose the department, in 1941, purchased 91 plows, 24 cultivators, 911 pounds of vegetable seeds, 300 pounds of improved seed rice, and various kinds of livestock. All were sold at cost to various farmers. The department, moreover, was responsible for inspecting plants and animals introduced into Guam or exported from the island. It also prepared and distributed medicines for the control of plant and animal diseases and inspected food products sold to the public.

An agricultural farm, maintained by the department, raised purebred cattle, swine, and poultry for distribution to progressive farmers. In 1941 the farm's herds were enlarged by the importation of Indian cattle. They were purchased in order to produce a breed better adapted to local conditions. Local cattle were especially plagued by the tropical heat and diseases. A liver-fluke campaign, inaugurated during the year, proved very successful. A total of 1,038 head of cattle and 42 carabao were given treatment. Ticks were controlled by either spraying or dipping the cattle in a solution of arsenic. The island government owned two dipping vats, and three others were owned by private individuals. The farm's herds included purebred Jersey, Holstein, Red Scindi, and Nellore bulls, the last two being Indian breeds.

Despite government efforts, Guamanian farmers were reluctant to visit the farm and acquaint themselves with the latest agricultural information. It became necessary, therefore, to reach the farmers by personal contact. This was done effectively by extension agents. The extension service, already established, was completely reorganized in December 1940. The island was divided into four districts and an extension agent was assigned to each. Duties of each agent included work with agricultural clubs and farmers' cooperatives. The agent also inspected government land leased by private individuals, supervised forestry matters, and served as a deputy game warden. Forest activities of the various agents dealt with the investigation of requests to cut timber, bamboo, and nipa leaves on government land; inspection of sawmills; checking timber cut on private property; and patrolling of forest areas.

The public market in Agana was under the general supervision of the Department of Agriculture. The market was open three days a week: Tuesdays, Thursdays, and Saturdays. Fruits, vegetables, and foods of all kinds were sold. Prices of produce sold were decided upon each Saturday morning by the producers. Such prices were in effect during the following week. Three times a week a government-owned truck visited various villages to pick up produce. Farmers were charged a ten per cent commission on all sales of produce transported. This was used to pay the operating expenses of the truck. In addition, five per cent commission was charged on all sales to cover costs of operating the market. A total sale of $7,852.43 was made in the Agana market during 1941. A second public market building in Sumay, owned by the island government, was leased during the year to a private contractor. Besides the public markets, a slaughterhouse was also operated in Agana. In 1941 a total of 184 hogs and 516 head of cattle were butchered there. The meat was sold in privately owned markets. All meat was inspected by the Health Department immediately after butchering.

POLICE DEPARTMENT: The Police Department was the law-enforcement body of the island. It was responsible for the custody, maintenance, and labor of all civil prisoners. In terms of organization, it consisted of two major parts—the Insular Patrol and the Native Police. According to the governor's report for 1941, the Insular Patrol consisted of the following U.S. Marine Corps personnel:[40]

| Number and rank | Duty |
| --- | --- |
| 1 first lieutenant | head of Police Department and chief of police |
| 1 sergeant | assistant chief of police and in charge of Police Department transportation |
| 1 corporal | inspector of police, corpo- |

1 private first class

1 private first class

1 corporal and 7 privates
first class and privates

5 privates first class

6 privates first class

11 privates first class and
privates

(Total: 1 officer, 34 enlisted men)

ral of the guard, Agana
Navy Yard guard; chief
orderly and special watch,
Civil Jail
warden, Civil Jail
traffic patrolman
Agana patrolmen

commandant's orderlies
Agana Navy Yard guard
outstation patrolmen

During the same year (1941) twenty-eight Guamanians served as members of the Native Police force. The force consisted of one desk sergeant, one street sergeant, two corporals, two police detectives, three policemen, six policemen second class, and thirteen probationary policemen. They served as interpreters, did clerical work, were farm overseers, supervised prison work parties, policed Agana, acted as sanitary inspectors, and served as turnkeys at the civil jail.

The Insular Patrol was the primary law-enforcement body of the island. An insular patrolman was stationed in eleven of the twelve municipal districts outside of Agana. A native policeman was stationed in Sinajana. The patrolmen and policemen were responsible for maintaining peace and order in their districts. Minor offenses, for which the fine was not more than five dollars, were usually handled in the district by the patrolman and the commissioner. More serious offenses were reported to the head of the Police Department for further action. All criminal offenses, being assigned to one of the courts, had first to be investigated by the chief of police.

The patrolman in charge of each district had to submit bimonthly reports to the chief of police. His reports dealt with water supplies, roads, trails, offenses committed and action taken, condition of crops, cattle, and any other information that might be of interest.

During 1941 an average of eighty-seven cases per month were

investigated by the chief of police. The most common offenses were traffic violations, infractions of the sanitary regulations, simple battery, and disturbing the peace. Two cases of suicide by hanging occurred during the year. The status of prisoners in the civil jail as of June 30, 1941, was as follows:[41]

| | Male | Female |
|---|---|---|
| Confined in jail serving sentence | 33 | 0 |
| Confined at Libugon Farm serving sentence | 9 | 0 |
| Confined at Naval Hospital as patients | 4 | 0 |
| On parole | 7 | 3 |
| Confined in jail working off fines by public labor | 6 | 0 |
| Confined at Libugon Farm working off fines by public labor | 2 | 0 |
| Paying fines in monthly installments | 12 | 1 |
| Arrested and confined pending action | 3 | 0 |
| | 76 | 4 |

Upon recommendation of the Board of Pardons and Parole, prisoners could be released from jail and placed on parole for the unexpired portion of their sentences. Parolees were required to report in person to the chief of police on the first day of each month. At that time the parolee was required to fill in a blank form. On the form he listed his address, employment, earnings and expenditures during the previous month, and other pertinent information that enabled the police to keep a close check on him at all times. Upon being placed on parole, a prisoner was issued a ticket of leave by the governor. The ticket was similar to the form used in the state of California.

Prisoners working off their fines by public labor were credited with eighty cents a day for each day of confinement. Six prisoners were regularly employed in collecting trash and garbage in Agana, Asan, Tepungan, and Piti. Garbage was deposited at the San Ramon dump and covered with *cascajo*. Prisoners were used to cover the dump grounds as a sanitary measure. Fourteen prisoners were also detailed to work at the prison farm and the Naval Government Tile Factory at Libugon. Others were used to maintain the bleachers, buildings, and grounds at Bradley Park.

TRANSPORTATION: By 1941 air transportation had become an important factor in establishing and maintaining contact between Guam and the outside world. The Navy Department now used this means of transportation for officers being detached from the naval station. Water transportation, however, continued to be inadequate. Specifically chartered vessels were obtained on occasion to bring in materials needed for the completion of federal projects on the island. Ocean transportation available during the year was as follows:

1. Navy transports *Chaumont* and *Henderson,* both eastbound and westbound, carrying naval personnel and freight for the federal and naval governments.

2. Army transport *U.S. Grant,* westbound only. It was the only carrier that provided frozen meats and cold-storage supplies (for federal use) direct from the United States.

3. Steamship *Admiral Halstead,* westbound, calling about once a quarter, with facilities for carrying heavy cargo but no cold-storage facilities.

4. USS *Gold Star,* station ship at Guam. It made frequent trips to the Philippines to obtain coal for the power plant and supplies for the island's merchants.[42]

Besides these, two smaller vessels were stationed at Guam. One, the USS *Penguin,* was the station tug. It carried the governor on inspection trips, made security patrols around the island, and transported passengers and supplies between Apra Harbor and Merizo. The other, the USS *Robert L. Barnes,* was a floating oil depot and mess attendant training ship. Beginning July 1, 1937, mess attendants recruited on the island were given their training on the *Barnes.* A total of 616 mess attendants were trained and transferred to the United States fleet for duty.

TYPHOON: On November 3, 1940, Guam was struck by one of the most severe typhoons on record for the island. The day before, Governor McMillin instructed all commissioners and insular patrolmen to warn their people that a typhoon would strike the island within twenty-four hours. True to his prediction, the typhoon struck with devastating force. Throughout much of the storm, wind velocities exceeded 100 knots. At times, gusts were estimated to reach 130 knots.

During the typhoon, houses were blown away, crops were destroyed, and animals and poultry were killed. Life on the island was completely disrupted. The American Red Cross donated $10,000 to help relieve distress among the islanders. Other funds were donated by the local chapter of the Society of St. Vincent de Paul. This assistance, however, quickly proved to be inadequate, and naval government funds were spent, as necessary, to aid the civil population. The government canceled payment of taxes on rural property for a period of six months in order to help the people re-establish themselves. Although the government acted quickly, Governor McMillin reported that "Guam's largest industry, the production of copra, will not be normal for five years, due to the destruction of cocoanut trees. Swine herds on the island have of necessity been reduced, as well as poultry flocks, due to the lack of locally produced feed. It has been necessary to commence importation of copra-cake from the Philippines in order to supply proper feed for popultry raisers. It will be approximately 18 months from the date of the tyhoon before tree crops, such as bread-fruit, avocados and bananas can be expected to produce a normal crop."[43]

On November 2, the day before the typoon struck, the Greek freighter *Axios* entered Apra Harbor. Her cargo consisted of phosphates which she was carrying from Nauru in the Marshall Islands to Japan. She was in need of urgent repairs to her pumps. During the height of the typhoon the *Axios* parted her moorings and was under way for some four hours, generally at full speed ahead. Without a suitable chart of the harbor or a pilot on board, it was somewhat of a miracle that she did not founder on the reefs.

As a result of the typhoon, damage to private property and government installations was very heavy. In Agana the Susanna Hospital lost all its roofing, and portions of other hospital buildings were damaged. Telephone and electric wires were down all over the city. Practically all government buildings suffered some damage. Fires under the boilers in the central power plant were allowed to die out. For the first time in forty-two years the plant was dead—no steam, no electricity, no refrigeration.

The Piti Naval Yard suffered severe damage. All buildings were either unroofed or entirely destroyed. Storehouses were full of stores that had been received a few days earlier from the USS *Chaumont*. Perishable goods like flour and sugar were a total loss. One thousand barrels of cement were spoiled. Both landing docks were badly damaged. Small boats were blown aground, and one was sunk.

The typhoon struck Sumay with full force. A hangar that had just been repaired was smashed flat. The Pan American Airways hotel was reduced to kindling wood, and other buildings were badly damaged. All government quarters leased by the company were either damaged or completely destroyed.

Immediately after the typhoon Governor McMillin notified the Navy Department by dispatch and requested funds to repair the damage. Within a matter of months the Bureau of Yards and Docks, as well as other bureaus concerned, allotted $128,750 for rehabilitation work. The last allotment came through on June 19, 1941. Just six months later, when the island was well on its way to recovery, the Japanese unleashed their sneak attack on Guam and Pearl Harbor.

### Governors of Guam during the Period of Naval Government

| Governor | Date of Accession |
| --- | --- |
| Don José Sisto (acting) | June 23, 1898 |
| Don Francisco Portusach (acting) | June 23, 1898 |
| Don José Sisto (acting) | January 1, 1899 |
| Don Joaquín Pérez (acting) | February 1, 1899 |
| Mr. William Coe (acting) | April 20, 1899 |
| Captain Richard P. Leary | August 7, 1899 |
| Commander Seaton Schroeder | July 19, 1900 |
| Commander W. Swift | August 11, 1901 |
| Commander Seaton Schroeder | November 2, 1901 |
| Commander W. E. Sewell | February 6, 1903 |

| | |
|---|---|
| Lt. F. H. Schofield (acting) | January 11, 1904 |
| Lt. Raymond Stone (acting) | January 28, 1904 |
| Commander G. L. Dyer | May 16, 1904 |
| Lt. Luke McNamee (acting) | November 2, 1905 |
| Commander T. M. Potts | March 2, 1906 |
| Lt. Commander Luke McNamee | October 3, 1907 |
| Captain Edward J. Dorn | December 28, 1907 |
| Lt. F. B. Freyer (acting) | November 5, 1910 |
| Captain G. R. Salisbury | January 12, 1911 |
| Captain Robert E. Coontz | April 30, 1912 |
| Commander A. W. Hinds (acting) | September 23, 1913 |
| Captain W. J. Maxwell | March 28, 1914 |
| Lt. Commander W. P. Cronan (acting) | April 29, 1916 |
| Captain Edward Simpson (acting) | May 9, 1916 |
| Captain Roy C. Smith | May 30, 1916 |
| Captain William W. Gilmer | November 15, 1918 |
| Lt. Commander W. A. Hodgman (acting) | November 22, 1919 |
| Captain William W. Gilmer | December 21, 1919 |
| Captain Ivan C. Wettengel | July 7, 1920 |
| Lt. Commander James S. Spore (acting) | February 27, 1921 |
| Captain Ivan C. Wettengel | April 15, 1921 |
| Lt. Commander James S. Spore (acting) | October 28, 1921 |
| Captain Adelbert Althouse | February 7, 1922 |
| Commander John P. Miller (acting) | November 8, 1922 |
| Captain Adelbert Althouse | December 14, 1922 |
| Captain H. B. Price | August 4, 1923 |
| Commander A. W. Brown (acting) | August 26, 1924 |
| Captain H. B. Price | October 14, 1924 |
| Captain L. S. Shapley | April 7, 1926 |
| Commander Willis W. Bradley Jr. | June 11, 1929 |
| Captain Edmund S. Root | May 15, 1931 |
| Captain George A. Alexander | June 21, 1933 |
| Commander Benjamin V. McCandlish | March 27, 1936 |
| Commander James T. Alexander | February 8, 1938 |
| Captain George J. McMillin | April 20, 1940 |
| Rear Admiral Charles A. Pownall | May 30, 1946 |

SUMMARY: The years from 1914 to 1941, the period between two world wars, thrust Guam into close and sometimes violent contact with the outside world. During the same period, however, giant strides were made in terms of economic and political development. Among the violent incidents were the circumstances surrounding the arrival, the internment, and the sinking the German cruiser *Cormoran* in Apra Harbor. This incident stirred the patriotic fervor of the Guamanian people, hastened their buying of Liberty Bonds, and gave impetus to the desire of their young men to enlist for military training.

The movement for a greater measure of self-government in Guam received tremendous impetus on February 3, 1917, when Governor Roy C. Smith convened the First Guam Congress. Although the Congress had no authority whatever with respect to taxation or the appropriation and expenditure of local tax and customs receipts, in the eyes of the islanders it was, nevertheless, a step in the right direction. It was not until the passage of the Organic Act in 1950, thirty-three years later, that most of the demands of the Guamanian people for a greater measure of self-government were finally met.

The period between the two world wars saw Guam emerge from behind a vast sea barrier and enter upon an era of expanded contacts with the outside world. This was due, in the main, to the advent of commercial aviation in the Pacific region, which began on November 22, 1935. On that date the Pan American Airways *China Clipper* began the first airmail flight from Alameda, California, to Manila.

By 1940, substantial improvements had been made in Guam's economic life, its health and sanitary conditions, its judicial and educational systems, and in various other departments and agencies of government. Unfortunately, however, many of the physical improvements were wiped out by a disastrous typhoon which struck the island late in 1940. Guam was well on the way to recovery from the typhoon when the Japanese attack and invasion began. In the next chapter we will see what happened in Guam during World War II.

## NOTES

1. Governor of Guam, *Annual Report, 1917*, p. 29.
2. *Ibid.*, p. 37.
3. *Ibid.*, p. 35.
4. Roy E. James, "The Guam Congress," *Pacific Affairs*, Vol. XIX, No. 4 (December 1946), p. 409.
5. Governor of Guam, *Annual Report, 1917*, p. 35.
6. Governor of Guam, *Annual Report, 1925*, p. 1.
7. Robert Sherrod, *History of Marine Corps Aviation in World War II* (Combat Forces Press, Washington, 1952), p. 27.
8. Governor of Guam, *Annual Report, 1922*, p. 51.
9. Governor of Guam, *Annual Report, 1930*, p. 124.
10. *Ibid.*, p. 123.
11. *Ibid.*, p. 4.
12. *Ibid.*, p. 30.
13. *Ibid.*, p. 29.
14. *Ibid.*, p. 30.
15. Governor of Guam, *Annual Report, 1931*, p. 8.
16. *Ibid.*, p. 7.
17. Governor of Guam, *Annual Report, 1932*, p. 4.
18. Governor of Guam, *Annual Report, 1933*, p. 1.
19. *Ibid.*, p. 1.
20. *Loc. cit.*
21. Governor of Guam, *Annual Report, 1933*, p. 2.
22. *Ibid.*, p. 3.
23. Governor of Guam, *Annual Report, 1934*, p. 1.
24. Governor of Guam, *Annual Report, 1937*, p. 4.
25. *Ibid.*, p. 4.
26. *Loc. cit.*
27. Governor of Guam, *Annual Report, 1936*, p. 30.
28. *Ibid.*, p. 31.
29. Governor of Guam, *Annual Report, 1934*, p. 13.
30. *Ibid.*, p. 13.
31. *Twenty Years of Progress: History of the Pacific-Alaska Division, Pan American World Airways* (Public Relations Department, Pan American World Airways System, November, 1955), p. 1.
32. *Ibid.*, pp. 3–4.
33. Governor of Guam, *Annual Report, 1938*, p. 2.
34. Governor of Guam, *Annual Report, 1940*, p. 7.
35. Governor of Guam, *Annual Report, 1941*, p. 40.

36. *Ibid.*, p. 37.
37. *Loc. cit.*
38. Governor of Guam, *Annual Report, 1941*, p. 21.
39. *Loc. cit.*
40. Governor of Guam, *Annual Report, 1941*, p. 60.
41. *Ibid.*, p. 63.
42. *Ibid.*, p. 7.
43. *Ibid.*, p. 9.

## CHAPTER EIGHT

## GUAM DURING WORLD WAR II

ON SUNDAY morning, December 7, 1941, Japan attacked Pearl Harbor. The next day President Franklin Delano Roosevelt called on the Congress of the United States for a formal declaration of war against Japan and Germany and Italy as well.

At the outbreak of hostilities Guam, being almost completely defenseless, was unable to resist the impending Japanese attack. Her state of unpreparedness was due in large measure to her isolation and to inaction on the part of responsible officials in Washington. They had feared that any move to fortify Guam would be considered by the Japanese as an unfriendly act. As the clouds of war gathered on the horizon, however, Congress in May 1938 authorized the appointment of a board of naval officers for the purpose of investigating and reporting the need for additional naval and air bases in the United States and its possessions. When the board, headed by Rear Admiral A. J. Hepburn, submitted its report, it recommended, among other things, that Guam, "at present practically defenseless against determined attack by any first-class power based in the western Pacific," could, by means of adequate air and naval installations, "be made secure against anything short of a major effort. . . ." Guam, continued the report, "is adapted naturally to development as a major advanced fleet base."[1] Congress, however, failed to act.

### ATTACK AND SURRENDER

On December 8, 1941, at 5:45 in the morning, the governor of Guam, Captain George J. McMillin, USN, received word from the Commander-in-Chief, Asiatic Fleet, of the Japanese attack on

Pearl Harbor. Naval and Marine Corps officers and personnel were alerted. By 6 a.m. top American and Guamanian civilians had been officially informed of the hostilities between Japan and the United States. There was, however, no way of informing the general public. There was no radio station on Guam at that time, and the mimeographed daily *Guam Eagle* was not distributed until the late afternoon hours. Governor McMillin also ordered the arrest and imprisonment of a small number of enemy nationals living on the island. Among them were the Japanese who "owned the largest and most popular saloons, where the sailors and marines liked best to hang out and argue the fine points of their professions."[2] The Insular Force Guard,* composed of young Guamanian men, was assembled at headquarters on the Plaza de España in Agana and prepared to defend the palace and government buildings. The marines of the garrison force, except for a few in the Insular Patrol (police) who remained on duty in the villages and at other posts, took up positions at the butts of the rifle range on the marine reservation on Orote Peninsula. This force, commanded by Lieutenant Colonel William K. McNulty, consisted of 6 officers, 1 warrant officer, and 118 enlisted marines.

After all orders had been issued, the Insular Force Guard and naval and marine personnel manned their posts, waiting for the impending attack. The defenses of the island were hopelessly inadequate. There was no weapon larger than .30-caliber guns and .45-caliber pistols. Naval craft consisted of a small patrol boat, the USS *Penguin;* a YP-16 and a YP-17; and one old decommissioned oiler, the *R. L. Barnes.*

Several months prior to December, the threatening situation in the Pacific had led the government to order the evacuation of all American dependents from Guam. All but one woman, the wife of a Navy chief petty officer, had left the island by October 17, 1941.

---

* The Insular Force Guard (known by the Guamanians simply as the Insular Guard) consisted of about 80 men who had been organized in early 1941 as an infantry unit. They were in U.S. government service. Another group of Guamanians in uniform were the Insular Navy Force, known collectively as the Insular Force. They performed various duties of naval enlisted men and dressed like Navy personnel but were not considered to be regular members of the U.S. Navy. There was also a volunteer organization, known as the Guam Militia, which served without pay.

On December 6, all important papers and classified matter were destroyed. Then Guam, like all other American outposts in the Pacific, waited for word of the outcome of the negotiations that were taking place between the diplomats of Japan and the United States in Washington. Upon the failure of negotiations, Japan carried out her prearranged attack on American possessions in the Pacific. On December 8, 1941, when the Japanese struck at Guam, the island's population and defenders consisted of about 22,000 Guamanian civilians, 246 members of the Insular Force and Guam Naval Militia, 30 naval officers, 6 naval warrant officers, 5 naval nurses, 230 regular naval enlisted men, 7 marine officers, 1 marine warrant officer, and 145 marine enlisted men.[3]

The first Japanese bombs, carried by nine Saipan-based planes, fell on Guam at about 8:30 a.m. on December 8. At that time, the Most Reverend Miguel Angel de Olano y Urteaga, Bishop of Guam, was celebrating a High Mass in the Agana cathedral in honor of the Feast of the Immaculate Conception, one of Guam's most solemn religious festivals. While the Mass was still in progress, the bishop was told that the Piti Navy Yard, Apra Harbor, and Sumay were being bombed. Turning to the assembled people, the bishop calmly advised them to leave the cathedral. He then returned to the altar to complete the Holy Sacrifice of the Mass.

One of the first targets of the Japanese was the patrol vessel USS *Penguin*. She was attacked and sunk off Orote Point. Her skipper, Lieutenant J. W. Haviland, and several members of the crew were wounded but got ashore on life rafts. In the Sumay and Orote Peninsula areas, principal targets were the United States Marine Barracks, just outside the town, the Pan American Airways station, and naval installations in the harbor area. The Pan American Hotel, the cable office, and parts of the marine barracks were severely damaged. In Piti, the docks were bombed but only slightly damaged.

News of the bombing of Sumay and Piti signaled the beginning of a mass exodus of approximately 11,000 Guamanians from Agana. As the people poured out of their homes and from the cathedral and other churches in Agana, survivors from Piti and

269

Sumay began streaming into the capital. They spread frightening and exaggerated stories of the Japanese attack on the military installations in the Piti-Sumay area. From out of nowhere, seemingly, a rumor that Agana would be bombed within half an hour spread through the city. Panic resulted, and the cries of women and children could be heard everywhere. All major roads and trails out of the city were suddenly crowded with refugees. Fortunately, there were but few cars to crowd the highways. These were used most effectively to carry people out into the country. Within an hour's time, Agana was almost deserted. In the rush to escape, houses were left open, husbands were separated from their wives, and children from their parents. All was in utter confusion. Since Sumay and Piti were the first Japanese targets, Agana was spared during the morning of December 8th. During that afternoon, however, the city was attacked. One bomb fell in the San Ramon district, hitting the houses of George R. Tweed* and Don Luis Baza. Another bomb damaged the house of Dr. Thomas Mesa, the Underwood Store, and the Agana police lockup. On December 9, the planes returned but concentrated their attacks on the Agana Heights area. Damage was not extensive.

The Japanese invasion fleet, commanded by Rear Admiral A. Goto, appeared off Guam early in the evening of December 9. By midnight the island was surrounded by Japanese naval craft. Between three and four o'clock in the morning of December 10, an estimated 5,000 enemy troops began landing on the beaches of Aporguan, Tumon, Togcha, Agat, and other areas. Except for a machine-gun nest in Aporguan, the Japanese met no major opposition. In Aporguan (now lower Tamuning), a principal road of the island skirted the coastline. Guamanians fleeing from Agana before dawn met head-on with invading troops on a lonely stretch of the road. Without warning, the Japanese opened fire on them. Later, the bodies of about twenty men, women, and children were found piled on the road beside their overturned cars and jitneys.

---

* Tweed, Radioman First Class, USN, escaped into the jungle and remained in hiding throughout the occupation. He was the only American not killed or captured by the Japanese.

From Aporguan and Tumon, the invading forces marched towards Agana without meeting any of the island's defenders. In east Agana, in the districts of San Antonio and Padre Palomo, the Japanese met more Guamanians fleeing the city. Some were killed and others were wounded. Among the wounded were Luis Untalan, then principal of Padre Palomo School, and his brother, Jesús. In San Antonio, one house was burned to the ground. Near the San Antonio-San Nicolas Bridge, a truck loaded with Guamanians was attacked by the Japanese. All of the passengers were killed.

Enemy troops, consisting of about 700 of the Special Naval Landing Force, advanced rapidly on the Plaza de España. There they were met by Guamanians of the Insular Force Guard and a handful of sailors and marines. After a brief but brave resistance, the small band of defenders was overwhelmed. Shortly thereafter, at about 5:45 a.m., Governor McMillin decided to surrender.[4] Lack of arms and defensive forces made further resistance impossible.

After papers of surrender had been signed by Governor McMillin on December 10, the commander-in-chief of the Japanese forces issued a proclamation. This document was given wide distribution in Agana and in villages throughout the island. The following is an exact rendering of the proclamation which was posted in Agana and preserved to the present time by a Guamanian:

We proclaim herewith that our Japanese Army has occupied this island of Guam by the order of the Great Emperor of Japan. It is for the purpose of restoring liberty and rescuing the Whole Asiatic people and creating the permanent peace in Asia. Thus our intention is to establish the New Order in the World.

You all good citizens need not worry anything under the regulations of our Japanese authorities and my [sic] enjoy your daily life as we guarantee your lives and never distress nor plunder your property. In case, however, when we demand you [sic] accommodations necessary for our quarters and lodgings, you shall meet promptly with our requirements. In that case our Army shall not fail to pay you in our own currency.

Those who conduct any defiance and who act spy [sic] against our

271

enterprises, shall be courtmartialled and the Army shall take strict cause to execute such criminals by shooting!

Dated this 10th day of December 2601 in Japanese calendar or by this 10th day of December 1941.

BY ORDER OF THE JAPANESE COMMANDER-IN-CHIEF

News of the surrender of Guam to the Japanese spread rapidly to all parts of the island. As enemy troops spread out from Agana, Americans, individually or in groups, surrendered to them. Permanent American residents, among them Chester Butler, A. W. Johnston, Albert P. Manley, William Gay, Arthur Jackson, and others, were interned in Agana along with Bishop Olano, who was a Spanish citizen, and American members of the Catholic clergy. Guamanian members of the Guam Police Department, the Insular Force, and the Insular Naval Force were interned in Dorn Hall School on the west side of the Plaza de España. Most of the Americans were interned in the Agana cathedral and in the St. Vincent de Paul building. Governor McMillin and some of his aides, however, were confined to the Naval Hospital. For several days after the fall of Guam, Americans surrendered or were captured in the outlying districts and were brought into town in trucks. Some Americans, stripped of all clothing, were made to stand in the hot sun. Others were forced to run around the plaza so as to be made to appear ridiculous in front of Guamanians who had been herded into the area for the purpose of obtaining passes. Navy nurses did not fare much better than the other prisoners. The Japanese disregarded all international rules and regulations governing the conduct and care of prisoners of war. They also disregarded many of the laws of human decency and showed nothing but contempt for their American prisoners. The Guamanians were shocked and frightened by their deeds.

On January 10, 1942, Bishop Olano, the American priests, and the women were loaded on trucks and taken to the docks at Piti. Governor McMillin, marines, sailors, civilian construction workers, and American residents of Guam were compelled to march from Agana to Piti. Upon arrival at the docks, they were loaded on board the *Argentina-maru* and sent to prison camps in Japan.

272

22. Mouth of the Agana River, 1918, prior to the great typhoon of that year from which only the palm tree at the left survived. This tree inspired the design of the official seal of Guam, adopted in 1930. The shape of the seal is that of the sling stones used by the ancient Chamorros in hunting and fighting. Also included in the seal is a sketch of a typical flying prao boat, with Point Ritidian in the background.

23. Village of Sumay, 1925. Fort Santa Cruz was situated on the small island in the background.

24. The capital city of Agana as it appeared in 1925.

25. Historic Fort Santa Cruz, located on a small island in Apra Harbor, as it appeared in 1925. Today only a plaque marks the spot.

26.  Marine Barracks at Sumay in 1925

27. The Governor's Palace, Marine Barracks, and the old bandstand in the historic Plaza de Espana in 1925.

28. The most common means of transportation in 1925

29. Old schoolhouse west of Agana, 1925

30. General Baptist Mission in Agana, 1925

31. Church of Our Lady of Guadelupe at Sumay, 1925

32. Guam's first legislature

33. Gov. McMillin and family, 1941.

## ARMY RULE

Guam was captured by units of the Japanese army. Shortly after American prisoners had been sent to Japan, however, the army units departed for Rabaul, leaving the island to be garrisoned and governed by the navy. Because they believed that Guam would remain theirs forever, the Japanese set out to incorporate it into their new Greater East Asia Co-Prosperity Sphere. The island's name was changed to Omiyajima (Great Shrine Island), and Agana was renamed Akashi (Red or Bright Stone).[5] During the period of army rule especially, the Guamanian people were subjected to acts of brutality and to indignities of the worst sort.

On the day of the invasion, several Guamanians were captured by Japanese troops and taken to Agana, where they were given identification passes. The pass was a piece of cloth about two inches wide and from four to six inches long. It bore Japanese inscriptions indicating that the bearer was a native. It was stamped with two red marks. One stamp, about an inch square, was the stamp of the *minseisho*, a civilian section of the army. The other square, a smaller one, was the stamp of the issuing officer. Upon receiving their passes, these few Guamanians, as well as some members of the Naval Militia, were released and sent out to call the people from their hiding places. For several days the Guamanians came by the thousands and stood in lines for hours waiting for passes. The old Leary School and the plaza areas were crowded with frightened islanders. They were unprepared to face their conquerors, for they had never fully believed that Japan would really fight against the United States. That Japan would ever capture Guam was something no Guamanian ever thought possible. Now that the war was really upon them, they did not know what to do. They were confused and they were frightened. Getting the pass and the first encounter with the Japanese was, for many, a terrifying ordeal.

The cloth pass was the only identification that the Japanese required. Since it was issued only once, great care was taken to prevent losing it or getting it dirty. The identification pass was pinned on the chest, ready for viewing by any of the thousands of Japanese soldiers who might wish to check it. Some people put cellophane around the pass and a piece of cardboard behind it to keep it from getting wet, wrinkled, or dirty. The pass was required to be worn at all times, for about a year. By this time many passes had become extremely dirty. Yet they had to be pinned on clean shirts or dresses. Many were embarrassed because they had to wear the passes wherever they went. Needless to say, the identification tags occasioned many jokes at the expense of the unsuspecting Japanese.

During the first few days of Japanese occupation the Guamanians learned, by force of arms, sticks, and fists, the Japanese custom of bowing. There were three degrees of bowing: (1) the *rei*, a slight nodding of the head for a friend or a common man; (2) the *keirei*, bending forward from the waistline at a 45-degree angle, for members of the armed forces, police, and other officials —virtually all Japanese on Guam; and (3) the *saikerei*, bending the body at a 90-degree angle for the emperor and his immediate family.

Bowing was not practiced on Guam before the war, so the custom was entirely foreign and new to the people. When the Japanese armies occupied Guam, signs were placed all over the island—Agana especially was flooded with them—reading: "You Must Stop Here and Bow to Us." Every sentry box, office, and important military area bore such signs. Many Guamanians, not knowing what the signs meant, went about their business without paying much attention to them. As a result, many people, young and old, men and women, were slapped, kicked, or hit with sticks and the butts of rifles for failing to bow. Many were punished for not bowing properly. The custom required that a person make a full stop, turn to the sentry box or individual, and make the appropriate bow. If one bowed too low, he was punished. If he bowed too slightly, he was punished. The bow was required to be appropriate to the person and the occasion. Although it was done begrudgingly, the Guamanians learned how to bow.

During the short-lived but ruthless period of army rule, two young Guamanians met death before firing squads. They were Alfred León Guerrero Flores, of Agana, and Francisco B. Won-Pat, younger brother of the first speaker of the Guam legislature, the Honorable Antonio B. Won-Pat. Alfred Flores was accused of smuggling a note to one of the American prisoners of war. During the period of internment Guamanians were permitted to bring gifts of food, candy, fruit, cigarettes, and clothing to the American prisoners. So many did so that the temporary prisons were always crowded during visiting hours. Alfred Flores was among those who regularly brought gifts. One day, according to the charges read before his execution, Alfred smuggled a note, buried under some rice in a lunch pail, to one of the prisoners. The note, according to a reliable source, requested from one of the American prisoners information concerning the locations of dynamite and other materials which Flores did not wish to fall into Japanese hands. He wanted to destroy the dynamite.

Francisco Won-Pat was accused of stealing food and other items from the Pomeroy Company warehouse at Sumay. It was generally known among the Guamanians, however, that young Won-Pat was falsely accused. Nevertheless, both he and Alfred were taken to military headquarters. There they were beaten with fists, clubs, and water hoses until they "confessed" to the charges.

On the day set for the execution, people who had come to Agana in search of food, the handful who were staying in town, and others from the vicinity of Agana were ordered to proceed to Pigo Cemetery. A great number of men, women, and children were forced to walk to Pigo. Among the spectators were relatives of the accused.

The two men were taken to the cemetery in an armed truck, followed by a firing squad. For the benefit of the assembled Guamanians, a Japanese officer read the charges against the accused, in English. The accused were then blindfolded. As the blindfolders moved away from the two, Flores, then Won-Pat, waved goodbye to the crowd. The firing squad took their positions; the squad leader raised his sword above his head. When the sword dropped, a chorus of shots resounded through the still air. Won-

Pat, the smaller of the two, was thrown backward and fell into his grave. Flores, a larger man, crumpled under the shots. The squad got ready to fire again, but it was unnecessary. Both men had died instantly. The crowd, which came not knowing what to expect, dispersed quietly. They were too stupefied to speak. They had witnessed Japanese justice and were afraid. This event was one that was hardly ever mentioned either during or after the Japanese occupation.

The major concern of the Japanese army was to establish peace and order. This it did with little difficulty. Troops were stationed as far south as the Talofofo River and in Sumay, Piti, Asan, Sinajana, Barrigada, Dededo, Tumon, and Agana Heights. Army trucks, motorcycles, bicycles, and horses thronged Agana and its vicinity. Curfew hours were set from sunset to sunrise, and complete blackouts were ordered. Agana was virtually a Japanese army camp. All government buildings in the plaza area, all school buildings in Agana, and a great many houses were occupied by Japanese troops without compensation, in spite of the proclamation. All cars, radios, and cameras were confiscated. Houses and stores were looted, and not a few were stripped of their lumber for firewood.

Civilian affairs of the island were delegated to a minor branch of the army called the *minseisho*. The *minseisho* was responsible for issuing passes and ration tickets and, in general, seeing to it that civilian needs were met. It was the *minseisho* which ordered all American currency turned into Japanese currency, at the ridiculously low rate of four and five to one. Because the people were convinced of the immediate return of the Americans, the amount of money exchanged was very small. In time, the American bills and coins became quite useful as a medium of exchange for scarce commodities. This was especially true near the middle and close of the Japanese period of occupation.

The *minseisho* ordered all Guamanian store owners to open their stores to the general public and sell their goods for Japanese currency. People flocked into Agana each day to obtain rice, sugar, and canned goods. Standing in line to buy commodities became a common experience. Since no replacements were available, however, the stores soon ran out of supplies. One by one they closed, until only the Japanese Kohatsu Company, located at the Atkins-Kroll store in Agana, remained open. As the end of the war drew nearer, even this store was closed to the general public.

## NAVY RULE

THE KEIBITAI: In March 1942, the last units of the Japanese army departed from Guam. Control of the island was turned over to a navy unit called the *keibitai*. Commander Hayashi, commandant of the navy troops, occupied the Governor's Palace in Agana. Officers and men of his command occupied other government buildings around the plaza. Unlike the army, officers and men of the naval unit were well disciplined. They generally kept to their quarters during the greater portion of the week. When enlisted men went on leave, they neither molested the populace nor disturbed them. They cultivated friendships everywhere. In exchange for hospitality, they gave the people candy, cigarettes, and other articles which they were able to get from their stores.

Naval personnel were not all sweetness and light, however. In their search for six or seven Americans who escaped into the woods, they were relentless and ruthless. Searching for the Americans was the navy's biggest job. Every day squads of men scoured the woods. In about a year's time, they succeeded in killing every American except one: Navy radio man George R. Tweed, who survived the war in Guam.

In their quest for the Americans, the *keibitai* searching parties were overzealous. Scores of Guamanians were punished until they were near the point of death. Many more suffered permanent injury. Innocent men, women, and children were questioned. In the process they were slapped, hit with fists, or clubbed. Many were taken to Agana for more questioning and grilling. The more vigorous the denial, the more brutal the punishment. For many people there was simply no way to escape punishment.

During the first year and a half of naval rule, Guam was "governed tolerably well."[6] The people were left pretty much to themselves. Except for those who were accused of aiding Tweed and other Americans, or those who were accused of committing crimes, the majority of the people were not bothered at all. Those who worked for the Japanese were paid for their work. Payment was low and in Japanese currency (yen); nevertheless, they were paid. Those who wished to remain on their farms were permitted to do so. Some of Guam's prewar leading citizens elected to stay on their farms. They planted food, vegetables, and fruits and raised what livestock they could. What they couldn't grow, they secured from their neighbors through barter. Trading or *kokan* (Japanese, meaning "exchange"), as it was called, became a common practice. Cigarettes, clothes, and rice were in great demand. *Kokan tamago* (exchange eggs) was a common expression, since eggs had become a popular medium of exchange. Throughout this period, the people of Guam managed to live off the land and the sea—something they had not done before, nor have done again since the war. Men and women who had never worked on farms found themselves working there in order to survive. Guam was able to produce, in time, enough food for its population—and some over for the Japanese army.

The period of Japanese occupation was not all work and struggle. In the evenings the people, most of whom had moved away from Agana and other towns to their farm areas, amused themselves with dancing and singing. Parties were held on numerous occasions. Movies could be seen without charge by those who cared to see Japanese films. On various occasions the Japanese authorities presented variety programs for the entertainment of the *keibitai* officers and men and for the general public as well. Such programs were usually presented in the Plaza de España. They were generally well attended by both the Japanese and the local people. Baseball games and other games of sport, such as Japanese *sumo* wrestling, were usually open to the public. School contests were also held on three or four occasions, and prizes were given to the top teams. These were always well attended. The vast majority of the Guamanians, however, entertained themselves in their own ways. Novena parties were frequent. So were birthday parties and wedding feasts—when priests were available. Dancing in the moonlight and other forms of merrymaking and entertainment were plentiful throughout the first year and a half of Japanese naval administration.

The *keibitai* had ultimate responsibility for everything that happened on Guam during the period of naval administration. Immediate administration and control of civilian matters, however, rested with civilian authorities collectively known as the *minseibu*. The change from *minseisho* to *minseibu* occurred when the army left Guam. While the *minseisho* was a minor section of the army, the *minseibu* was virtually independent of the *keibitai*. The latter, however, had some measure of control over the *minseibu* in matters pertaining to the security of the island. The *minseibu* occupied the St. Vincent de Paul building, adjacent to the cathedral in Agana, after American prisoners of war had been sent to Japan. The cathedral was used as an auditorium.

The head of the *minseibu* was an elderly man known only by his last name and his rank in the Japanese navy. He was Lieutenant Commander Homura. Homura was recalled to active duty when war broke out and was assigned to Guam as the *minseibucho* (head of the *minseibu*). The *minseibucho* was an emotional old man who walked is if he were carrying a heavy load on his shoulders. He had virtually no contact with the Guamanians except for a few individuals who had to see him for one reason or another. He met the vast majority of the people only in mass meetings and delighted in talking to them about the mighty Japanese armed forces. He was Japan's number one propagandist on the island.

During the early part of his administration, Homura ordered mass meetings to be held in the Agana cathedral. The Guamanians were compelled to attend. At such gatherings Homura told the people about the "progress" of the war. On every occasion he was sure to extol the virtues of Japan and the might of its military forces. He never failed to put in a word for the "spirit of Japan." *Nippon seishin* (spirit of Japan), he often said, was what made Japan the great nation that she was. He never failed to end his propaganda meetings with the traditional three cheers for the emperor: *"Tennoheika, banzai!"* When Singapore fell to the Japanese, he forced hundreds of people to assemble with Japanese flags in front of the palace. These people were compelled to march through the main streets of Agana shouting *"Banzai! Banzai! Banzai!"* every few hundred yards or so. On several occasions he forced many people to line up on both sides of the street in front of the palace to greet visiting dignitaries. Homura loved his country so much that tears often ran down his cheeks and his voice often trembled with emotion as he spoke to the assembled Guamanians.

During the height of the Japanese victories, when conditions were relatively quiet on Guam, Homura called together Guam's leading citizens and organized them into a club known as the Kyowakai (Peace Club). Without consulting him, Homura appointed a Guamanian to be chairman of the new organization. Homura outlined the club's purpose, namely, to co-operate with Japan in winning the war and in making Guam a part of the Greater East Asia Co-Prosperity Sphere. Neither the "chairman" nor the members really understood what the club was all about. Many were surprised to learn that they were members at all. No one had volunteered to join the organization. Since the *minsei-bucho* or his representative conducted all its monthly meetings, the Guamanian chairman never exercised the duties of a presiding officer. The meetings were usually devoted to propaganda lectures. On one occasion, members of the organization were called together and marched to the present Naval Air Station, Agana area. There they were forced to pull weeds and help in clearing the area for an airfield.

During the peak of his propaganda activities, Homura told the people that "never in a hundred years" would the Americans return to Guam. He told them that California was a Japanese colony and that the fall of Washington, D.C., was just a matter of time. Some of his statements were so ridiculous that they offered the people of Guam their only comic relief in a rather difficult situation. Toward the close of the war, Homura was more helpful to the Guamanians than he intended to be. His tales of Japanese "victories" were concerned only with "gains." Many of the people, however, were able to read more between the lines than Homura realized. During the closing months of 1943 and the beginning of 1944, Homura announced the results of various battles in the Pacific. According to his story, Japan was winning all of them. Little did he know that each "victory" seemed, to some Guamanians familiar with Pacific geography, to be drawing the area of conflict closer and closer to Guam. From such information they concluded that the Americans were winning some battles and were slowly pushing across the Pacific toward Guam.

Homura was not considered to be a cruel man. He generally kept to his post and attended to civilian affairs without fanfare. He visited every village regularly and kept himself informed of general conditions on the island. The *minseibucho* remained in Guam for the duration of the war. It is believed that he died on the island, a victim of his own sword.

For purposes of administration, the Japanese authorities divided rural Guam into several districts. Such districts were usually about the same as those that prevailed before the war. In every district a Guamanian commissioner, called the *soncho*, was appointed. In Agana, where the districts followed the old *barrio* boundaries, the head of the district was known as the *kucho*. Like the *soncho* in the outlying districts, the *kucho* were appointed without consultation and were given no choice in the matter. Some of the men who were appointed district commissioners in Agana were Vicente Herrero, Manuel Lujan, Matias L. G. Pérez, Juan Manibusan, Antonio Baza, and Vicente Rosario. These men, like their counterparts in the outlying districts, distributed electric light bills, passed information to the population, notified people to attend lectures, and attended ceremonies of a civil and religious nature. They were without real authority and had virtually no voice in government affairs. Indeed, their principal duty was to serve as messengers for the Japanese. Yet they were subjected to great pressures to produce for one thing or another. They were expected to assemble people whenever the *minseibucho* so desired. Yet they had no authority to compel the people to obey. Lacking such authority, they were themselves subjected to punishment for their "failure to produce."

The most dreaded and feared of all Japanese were the members of the civilian police force. The force was part of the *minseibu* and was quartered in the old Agana Police Station across the plaza from the Governor's Palace. The office of the Japanese civilian in charge of the force was situated nearby. There were three to five Japanese in the main station. About ten others were stationed in the outlying districts. The Japanese policemen were assisted by a crew of Saipanese interpreters. Some of them were as much dreaded as the Japanese themselves.

The main task of the police force was to maintain peace and order among the inhabitants. The Agana station, as well as those in the outlying districts, served as a listening post for the *keibitai* and for the main office of the *minseibu*. It was the duty of the police to investigate all criminal acts and prepare violators for trial. In this function, they had one general procedure. When a person was accused of a crime—and there were a thousand and one crimes, from speaking English to murder and spying—the police would seize him for questioning. They assumed that a man was guilty until he proved himself innocent. This was in conflict with the concept of justice which the Guamanians had learned through experience with the American court system. Questioning was always accompanied by physical punishment such as kicking, punching with the closed fist, clubbing, suffocating with a cold wet towel on the nose and mouth, and drowning with a water hose. There was no way of escaping the punishment. If a person admitted his guilt, he was punished for the offense. If he denied the charges, he was accused of lying and punished accordingly. If he elected to remain silent, he was punished for "hiding something." In many cases, the easiest way out was to admit guilt whether guilty or not. Those released after going through such an ordeal were usually warned not to discuss the punishment.

After a "confession" of guilt had been wrung from a person, one of two things might happen to him. He would either be brought to trial in a Japanese court or released by the police. If he was taken to court, the judge would read the charges, and the accused would admit his guilt. He then would receive his sentence, usually a prison term. Towards the close of the Japanese occupation there were from thirty to fifty Guamanians in prison. They were used as farm workers, house-builders, and in other kinds of manual labor.

In April 1942, schools were opened in Agana for the purpose of teaching the Japanese language. Adults as well as children were compelled to attend. Among the first students were some of the island's most prominent prewar citizens. Compulsory attendance was permitted to lapse at times, but at other times it was strictly enforced, particularly in Agana. Many were punished for missing school.

The first schools were conducted by Japanese sailors attached to the *keibitai*. On the whole, they were patient with their students as they attempted to teach Japanese vocabularies, simple sentences, and phrases. In July or August 1942 a group of civilian instructors from the Micronesian islands under Japanese control arrived on Guam. They replaced the sailors as instructors and enlarged the program. The schools were more efficiently organized, and outlying district schools were opened. Every school had a Japanese instructor who taught reading, writing, arithmetic, and Japanese games and songs. Children were in attendance from 7:30 to 11:30 in the morning. Adults attended school for about an hour and a half in the evening.

With the arrival of civilian instructors and the opening of schools in each village, along with three in Agana, it soon became necessary to employ more teachers. In September 1942, Japanese superintendent S. Takenaka announced a plan for training Guamanian teaching assistants. Volunteers were sought, but none were forthcoming. Realizing that the plan might fail for lack of volunteers, the village and district commissioners were ordered to select a candidate from each district. In October the first of the teaching-assistant candidates entered the training school in Agana. There were twelve young men and thirteen young women in the first class. They were in their late teens or early twenties and represented almost every major village on the island. The students stayed in dormitories throughout the six months of training, except weekends, when they were permitted to go home. The boys stayed on the first floor of the Bishop's House in San Ramon, and the girls were quartered in the naval station library. Classes were held at the library from 8:00 in the morning until about 2:00 in the afternoon. The training included reading, writing, some elements of arithmetic, geography and Japanese history, Japanese patriotic and school songs, and calisthenics. The instructors were all Japanese, except for a Guamanian who came in periodically to teach music, and everything was taught in Japanese. At the close of the six-month training period, the students were awarded certificates and assigned to various schools. In Agana, two boys were assigned to the Padre Palomo School, two girls to Althouse School, and two girls to Anigua School. The others were assigned to village schools so that every school had at least one Guamanian teaching assistant.

The second group of trainees was a little larger than the first. They began their training in April and were graduated in October 1943. The third group entered the school in November 1943, but was unable to complete its work because of frequent interruptions due to the great pressure of plantation projects and defense work. Moreover, the American forces were beginning to make their presence felt in the area. As a result, the students spent most of the latter part of their training period out in the forests hiding from aircraft. The teaching assistants were used almost exclusively for school work and occasionally as interpreters. Toward the close of the occupation period, they were used as interpreters and as supervisors in agricultural projects.

Throughout most of the occupation, religious needs of the people were cared for by three Guamanians; two Catholic priests and one Baptist minister. When Bishop Olano and members of the Catholic clergy were sent to prisons in Japan, the spiritual welfare of the overwhelming majority of the Guamanians was entrusted to two native priests. They were Fathers Jesús Baza Duenas and Oscar Lujan Calvo. After the war Father Calvo was raised to the rank of Monsignor. Shortly after the bishop's departure, Father Duenas was named pro-vicar apostolic of Guam. He

284

and Father Calvo divided the island between them. Father Calvo administered to the needs of the people who lived in the area north of Chalan Pago and east of Piti. Father Duenas served the southern area, with headquarters at the church of St. Joseph in Inarajan. Both priests covered the island quite thoroughly on foot, horseback, and occasionally in borrowed jitneys or in buses. In spite of their efforts, however, many of the faithful died without the benefit of the church's sacraments.

In November 1942, two Japanese priests arrived on Guam. They were Monsignor Fukahori and Father Peter Komatsu. Monsignor Fukahori brought a letter from Bishop Olano in Tokyo. The letter named Father Duenas pro-vicar.

Father Duenas was one of the most respected persons on the island during the Japanese occupation. He was born in Guam in 1914. After attending elementary school in Agana, he studied under American Jesuit priests in Manila. By 1938 he returned to Guam and was ordained to the priesthood by Bishop Olano. Father Duenas did not always co-operate with the Japanese. One account says:

> They "suggested" that he submit his sermons to a censor. They asked him to make official announcements during the services.
> Father Duenas replied by omitting sermons from his services. He refused to read any announcements other than routine notices of meetings and new regulations.
> Once a month he and Father Calvo met at Agana with the Minseibu, which was composed of the Japanese civil governor and his staff, to discuss the welfare of the people of the island. At each session Father Duenas suggested improvements: The people needed more food and new clothing. The prices set by the Kohatsu Company were high. The people were being terrorized, treated like slaves. Women, forced to work long hours in the rice fields, were slapped across the face and beaten. There was inadequate medical care.
> Each time the governor promised to look into these matters, and each time he did nothing.[7]

On one occasion, when Father Duenas was absent, the Japanese priests held a meeting in Inarajan. They told the people that the American forces had been defeated and that Japan wanted only peace for Guam. When everyone co-operated, they said, the people would enjoy great prosperity and happiness. Upon his return to Inarajan, Father Duenas wrote an angry letter to the Japanese priests. He told them that the Guamanians "did not believe they were Catholic priests, but Japanese spies. He quoted the late Pope Benedict XV, who during the First World War had said that it was not proper for a priest in a foreign country to preach of his own country's greatness."[8] What the Japanese priests did with the letter is not known.

On July 2, 1944, nineteen days before the American reoccupation of Guam began, Father Duenas was ordered once more to appear at the office of the *minseibu*. When he arrived, he found that his nephew, Edward Camacho Duenas, the 31-year-old island attorney, was also there. Both men were questioned about the American sailor, George Tweed, who was still in hiding on the island. Both denied knowing Tweed's whereabouts. Then "they were beaten, whipped and tortured. Water was poured in the Father's nose from a hose, and afterwards his bruised and bloody body was placed in the broiling sun for the ants and flies to do their worst."[9] About midnight the *minseibu* turned the two almost unconscious men over to the secret police. After more torture they were taken to Tai. There, at about four o'clock in the morning, both were beheaded. Thus, at the age of thirty, was ended the life of Father Jesús Baza Duenas.

In March 1945 Father Duenas' body was exhumed. In a solemn ceremony, attended by the people and the highest military and civic leaders of Guam, he was buried under the high altar of St. Joseph's Church, Inarajan. Since that time the church has been enlarged and the altar moved back. In front of the altar, however, is a marble slab marking the burial place of this beloved Guamanian martyr.

During the occupation, the Baptist mission continued to be under the care of the Reverend Joaquin F. Sablan. Like the Catholic priests, Reverend Sablan was hampered by too large a territory to cover and by lack of transportation. His ministry was made more difficult near the end of the occupation period. At that time the Japanese authorities, ignoring his clerical position, forced him to work on defense projects.

Local businessmen were ordered to open their stores and sell goods to the general public. As a result, all goods were quickly sold. In time all the stores were closed, and the Kohatsu Company remained as the only business firm on the island. One local meat market, belonging to Pedro Martinez, was forced to open during most of this period. Japanese personnel, however, had top priority in buying. The market was opened once a week. After the Japanese had bought up all the choice items, the remainder was sold to the Guamanians. The demand for meat far exceeded the supply. A tuna-fishing company entered the island about the middle of the occupation. The same priority system prevailed and, as far as the local people were concerned, business was nonexistent.

PERIOD OF THE KAIKONTAI: The third and final period of Japanese rule, the last six or seven months of the occupation, may be called the period of the *kaikontai*. The *kaikontai*, an agricultural group, came to Guam early in 1944. Its purpose was to provide food for thousands of returning army troops sent to defend the island against American forces whose island-hopping campaign was bringing them ever nearer to Guam. Because the prosecution of the war was more important than civil administration, almost every Japanese civilian employed by the *minseibu* was drafted into agricultural projects. Guamanian men, women, and children were forced to work in the fields. Schools were closed, and children under twelve years of age were sent home. If they were over twelve, they were made to work with the adults. All available hands were drafted into the fields. Only invalids and those gravely ill were spared.

The headquarters of the *kaikontai* was located at Tai, near where the present Father Duenas Memorial School is located. It was there, in fact, and at the hands of the *kaikontai*, that Father Duenas was beheaded. In their headquarters area, high-ranking members of the *kaikontai* committed some of the worst crimes that occurred during the occupation. Toward the close of this period, several of Guam's leading families were interned at Tai. These Guamanians were made to serve the Japanese officials and were compelled to submit to indecencies and indignities. It was in this camp, too, that several Guamanians were beheaded, for reasons known only to the Japanese.

The *kaikontai* was caught between two mighty forces. On the one hand, American forces were drawing nearer each day. On the other, Japanese army authorities were demanding more and more food as supplies went lower and lower. In an attempt to remedy the food situation, the *kaikontai* began pushing the people harder. The *taicho* (district supervisors) began using clubs and rifle butts to get more work out of the Guamanians. Brutalities were reported everywhere. In Barrigada and Mangilao, where some of the worst incidents were reported, young and old alike were punished almost daily. In Merizo and Agat, scores of Guamanians were herded into caves and air-raid shelters and blasted with hand grenades. Some lived to tell of the horrible experience, but most of them died.

The people of Guam, like their fellow Americans on the mainland, had no idea how long the war would last. The general consensus at the outbreak of war was that the Japanese would be defeated in about a month's time. This childlike belief in the immediate defeat of Japan provided a basis for hope during the hard years of the occupation. Just before Christmas 1941, about two weeks after the Japanese invasion, rumors of a pending American reoccupation of Guam spread throughout the island. The Americans were massing in great strength just off Guam, the rumor went. They were coming in on December 25 to recapture the island as a Christmas gift for the people. On Christmas Eve, the people waited impatiently for the first sign of the American forces. They also waited throughout Christmas Day, but of course, the Americans did not return. The Guamanians had no way of knowing that the Japanese sneak attack on Pearl Harbor had almost wiped out the Pacific fleet. That the Americans did not come back on Christmas of 1941, however, was considered to be no cause for alarm. The people went on hoping. In February another rumor spread throughout the island. This time the Americans were coming in on

Washington's Birthday. No Americans came. This, too, did not dampen their hopes. Again in July 1942, rumors of an American invasion cropped up on the island. Each time it was scheduled to occur on a major American holiday. By Christmas of 1943 there was still hope, but no more rumors. The Guamanian people, driven to despair by their conquerors, could only utter silent prayers for the return of the Americans.

During the latter part of 1943 and the remainder of the occupation period, two anti-Japanese songs were sung by the Guamanians. One, a satire directed at the Japanese teachers, was entitled "Sensei Na Sensei, Hafa Nanamu" (Teacher, Teacher, What Have You to Eat?). The most popular and perhaps most daring of Guamanian songs, however, was "Uncle Sam, Please Come Back to Guam." The song was sung to the tune of an old American ballad popular on Guam before the war. The Japanese became frantic over the effects of the underground song, and many people were punished for singing it. During the war, no one seemed to know who wrote it. After the war, however, several persons claimed authorship. Sung in English, a language despised by the Japanese, the song went as follows:

Early Monday morning
    The action came to Guam,
Eighth of December,
    Nineteen forty-one.

        Oh, Mr. Sam, Sam, my dear Uncle Sam,
        Won't you please come back to Guam?

Our lives are in danger
    You better come
And kill all the Japanese
    Right here on Guam

        Oh, Mr. Sam, etc.

And on and on, with numerous verses added, to the despair of the Japanese.

## THE RETAKING OF GUAM

PROLOGUE TO A LANDING: On February 23, 1944, twelve American carrier-based planes bombed the Orote airstrip. This preliminary attack was the answer to the Guamanians' prayers. It marked the beginning of the end for the Japanese on Guam. The attack brought real joy to the people of Guam. It also ushered in the worst period of Japanese rule. All local able-bodied men were recruited for work on defense projects. Before this time, some men had worked at the Orote air base and in other defense activities, but such work had been partially voluntary. Many were compelled to work for the Japanese in order to secure Japanese money with which to buy rice—the only means by which rice could be obtained. For a day's work, the men received one cup of rice and from one to five yen. The money was valueless, but the rice was carried home with great care.

After the first raid, the Japanese worked feverishly to strengthen the defenses on the island. Every male from twelve to sixty years of age was drafted into labor battalions. These battalions completed the airstrip at Orote and built one at Jalaguag, the present location of the Agana Naval Air Station, and started a third one in Dededo. They paved roads, dug air-raid shelters in the hillsides, and built pillboxes and gun emplacements on the beaches and in other areas. Such work was done without heavy equipment. Only wheelbarrows, picks, and shovels were available. Men worked throughout the day under the worst conditions. They were often kicked, slapped, punched, and clubbed by their Japanese and Korean supervisors. The Guamanians worked side by side with hundreds of Koreans brought as laborers to the island by the Japanese. These Koreans were treated the same as the Guamanians. Like the Guamanians, they were driven like slaves by both Japanese and Korean supervisors. The only relief from the heavy work was afforded when American planes attacked Guam in force.

When the preliminary attacks on Guam became sustained, most of the people were moved to concentration camps located at Maimai, Tai, Manengon, Talofofo, Inarajan, and several other places. The removal order was issued on July 10, 1944. Since the Japanese expected to make their strong defense against the Americans on the northern plateau, the people of Yigo were the first to be moved. Residents of the Mt. Santa Rosa area were sent first to waterless Maimai. They were joined later by people from other parts of the Yigo region. The people took with them as much food as they could carry on bullcarts, on the backs of cows and carabaos, and on their own shoulders and backs. Before the march they were assembled in front of the Yigo School. At about 7:30 p.m. the long walk began. Men, women, and children, the well and the sick, marched throughout the night. From Yigo some went one way, some another. One group walked to Dededo and then across to Barrigada, following approximately the present Harmon to Barrigada road. The other group walked as far as Asatdas, where Marbo is now located, and cut left on a trail to Barrigada. The first group reached Barrigada by morning and continued on to Mangilao, where they waited for the rest. The second group, a larger one, reached Mangilao about 4:30 in the afternoon. The wretched column consisted of exhausted men, women, children, the sick who were hardly able to carry themselves, and invalids on stretchers borne on the shoulders of tired men. The Japanese civilian guards were relentless, permitting no one to stop by the wayside. Now and then the spine-tingling sound of club against flesh and the painful cries of men and women resounded through the line of march as the Japanese guards punished those who fell behind. Many who dropped from exhaustion were picked up by relatives and friends and dragged along the way.

From Maimai, the people of Yigo marched along the Price-Tai road to Manengon, behind Yona. The people of Dededo, Barrigada, and Mangilao followed behind them. The latter group proceeded all the way to Talofofo, where they stayed until their liberation. Residents of Agat and Apla moved into the Yona region. Those who lived in Inarajan, Merizo, and Umatac were grouped in Malolo and other locations. Almost no one was spared the march. There were a few, however, who either refused to obey the Japanese order or did not know about it. On all marches and in all camps, the same harsh treatment was meted out to the Guamanians.

Once the people reached the camp sites, they hurriedly gathered coconut fronds for building shelters. Almost every camp was a sea of mud. It seemed that two prayers were answered at once: rain and the Americans. For about a year, Guam had received little rain. Fields were dry and crops were dying. The people had prayed for rain about as much as they had prayed for the return of the Americans. As the steady drone of American planes sounded in the skies, dark clouds gathered above the island, and rain began to fall. The rain fell steadily throughout most of the American invasion period and during the mopping-up operations that followed. As a result, the concentration camps, which were spared attacks by American planes, were constantly wet, and the people in them lived in utter misery.

Fortunately for the Guamanians, their stay in the concentration camps lasted only a few weeks. It was, however, perhaps one of their worst experiences during the war. No one except the Japanese knew why the people had been confined in the camps. It was believed by many that the Japanese intended to slaughter the island's entire population. Others believed that the only purpose of the Japanese was to remove the Guamanians from areas where they might have been able to help the Americans. It would seem, however, that if the Japanese had wished to destroy the Guamanians, there was nothing at the time to prevent them from doing so. Regardless of their motives, their action proved to be a blessing in disguise. If the people had been permitted to remain on their farms or in their homes, especially in Agana, Asan, Agat, Sumay, and Piti, and the northern communities of Barrigada, Dededo, and Yigo, large numbers of them might have been killed or wounded in the heavy fighting which occurred in those areas.

On July 21, the day American forces landed on Guam, eight men in Merizo hastened their liberation by revolting against their Japanese guards and killing about sixteen of them. The men then paddled their canoes out to sea, where they were picked up by

American naval forces. They were reportedly used as observers and guides for the bombing operations.

Guamanians in the camps got their first look at American troops about a week after the invasion began. Some men who were out gathering food in the jungle near Yona and Manengon met an American patrol. They immediately received cigarettes, chocolate, and other American goods to show to the people as proof that the Americans had landed on the island. Within a few minutes of their return to camp, a number of young men went out in search of the Americans. By noon, the first American patrols were led to the camp sites. Japanese guards still remaining in the area were shot on sight.

The arrival of American patrols was a happy occasion for the Guamanians. At last their prayers had been answered. The sick were immediately better, and smiles appeared once more on happy faces, but the ordeal was not yet over. The march to freedom still lay ahead. The people were overjoyed, but they were too weak and tired to engage in wild celebrations. The following day some members of the Insular Force, with renewed courage and vigor, took upon themselves the task of directing the evacuation of the people from Manengon and Yona to Anigua and Agat. The people took up their few possessions and marched out of the camps. From Yona some walked across the mountains to Anigua. Others walked to Piti, where waiting trucks carried them to Agat. There, in temporary shelters, they settled down to await the completion of the American reoccupation of Guam.

By late February 1944 American military forces completed the capture of Eniwetok in the Marshall Islands. In a bold and daring move, they planned to strike at Guam and the Marianas, more than a thousand miles to the westward. Before the returning Americans could strike at the homeland of the enemy, it was necessary for them to destroy Japanese forces in the Marianas. Thereupon it would be possible to establish bases there for large-scale air attacks on Japan. As soon, therefore, as the Americans had secured the Marshalls, they launched air and naval attacks against the Carolines and the Marianas. "Large carrier-plane formations hit

Truk in the Carolines late in February, sinking 19 ships and seriously damaging shore installations. A strong task force, including hundreds of carrier-based aircraft, attacked Saipan and nearby Tinian on 23 February; a small raid by 12 fighters was made on Guam. These were the preliminary actions toward neutralizing the Carolines and preparing for an invasion of the Marianas."[10]

The American air raid that occurred on February 23, 1944, was a sure sign to the Guamanians that the event they desired most, the return of the Americans, was about to take place. The Japanese, however, had known for a long time that the Americans were coming. As early as September 1943, heavy allied air strikes against the Gilbert Islands had alerted the Japanese Imperial Headquarters to the possibility of an American advance through the central Pacific to Guam and the Marianas. In an attempt to strengthen the islands' defenses, the Japanese started moving some of their best troops from Manchuria to the Marianas. All of them, however, did not arrive as scheduled. American submarines, lying in wait, caught a convoy about forty-eight hours out of Saipan and torpedoed two of the troop transports, sinking one. This ship, the *Sakito-maru*, went to the bottom carrying almost 1,400 men and large amounts of military equipment. Enough reinforcements arrived, however, to swell the enemy military strength to formidable proportions.

When Japanese army units began returning to the island as reinforcements in the spring of 1944, the enemy dropped all pretense of getting along with the natives. The military closed schools, forbade church attendance and took over all government functions. As the garrison grew larger, an acute shortage of food developed and the Japanese seized all available stockpiles. In addition, they drastically increased forced labor demands and further reduced the already small pittance of food supplies of the natives. A bare subsistence ration was issued to the worker, and those too sick or weak to produce had even this withheld.

Finally, the Japanese ordered all people living in the military areas to evacuate their homes, and herded them into concentration camps in the interior. Medical supplies were limited, sanitation non-existent, and food inadequate. Hundreds died, and small children who did survive became stunted and deformed from disease and malnutrition. Human bodies were beaten and broken, but within them the spirit remained alive. Every bow to a Japanese officer, every blow received for some real or fancied offense, every violation of native customs and traditions only served to heighten the resentment against Japanese rule.[11]

The reinforcing army units from Manchuria, organized under the South Marianas Area Group, arrived on Guam in March 1944. Lieutenant General Hideyoshi Obata, commander of the area group, was stranded on Guam when the American invasion of Saipan caught him returning from an inspection tour of the Palau Islands. General Obata, an elderly man who was described by his opposite number in the navy as "extremely intelligent and, for an army officer, of extremely broad vision," supervised plans for the fixed defenses of the island. However, he left command of the actual fighting to Lieutenant General Takeshi Takashina. Thus General Takashina, commander of the 29th Infantry Division, the core of the defense force, was island commander as well.

In June, for purposes of defense, the Japanese had their troops deployed in the following areas. The 2nd Battalion, 18th Infantry, was in the northern part of the island, near the present Anderson Air Force Base. The 48th Independent Mixed Brigade and part of the 29th Division surrounded the Tumon Bay area. The rest of the 29th Division occupied the narrow waist of the island between Agana and Pago Bay. Further south, the 54th Independent Guard Unit held Orote Peninsula; the 38th Infantry, except for the 5th Company, which was on Cabras Island, occupied the Agat area; and the 10th Independent Mixed Regiment spread out from Umatac, around the southernmost part of the island, to as far north as Yona.[12]

Although in June the enemy had stationed his forces to cover the entire island, during July he began to shift them to the areas most vulnerable to an attack from the sea.

Captured documents indicated that the enemy considered these areas to be along the central portion of the west side of the island, where the coastal features presented the least formidable barrier to an invading force . . . the enemy in the sector from Agana to Agat Bay had about twenty-five 75-mm mountain guns, ten 70-mm to 90-mm howitzers, two 37-mm antitank guns, and more than thirty-five machine guns. These

295

were supplemented by at least 25 naval coastal defense and dual-purpose guns. Rifle pits, trenches, and barbed wire added to the strength of the beach defenses, and mid-July studies indicated that the enemy was increasing their depth daily. The Japanese were also believed to have a large amount of mobile artillery and some tanks to lend support to their fixed positions along the shore.

Planning staffs . . . knew that the enemy's defense of the island would be favored by the reef and the hills overlooking the most likely landing beaches, and that enemy defenses in those areas might indicate the intention of fighting hard at the shore. They later learned that the Japanese commanders were ordered: "While the enemy is advancing from the line of coral reefs to the shore, the combined artillery and infantry fire power will be developed. In particular when they reach the water obstacle, oblique and flanking fire will be employed to establish a dense fire net and thus annihilate them on the water."[13]

When the American reoccupation forces landed on the beaches of Guam, they were met by a strongly fortified and determined enemy whose forces numbered almost 18,500 men.

THE CAMPAIGN: Early in December 1943, at a conference in Cairo, Egypt, the combined chiefs of the nations allied against Germany and Japan approved the plan of the United States for striking at Japan by way of Guam and the Marianas. This plan, after several revisions, called for the seizure of Saipan and Tinian by the Fifth Amphibious Corps, consisting of the 2nd and 4th Marine Divisions, and the Army's Twenty-fourth Corps Artillery. This group was to sail from Hawaii. At about the same time, a second group, the Marine Third Amphibious Corps, moving out from Guadalcanal, was to attack and recapture Guam.

Acting in his dual capacity as Commander-in-Chief, Pacific Fleet (CINCPAC) and Pacific Ocean Areas (CINCPOA), Admiral Chester W. Nimitz assigned Admiral Raymond A. Spruance to over-all command of operation FORAGER, the name given to the campaign to take the Marianas from the Japanese. Rear Admiral Richard L. Conolly was given responsibility for landing and protecting the troops of the Third Amphibious Corps.

As finally worked out, the plan to recapture Guam called for simultaneous landings at two points on the west side of the island.

"To accomplish this, Admiral Conolly divided TF [task force] 53 into Northern and Southern Attack Groups, the former under his own command and the latter under Rear Admiral Lawrence F. Reifsnider. In the north, the 3rd Marine Division would land on beaches between Adelup Point and the Tatgua River; in the south, the 1st Provisional Marine Brigade, followed by Third Corps Artillery, would land on beaches between Agat Village and Bangi Point. Both units were then to advance inland and establish the FBL [force beachhead line] along the commanding ground, Adelup-Alutom-Tenjo-Alifan-Facpi Point. Control over the important Orote Peninsula–Apra Harbor area was to be gained as rapidly as possible, and then further operations conducted to seize the remainder of Guam."[14]

After many months of intensive preparations, operation FORAGER began. No operation in all of World War II was conducted on so vast a scale. Five hundred and thirty-five ships of all descriptions, carrying 127,571 troops, took part in the operation. On June 15, 1944, troops of the Northern Attack Force landed on the beaches of Saipan. There they were met by 32,000 enemy troops, and one of the bitterest battles of the Pacific war ensued. As originally planned, it was intended that the invasion of Guam would begin on June 18, but the date had to be changed. The change was made necessary by the fact that the Japanese fleet moved out toward the Marianas to challenge the invaders. As the result of a two-day naval battle, the Japanese lost 426 carrier-based planes in the Battle of the Philippine Sea and fled in hasty retreat toward the safety of the Japanese islands.

On July 8, ships of the U.S. Navy began a systematic "softening" of enemy defenses on Guam. Originally the plan had called for only two days of naval bombardment. Because of the postponement of the invasion of Guam, however, it was possible to blast the enemy positions for thirteen days instead of two.

On 8 July four cruisers of Southern Attack Force led off with a three-day bombardment, firing five thousand five hundred 5- and 8-inch shells on the coastal defenses. From the 12th through the 16th, four battleships fired more than three thousand 14- and 16-inch shells. During the next four days three battleships were joined by two others and by six cruisers, and they blasted the island with more than 16,000 shells. LCIG's [landing craft, infantry gunboats], closing to within a few yards of the reef, raked trenches and pillboxes and reported the location of enemy positions to the heavier ships. Destroyers screened the larger ships and delivered harassing fires at night. Admiral Conolly, directing the bombardment from the flagship, supervised the destruction of every known gun emplacement that could seriously endanger the assault landing.[15]

On July 14, while the Navy's softening-up process was in full swing, underwater demolition teams, the navy's famous frogmen, swam in and checked the barriers that the enemy had built along the assault beaches. They were so protected by covering fire from ships offshore that only one man was killed in the operation. When, on the 17th, other frogmen arrived from Eniwetok, they began four days of blasting tank traps and other obstacles from the reefs. "Off Agat the obstacles consisted mostly of palm-log cribs filled with coral, joined together by wire cable. On the northern reef (Asan Point to Adelup Point), teams found wire cages four feet square and three to four feet high filled with cemented coral. Very little barbed wire and no underwater mines were located. By midnight of W minus 1, hand-placed demolition charges had blown 640 obstacles off Asan and 300 off Agat."[16] Without the effective work of the frogmen, landings at the Agat and Asan beaches would have been extremely difficult, if not impossible.

July 21, 1944, will long remain a day of historic importance to the Guamanian people. It will also be long remembered by their fellow Americans in the armed forces of the United States who, on that day, prepared to end the Japanese occupation of Guam—an occupation that had lasted more than two and one-half years.

By 6 o'clock in the morning, July 21, all assault units of the American liberating forces had reached their assigned positions off Asan and Agat beaches. The total number of ground forces poised for the attack amounted to 54,891 men: 36,933 marines and 17,958 army troops of the 77th Infantry Division. Before the men left their transports, and later, as landing craft carried them to the shore, battleships and cruisers blasted the beaches with high explosive shells. Eighty-four fighter planes and sixteen torpedo bombers from the carriers *Wasp* and *Yorktown* wreaked havoc among the enemy with shells and bombs. At the same time, landing craft opened up with a tremendous rocket barrage along all beaches. When the landing waves were 1,200 yards from shore, the barrage lifted. At 8:29 a.m., troops of the 3rd Marine Division "hit the beach" at Asan. Three minutes later, men of the 1st Provisional Marine Brigade waded ashore at Agat. Thus began the liberation of Guam.

The northern invasion sector lay between a pair of "devil's horns," Adelup Point on the north and Asan Point to the south.[17] In this sector the 3rd Marine Division had orders to move forward in a three-pronged attack. It was to attempt, on the left, to capture Adelup Point and the Chorito cliffs behind it; in the center, the line of cliffs behind Asan; and to the right, the Asan Point region, and if possible, Cabras Island as well. In spite of withering fire from Japanese machine guns, mortars, and artillery, the marines advanced rapidly in the center of the line. Their drive toward Adelup and Asan Points, however, was much slower. "The 3rd Marines, landing on the left flank of the division, soon found that the devil's left horn, Adelup Point, held plenty of the enemy. Support from Chorito Cliff, the high ground immediately off the beach, added to the effectiveness of the point's defenses. The Japanese had survived the tremendous pre-invasion bombardment by holing up in a complex cave system in and behind the cliff. From their perfect observation posts on the height, the enemy directed mortar and artillery fire on beaches being used by the 3rd Marines."[18] Meanwhile, a similar situation at Asan Point had brought the marines to a temporary halt. Reinforcements, however, were streaming ashore all afternoon. By the end of the first day's fighting, Adelup Point was taken, and the marines were dug in on the ridges behind Asan Village and Asan Point.

At dawn the next day (July 22), the enemy launched a counterattack against the 3rd Division's left flank, from Agana and the hills behind Chorito Cliff. Fire from tanks, carrier planes, and ships helped to break up the attack and turn it back. Later in the day, Cabras Island was taken. The marines in the center of the line then moved up the steep hills behind Asan Village toward Mt. Chachao. The Japanese, holed up in caves and entrenched positions, fought them every step of the way. Casualties, as a result, were heavy on both sides. Attacks and counterattacks continued for the next two days and nights. On the night of July 25, the Japanese delivered their most serious counterattack against the northern beachhead.

After the counterattack was stopped, 3,500 enemy dead were counted on the battlefield. Although much bitter fighting still lay ahead, this was the battle that broke the back of enemy resistance on Guam. Lieutenant Colonel Hideyuki Takeda, former operations officer of the Japanese 29th Division, who surrendered on Guam, later wrote: "It was estimated that it was no longer possible to expel the American forces from the island after the results of the general counterattack on the night of 25 July were collected in the morning to about noon of the 26th. After this it was decided that the sole purpose of combat would be to inflict losses on the American forces in the interior of the island."[19]

When the 1st Provisional Marine Brigade landed on the beaches of Agat on the morning of July 21, they encountered much stiffer resistance than had the landing in the northern sector. From the moment their landing craft hit the reef, enemy guns on Gaan and Bangi points raked them with murderous cross fire. Enemy pillboxes and gun emplacements ashore, in spite of the preliminary naval and air bombardment, had survived the onslaught. They were in position to exact a heavy toll from the advancing marines. Twenty landing craft were sunk before they could reach the shore. Others, caught in the coral boulders on the reef, became sitting ducks for the determined enemy. Thirty minutes after the invasion began, however, tanks and artillery were ashore to lend much-needed support to the slow advance of the American troops.

As the marines pushed inland, Japanese mortar and artillery fire became more intense. Two small but spirited enemy counterattacks were beaten back. These counterattacks led the marines to believe that the Japanese might be able to counterattack at any time. It was believed that they were just waiting for more American troops and supplies to be brought ashore in order to make the effort worthwhile. By the end of the first day's fighting, however, no major counterattack had developed. By that time the marines had pushed inland 2,000 yards on a 4,500-yard front. For support in holding their beachhead against an expected counterattack that night and in expanding the area the next day, the marines had, during the afternoon, summoned help from the army troops of the 77th Infantry Division. These troops were being held aboard their ships for just such a purpose. When all forces were committed, the combined total of marines and army personnel engaged in the Agat–Orote Peninsula area numbered 34,563 men.

Plans for the southern sector operation called for units of the marines, once they had secured the Agat area, to turn north and cut off Orote Peninsula. This they succeeded in doing on July 25. When the marines secured the area between Agat Bay and Apra Harbor, they had approximately 3,100 Japanese troops trapped on the eight square miles of Orote Peninsula.

While the 1st Provisional Marine Brigade, commanded by Brigadier General Lemuel C. Shepherd, Jr., prepared for the assault on the peninsula, army troops took over defense of the Agat beachhead. They moved northward to meet the marines from the Asan beachhead who were pushing southward toward Orote. On July 27 the two groups met and closed the gap between them. Thus they secured control over an area extending from Adelup Point on the north to Facpi Point on the south. With the final beachhead line attained, the next objective was to clear the Japanese out of the northern half of the island, to which they had slowly withdrawn. Their units on Orote Peninsula were left behind to fend for themselves.

The brigade, in the meantime, concentrated on taking Orote Peninsula. On the morning of July 26, General Shepherd's marines began the final phase of their push to destroy the Japanese on the peninsula. The enemy was commanded by Air Group Commander Asaichi Tamai, Imperial Japanese Navy. He succeeded to the command of the Orote defenses after Colonel Tsunetaro Suenaga was killed. He was prepared to contest the marine advance every foot of the way. The Japanese, knowing they were trapped, were determined to die rather than surrender. On the day before, however, Commander Tamai had tried to evacuate some of his troops from the peninsula. Their barges were seen as they moved out into Apra Harbor from Sumay, and American planes and artillery had wiped them out. Failing in the escape attempt, the remainder of the trapped Japanese had tried to break through the marine lines in a vicious but highly disorganized *banzai* charge.

> After dusk, the intermittent showers that had been falling all day became more frequent. A heavy downpour hampered organization of the brigade's defense for the night. On the other hand, the pitch blackness and the unpleasant weather aided the Japanese in making preparations for their supreme effort.
>
> Marines in the front lines could hear screaming, yelling, laughter, and the breaking of bottles as the Japanese made final arrangements. At times so much clamor could be heard that reports reached the command post that the assualt had started. . . .
>
> While the enemy made ready and drank, Marine artillerymen laid down normal barrages along the swamp's edge and at all other points of possible penetration. Shortly before midnight the Japanese commanders felt that their men had reached the proper emotional state, and the assault began. Sake-crazed attackers swarmed from the cover of the mangroves in front of the 3rd Battalion, 22nd Marines. Led by flag-waving, sword-swinging officers, the enlisted men stumbled forward, carrying everything conceivable. Unsteady hands clutched pitchforks, sticks, ballbats, and pieces of broken bottles, together with the normal infantry weapons.
>
> When the surging Japanese mass came within range, Marine forward observers and company commanders gave the order to commence firing.[20]

The *banzai* charge, like the escape attempt, had been a costly failure.

Air attacks and naval and artillery fire preceded the push of the marines against the Japanese on Orote Peninsula. Dense undergrowth and jungle at the base of the peninsula slowed the progress of the attackers. Japanese troops who had survived the preliminary bombardment resisted vigorously with mortars, machine guns, and small arms. When the marines knocked out one line of strongly defended bunkers and pillboxes, they moved forward to other lines that were just as strongly defended. The enemy resisted the advance so bitterly that on the second day of the attack General Shepherd had to call in army tanks to support the drive. By the evening of the 28th, the advancing troops gained control of the old marine rifle range and marine barracks as well as the town of Sumay. In the ruins of the buildings of the former barracks they found a large bronze plaque bearing the inscription "U.S. Marine Barracks, Naval Station, Guam." This was a grim reminder of the small band of valiant marines who, more than two and one-half years before, had been overwhelmed by the Japanese invaders. Although they faced little resistance as they entered the ruins of Sumay, the marines found that extensive mine fields made the streets impassable. The town was probably the most heavily mined area on Guam.

Because he wished to conclude the Orote campaign on the 29th, General Shepherd called for the heaviest preliminary bombardment of remaining enemy positions that had occurred since W-day. The final bombardment was so effective that by early afternoon the marines, encountering little resistance, captured the Orote airstrip and swept on to the tip of the peninsula. With this task accomplished, General Shepherd reported Orote Peninsula secured. At 3:30 in the afternoon, high-ranking naval and marine officers, and other officers and men who could be spared from mopping-up operations, gathered on the site of the former marine barracks. There, as a marine sounded "To the Colors" on a captured Japanese bugle, the flag of the United States was raised once more over Orote Peninsula. "On this hallowed ground [said General Shepherd], you officers and men of the First Marine Brigade have avenged the loss of our comrades who were overcome by a numerically superior enemy three days after Pearl Harbor. Under our flag this island again stands ready to fulfill its destiny as an American fortress in the Pacific."[21]

Of the more than three thousand Japanese on Orote Peninsula at the beginning of the bitter four-day campaign, only four surrendered; the others were dead. The brigade's casualties were 874; of these, 115 were killed in action.

DRIVE TO THE NORTH: On July 28, General Takashina, commander of all Japanese troops on the island, was killed while directing the withdrawal of his forces from the Fonte Plateau region. In the course of the bitter struggles at the Asan and Agat beachheads, Takashina had drawn troops from the Tumon, Agana, and Pago areas and concentrated them as reserves on the plateau. By the time he was killed, his reserves had been so depleted that only about 6,000 combat troops of the original 18,500 on the island were left to carry on the fight. At this point, the elderly General Obata took direct control of the remaining forces and ordered a general withdrawal to the Mt. Santa Rosa area for the final defensive stand on Guam.

To destroy the remaining enemy forces, Major General Roy S. Geiger planned to cut the island in half on a general line running from Agana on the west coast to Pago Bay on the east and then move northward on a solid front. This plan called for the 3rd Marine Division at the Asan beachhead to spread out over an area about half the width of the island and move northward to capture Agana and the Tiyan airfield (NAS Agana area). At the same time, Army troops of the 77th Infantry Division, covering the eastern half of the island, would move northward to take the high ground south of the Pago River and also Yona village.

The push to the north was to begin at 6:30 a.m. on July 31. While the troops were making final preparations for the attack, artillery and naval gunfire blasted enemy positions for two days. At the appointed hour marines, covering the western half of the island, moved out with three battalions abreast. The units approaching Agana from the south met with little enemy opposition. Although the thickly mined roads into the former capital caused some casualties, by midmorning the marines were in the Plaza de España, and by noon the remainder of the city was occupied. Further inland, other marine units swept through the ruins of Sinajana and Ordot. The only real fight took place near Ordot, where a detachment of Japanese had been left behind to protect dumps containing hundreds of tons of supplies and equipment. Two days later, on August 2, the marines captured Tiyan airfield. As soon as it was secured, work was started to convert it into one of the finest fighter strips in the Pacific. Leaving Tiyan airfield on the morning of August 3, the marines entered the jungle of the northern half of Guam. At about midmorning, Company B, 1st Battalion, 9th Marines, was ambushed by a large group of Japanese just west of Finegayan village. In the ensuing battle, Private First Class Frank P. Witek was struck down by an enemy rifleman. Before he was killed, he had covered the temporary withdrawal of of his platoon, exposed himself to enemy fire to protect a wounded buddy, and then led an attack, personally killing sixteen Japanese and wiping out a machine-gun position. For his heroic action, he was posthumously awarded the Medal of Honor.

The northward push of the marines was co-ordinated with a similar drive by the Army troops of the 77th Division. Moving out from the Mt. Tenjo region on July 31, Army units pushed along the eastern side of the island toward Yona, the Pago River, and Barrigada. Lack of organized enemy resistance permitted the troops to move in columns. Even so, the march was extremely difficult because the way lay through rugged mountain terrain. For a while, the troops were supported by vehicles. After a short time, however, the terrain became so rough that not even jeeps could get through. For a distance of about six miles, no roads existed. As a result, much of the march had to be cross-country, down the steep slopes and through the mountains to the east coast. One infantryman wrote later:

> The distance across the island is not far, as the crow flies, but unluckily we can't fly. The nearest I came to flying was while descending the slippery side of a mountain in a sitting position. . . . After advancing a few yards you find that the handle of the machine gun on your shoulder, your pick and shovel, canteens, knife, and machete all stick out at right angles and are as tenacious in their grip on the surrounding underbrush as a dozen grappling hooks. Straining, sweating, and swearing avails you nothing so you decide on a full-bodied lunge— success crowns your efforts as all the entangling encumbrances decide

305

to give up the struggle simultaneously.... You untangle your equipment, retrieve your helmet, and move on. The flies and mosquitos have discovered your route of march and have called up all the reinforcements including the underfed and undernourished who regard us as nothing but walking blood banks. We continue to push on....[22]

As the weary columns pushed slowly forward, faster-moving patrols went along to scout the terrain and report on any enemy activity in the area. One of these patrols had the distinction of freeing the first large group of Guamanians. An account of the event describes the liberation as follows:

> An outstanding event of the day for the "Statue of Liberty" Division was the liberation of 2,000 Chamorros who were huddled in a concentration camp near Asinan. Patrols ... found the camp unguarded. They let the natives out and directed them back toward their homes on the west side of the island. The ex-captives were almost beside themselves with joy. Not knowing whether to kiss their liberators, bow to them, or shake hands with them, they tried to do all three at once. Many carried tiny American flags which they had hidden from the Japanese. ...Their faith in the return of the Americans had apparently never faltered, although as one Chamorro scornfully said, "We were told by the Japanese that the U.S.A. was being defeated, that Japan had control of the Hawaiian Islands, and that the Americans had only one ship left as the rest had been sunk."
>
> The weary infantrymen were immensely moved by the joy of the natives as they passed back through the lines. Soldiers who had been complaining because their rations were low gave away what few cigarettes they had. While watching the tiny children who carried huge baskets, and the women who trudged along with half their household possessions on their backs, the soldiers realized the meaning of liberation for these enslaved people.[23]

The Pago River was the first natural barrier where the Japanese might make a stand, but patrols crossing the river found none of the enemy there. Guamanians who were questioned revealed that the Japanese had withdrawn from the Yona area toward Barrigada. It now became clear that the major battle for Guam had been fought at the beachheads and that the enemy was withdrawing to the northern part of the island for a last stand. Consequently, the pursuit was stepped up in order to keep the Japanese on the run and thus prevent them from regrouping.

As the advance moved farther north, troops began to run low on food and water. The route of march led through such rugged terrain that vehicles were unable to bring up supplies. The lack of water, especially, made it necessary to capture Barrigada quickly in order to gain possession of its deep well that could provide 30,000 gallons of pure water daily.[24] It was expected, however, that the enemy, as a delaying action, would defend Barrigada so as to gain more time for the construction of defenses at Mt. Santa Rosa.

At 8:00 a.m. on August 2, Army tanks and infantry resumed their push toward Barrigada. When they arrived at the southern edge of the village, they met with determined enemy resistance. Throughout the rest of that day and most of the next, they made little headway against Japanese who resisted fanatically with tanks, mortars, grenades, and small arms. By the evening of August 3, however, the battle of Barrigada was over. The victorious American troops then pushed on toward Finegayan, the outer bastion of the Mt. Santa Rosa defenses. In the Finegayan region, Army troops on the east made contact with the marines on the west. There the combined force prepared for the final push that would drive the Japanese from Guam.

On August 7, the marines resumed their drive toward Ritidian Point, at the northern tip of the island. At the same time, troops of the Army's 77th Division began their attack on Mt. Santa Rosa. Intelligence gathered from various sources indicated that the Japanese strength in the Mt. Santa Rosa area alone numbered 1,500 army troops, 1,000 navy, and about 2,500 laborers. Their arms consisted of 7 large guns, 13 tanks, mortars, rifles, machine guns, and other automatic weapons. Before the American push began, the Japanese positions were blasted by aerial bombs, artillery, and naval gunfire. After a bitter battle that lasted two days, the Americans gained the summit of Mt. Santa Rosa. There, and on the slopes of the mountain, they counted the bodies of 528 enemy dead. The rest of the enemy force had escaped into the jungle in small groups.

The marines completed their drive to Ritidian Point on August

8. The next day Army troops reached Pati Point. On August 10, 1944, at 11:30., General Geiger announced that organized enemy resistance on Guam had ceased. His announcement was somewhat premature, however, since it was not until August 12 that General Obata's last command post near Mt. Mataguac was stormed by Army troops. Everyone, including Obata, was killed.

MOPPING UP: After twenty-one days of bitter fighting, Guam was in American hands once more. The price of victory, in terms of human life and suffering alone, was staggering. The American losses were 1,283 men killed in action, 5,719 wounded in action, and 329 missing in action. For the same period the Japanese had, by actual count, lost 10,971 men.[25] Hundreds of others were sealed in caves and never counted. In spite of their losses, however, over 7,000 Japanese still remained on the island. They were scattered and hiding in small groups. Strong American patrols, reinforced by armed Guamanians, hunted them down and destroyed them. From the 10th of August to the end of the month, an average of 80 Japanese were killed or captured daily. For months and even years after the American reoccupation of Guam, enemy troops were being rounded up on the island. As recently as 1960, more than 15 years after the war ended, Japanese stragglers were still believed to be in hiding in the mountains and jungles of Guam. One straggler was captured by two Guamanians in May 1960. Within three days his companion surrendered. Both were returned to Japan early in June 1960.

After organized enemy resistance had ceased, Major General Henry L. Larsen, at noon on August 15, took over control of the island. Besides the job of hunting down Japanese stragglers, he was also responsible for completing work on airfields, highways, and harbor improvements. This work had been started by the Seabees and army engineers while the fighting was still in progress. To complete the gigantic task, Larsen had nine naval and three special (stevedore) naval construction battalions (Seabees), one marine special engineer battalion, and four army aviation engineer battalions at his disposal. Working day and night, the construction battalions quickly developed the facilities of Apra Harbor so that medium-sized cargo ships could land supplies and equipment onto quays leading from Cabras Island. A year later, with more construction and improvements, this harbor handled more cargo than any other forward-area port in the world.[26] Air facilities too were expanded rapidly. Within a few months B-29's were making daily flights from Guam airfields to dump their bombs on targets in Japan. By early 1945, five large air bases and eight air strips were in operation on the island. At the same time that this work was in progress, Marine Drive, Guam's principal highway, was being built. It was followed by the construction of a network of secondary highways that spread to all parts of the island.

General Larsen's island command changed Guam from a devastated, war-torn island into a strong and revitalized outpost of democracy in the Pacific.

By the end of the war the entire face of Guam had been changed. A busy naval operating base occupied Apra Harbor, and Navy planes crowded the fields at Agana and on Orote Peninsula. On the northern plateau B-29's of the Twentieth Air Force rested on fields bulldozed from the jungle that had impeded the advance of the Third Amphibious Corps. On the heights above Agana was the advance headquarters of the Pacific Fleet, nerve center of Nimitz's strikes against the Japanese homeland. Scattered throughout the island were vast naval and military supply installations. ... The island population on 31 August 1945 had swelled to over 220,000, with 21,838 natives, 65,095 army, 77,911 Navy, and 58,712 Marine troops.[27]

## MILITARY GOVERNMENT, 1944–46

While the recapture of Guam was still in the planning stage, a small military government team was organized. It was assigned the duty of planning for the government of the civilian population after the island had been recaptured. The original group in Guam was patterned after military government units in the Gilbert and Marshall islands. From such a small beginning, military government in Guam, Tinian, and Saipan became the largest of such operations conducted by the navy in the Pacific.

The first phase of military government was the assault phase.

At that time the military government unit was known as the civil affairs unit. Civil affairs officers landed on Guam on the first day of the invasion. At the first sign of civilian activity, they posted a number of proclamations. The first declared that Admiral Chester W. Nimitz, as Commander-in-Chief Pacific Fleet and Pacific Ocean Areas, had become the military governor of Guam. A second proclamation defined war crimes, and a third established "exceptional military courts" for Guam and the Marianas. Other proclamations came in rapid order. They dealt with matters of civilian property, operation of a labor pool, and regulations concerning refugee camps. At about the same time, all Japanese powers, laws, and regulations were rescinded.[28]

For the first few days after the invasion the civil affairs unit had very little to do. Soon, however, small groups of islanders began passing through the American lines. They were sent to the rear for badly needed care. An account of the marines' first contact with Guamanian civilians runs in part as follows:

> The first contact we had with civilians came soon after we widened our perimeter to include the outskirts of the battered city of Agana. One day a radio message came back from one of our outposts: "Twenty women, several babies, one cow, and a sewing machine coming through our lines."
>
> More groups followed—old, gnarled men with sticks; crones with wispy white hair, lace dresses, and no shoes; young girls in mud-stained rags, carrying naked babies; little boys and girls holding onto each other's hands fearfully. Coming out of hiding places near the shore, they told us they had seen us land and had waited for us to come near enough for them to emerge and enter our lines. One woman had a tiny American flag that she had made on her sewing machine in a cave; it had seven red and white stripes and a field of blue, and was fashioned from a dress. She had waved it at our ships from her cave, hoping to be rescued, but none of our vessels had seen her.[29]

After all Guamanians had been released from Japanese concentration camps, they were cared for in refugee camps hurriedly set up near Anigua, Agat, Yona, Talofofo, and Dededo. They numbered more than 18,000. As soon as an area was cleared of Japanese stragglers, the Guamanians were encouraged to return to their homes and farms. Because of war damage, however, and in view of the need of the military forces for vast tracts of land, most of the Guamanians had no homes to return to. To remedy the situation, Island Command was given the additional task of building new villages. As quickly as possible, temporary houses and schools were built. The new villages and other nonmilitary areas were policed by former members of the Insular Patrol and marines from Island Command.

After the assault phase, Guam's military government underwent two major revisions. In October 1944 the government dropped the name "civil affairs" and became the military government of Guam. At the same time, the number of government departments was expanded. A second reorganization occurred in April 1945. Some departments were consolidated, and others were given extra duties. The government's name was changed to United States Naval-Military Government. From August 1944 to May 1946, a period of about two years, military government affairs were conducted through ten separate departments. Among these was the Legal Department.

A Legal Department was included in the early plans for the reoccupation of Guam. Its first duty was that of drafting proclamations to be posted on the island. When the island had been secured, the Legal Department began a study of all laws that had been in effect before the war. Such laws were revised to meet the needs of the new situation. Guamanians who had worked for the prewar Legal Department were called upon to help with the task. As quickly as possible, the old island court system was re-established. These courts were staffed entirely with Guamanians. Because of the confusion that prevailed at the time, many military government regulations were violated by the islanders. However, cases that required trial in the criminal courts were few in number.[30]

The Legal Department was the custodian of all enemy property on the island. It also had the right to seize any property needed for military use. In doing so, it was required to keep complete records of all property seized. It could also return private property to its legal owners when it was no longer needed for military purposes.

311

During and immediately after the reoccupation, civil affairs officers were faced with a tremendous welfare and relief problem. Food, clothing, and shelter had to be provided for thousands of people. In time the American Red Cross and other mainland organizations sent several shipments of clothing. The military forces provided food for the people in the refugee camps. In addition, the large quantities of rice found among captured Japanese stores made a welcome addition to the Guamanian diet. As soon as possible, military government built makeshift houses at Agat, Sinajana, Barrigada, Talofofo, Yona, Santa Rita, Asan, and Dededo. These houses were crudely built, temporary structures. Eighteen years after the war, however, many of these "temporary" houses were still in use—until the typhoon of 1962 destroyed almost all of them.

Perhaps the most difficult task of the Welfare Department was that of relocating the civilian population. This problem was complicated by the ever-increasing demands of the military for land. In many instances, large groups of people were moved several times in order to satisfy the needs of the military. "Nevertheless, in the hundreds of relocations made necessary," wrote Friedrich, "only two or three families objected to the necessity for moving. It is to the lasting credit of the civilians that they regarded the misery of moving as a price to be paid for advancing the cause of the war."[31] In later years, however, the taking of land for military or other government use was bitterly contested in the courts.

The Department of Education was one of the most important departments of the military government. During the war, school buildings and facilities throughout the island were almost completely destroyed. In an attempt to remedy the situation the government hastily built a number of temporary schools. This building program, as well as other matters regarding postwar education, is discussed at length in a later chapter.

A Department of Economics and Labor was set up immediately after the island was once more in American hands. This department performed the duties of the prewar Executive Department and the Department of Agriculture. In October 1944 a separate

Labor Department was established. Because of numerous construction projects on the island, local civilian labor was in great demand. In an attempt to help meet the labor needs of the military, the Labor Department maintained a register of all available civilian workers. Full-time farmers were the only persons whose names were not included in the register. Teams of recruiters were sent to all parts of the island to find workers. These workers became part of a civilian labor pool. Even though, in time, most Guamanians were employed by the government, the labor needs of the military were never fully met. Because of the many jobs available, Guamanian women were employed in large numbers outside the home for the first time. Before the war, a few working women were housemaids, nurses, or teachers. After the war, besides filling those jobs, they also became clerks, telephone operators, and stenographers.

The Department of Commerce and Industry was given the task of rebuilding the commercial life of the island. In view of the widespread damage that had occurred during the war, that was not an easy thing to do. Nevertheless, a start was made. Two private wholesale companies were permitted to buy government food and supplies on credit. They, in turn, sold to a small number of private retail stores. In the main, the retail stores were operated by persons who had such stores before the war. All merchandise was brought to the island in military vessels. Thus, it was possible for the government to maintain strict control over all trade. Later, this resulted in a bitter conflict between the government and the island's businessmen. Until late 1947 or early 1948, military personnel were not permitted to make purchases in village stores. This was another source of conflict. Aside from the merchandising of goods, the Department of Commerce and Industry also tried to revive the copra, soap, tile, and handicraft industries. These attempts, however, met with only limited success.

Some of the most successful business firms in present-day Guam owe their beginnings to the efforts of the military government. One such firm is that owned by Pedro M. Ada, a Guamanian. Shortly after the reoccupation, Ada opened a small store in the ruins of

Agana. In the beginning his stock consisted mostly of canned goods. Later, he was able to get supplies from mail-order houses in Hawaii and the mainland. Thereupon, his small business grew in size until today it is the largest individually owned firm in Guam. At present the Ada establishment consists of a wholesale business and three retail stores. The stores are located in Agana, Tamuning, and Barrigada. In 1955 Ada completed the construction of a $200,000 building in Agana. It houses his main retail store, the wholesale establishment, and numerous offices.

Through the Department of Agriculture and Fisheries the military government encouraged farmers to return to the land. Its main goal was the production of enough food to meet the needs of the Guamanian people. Rice was a staple food. In view of the fact that Guam was not, and had never been, a large rice-producing area, this goal was never attained. The problem of food production was complicated by the fact that much of the island's best agricultural land was taken over by the military. Farmers, who knew from sad experience that their land might be taken from them at any moment, were not inclined to return to the land. Moreover, plenty of high-paying jobs were available on military construction projects. As a result, the land was neglected, and the island quickly changed from an agricultural to a money-based economy. Today, more than twenty years since the end of the war, the same situation prevails.

Upon its establishment, military government included a Finance Department. Later, the name was changed to Supply Department. This department did the work that was formerly done by the immigration, records and accounts, and bank and supply sections of the prewar government. Until the Bank of Guam was re-established, the Supply Department handled all of the government's banking matters. One of its most difficult tasks was that of redeeming Japanese yen.

The Department of Public Health was under the supervision and control of a United States Navy medical officer. He was assisted by other officers and corpsmen. Whenever possible, Guamanian nurses and prewar employees of the department were rehired.

314

Dispensaries were established, and vaccination and inoculation programs were carried on throughout the island. In time the department established a school for the training of native nurses and medical practitioners. Natives of Guam, American Samoa, and the Trust Territory of the Pacific were admitted. The school was discontinued in 1950.

The Department of Public Works performed one of the island's biggest postwar jobs. It restored damaged villages and built new ones. It had charge of all government buildings and was responsible for the operation of the government motor pool. Since civilian automobiles were few in number, the Public Works Department set up a government-owned bus system that served most of the villages.

The Department of Public Safety, under the control of Marine Corps personnel, was assigned the duty of policing the island's nonmilitary areas. It was assisted by Guamanian members of the Insular Patrol. One of its principal tasks was that of hunting down and either killing or capturing Japanese stragglers. In this it proved to be very successful.

In little less than two years, the work of the military government came to an end. Conditions which required its establishment no longer existed. The war had ended in the Pacific. Most Guamanians had been relocated and almost all were housed, if only poorly. The island's commercial life was well on its way to recovery. Guam had resumed as normal a way of life as the situation permitted. Consequently, on May 30, 1946, the military government was declared at an end and the naval government of Guam was re-established.

SUMMARY: On December 10, 1941, the island of Guam was surrendered to invading Japanese forces. For a period of 31 months the people of Guam were subject to the iron-fisted rule of the foreign invaders. At times, especially during the period of Japanese army rule, the Guamanian people were subjected to acts of brutality and to indignities of the worst sort. Despite that fact, the Guamanian people attempted to keep their lives on an even keel.

315

That, however, was oftentimes difficult to do. Nevertheless, they did what had to be done for survival. In March 1942, when the last units of the Japanese army departed from Guam, control of the island was turned over to the Japanese navy. For a time, the lot of the Guamanian people became somewhat easier. Schools were reopened in Agana, primarily for the purpose of teaching the Japanese language, and adults as well as children were compelled to attend. Although religious services were permitted to continue for a time, their number and scope were drastically curtailed. This was due, in large measure, to the fact that all American priests had been removed from the island as prisoners of war. Business activities were permitted to continue, but in time they too were severely restricted. By July 1944 the conditions under which the Guamanian people lived had become almost unbearable. Fortunately for them, the Americans began the reoccupation of the island at that time.

American reoccupation forces landed on the beaches of Guam on July 21, 1944. The northern beachhead extended from Asan Point to Adelup Point; the southern beachhead extended from Facpi Point to Orote Peninsula. After a fairly short but savage period of fighting, forces in the two beachheads were joined up and began their push to the north. As American forces moved steadily northward, the ever-diminishing Japanese forces fell steadily backward. In time the American forces reached the northernmost coast of the island, extending from Ritidian Point to Pati Point. The Japanese forces, needless to say, had been wiped out, and the island of Guam was once more in American hands.

On May 30, 1946, the military government of Guam, which had been established as the result of dire military necessity, was declared at an end and the naval government of Guam was reestablished. The next chapter will deal with the last years of naval administration in Guam.

## NOTES

1. *Hepburn Report* (printed as House Document No. 65, 76th Congress of the United States, 1st session, December 27, 1938).

2. L. W. Johnson, "Guam Before December 1941," *United States Naval Institute Proceedings*, Vol. LXVIII, No. 7, July 1942, p. 998.

3. G. J. McMillin, "Surrender of Guam to the Japanese" (official report to Chief of Naval Operations, September 11, 1945).

4. Samuel Eliot Morison, *History of United States Naval Operations in World War II*, Vol. III: *The Rising Sun in the Pacific, 1931–April 1942* (Little, Brown and Co., Boston, 1948), p. 186.

5. O. R. Lodge, *The Recapture of Guam* (Historical Branch, G-3 Division, Headquarters, U.S. Marine Corps; U.S. Government Printing Office, Washington, 1954), p. 8.

6. Julius O. Sullivan in the *Guam Daily News*, July 21, 1953.

7. Alvin M. Josephy, Jr., *The Long and the Short and the Tall* (Alfred A. Knopf, New York, 1946), p. 83.

8. *Ibid.*, p. 84.

9. *Guam Daily News*, July 21, 1952, p. 4.

10. "Guam: Operations of the 77th Division, 21 July–10 August 1944" (Bulletin, *American Forces in Action* series, Historical Division, War Department, Washington, 1946), pp. 3–4.

11. Lodge, *op. cit.*, p. 9.

12. "Guam: Operations of the 77th Division," p. 21.

13. *Ibid.*, pp. 21–23.

14. Lodge, *op. cit.*, pp. 18–19.

15. "Guam: Operations of the 77th Division," p. 29.

16. Lodge, *op. cit.*, pp. 34–35.

17. Samuel Eliot Morison, *History of United States Naval Operations in World War II*, Vol. VIII: *New Guinea and the Marianas, March 1944–August 1944* (Little, Brown and Co., Boston, 1953), p. 386.

18. Lodge, *op. cit.*, pp. 42–43.

19. *Ibid.*, p. 87.

20. *Ibid.*, p. 78.

21. M. Kaufman, "Attack on Guam," *Marine Corps Gazette*, April, 1945, p. 63.

22. "Guam: Operations of the 77th Division," p. 65.

23. *Ibid.*, pp. 68–69.

24. Andrew D. Bruce, "Administration, Supply, and Evacuation of the 77th Infantry Division on Guam," *Military Review*, December 1944, p. 8.

25. At the end of August 1945, a recapitulation of Japanese casualty figures showed 18,377 dead and 1,250 prisoners taken.

26. "Guam: Operations of the 77th Division," p. 134.

27. Lodge, *op. cit.*, p. 164.

28. Carl J. Friedrich and Associates, *American Experiences in Military Government in World War II* (Rinehart and Co., Inc., New York, 1948), p. 307.

29. Josephy, *op. cit.*, pp. 75–76.

30. Friedrich, *op. cit.*, p. 308.

31. *Ibid.*, pp. 302.

## CHAPTER NINE

# THE LAST YEARS OF NAVAL ADMINISTRATION

THE YEARS BETWEEN 1946 and 1950 ushered in a period of rapid change in the affairs of Guam. In 1946 military government came to an end and naval government was re-established. Despite efforts of the naval government to restore the old order, affairs in Guam could never be the same again. Too many changes had been wrought by the war. Destruction of towns and villages was accompanied by the destruction of old ideas. This was especially true in the realm of politics and government. On the whole the Guamanian people were grateful for the many benefits that had come to them under naval rule. Nevertheless, a small group of islanders were resentful of the fact that American citizenship and other civil rights had been denied them for almost half a century. Consequently, the latter looked upon the re-establishment of the naval government as a temporary measure. Indeed, in 1945 a process had been started in Washington that was to bring about the end of naval rule five years later.

In 1950 an Organic Act for Guam was passed by the Congress of the United States. By this act Guamanians acquired American citizenship and, for the first time in 300 years, a civilian administration and a limited measure of self-government. Thus the long period of military rule, under both Spanish and American jurisdictions, was brought to an end.

This chapter is concerned with the years from 1946 to 1950. Topics discussed include the re-establishment of naval government and the events that occurred during the closing years of naval administration under Rear Admiral Charles A Pownall.

## NAVAL GOVERNMENT RE-ESTABLISHED

The naval government of Guam was re-established on May 30, 1946. The order for its re-establishment was issued by Secretary of the Navy James Forrestal. On the same day that the order was issued, Rear Admiral Charles A. Pownall was appointed governor of Guam. He was the first admiral to hold the office of governor. Formerly, no naval governor of Guam had held a rank higher than that of captain. On the day that he became governor, Admiral Pownall proclaimed: "The Naval Government of Guam is hereby re-established, and all powers of the Government and jurisdiction in Guam and adjacent waters and over the inhabitants thereof, and final executive, legislative and judicial responsibility are vested in me as Naval Governor of Guam and will be exercised through subordinate commanders by my direction."

The powers granted to Admiral Pownall were greater than those held by any previous governor. He was governor of Guam's civilian population as well as commander of all military forces in the entire Marianas area. "In his military capacity he exercises the authority of commanding officer over thousands of service personnel in the Marianas, Carolines, and Marshalls. In his capacity as civil administrator, the governor of Guam exercises supreme authority over the civilian native population of the island (now numbering some 23,000) and the American civilian population, employees of the Navy, Army, and construction companies, now numbering several thousands (the exact figures have not been made public). From the point of view of governmental structure, the dual function of the top island administrator reinforces his civil authority with military prestige and power obviously far greater than that of any pre-war governor."[1]

In almost all respects government organization under Admiral Pownall was the same as that of the naval government that had prevailed for forty-three years before the war. One difference, however, was the addition of the office of civil administrator. The principal duty of the civil administrator was to help the governor in the administration of all civilian affairs. The civil administrator and all department heads in the newly re-established government were naval officers. There were twelve departments of the government:

The Department of Law was responsible for all legal matters in which the government of Guam was interested. Moreover, it had charge of all public prosecutions. Much of this work was handled by the island attorney and deputy island attorneys. These officials were usually Guamanians. They were under the jurisdiction and control of the attorney general, who was a naval officer.

The Judiciary Department maintained the island court system and court records. It conducted all criminal and civil cases involving civilians under the jurisdiction of the island's courts. It was also responsible for enforcing the judgments of the courts as well as all the laws of Guam. The courts consisted of the Court of Appeals, the Island Court, the Justice Court, and the Police Court. In operation, they were very much like the island's prewar courts.

The Department of Education maintained all public elementary and secondary schools on the island. It provided vocational training for qualified students. Vocational training was offered in agriculture, business, mechanics, carpentry, automobile repair, and related fields. The department, moreover, conducted annual teachers' institutes. Immediately following the re-establishment of naval government, the Department of Education was headed by a Navy chaplain. He was assisted by a Guamanian superintendent of schools. The governor, however, as director of education, established school policy, decided how all money was to be spent, and selected key personnel.

The Department of Health was headed by a naval medical officer. This department was responsible for public health and sanitation. It also supervised the Naval Medical Center and maintained a maritime quarantine station. Moreover, it conducted a never-ending campaign for insect and rodent control.

The Department of Internal Affairs was made up of the former Departments of Commerce and Industry, Fishing and, Agriculture and Labor. This department maintained strict control over the island's economy. Its principal purpose was to bring about the "planned" development of the island's business, industry, labor, and agriculture. It issued business licenses, operated an agricultural experiment farm, supervised fishing, and controlled labor and wages.

The Department of Public Works supervised all civilian engineering and construction work. It maintained and operated public utilities such as the bus lines and the ice plant. It also built and maintained public utilities and facilities in the villages.

The Department of Civil Police supervised the Island Police Force. This force policed all areas outside of military reservations. Headquarters of the police force was the Central Police Station in Agana. At least one patrolman, an enlisted marine, was stationed in each village. Patrol cars, fitted with radio receivers and transmitters, maintained constant touch with the central station. Besides these duties, the police department maintained and supervised the civil jail in Agana.

The fire marshal was charged with fire prevention and control. In this task he was assisted by fire departments from Navy and Army bases.

The Department of Records and Accounts served as the island treasury and as custodian for all government property. It collected taxes, disbursed government funds, issued certain licenses, and served as a depository for land registration and vital statistic records of the naval government.

The Land and Claims Commission, which began operations on April 23, 1945, served as a real-estate agency for the government. It administered the Guam Meritorious Claims Act (Public Law 224, 79th Congress), passed on November 15, 1945. This commission processed claims which arose as a result of World War II. Such claims were for damage to real and personal property and for injury and death. In 1946 a total of 2,841 claims were filed with the commission. These amounted to $7,859,770.55 for loss and damage to property. Besides these, 310 injury and death cases were filed. By 1947 the number of property claims rose to 5,935. They amounted to $10,427,403.55. Moreover, 711 injury and death claims in the total amount of $1,396,005 were filed with the commission.

The City Planning Commission was responsible for drawing up plans for the rebuilding of Guam's war-torn towns and villages. It was also assigned the task of planning for new military bases and installations. One of its most important tasks was to prepare plans for rebuilding Agana. The capital city had been almost completely destroyed during the war. Besides these duties, the commission prepared plans for houses and buildings. These structures were designed to withstand the rigors of Guam's climatic conditions. Plans drawn up by the commission were used for both public and private construction. The name of this commission was changed later to the Guam Planning Commission.

The Bank of Guam, operated as a branch of the naval government, was the only bank on the island. It conducted a general banking business which included services in connection with commercial and savings accounts; issuance of bank drafts, cashier's checks, and traveler's checks; loans; discounts and commercial letters of credit; services related to trustee and guardianship accounts; cable transfers. It served as the United States government depository, accepting deposits for the account of the United States Treasury.

In addition to these twelve departments, naval government included a United States Post Office and the commissioners of Guam. The Guam Post Office operated under regulations of the federal Post Office Department. The commissioners, one for each municipality, were appointed by the governor. They served at his pleasure and received a salary determined by him. They were the direct representatives of the governor in the villages and municipalities.[2]

## SOCIAL CONDITIONS

POPULATION: In 1710, when the first official census of Guam was taken by the Spanish government, there were but 3,678 persons living on the island. By 1901, when the first census was taken by naval government, the island's population had grown to 9,630.

Under naval rule major improvements were made in the field of public health and sanitation. As a result, by 1941 the Guamanian population had increased to 22,000. As of March 1946, the resident population of Guam totaled 23,136. It was comprised as follows:[3]

| | |
|---|---:|
| Guam males (16 years and above) | 5,796 |
| Guam females (16 years and above) | 6,484 |
| Guam children (males 15 years and under) | 5,348 |
| Guam children (females 15 years and under) | 5,070 |
| Japanese and part-Japanese males | 148 |
| Japanese and part-Japanese females | 150 |
| Japanese and part-Japanese children | 69 |
| Hawaiian males | 1 |
| American males | 38 |
| Filipino males | 3 |
| Marshallese males | 2 |
| Samoan males | 6 |
| Gilbertese males | 1 |
| Saipanese males | 2 |
| Rotanese males | 1 |
| Rotanese females | 6 |
| Danish males | 1 |
| Yap-Chamorro males | 3 |
| Yap-Chamorro females | 1 |
| Carolinian females | 6 |
| | 23,136 |

After World War II the island's resident population entered upon a period of steady growth. The trend has continued to the present. As of February 1947, the Guamanian population had grown to 24,139. This was an increase of almost one thousand over the previous year. The island's non-Guamanian population consisted of Army, Navy, and Marine Corps personnel, their dependents, civil service workers and contractors' employees. They numbered 36,388 as of February 28, 1947. By June 30, 1950, the Guamanian population had increased to 27,985. As of the same date, the island's total population was 58,754.

HEALTH AND SANITATION: During the period from 1946 to 1950, public health and sanitation was a major concern of the naval government. Indeed, it had been a matter of real concern to all American governors. Although reliable accounts are not available, some Spanish governors, too, were interested in matters of public health and sanitation. The interest of American governors was shown by their efforts to construct hospitals and dispensaries. As mentioned in an earlier chapter, a hospital for lepers was constructed in 1899. In 1905 the Susanna Hospital was built in Agana. Four years later the hospital buildings were destroyed by earthquake. Following this, the Navy Department provided funds for the construction of a new hospital. It was known officially as the Naval Hospital, Guam. The Susanna Hospital Association, however, continued to care for women and children in a building erected on its own land and from its own funds. In 1922 an eight-room annex was added to the Susanna Hospital. Affairs of the Susanna Hospital were managed by a board of directors, of which the governor of Guam was ex-officio chairman. A Navy medical officer served as the hospital's executive director. Thus, the Susanna Hospital occupied a semiofficial position in the affairs of Guam.

During the American assault on Guam in 1944, the Naval Hospital and the Susanna Hospital were destroyed. While fighting on the island continued, a temporary hospital to care for the civilian population was erected near the site of the old Susanna Hospital. When hostilities ceased, the civilian hospital was moved to the site of one of the Navy's fleet hospitals in the Oka (Tamuning) area. Although housed in Butler huts and other temporary buildings, the 300-bed hospital was well staffed and well equipped. On March 15, 1946, this hospital was named the Guam Memorial Hospital "in honor of the Guamanians who fervently and loyally supported the Allied cause."[4] Ten years later, in 1956, the Guam Memorial Hospital moved to a new modern structure at Saupon Point, beyond the old Oka site. At the time of the move, a modern, six-story tuberculosis wing had already been erected at the new hospital site.

In addition to the facilities at the Guam Memorial Hospital, in 1947 the naval government maintained dispensaries in 14 outlying districts. These dispensaries were supervised by Navy medical corpsmen who were assisted by Guamanian nurses. Medical officers made periodic visits to the outlying districts. They conducted clinics and attended to the needs of the seriously ill. Guamanian nurses visited village homes regularly. During 1947, from 1,000 to 1,200 monthly visits were made to the homes of Guamanians by the Guamanian public health nurses. The work of these nurses was supervised by Navy nurses. In the district clinics immunization against typhoid, smallpox, tetanus, diphtheria, and whooping cough were given to the extent of about 1,000 injections monthly. In addition to these services, inspections of all public sanitary facilities, food-handling establishments, and stores were held monthly.

On January 23, 1947, by order of the Secretary of the Navy, a school for dental assistants was established at the Naval Hospital. Students accepted by the school came from the islands of the Trust Territory of the Pacific, Guam, and American Samoa. This school was a welcome addition to the school of medical practitioners, organized during the period of military government, and the native school of nurses, established in 1907 and re-established in 1945. The number of dental school students from the various islands was determined by each island's population and its dental needs. The first dental classes began on April 5, 1948.

The number of deaths from all causes among the local population during 1947 was 281. Diseases most common among the islanders during the same year are shown in the following list of hospital admissions for the year.[5]

| DISEASE | NUMBER OF ADMISSIONS |
|---|---|
| Gastroenteritis, acute | 154 |
| Tuberculosis, all types | 100 |
| Pneumonia, broncho | 99 |
| Catarrhal fever, acute | 73 |
| Asthma | 64 |
| Hookworm disease | 47 |

| Bronchitis, acute | 43 |
| Anemia | 33 |
| Mumps | 19 |
| Yaws | 24 |

Diseases causing the highest number of deaths among the local population in 1947 are listed below.[6]

| DISEASE | NUMBER OF DEATHS |
|---|---|
| Tuberculosis | 60 |
| Pneumonia | 37 |
| Hookworm | 11 |

Early in 1948 the island experienced a small outbreak of Japanese B encephalitis. This was the first time that the disease had occurred in Guam. To study the disease, a specially equipped laboratory was set up. It was manned by Army and Navy medical men. Before the outbreak subsided, 35 cases of encephalitis had developed among the local population. Three of the victims died. There were also four cases among the nonresident population, with two deaths. A vigorous mosquito-control campaign was started, and the outbreak was brought under control.

During the fiscal year 1950 the naval government appropriated $661,386.33 for medical care, public health, and sanitation. This sum did not include the expense of naval medical officers and other services and supplies furnished by the Navy.

LABOR: After the American reoccupation of Guam it became necessary for the government to provide the Guamanians with most of the necessities of life. These included food, medical care, and shelter. Because of widespread war damage, most of the people were unable to earn a living. Consequently, the government was compelled to provide them with jobs. In view of the many construction projects that were begun, plenty of jobs were soon available. In a short time large numbers of Guamanians were employed by the government. Under these conditions "wage scales were established which differentiated between local labor and United States citizens employed for work on Guam."[7] This dual wage scale was bitterly resented by Guamanian workers. "Equal pay for equal work" became a popular cry. Over and above their base pay, most workers recruited from the mainland were granted a territorial post differential, or TPD, as it was commonly called. In many instances the TPD amounted to 25 per cent of the base pay. It was this bonus that was especially resented by the Guamanians. They felt, moreover, that the dual wage scale placed them in the position of inferiors. This too was cause for resentment. In 1947 the naval government salary scale ranged from 35 cents an hour for a common laborer to $3,000 a year for the senior judge of the Island Court. Although the salary scale for Guamanians was revised upwards several times, a single uniform scale was not established until after passage of the Organic Act.

Under the government's labor program, working conditions for Guamanians were the same as those for United States citizens. A 40-hour week and an 8-hour day were in effect. This work schedule applied to all government employees except nurses, policemen, teachers, commissioners, and others whose work demanded an irregular schedule. Overtime pay at the rate of time and one-half for each hour over 40 hours in any work week was provided. Provision was also made for rest periods, annual leave, and accumulated leave. A civil service retirement and disability fund was established for full-time employees. Any worker discharged from his job was guaranteed the right of appeal.

In June 1948 the Navy Department submitted its annual report to the United Nations. In the report it declared that the Navy's labor policy in Guam was intended to give maximum benefits to the Guamanian people. Part of its policy statement follows:

1. Guamanians are granted preference over stateside or other foreign personnel at all levels and types of employment in government service where equally qualified or qualified to the extent that would permit accomplishment of a job in a reasonably successful manner.

2. Except for contract stevedores and workers for Federal projects not available on Guam, all entries of outside labor are denied in order to safeguard the Guamanian economic and social life.

3. The wage policy of the Island Government is briefly:
   a. The Island Government will not compete unfairly for labor against private enterprise on Guam.
   b. The Island Government will not give preference to its own requirements over the normal development of the island's natural resources and its own natural economy.[8]

By 1948 about 39.5 per cent of available Guamanian workers were employed by the naval government or by various federal installations on the island. In 1950, when naval rule was ended, there was a total of 8,732 employable persons out of a population of 27,985 Guamanians. Of this number, 3,013 were employed by the United States armed forces, 2,818 by private enterprise, 1,154 were self-employed, 1,250 were farmers, 193 were fishermen, and 60 were unemployed. Persons working for the federal and local governments were the so-called white collar workers and skilled and unskilled laborers. The former earned an average of $195.22 a month, the latter an average of $119.50 a month.

Under the labor policy of the naval government, employees' and workers' organizations were not forbidden. But they also were not encouraged. As of 1950 there were no local labor unions on the island. The Chamber of Commerce and the Guam Teachers' Association were representative local organizations. The first was interested primarily in promoting commerce and trade, the second in raising teaching standards.

From 1946 to 1950, Guam had no real unemployment problem. In fact, there were not enough workers to fill the labor needs of the government and of local businesses. To meet its labor requirements, the naval government had to adopt the same measures followed by the military government immediately after the war. It recruited skilled and unskilled workers from the United States, Hawaii, the Philippines, and other parts of the Pacific Ocean area. Recruitment was voluntary and was on a contract basis. In the beginning, most contracts were for one year. Later, in many instances, they were changed to two years. Workers were required to leave the island at the end of their contracts. They were not prohibited, however, from leaving Guam and returning to their places of origin at any time. In most cases, if a worker left before the end of his contract, he was required to pay his own way home. Few left early. In fact, if permitted to do so, most of them renewed their contracts. Wages paid in Guam were much better than those in the areas from which many of the workers came. Thus employment in Guam was eagerly sought after. Concerning one phase of this matter, Stevens wrote:

> During the postwar reconstruction and rehabilitation period, the Navy was faced with an acute labor shortage. Not only was labor inadequate for such rehabilitation and reconstruction, but also for proposed military expansion in the area. Many projects of a substantial and permanent nature were planned for Guam, including barracks buildings, a hospital, permanent living quarters, reservoirs, dams, power plants, and others. Brown-Pacific-Maxon, a joint adventure, came to Guam under contract with the Navy to construct these military projects and others. There was no local labor in quantity, and the cost of importing labor from the United States is excessively high. Therefore, the contractors desired to turn to foreign labor. There being a surplus of labor in the Philippines, the Navy granted the contractors permission to import alien Filipino laborers. During the construction period alien Filipinos [laborers] began pouring into the island by the thousand, and continue to do so. Theoretically, they are given a security check in the Philippines and only desirable aliens are brought in. However, many of them later prove undesirable and also, some are discovered to be security risks and must be returned to the Philippines. The Navy exercises absolute control over the Filipinos. They are brought in under naval supervision and jurisdiction and are housed and paid with the approval of the Navy. They are kept within compounds, and within large barracks buildings which are supplied with the necessities of life. In spite of the fact that their wages are low by our standards, they are high by Filipino standards and since their standard of living is low they are able to save a considerable portion of their wages and to spend more than they have been accustomed to spend in the past.[9]

WELFARE AND RELIEF: Before World War II, Guamanian orphans, the aged, and the needy were usually cared for by family and close relatives. As a result, there was no pressing need for public welfare and assistance programs. After the war, however, frequent cases of temporary need arose. Such emergencies were generally cared for by the Guam Chapter of the American Red

Cross. The Society of St. Vincent de Paul, sponsored by the Roman Catholic Church, also lent its assistance. By 1947 the local Red Cross chapter was engaged in an active assistance program. The Home Service Department of the chapter rendered social services to people in their own homes. Both Guamanians and non-Guamanians were helped. Needy cases were contacted and investigated. Help was given as needed. When necessary, financial assistance in the form of loans was given. Individuals and families were helped in the dispatch of emergency messages connected with illnesses or deaths. The chapter also helped military personnel with the filing of claims for government benefits. Perhaps the most important service rendered by the chapter was that of helping needy Guamanian civilians to receive early payment of claims from the Land and Claims Commission. During the eleven months ending February 1, 1948, the Red Cross Home Service Department served 676 cases of various types.

In addition to its Home Service Department, the local Red Cross maintained a home nursing service. This service aided the training of Guamanians in public health and sanitation. The work was done through the combined efforts of the public health doctors and nurses and Red Cross nurses, who were hired by the chapter. An outstanding service rendered by them was the gathering of records on Guamanian amputees. Five of these amputees were later sent to the United States Naval Hospital, Mare Island, California. At a cost of $8,505.45 they were provided with artificial limbs and then returned to Guam.

Until early 1948 the local Red Cross was controlled by a board of officers consisting of Chairman Rear Admiral Charles A. Pownall, governor of Guam; Vice-Chairman Captain M. H. Anderson, USN, civil administrator; Secretary-Treasurer Jose S. Perez, the highest Guamanian officer with the Bank of Guam and later with the Bank of America on Guam; and Executive Secretary Miss Lagrimas P. Leon Guerrero, one of Guam's outstanding feminine leaders. From the time that the Red Cross was established on the island, it was the custom for the governor to serve as chairman of the local chapter. The practice ended in 1950, however, when Mr.

Manuel U. Lujan, a highly respected Guamanian educator and political leader, was elected chairman for 1950–51.

On November 17, 1949, Guam was struck by a disastrous typhoon. The local chapter of the Red Cross went into immediate action. Emergency issues of food, clothing, and supplies were distributed. This was followed by a long-range feeding program. In response to an appeal from the local chapter, the national chapter of the American Red Cross appropriated $150,000 for Guamanian relief. Of this amount $83,543.11 was spent for immediate typhoon relief. The sum of $62,586.10 was spent later for the rebuilding and repair of damaged or destroyed homes.

In 1950 the island's Red Cross fund raising campaign, under the chairmanship of Mr. William U. Lujan, Guam's leading sports promoter, raised $29,376.29. This was more than $1,000 over the established goal. For this effort the local chapter gained national recognition as one of the first Red Cross chapters to exceed their 1950 goal.

POLICE DEPARTMENT: The Department of Civil Police was reestablished immediately after the American reoccupation of Guam. On September 1, 1944, the department resumed operations as the Guam Police Department. As of December 31, 1947, personnel of the department consisted of one Marine Corps major, a Navy lieutenant commander, a second lieutenant of marines, a Marine Corps warrant officer, 96 enlisted marines, 137 civilian patrolmen, 1 police matron, and 2 civilians. Until 1949, the head of the department was an officer of the Marine Corps.

For several years after the war, the civil jail was one of the principal establishments in the ruins of Agana. In 1948 it consisted of four Quonset huts, size 20 feet by 56 feet. Two of the huts were used for male prisoners. They contained four solitary confinement cells. One hut, apart from the others, was for women prisoners. The other hut was used as a combination galley and mess hall. The jail was enclosed by an elephant-wire fence and barbed-wire entanglements. Guard stations were posted at points of vantage around the compound. In reality the civil jail was a wartime emergency stockade. By late 1948 it had outgrown its usefulness. At that time plans for a new and permanent structure were drawn up by the Guam Planning Commission. Construction was begun a short time later. While the new jail was being built, prisoners were confined in a temporary jail at Ordot. This interim jail was expanded later and became the island prison.

Shown below is a summary of prisoners in order of confinement in the civil jail during 1948:[10]

| MONTH | SERVING JAIL SENTENCES | PENDING ACTION |
|---|---|---|
| January | 44 | 20 |
| February | 37 | 21 |
| March | 45 | 12 |
| April | 33 | 8 |
| May | 32 | 24 |
| June | 30 | 26 |
| July | 30 | 10 |
| August | 28 | 10 |
| September | 30 | 30 |
| October | 35 | 21 |
| November | 37 | 27 |
| December | 39 | 16 |
| | 420 | 225 |

During 1948 the Bureau of Identification fingerprinted and classified 1,494 persons who were booked for offenses other than motor-vehicle violations. Also, 947 persons were fingerprinted in accordance with the Federal Employees' Loyalty Program. This work was done under the supervision of a fingerprint expert from the mainland. He was assisted by five Guamanian patrolmen who were instructed in fingerprinting.

Under the laws of the naval government, persons convicted of crimes could address petitions to the governor. The governor had the power to grant reprieves, commutations, and pardons. He could also grant persons sentenced to pay a fine the privilege of paying such fines in installments. If a person convicted of a crime felt he was being treated unjustly in Guam, he could appeal to the Secretary of the Navy for a review of his case.

DEVELOPMENT PROGRAMS: In October 1945 the Congress of the United States appropriated $6,000,000 for rebuilding Guam's towns, especially Agana and Agat. Rebuilding plans were approved by the Guam Planning Commission and the Guam Congress, and reconstruction was well under way by the end of 1946. Included in the program were plans for a new congress building and an entirely new capital city. Problems connected with the rebuilding of Agana were described by Stevens as follows:

When our troops stormed ashore they came into a city which consisted of nothing but rubble, broken glass, burned roofing, metal, and ashes. Here and there the shattered walls of more substantial concrete buildings could be seen above the ruins. Prominent among these walls were those belonging to the church and those of the Agana hospital, which building remained virtually intact and which later was to be utilized as the Administration Building for the government of Guam.

Immediately after the landing, bulldozers began to clear the rubble from the area and much of it was pushed into the sea to form a peninsula jutting into the ocean from the city, which later became an area known as the Paseo de Susana....

...One of the first phases of reconstruction was to lay out a system of roads and sidewalks, together with utility facilities throughout the city. The entire area having been bulldozed and cleaned, it was a simple matter to lay out the streets and sidewalks in perfectly straight, even squares in the fashion of our modern American towns and cities. The latest designs were used, streets were broad, blocks were of standard size, and the general pattern in which the city was laid out was one conforming to the most modern conception of city planning. In conjunction therewith, certain public buildings were planned and their construction started, including the buildings now housing the Guam Legislature and the police station....

Prewar Agana did not have straight streets, nor did it have a regularized block and lot pattern. The roads often twisted where fancy led them, and there was no practical system of arrangement.

The lots were of uneven size and shape. Some of them would be considered far too small by American standards, yet housed substantial dwelling structures. Other lots were large and contained little or no construction. Some lots were shaped as triangles, squares, rectangles, and otherwise, and adjoining lots rarely were the same in size and shape....

When the postwar planners laid out streets in straight, evenly divided blocks they ignored all the old ownerships. Streets crossed through former lots, streams were filled and bulldozed and the water diverted, and the former property lines were abandoned. . . .

All the above resulted in a legal nightmare upon the laying of even blocks and lots. New lots include as many as thirty owners within the confines of one lot. The most common multiple ownership is five or six owners per lot, but often it rises to ten or twelve. . . .

As a result of the confused property title situation and the difficulty of one person obtaining clear title or possession of an entire lot for building purposes, only a limited number of buildings has been constructed in new Agana. Entire blocks may be seen with no buildings on them, although they are surrounded by wide, attractive streets and handsomely constructed curbs and sidewalks. Other blocks have a handful of buildings interspersed here and there. A few blocks have been substantially built up through the consistent efforts of a few persons over several years' time. . . . Although this city has one of the greatest potentialities of any city in the Pacific today, its development is proceeding laboriously, and it is an open question whether it will ever be completely built up. . . .[11]

At this writing the land problem in Agana is still unsolved.

By 1948 an additional sum of nearly $1,000,000 had been appropriated for building temporary facilities in the remaining villages of Guam. This program, a continuation of work begun shortly after the reoccupation, included repairs to power plants, water systems, schools, and medical and public safety facilities.

## ECONOMIC CONDITIONS

LAND: When the United States acquired Guam from Spain, the Spanish crown lands consisted of 14,581 hectares. This land, about one-fourth the total area of the island, became the property of the federal government. Much of it was grass and timber land in the northern part of the island. Most of the good farm land was privately owned. As American rule progressed, however, large tracts of private land passed into the hands of the naval government. This land was either bought from the owners or acquired for non-payment of the land tax. The federal government, moreover, bought up more and more land, especially around Agana and in the Apra Harbor area. As a result, by 1937 the naval government

335

owned about 2,924 hectares of land and the federal government owned 16,507 hectares. This amounted to 48,014 acres. After World War II, more land was needed for military purposes. Consequently, private land was condemned in many parts of the island. By 1948 the government, federal and local, owned or controlled about 42 per cent of the total land area of the island. Much of the land was not used by the military and was permitted to lie idle. This was cause for bitter resentment among the Guamanians. Agitation soon developed for return of some of the land to private ownership.

Under the naval government, aliens were forbidden to own land in Guam or to lease land for more than five years. With the government's permission, American citizens could lease privately owned land for any length of time. Churches, schools, and other nonprofit organizations could buy land if the purchase was approved by the local government. The government could buy privately owned land for public use or could acquire it by eminent domain. In 1948 the total land area of Guam could be roughly divided as follows:[12]

> 24.5% arable (including coconut groves)
> 22.5% forest (containing very little useful timber)
> 40% pasture and meadow
> 13% wasteland

In that year about 58 per cent of the above land was privately owned. The rest was owned either by the United States or by the naval government.

AGRICULTURE: In 1946 a total of 1,250 acres of land was under cultivation. This figure did not include coconut groves. An additional 1,600 acres was available for farming. However, since most of the Guamanian workers were employed by the government, much of the land was permitted to lie idle. Nevertheless, small plots of land were cultivated in order to add to the wage income. Crops grown in these small gardens were yams, taro, eggplants, red peppers, bananas, plantains, squash, watermelons, peanuts, tomatoes, mustard, radishes, beans, onions, garlic, and lettuce.

Corn was the most important food crop after breadfruit and coconuts, and the island produced about 500,000 pounds of it during the calendar year 1947. Aside from corn, no other cereal crops were grown. Rice, the most important food crop before the war, was not grown after the reoccupation. Small amounts of corn, sweet potatoes, and cassava, combined with the meat of coconuts, were used for animal feed. Generally it was possible to produce two crops a year in spite of the fact that temperatures remain about the same throughout the year. Shown below are agricultural statistics as of December 31, 1946.[13]

| | |
|---|---|
| Area under cultivation | 1,311 acres |
| Area cleared but not under cultivation | 1,461 acres |
| Number of farmers | 435 |
| Number of swine | 3,768 |
| Number of chickens | 30,132 |
| Number of ducks | 185 |
| Number of cattle | 2,546 |
| Number of carabao | 580 |
| Number of goats | 280 |
| Number of horses | 54 |

All crops on the island were plagued by the destructiveness of the giant African snail. Control measures, consisting mostly of the spreading of poisoned bait in infected areas, were not too successful. Other agricultural pests were the rhinoceros beetle, the Saipan coconut beetle, and the banana root borer.

By 1948 the Department of Agriculture was supervised by a trained and experienced director. Included on the staff were three agricultural agents and one club leader. They carried on farm demonstrations and supervised the activities of boys' and girls' agricultural clubs. In general, their work was similar to that of Agricultural Extension Service agents in the United States. However, no formal connection existed between the local and the federal departments of agriculture.

In addition to strictly agricultural affairs, the Department of Agriculture had other duties as well. These included the licensing of fish weirs, issuance of slaughter permits, livestock and plant import permits, plant and animal inspection, quarantine regulations, etc. The department also operated the Agriculture Demonstrational Farm and Quarantine Station, which consisted of about 75 acres of land, both developed and undeveloped. The principal purpose of the farm was to provide a source of livestock, poultry, and plants necessary for the agricultural rehabilitation of the island.

Two typhoons, one in November 1949 and the other in May 1950, did severe damage to the island's crops. Field crops were just being replanted when the second typhoon struck. Despite typhoon damage, crops produced during the fiscal year 1950 totaled 1,685,614 pounds.

During the Japanese occupation and the period following liberation, livestock and poultry were greatly reduced in numbers. By 1948 the number of cattle and carabao was only a little more than 40 per cent of that of the prewar period. Pigs numbered only one-third of the previous level. Poultry numbered less than one-fifth the number on hand in 1940. After the war considerable numbers of pigs were imported for feeding and breeding. The rate of increase, however, was slow. This was due to the demand for fresh pork for local consumption and to repeated outbreaks of hog cholera. In 1949, the island imported 144 head of cattle from Maui, Hawaii, and, during the latter part of the same year, 129 head from the United States. Imported cattle were bothered by ticks and liver flukes but otherwise were generally free of diseases. There were a few horses on the island after the war but no mules or burros. Chicken production was aided by the operation of a hatchery at the demonstration farm. In spite of all efforts, from 1946 to 1950 locally produced meat and meat products were far below demand.

STANDARD OF LIVING: During the years following the war the Guamanian economy changed from an agricultural to a money economy. This brought about a very marked improvement in the standard of living. As of December 31, 1947, Guamanians working for the government—local and federal—were being paid a total of about $225,000 a month or $2,700,000 a year. Large sums of money were spent by Americans and other nonresidents temporarily stationed in Guam, and much of this money ended up in Guamanian hands. In general, Guamanians employed in private enterprise earned more money than those working for the government. Privately employed Guamanians were paid at the following wage rates in 1948:[14]

| OCCUPATION | RATE PER HOUR | | |
|---|---|---|---|
| Labor | $0.50 | to | $0.875 |
| Carpenter | .69 | to | 1.50 |
| Automotive mechanic | .67 | to | 1.50 |
| Plumber | 1.10 | to | 1.40 |
| Heavy equipment operator | 1.10 | to | 1.40 |
| Painter | .77 | to | 1.40 |
| Truck driver | .65 | to | 1.16 |
| Gardener | .76 | to | ? |
| Cook | 1.00 | to | 2.50 |
| Salesgirl | .70 | to | 1.00 |

| OCCUPATION | RATE PER MONTH | | |
|---|---|---|---|
| Clerk | $90.00 | to | $200.00 |
| Assistant manager | 275.00 | and | up |
| Storekeeper | 75.00 | to | 200.00 |
| Waitress | 75.00 | to | 150.00 |
| Chauffeur | 100.00 | to | 150.00 |
| Salesman | 125.00 | to | 220.00 |
| Cashier | 69.60 | to | 140.00 |

An over-all rise in the cost of living occurred during 1948–49. Price increases on canned and imported foods averaged from 10 to 50 per cent. The greatest increases were noted in the prices of such foods as fresh meat and dairy products. The following is a table of retail prices on certain items in 1949:[15]

| ITEM | UNIT | AVERAGE RETAIL PRICE |
|---|---|---|
| Kerosene | gal. | $0.60 |
| Sugar | lb. | .15 |
| Coffee | lb. | .90 |
| Milk, evaporated | 14-oz. can | .23 |
| Salmon, pink | 1-lb. can | .80 |
| Sardines | lb. | .18 |
| Bread | 1-lb. loaf | .25 |

| | | |
|---|---|---|
| Fish, fresh | lb. | .75 |
| Coconuts | ea. | .03 |
| Beans, Kentucky Wonder | lb. | .35 |
| Chicken, fresh | lb. | 1.00 |
| Beef, fresh | lb. | 1.00 |
| Cigarettes | pack | .18 |
| Soap, laundry | bar | .12 |
| Flour | lb. | .18 |
| Eggs, fresh | doz. | 1.50 |
| Onions, fresh | lb. | .20 |
| Cabbage, fresh | lb. | .10 |
| Gasoline (4¢ tax) | gal. | .25 |
| Shortening | lb. | .80 |
| Vinegar | qt. | .45 |
| Butter | lb. | 1.45 |

TRADE AND COMMERCE: By 1946 over 300 firms were licensed by the naval government to do business in Guam. Included among them were wholesalers, retailers of all types of merchandise, beauty parlors, barbershops, cobblers, bakeries, and many others. All of the licensed businesses were owned by Guamanians. Under government regulations non-Guamanians could not engage in business. Since almost all merchandise was brought to the island in Navy ships, most goods sold in the stores were purchased from the Naval Supply Center. Some trade figures for April 1946 are as follows:[16]

| TYPE OF BUSINESS | NUMBER OF ENTERPRISES | APRIL 1946 RECEIPTS |
|---|---|---|
| Wholesaler | 4 | $155,157.00 |
| Retailer | 53 | 158,280.27 |
| Restaurant | 20 | 14,332.13 |
| Lumber and building materials | 1 | 26,310.45 |
| Arts and crafts | 1 | 4,477.68 |
| Bakery | 33 | 7,007.50 |
| Taxicab | 18 | 1,458.39 |
| School lunch counter | 21 | 4,028.68 |
| Cargo hauling | 13 | 2,206.93 |
| Gas station and auto repair | 3 | 3,597.28 |
| Importer and distributor, motor vehicles, parts | 1 | 4,480.36 |

| | | |
|---|---|---|
| Beauty shop | 7 | 1,386.65 |
| Barbershop | 34 | 1,811.75 |
| Silversmith | 12 | 1,889.00 |
| All other miscellaneous types of business, including watch repair, instrument repair, poolroom, private school, tailor, seamstress, refreshment stand, retail produce, blacksmith, cobbler, carpenter, and wood carver | | 6,953.07 |
| TOTALS | 335 | $393,377.14 |

As the island's reconstruction projects increased in number, more space aboard Navy ships was needed for bringing in supplies and equipment. As a result, civilian businesses were encouraged to secure their goods through private imports. By early 1947, private imports had increased considerably. Because of the lack of nonmilitary docks and storage space, however, most goods continued to reach the island in Navy ships. The situation was not greatly improved until after establishment of the commercial port. During the year 1947, imports into Guam were valued at $6,803,445. For the last six months of the same year, the classification and value of imports were as follows:[17]

| IMPORT | AMOUNT |
|---|---|
| Food products | $ 994,271.00 |
| Petroleum products | 158,210.00 |
| Beer | 903,474.00 |
| Liquor | 673,877.00 |
| Dry goods | 339,189.00 |
| Building materials | 134,857.00 |
| Motor vehicles and accessories | 217,085.00 |
| Miscellaneous | 329,686.00 |
| TOTAL | $3,750,649.00 |

During the last years of naval rule commercial activities developed rapidly. By June 1950 there were 1,523 licensed businesses on the island. The following table presents a partial list of commercial interests at that time:[18]

341

| ACTIVITY | NUMBER OF ENTERPRISES |
|---|---|
| Accounting, advisory | 3 |
| Arts and crafts | 4 |
| Attorney | 9 |
| Auto dealer | 12 |
| Surveying (land) | 3 |
| Tailoring | 8 |
| Taxi | 241 |
| Theater | 12 |
| Trader, first class | 72 |
| Trader, second class | 175 |
| Cargo service | 4 |
| Carpentry | 5 |
| Chicken ranch, commercial | 2 |
| Construction | 6 |
| Dentistry | 3 |
| Drug store | 2 |
| Dry cleaning | 2 |
| Dry goods store | 4 |
| Electrical installation and repair | 16 |
| Electrical supplies | 1 |
| Electrical trade school | 1 |
| Engineering consultation | 3 |
| Equipment rental | 3 |
| Feed store | 1 |
| Fishing, commercial | 4 |
| Fish weir | 24 |
| Florist | 5 |
| Frozen confection manufacturer | 1 |
| Gasoline filling station | 40 |
| General repairs | 7 |
| Generator repairs | 6 |
| Ice manufacturing | 2 |
| Insurance agency | 8 |
| Interisland steamship line | 4 |
| Instrument repair shop | 1 |
| Manufacture of concrete buildings | 1 |
| Photography | 10 |
| Plumbing | 19 |
| Printing | 4 |
| Public market | 9 |

| | |
|---|---:|
| Radio parts store | 1 |
| Rattan assembly plant | 1 |
| Refrigeration repair | 3 |
| Restaurant | 125 |
| Sawmill | 1 |
| Sheet metal supply | 2 |
| Shoemaker | 8 |
| Silversmith | 5 |
| Soap manufacturing | 1 |
| Soft drink manufacturing and distribution | 2 |
| Auto repair shop | 46 |
| Bakery | 30 |
| Banking | 1 |
| Blacksmith | 3 |
| Broker agents | 5 |
| Building materials supply | 4 |
| Travel service | 2 |
| Watch repair | 4 |

Rapid business expansion after the war may be credited in large part to the Navy's favorable and co-operative attitude. The effects of the postwar boom on some businessmen were described by Stevens as follows:

> Following the war, some merchants were able to finance purchases interest free. Huge amounts of stores and supplies of all kinds were issued from Navy supplies and quickly turned into profits. In addition, war claims were paid out in the amount of several million dollars, and some individual claims rose to very high figures. As a result of this large supply of circulating dollars, within a few years following cessation of hostilities Guam had some merchants whose fortunes were almost beyond their own belief. For the most part, such persons had only minimum obligations to pay. Their houses and stores were constructed largely of salvaged material; their standard of living was not high; they paid no income taxes; and in general it was possible not only to make large profits but to retain virtually all of them. Most of the merchants kept their profits in cash rather than investing their surplus.[19]

BANKING AND PUBLIC FINANCES: The Bank of Guam was re-established in January 1946. It had been closed throughout the period of the Japanese occupation. As of April 1946 its deposits totaled more than $4,500,000. Its investments were mainly in United States government securities. The bank performed the usual functions of mainland banks. It advanced loans, issued bank drafts and cashier's checks, and sold and redeemed defense bonds. By 1949 it maintained an active branch on the island of Saipan. In 1950 the naval government sold the bank, with all its facilities, to the Bank of America. At that time the bank held local gross deposits amounting to about $20,000,000.

In 1948 revenues for operating the naval government came mainly from four tax sources. They were an internal revenue tax, a personal tax, trade and license fees, and a general gross sales tax. The internal revenue tax was levied on soft drinks, beer, cosmetics, cigarettes and tobacco, and gasoline. Each person between eighteen and sixty years of age living in Guam was required to pay a personal tax of $3 a year. Most business establishments were required to pay trade and license fees ranging from $10 to $100 a year. Pawnshops, under the law, had to pay an annual fee of $300. The general gross sales tax was levied on property and professional services. It included a 20 per cent tax on admissions to theaters and other amusement places. Charitable and religious organizations, as well as agricultural products and fisheries, were exempted from this tax. The table below shows the sources and amounts of revenue collected during fiscal year 1950.[20]

| TAXES | |
|---|---|
| Internal revenue tax | $ 634,300.52 |
| Gross sales tax | 595,879.49 |
| Gasoline tax | 201,146.62 |
| Personal tax | 18,450.50 |
| Other taxes | 300,724.11 |
| | $1,750,501.24 |
| LICENSES | |
| Vehicle licenses | $138,815.01 |
| Business licenses | 122,067.24 |
| Others | 85,733.07 |
| | $346,615.32 |

| FINES AND PENALTIES | |
|---|---:|
| Court fines | $105,283.00 |
| Court fees | 20,522.50 |
| Other fines and penalties | 1,403.69 |
| | $127,209.19 |
| CUSTOMS | |
| Duties | $316,443.25 |
| Others | 296,202.77 |
| | $612,646.02 |
| UTILITIES | |
| Electricity | $ 42,918.83 |
| Water | 55,486.81 |
| Telephone | 8,879.74 |
| | $107,285.38 |
| MISCELLANEOUS | |
| Rental | $ 34,641.18 |
| Garbage collection | 17,769.50 |
| School assessment | 112,504.91 |
| Guam Memorial Hospital | 40,012.13 |
| Samoa | 13,326.00 |
| Others | 149,260.65 |
| | $367,514.37 |
| OTHER RECEIPTS | |
| U.S. appropriation | $447,000.00 |
| Eigloan (medical, dental, and nursing school) | 113,326.00 |
| | $560,326.00 |
| TOTAL REVENUES | $3,872,097.52 |

TRANSPORTATION AND COMMUNICATIONS: In 1946 a bus line was owned and operated by the naval government. Bus routes connected most of the major villages on the island. Most of the buses were old and in poor mechanical condition. As a result, bus service was poor. Despite several attempts by the government to improve the line, conditions gradually became worse, and the service was discontinued. After the Guam Bus Line ceased operations, military buses and private automobiles became the principal means of transportation.

By 1948 Guam was covered by a network of roads and highways. There were about 80 miles of paved highways on the island. These were two-, three-, and four-lane roadways. In addition, there were about 60 miles of improved secondary roads. Besides these, an unknown number of miles of unimproved roads spread to all parts of the island. During fiscal year 1950, a two-mile cross-island road was built from Talofofo Village to Base 18, overlooking Apra Harbor. This provided the southern end of the island with its first transisland road since before World War II.

In 1948 nonmilitary sea and air transportation to the island was extremely limited. As it had been since 1898, Guam continued to be a closed port. All nonmilitary vessels entering Apra Harbor were strictly controlled by the Navy. Port facilities and the entire harbor area were under military jurisdiction. A limited number of commercial cargoes were handled through the military port. At the same time, there were five military airfields on the island. Civilian airlines were permitted to land planes on two of the fields.

Communication systems were also controlled by the military. These included radio and wireless communication and an extensive telephone system. Whenever possible, the local population was permitted to lease telephone services. Guam, moreover, was a relay station for the Pacific Cable Company. Connections were available to Japan, China, the Philippines, Australia, the Hawaiian Islands, and the United States.

## POLITICAL CONDITIONS

GUAM CONGRESS: The limited political activity on the island centered around the Guam Congress. The congress did not meet during the Japanese occupation or during the period of military government which followed. Upon the re-establishment of the naval government, however, the prewar membership of the congress was convened. After talks with Governor Pownall, it was decided that they should be continued in office until an election for a new congress could be held. In June 1946, by popular referendum, the people of Guam expressed their desire to hold a general election for members of both houses of the congress. In view of the shift of population caused by the war, they also asked that representation in the congress be reapportioned. Before the election was held, Governor Pownall let it be known that he intended to ask the Navy Department to give the Guam Congress limited lawmaking powers. This aroused keen interest in the forthcoming election. Registration of voters took place on June 17, 1946. About a month later, on July 13, 1946, the first postwar congressional election was held. The thirteen seats in the House of Council and the thirty-three seats in the House of Assembly were filled. A matter of unusual interest was the fact that Miss Rosa T. Aguigui was elected to a seat in the House of Assembly. Representing the Merizo district, she was the first woman elected to the Guam Congress.

On August 7, 1947, Acting Secretary of the Navy John L. Sullivan issued a proclamation which granted certain home-rule powers to the Guam Congress. This proclamation came to be called the Interim Organic Act. By the terms of the proclamation, changes in the then existing laws could be made only by the Guam Congress. The governor had a veto power, but his veto could be overridden by a two-thirds vote in each of the two houses of congress. After a measure had been overridden, it was submitted to the Secretary of the Navy for final action. This proclamation granted considerable power to the Guam Congress. For the first time since 1898 a curb was placed on the absolute power of the governor. In the field of government finance, the congress was granted a right never before extended to earlier congresses. It was permitted to examine and approve the naval government budget. To carry out this task, budget and finance committees were formed in each house. Government officials appeared before the committees to justify their departmental budgets. In most instances the budgets were approved with little opposition from the congress.

At about this time Governor Pownall began to hold regularly scheduled conferences with the congress. At these conferences important problems of government were discussed and solutions proposed. Congressmen brought important questions to the attention of the governor. The governor, in turn, presented items for the consideration of the congress. Because of these friendly and constructive meetings, the governor found it necessary to veto few congressional measures.

The friendly relations that existed between the governor and the congress were broken on only one occasion. This resulted from the fact that the status and powers of the congress were uncertain. It did not know how far it could go in the lawmaking process. Because of the uncertainty, an unpleasant incident occurred in March 1949. At that time the House of Assembly ordered a civil service employee to appear before one of its committees. The employee refused to obey the order. The governor, feeling that the congress had exceeded its authority, sided with the employee. After a bitter debate, the assembly adjourned indefinitely against the wishes of the governor. The governor then ordered the assembly to reconvene. When it refused to do so, he removed all of the assemblymen from their seats. This incident received considerable national publicity which resulted in increased agitation for transferring Guam to the control of a civilian department of the federal government and for the passage of an organic act.

## Prelude to Citizenship and Civil Government

The road to American citizenship for the Guamanian people was a long and difficult one. As early as 1902 Governor Schroeder recommended to the Navy Department that an attempt be made to define the political status of Guam and its people. In 1925 the matter was brought to the attention of eleven members of the United States House of Representatives. They stopped at the island for two days while on their way to the Philippines. At that time members of the Guam Congress were invited to attend a meeting with the American congressmen. During the meeting Governor H. B. Price told the Americans of the desire of the people of Guam "to be accorded the right of naturalization as citizens of the United States." The governor's remarks were seconded by prominent Guamanian leaders, among them Don Atanacio T. Perez, Don Jose Roberto, and Dr. Ramon M. Sablan. Before they left, members of the American delegation expressed the belief that the subject of citizenship for the Guamanians would soon be presented to the United States Congress. However, no action on the matter was taken in Washington. Despite the lack of interest shown by officials in Washington, Guamanians and their leaders continued their efforts to gain American citizenship. In 1929 Governor Bradley recommended that "legislation be enacted permitting citizens of Guam to become citizens of the United States." He wrote:

> The greatest aspiration of the people of Guam is to become full-fledged citizens of the United States. Their present status is quite unsatisfactory, even the term 'Citizens of Guam' being almost meaningless at the present time, since there is no established system of acquiring citizenship in Guam and no law stating the exact requirements for such citizenship. ... Citizens of Guam now possess the privilege of freedom of entry and residence in the United States, and the extension of citizenship, in the same manner as is done in Territories of the United States, would be a just and generous act.

On December 19, 1933 a total of 1,965 Guamanian leaders signed a "Petition for American Citizenship" and sent it to President Franklin Delano Roosevelt. The petition read in part as follows:

> That the natives of the island of Guam have no other flag than that of the United States.
> That the natives of the island of Guam are not looking forward to separation from the protection and support of the motherland.
> That the natives of the island of Guam fervently aspire to become citizens of the United States.

As a result of this petition, Senator Ernest W. Gibson of Vermont introduced a citizenship bill for Guam. The bill was never voted out of committee. In November 1935 the Guamanian people again took up the cry for citizenship. They used the occasion of the visit of Secretary of War George H. Dern to express their wishes and to send their request to Washington. Secretary Dern was sympathetic and took back to Washington copies of the speeches made in behalf of citizenship for the Guamanian people.

The people of Guam decided in 1936 to send two Guamanian

representatives to Washington, D.C., to make a personal appeal for United States citizenship. The two-man delegation, consisting of the Honorable Francisco B. Leon Guerrero and the Honorable Baltazar J. Bordallo, was instructed to ask only for American citizenship. Members of the delegation were well received in Washington and were invited to the White House. There they presented a souvenir gift to President and Mrs. Roosevelt. As a result of their talks, on February 10, 1937, Senators Gibson of Vermont and Millard Tydings of Maryland introduced Senate Bill 1450 (75th Congress, 1st Session). The bill's principal purpose was to grant American citizenship to the people of Guam. The bill was approved by the Senate but failed of passage in the House, largely through the opposition of the Navy Department. In a letter to the Senate committee conducting hearings on the proposed bill, Secretary of the Navy Claude A. Swanson expressed his department's opposition, in part, as follows:

> The complicated international situation in the Far East, the questionable status of treaties, and the fact that the United States is withdrawing from the Philippines all contribute to the undesirability of any change in the status of the people of Guam or in the method of administration of that island during the present unstable conditions.
>
> The geographical location of Guam in the midst of foreign territory, with foreign commercial and colonizing interests to be considered, together with the racial problems of that locality, combine to provide a fertile field for international disputes. It is believed that the change provided for in the proposed legislation would aggravate the danger to peaceful international relations.
>
> At the present time, as citizens of Guam, the people of that possession enjoy the privileges of United States citizenship and have few, if any, of the obligations connected therewith. They are accorded passport privileges, have no Federal taxes or tariffs to pay, receive free medical and educational services, and are, in general, a particularly privileged people. . . . The general policy of the naval government is to guard them from exploitation by outsiders and protect their lands. The general policy of the naval government with reference to educational activities has been to enlighten the minds of the people and to stimulate their development through training and self-discipline. Emphasis is placed on industrial and agricultural training in order to improve the capacity of the native

350

population for self-maintenance and economic independence. However, as attested by the fact that they are not self-supporting and require not only Federal economic assistance but careful training and supervision from the paternal island government, there is every indication that these people have not yet reached a state of development commensurate with the personal independence, obligations, and responsibilities of United States citizenship. It is believed that such a change of status at this time would be most harmful to the native people. . . .

The Navy Department recommends against the enactment of S. 1450.

The bill was rejected by the House of Representatives. Consequently, the case for American citizenship for the Guamanian people rested until after the close of World War II.

Immediately after the war, the Guamanian people once more took up the cry for American citizenship. This time they received considerable support from various sources on the mainland. These included high-ranking officials in the Navy and Interior Departments, the *New York Times*, the Institute of Ethnic Affairs, and prominent individuals. Most of this support resulted from the manner in which the Guamanians had demonstrated their patriotism and loyalty to the United States while under the heel of the Japanese conquerors. Now the Guamanians asked not only for American citizenship but for a civil government as well.

On October 20, 1945, President Harry S. Truman called on the Secretaries of State, War, the Navy, and the Interior for advice on a matter of greatest importance to Guam. He asked them to submit recommendations to him concerning the administration of America's Pacific islands. For almost two years, Guam and other Pacific territories were the object of serious studies by official Washington. In February 1947 Secretary of the Interior Harold S. Krug visited the island, accompanied by Representatives Norris Poulson and Clair Engle of California and Delegate Joseph R. Farrington of Hawaii. In a speech to the Hawaiian legislature on his return, Secretary Krug stated that "the native populations of these islands Guam and American Samoa have made great progress under naval administration. But now they are ready for the next step in the American tradition, which is civil political administration, responsible to the people who are governed."[21]

At about the same time that Krug was visiting Guam and other Pacific islands, the Navy Department sent out a committee of its own. The purpose of this committee was to investigate the administration of the islands and make recommendations for self-government. Members of this committee were Dr. Earnest M. Hopkins, retired president of Dartmouth College, chairman; Maurice J. Tobin, former governor of Massachusetts; and Dr. Knowles A. Ryerson, dean of the College of Agriculture of the University of California. While in Guam the committee conducted a series of hearings, conferences, and studies. Upon its return to the mainland, it recommended full American citizenship for the peoples of Guam and American Samoa. It also expressed the opinion that the personal liberties of these people should be guaranteed by the passage of organic acts. The committee's report, called the Hopkins Report, contained many recommendations that were eventually incorporated into the Organic Act of Guam, passed three years later.

For almost two years the Secretaries of State, War, the Navy, and the Interior studied the matter of granting American citizenship and civil government to Guam and American Samoa. Finally, on June 18, 1947, they submitted their recommendations. With regard to Guam, they wrote: "Separate organic legislation for Guam to provide civil government and to grant citizenship, a bill of rights, and legislative power to Guamanians should be enacted this session."[22]

Final action on organic legislation for Guam, however, did not come through immediately. Lacking lobbyists or a well-organized effort in Washington, the Organic Act of Guam was not forthcoming for three years. In the meantime Acting Secretary of the Navy John L. Sullivan granted a measure of home rule to the Guam Congress in the form of an interim organic act. It granted the local congress legislative powers it had never enjoyed before. This move was welcomed by the Guam Congress as a transitional step toward a fuller measure of self-government. As the congressmen gained confidence in their newly acquired status, they became more vocal in their appeal for American citizenship and civil government. On January 15, 1949, the Guam Congress sent yet another petition to the Congress of the United States. It read in part:

> As we enter the second half-century period of unquestioning allegiance to the United States of America since the signing of the Treaty of Peace between the United States and Spain at Paris on December 10, 1898 ... we, the Ninth Guam Congress, on behalf of the native inhabitants of Guam, do hereby memorialize the Congress of the United States to so determine the civil rights and political status of the said native inhabitants of Guam by the passage of an organic act providing, among other things, the establishment of the Territory of Guam, and the representative government thereof, and conferring United States citizenship upon certain inhabitants thereof.[23]

This was but one of several petitions requesting passage of an organic act for Guam. The Organic Act of Guam, however, was not to come for another year and a half.

The drive for American citizenship and self-government received an unexpected spark in March 1949, when the House of Assembly of the Guam Congress walked out in dispute with the governor. The walkout and the subsequent dismissal of the congressmen by Governor Pownall received widespread publicity throughout the United States. By the time the congressmen and the governor had made their peace, self-government for Guam was a matter of general concern in a great many parts of the United States. Many mainland friends of Guam who were sympathetic to the island's desires for citizenship and home rule, brought personal appeals to the ears of many officials of both the United States Congress and the executive branch of the federal government. By this time, granting an organic act to Guam was a foregone conclusion. It was just a matter of time.

During the last half of 1949, two major events occurred which brought the island closer to its ultimate goal. On September 7, 1949, President Truman, on recommendations of the Secretaries of the Navy, War, the Interior, and State, issued Executive Order 10077, transferring the administration of Guam from the Secretary of the Navy to the Secretary of the Interior. The transfer from the Navy to the Department of the Interior was a great disappointment to the many Guamanians who had hoped for citizenship and a measure of self-government under the Navy Department. The average citizen was satisfied with the Navy control of Guam. The event, nevertheless, was a signal victory of the few, but highly vocal, political leaders of the island who widely proclaimed that civil government under a military department just wouldn't work for Guam.

The executive order revoked Executive Order No. 108-A of December 23, 1898, and broke the fifty-year history of Navy paternalism which the island had enjoyed. Executive Order 10077 read as follows:

WHEREAS the Island of Guam was placed under the control of the Department of the Navy by Executive Order No. 108-A of December 23, 1898; and

WHEREAS a committee composed of the Secretaries of State, War, the Navy, and the Interior recommended on June 18, 1947, that administrative responsibility for the Island of Guam be transferred to a civilian agency of the Government at the earliest practicable date as determined by the President; and

WHEREAS plans for the orderly transfer of administrative responsibility for the Island of Guam from the Secretary of the Navy to the Secretary of the Interior are embodied in a memorandum of understanding between the Department of the Navy and the Department of the Interior, approved by me on August 10, 1949, and it is the view of the two departments, as expressed in that memorandum, that such transfer should take effect on July 1, 1950; and

WHEREAS the transfer of administration of the Island of Guam from the Secretary of the Navy to the Secretary of the Interior, effective July 1, 1950,* appears to be in the public interest:

Now, THEREFORE, by virtue of the authority vested in me as President of the United States, it is ordered as follows:

1. The administration of the Island of Guam is hereby transferred from the Secretary of the Navy to the Secretary of the Interior, such transfer to become effective on July 1, 1950.

2. The Department of the Navy and the Department of the Interior shall proceed with the plans for the transfer of the administration of the Island of Guam as embodied in the above mentioned memorandum of understanding between the two departments.

3. When the transfer of administration made by this order becomes

* Later the date of transfer was changed to August 1, 1950.

effective, the Secretary of the Interior shall take such action as may be necessary and appropriate, and in harmony with applicable law, for the administration of civil government on the Island of Guam.

4. The executive departments and agencies of the Government are authorized and directed to cooperate with the Departments of the Navy and Interior in the effectuation of the provisions of this order.

5. The said Executive Order No. 108-A of December 23, 1898, is revoked, effective July 1, 1950.

Harry S. Truman[24]

Immediately after the President issued his transfer order, he appointed Mr. Carlton S. Skinner governor of Guam. On September 27, 1949, Mr. Skinner took oath of office as Guam's first civilian governor.

Within a week following the appointment of a civilian governor for Guam, the Committee on Public Lands approved on October 3, 1949, House Resolution 4499, introduced in the House of Representatives earlier. In November 1949 a special subcommittee from the public lands committee visited Guam. Its purpose was to conduct hearings on the proposed Organic Act. By the time the committee arrived in Guam, considerable discussion on H.R. 4499 had already taken place on the island. Interest was running high, and many persons were eager to be heard. About 100 witnesses testified. They included members of the Guam Congress, business leaders, and others. Statesiders as well as Guamanians appeared before the committee. During the hearing not a single person was opposed to the proposed bill. However, several changes were suggested. These changes were concerned with the compulsory school age, length of the governor's term of office, the right of the Guam Congress to give its advice and consent to the appointment of department heads, pay of Guam congressmen, and the organization of the island's courts. Much of the testimony was devoted to the subject of the settlement of land claims.

Many of the witnesses angrily denounced the government's land policies. During the war privately owned land had been seized by the Japanese and later by the Americans. The owners received no compensation at the time. Moreover, during the fighting on the

355

island, some title records and landmarks were destroyed. Upon the rebuilding of villages and towns, old property boundaries were disregarded. Consequently, the land-title situation was hopelessly confused. The situation in Agana was especially bad. There, new blocks and lots often contained portions of land that were formerly owned by several persons. Each person claimed the land as his own. A land court had been established for hearing and settling these claims. Because of the difficulty of proving ownership, however, little progress had been made. Members of the committee were unusually blunt with regard to this matter. They reported:

> The committee has no ready solution to this problem, but recognizes that winding up of the claims in a satisfactory manner must be among the first order of business. In many instances there is general dissatisfaction with the manner in which the military have handled land acquisition. For example, it was testified that some 14 acres on a most desirable site on Guam was on lease to the Navy, which paid the owner only $14.10 rent annually. The committee recommends that the need of the military for the land now held by it should be carefully re-examined, with the object of releasing at the first possible moment all lands not actually required for military purposes. At the hearings in 1947 on proposed organic legislation for Guam, then Under Secretary of the Navy Sullivan was questioned very closely by the committee as to the rate of settlement of the land claims. The committee was given the impression that it would not be long before substantially all the claims were settled, but the impression the committee received in Guam was that a great deal remains to be done.[25]

When the subcommittee members returned to Washington, they submitted a report to the Committee on Public Lands. This report recommended that certain changes be made to H.R. 4499. The public lands committee agreed to the changes, withdrew H.R. 4499, and introduced H.R. 7273 in its place. The new bill was introduced in the House of Representatives on February 13, 1950, by Representative J. Hardin Peterson of Florida. This bill was called "A Bill to Provide Civil Government for Guam, and for other Purposes."[26] During the Washington hearings on the new bill, members of the United States Congress, members of the cabinet, high-ranking officers of the Army and Navy, business people, and many others appeared before the committee. All were in favor of the immediate establishment of civil government in Guam. Not a single person spoke against passage of the bill.

On April 19, 1950, a subcommittee of the Senate Committee on Interior and Insular Affairs met in Washington, D.C. Its purpose was to hold a hearing on H.R. 7273 and its companion bill, S. 1892. Senator Clinton P. Anderson of New Mexico was the subcommittee chairman. Governor Skinner attended the hearing on behalf of the executive branch of the government of Guam. The Guam Congress was represented by the Honorable Antonio B. Won-Pat, speaker of the House of Assembly, and the Honorable Francisco B. Leon Guerrero, member of the House of Council. Other Guamanians at the hearing were Mr. A. T. Bordallo, president of the Guam Chamber of Commerce, Mr. Pedro M. Ada, a leading businessman, and Mr. Vicente R. Palomo, another businessman. During the hearing Mr. Leon Guerrero stated:

> . . . We are here today for the sole purpose of seeking the realization of a long-expected action on the part of the Congress of the United States. Before the treaty ceding Puerto Rico and Guam to the United States was ratified by Congress on April 11, 1899, we accepted American sovereignty without question pending congressional determination of our civil rights and political status. Our loyalty has never been questioned. There has been and always shall be only one "ism" in Guam and that is Americanism. We are proud of our record during peace and war. Without treachery to the former sovereignty, a few Guam boys are American veterans of the Spanish-American War. In World War I, Guam boys served in the Army, Navy, and Marines, and no one had to be drafted. We even had 17 percent of our total population voluntarily organized and actually performing military duty as ordered, before the United States joined the Allies. . . .
>
> During World War II . . . we were represented in the Army, Navy, Marines, Air Force, and Seabees. Our insular Guard, consisting of a handful of Guam boys, together with a couple of marines, fought a pitched battle in Agana, Guam, against overwhelming odds. Our country's casualties started simultaneously at Pearl Harbor and Guam. Our Guam boys overseas fought side by side with other American boys and for 32 long months the rest of us became prisoners in Guam—Guam, the only American soil ever captured and retained by an enemy throughout the entire history of the United States. We were physically helpless,

and were enslaved, tortured, and murdered. Yet throughout the 32-month nightmare, we kept faith in and with God and country.... Our island was shattered and is still shattered. But we have not complained and we are not here to complain.

Again, gentlemen, I repeat that we are here before you today to ask for simple justice in memory of our loved ones who died with undimmed faith and hope, and in behalf of our loyal people of Guam.... We are very hopeful that Congress shall, at long last, provide our people with a government under law, American citizenship, and a government in harmony with that to which Guam belongs....[27]

After Mr. Leon Guerrero had finished, Mr. Won-Pat addressed the committee. His remarks, like those of the first speaker, were eloquent in their appeal. Mr. Won-Pat said that he appeared before the committee in behalf of his people, the native inhabitants of Guam,

to speak, petition, and plead for their due and just cause the enactment of organic legislation for Guam by the Congress of the United States whereby we can have a legal form of government and be governed by laws and not men; and to become duly constituted citizens of a democracy whereby we can enjoy the blessings of liberty and justice inherent in all free peoples.

The desire and aspiration of our people to have a legally constituted government and to become citizens of the only country to which we owe unswerving allegiance have long been manifested. Time and again we have asked, petitioned, and supplicated with ever increasing fervency, and today as in the past we are here to reaffirm our belief in our just cause....

We have been under your benevolent protection and tutelage for over 50 years. We have learned your history, culture, customs, and traditions; we have adopted your language and assimilated your ideals and ways of life; we have never subscribed to any foreign ideologies or influences; we pledge allegiance to no flag except the Stars and Stripes; we have proven our loyalty, have demonstrated our valor, and have sacrificed for a common cause....

Are we as a people not deserving and entitled to just recognition and treatment of our aspiration to achieve social, economic, and political advancement as are the people of other Territories of the United States? Are we not ready and qualified in our understanding and assimilation of fundamental American principles and practices as are other people of other United States Territories?...

Gentlemen, in your judgment and wisdom hangs our fate. We appeal therefore to you with all the earnestness of which we are capable and implore your solemn sense of justice to exercise your legislative prerogative and responsibility in the determination of our just cause. . . .[28]

After all hearings were completed, Representative John McSweeney of Ohio, on May 23, 1950, called for immediate consideration of the Guam bill on the floor of the House of Representatives. Representative Clarence J. Brown of Ohio was recognized as the first speaker and started the debate.

I have always felt [said Brown] that in the life of an individual the thing that marks his greatness is the fact that that individual keeps his word. I think also that in the life of a nation the thing that marks the greatness of that nation is the fact that it keeps its word and keeps it promises. . . .

In 1898 under that same treaty [Treaty of Paris] we were given Guam by the Spanish Government and at that time we promised to the island of Guam that eventually it would have a civil government.*

During this long period of over 50 years Guam has been held as a naval base and has been under the supervision of the Navy Department. That has been absolutely necessary under the circumstances and we have held it up to this time. However, not only the President of the United States, not only the Secretary of State but the heads of our Army and Navy believe the time has arrived when America should grant to the people of Guam a civil government. So this bill introduced by the gentleman from Florida [Mr. Peterson] makes it possible for a civil government in Guam to be put into operation. . . .

It should be emphasized that this is not a preliminary step to the admission of Guam to statehood. It is merely granting them what we promised 50 years ago. I am especially interested in the fact that this bill incorporates a bill of rights so that these people will be amenable to the same protection that you and I as American citizens have under our American Bill of Rights.

I have gone over the bill carefully and I find it is drawn with the approval of every person who wants to treat the people of Guam fairly, but at the same time giving proper protection to our rights. In other words, it is interesting to find that under this law we will give to the people of Guam many of the fine improvements that we have placed upon that island, sewage, hospital facilities, and other things, but at

---

* According to the Treaty of Paris, Congress agreed only to define Guam's political status.

the same time the bill makes it possible for the President of the United States in case of an emergency to cause our armies and Navy to go in and again exercise their protection rights, both for the people of Guam and for the people of America, using Guam as part of our far-flung battle line in case of such emergency.[29]

From the very beginning of debate it was clear that some members of the House had some fears concerning the Guam bill. These fears were expressed by Representative John W. McCormack of Massachusetts. McCormack wanted the House to be assured that "this bill in no way can be considered as a precedent or to be construed in any way as a precedent for statehood."[30] Congressman Brown quickly reassured him. The bill, he said, definitely could not be considered "as an obligation on the part of either the Congress or the United States Government to even consider granting statehood. . . .We want to make it clear that there is no promise, direct or implied, as to statehood."[31] In order to reinforce the statements made by Brown, Congressman Peterson joined in the debate.

I want to make a brief explanation at the present time, so there will be no question in the minds of those who may be worried about the question of statehood.

I am going to put definitely in the Record a statement that this does not guarantee statehood and it is not a step toward statehood. . . .

In the recent debate in this House on the statehood bills for Alaska and Hawaii some statements were made to the effect that if Alaska and Hawaii were admitted to statehood we should be obliged to take in Guam, American Samoa, Puerto Rico, and the Virgin Islands as States, too. . . . Let me say categorically that enactment of H.R. 7273 will in no way commit the Congress to enactment of statehood legislation for Guam in the future. We have in no way made any promise to the people of Guam, or to Spain, from which Guam was acquired, that Guam would eventually be admitted to the union. . . . In the organic acts of both Alaska and Hawaii there is an express provision that the Constitution and laws of the United States, except those which are locally inapplicable, shall have the same force and effect in each of those Territories as elsewhere in the United States. Admission of Alaska and Hawaii, now incorporated Territories, to statehood, would complete the pattern set by the Northwest Ordinance* and carried over to the organic legislation of the Terri-

* The Northwest Ordinance of 1787 established the pattern whereby territories are

tories on the mainland, that a Territory once incorporated is destined for ultimate statehood. Alaska and Hawaii are our only remaining incorporated territories. We have given neither an express nor an implied pledge of incorporation or of statehood to the peoples of any of the other non-self-governing territories under our jurisdiction. After Alaska and Hawaii are admitted as States, no other area can come forward with a valid claim to statehood. . . .

You will note that the treaty provided that civil rights and political status of the inhabitants of Guam would be determined by Congress. And yet since 1898 Congress itself has taken no action. The President by executive order more than 50 years ago placed Guam under the Jurisdiction of the Navy Department, and the Secretary of the Navy, acting through a naval governor, has provided a naval government for Guam. This is not the government of laws to which the United States is pledged. It is contrary to American principles that the executive branch of the government should exercise complete legislative, judicial, and executive authority over peoples subject to the jurisdiction of the United States.[32]

When Peterson had finished his speech, Congressman McSweeney asked whether or not the Guam bill safeguarded American rights "so that in case of an emergency we can go in, without any restrictions upon the part of the citizens, and exercise our rights for our Navy and for our Army. . . ."[33] Congressman William Lemke of North Dakota, who had visited Guam a short time before as a member of the public lands subcommittee, answered the question with a positive statement. "Absolutely so!" he said. "There never will be any question about that, because the Guamanians are just as good citizens of the United States as any I have met in any State or Territory of the United States."[34]

For more than three months further work and debate on the bill continued. Finally, on May 23, 1950, the Guam bill was passed by the House of Representatives. About two months later the Senate began final consideration of the bill. It was especially interested in a number of amendments made by the Committee

admitted to the union. The ordinance provided, in part, that whenever the population of a territory numbered 5,000 free males the territory could elect a legislature and a nonvoting delegate to Congress. When the population reached 60,000 free inhabitants, the territory could draft its own constitution and be admitted to the union "on an equal footing with the original States, in all respects whatever."

on Interior and Insular Affairs. These amendments dealt with the powers of the governor, the form of the legislature, establishment of the District Court of Guam, and many other items. The committee recommended that the bill, with the amendments, be approved by the Senate. After brief discussion, and with no opposition from the floor, the Senate passed the bill on July 26, 1950. On August 1, 1950, H.R. 7273, the Organic Act of Guam, was signed by President Truman. It was declared to be effective as of July 21, 1950, the anniversary of the liberation of the island by the armed forces of the United States in World War II.

SUMMARY: The final years of naval administration were a most important period in the history of the people of Guam. It saw the island changed from an enemy-occupied territory into one where the rights of American citizens found a home.

When Guam was placed once again under the jurisdiction of the United States Navy and the naval government of Guam was re-established in 1946, the island was just about two years away from the end of the war. The physical rehabilitation of the territory was moving slowly, and the people were just beginning to look at their future. The re-establishment of the naval government was most welcome news.

During the next four years, the Navy Department began the task of getting the island rehabilitated from a disastrous war. Agana was cleared of its ruins, new streets were laid, and a completely new Agana was surveyed and laid upon the old. A new Agat rose from the ashes of the old, and other district centers grew. Employment became plentiful, and business boomed beyond Guam's wildest dreams. As the years of the war began to get dimmer in the minds of the people, a newer political horizon began to emerge. In 1947, the first of a series of major events took place. The Navy Secretary, through a proclamation, granted certain home-rule powers to the Guam Congress. Significantly, it was called the Interim Organic Act, and it signaled the beginning of the end of naval administration in Guam and provided a transitional step toward a fuller measure of self-government. During the final half of 1949, President Truman transferred the administration of Guam from the Secretary of the Navy to the Secretary of the Interior. Shortly after the transfer, the first civilian governor was appointed. On July 21, 1950, the Organic Act of Guam became effective, granting the inhabitants of Guam the privileges of United States citizenship and a greater measure of self-government.

## NOTES

1. Thompson, *Guam and Its People*, p. 75.
2. *Report to the United Nations on Guam, American Samoa, and Other Island Possessions Administered by the Navy Department* (OpNav-P22-100, U.S. Navy Department, Washington, July 1946), pp. 3–5.
3. *Ibid.*, p. 2.
4. *Ibid.*, p. 9.
5. *Information of Guam Transmitted by the United States to the Secretary-General of the United Nations Pursuant to Article 73 (e) of the Charter* (OpNav-P22-100C, Department of the Navy, Washington, June 1948), p. 16.
6. *Ibid.*
7. *Report to the United Nations* (OpNav-P22-100A, June 1947), p. 12.
8. *Report to the United Nations* (OpNav-P22-100C, June 1948), p. 10.
9. Stevens, *op. cit.*, pp. 110–11.
10. *Report to the United Nations* (OpNav-P22-100G, June 1949), p. 14.
11. Stevens, *op. cit.*, pp. 90–93.
12. *Report to the United Nations* (OpNav-P22-100C, June 1948), p. 29.
13. *Report to the United Nations* (OpNav-P22-100A, June 1947), pp. 24–25.
14. *Report to the United Nations* (OpNav-P22-100G, June 1949), p. 20.
15. *Ibid.*
16. *Report to the United Nations* (OpNav-P22-100, July 1946), pp. 13–14.
17. *Report to the United Nations* (OpNav-P22-100C, June 1948), p. 33.
18. *Report to the United Nations* (OpNav-P22-100K, June 1950), pp. 20–21.
19. Stevens, *op. cit.*, pp. 103–4.
20. *Report to the United Nations* (OpNav-P22-100K, June 1950), pp. 21–22.
21. *Guam Echo*, Vol. I, No. 3 (Institute of Ethnic Affairs, Guam), p. 1. p. 1.

22. *Congressional Record,* Vol. XCVI, Part 8 (81st Congress, 2nd session, 1950), p. 11080.

23. *Providing a Civil Government for Guam and for Other Purposes* (U.S. Congress, House Report No. 1677 of the Committee on Public Lands, 81st Congress, 2nd session, 1950), p. 2.

24. *Federal Register,* Vol. XIV, No. 174 (The National Archives of the United States, September 9, 1949), p. 5533.

25. *Ibid.,* p. 11.

26. *Congressional Record,* Vol. XCVI, Part 2 (81st Congress, 2nd session, 1950), p. 1779.

27. *Hearings on S. 1892 and H.R. 7273, An Act to Provide a Civil Government for Guam* (U.S. Congress, Senate, Committee on Interior and Insular Affairs, 81st Congress, 2nd Session, 1950), pp. 43–44.

28. *Ibid.,* pp. 48–49.

29. *Congressional Record,* Vol. XCVI, Part 6 (81st Congress, 2nd Session, 1950), p. 7560.

30. *Ibid.,* p. 7561.

31. *Loc. cit.*

32. *Congressional Record,* Vol. XCVI, Part 6 (81st Congress, 2nd Session, 1950), pp. 7562–63.

33. *Ibid.,* p. 7564.

34. *Loc. cit.*

# CHAPTER TEN

# GUAM UNDER THE ORGANIC ACT

UPON THE signing of the Organic Act by President Truman, Guam became an unincorporated territory of the United States. The act declared that the new territory should be known officially as Guam. Agana was designated the capital city and seat of government. The act additionally established a civil government, created a legislature with full lawmaking powers, established a District Court of Guam, enacted a bill of rights for the people of the territory, and granted them United States citizenship. The new government consisted of three branches: executive, legislative, and judicial. Its relations with the federal government were required to be supervised by a civilian department or agency of the government of the United States. In 1949 President Truman assigned such supervision to the Department of the Interior.

## PROVISIONS OF THE ORGANIC ACT

With the passage of the Organic Act, the people of Guam became American citizens. Citizenship was made possible by the addition of the following new section to Chapter 2 of the Nationality of Act of 1940:

Sec. 206 (a) The following persons, and their children born after April 11, 1899, are hereby declared to be citizens of the United States, if they are residing on the date of enactment of this section on the Island of Guam or other territory over which the United States exercises rights of sovereignty:

(1) All inhabitants of the Island of Guam on April 11, 1899, including those temporarily absent from the island on that date, who were Spanish subjects, who after that date continued to reside in Guam or other territory over which the United States exercises sovereignty, and who have taken no affirmative steps to preserve or acquire foreign nationality.

(2) All persons born in the Island of Guam who resided in Guam on April 11, 1899, including those temporarily absent from the island on that date, who after that date continued to reside in Guam or other territory over which the United States exercises sovereignty, and who have taken no affirmative steps to preserve or acquire foreign nationality.

(b) All persons born in the Island of Guam on or after April 11, 1899 (whether before or after the date of enactment of this section), subject to the jurisdiction of the United States, are hereby declared to be citizens of the United States, provided that, in the case of any person born before the date of enactment of this section, he has taken no affirmative steps to preserve or acquire foreign nationality.

By the terms of the Organic Act, all persons born in Guam on or after April 11, 1899, were not required to become citizens of the United States. Persons who were citizens of other countries and who wanted to retain their original citizenship were permitted to do so. However, within a period of two years after the act was passed, they were required to declare that they did not wish to become American citizens.

A bill of rights was included in the Organic Act. Among its twenty provisions were guarantees similar to those found in the United States Bill of Rights. It guaranteed freedom of religion, freedom of speech, and freedom of the press. It declared that no person could be deprived of his life, liberty, or property without due process of law. Although it guaranteed the right to a speedy and public trial, it did not specifically provide for trial by jury. However, in 1954 the Third Guam Legislature passed a jury bill, which became Public Law 42, providing for juries and trial by jury in felony and civil cases within the jurisdiction of the District Court of Guam.

The bill of rights forbade discrimination against any person in Guam on account of his race, language, or religion. It also guaranteed equal protection under law to all persons. Children under fourteen years of age were forbidden to work in occupations that might be harmful to their health or morals. The bill further provided for compulsory education for all children between six and sixteen years of age.

Section 27 of the Organic Act was included in order to aid the economic development of the island. This section provides that "articles which are the growth, production, or manufacture of Guam coming into any State, Territory, or insular possession of the United States from Guam shall be entered at the several ports of entry free of duty." Governor Skinner saw Guam developing as the Hongkong of the future. Businessmen of Guam and the United States interpreted this section to mean that cheaply produced raw materials and semifinished goods could be brought into Guam from foreign countries. They believed that such products could be changed on the island so as to make them a "manufacture of Guam." Then the finished product could be imported into the United States duty-free. That, however, has not been the case. A major problem involved here has been that of determining how much a product must be altered in order to make it a manufactured product of Guam. If this problem can be solved satisfactorily, Section 27 of the Organic Act might contribute greatly to the economic development of Guam.

Another important provision in the Organic Act is that dealing with the application of federal laws to Guam. Concerning this matter, Section 25 (b) of the Organic Act states:

Except as otherwise provided in this Act, no law of the United States hereafter enacted shall have any force or effect within Guam unless specifically made applicable by the Act of the Congress either by reference to Guam by name or by reference to "possessions." The President of the United States shall appoint a commission of seven persons, at least three of whom shall be residents of Guam, to survey the field of Federal statutes and to make recommendations to the Congress of the United States within twelve months after the date of enactment of this act as to which statutes of the United States not applicable to Guam on such date shall be made applicable to Guam, and as to which statutes of the United States applicable to Guam on such date shall be declared inapplicable.

To carry out this task a commission was appointed by the President. Members of the commission were former United States Congressman J. Hardin Peterson, chairman; Judge Jose C. Manibusan of the Island Court of Guam; the Honorable Francisco B. Leon Guerero, member of the Guam Legislature; Knight G. Aulsbrook, attorney general of Guam; Frank Chambers of the United States Department of Justice; Harold Seidman of the Bureau of the Budget; and Irwin W. Silverman of the United States Department of the Interior. The commission was required to submit its recommendations to the Congress by August 1, 1951, twelve months after passage of the Organic Act. In deciding whether to recommend the application of a federal law to Guam, the commission considered, among others, the following questions:

1. Can it be said that the Congress intended that the law should apply to the Territories?
2. Is the statute compatible with Guam's social and economic development and with its geographical position?
3. Will the application of the statute tend to place Guam in a position which parallels that of other Territories?
4. Is the function one which could be better performed by the Government of Guam?
5. Does the new law apply to Guam?[1]

While pursuing its work, the commission was assisted by representatives from many departments and federal agencies in Washington. The governor of Guam was consulted throughout. Moreover, the views of the people of Guam were sought and represented by the three commission members of Guam.

## THE EXECUTIVE BRANCH

By the terms of the Organic Act the executive authority in the new government of Guam is vested in a governor. The governor is required to be a civilian or a retired officer of the armed forces of the United States. He must live in Guam during his term of office. The governor is appointed by the President of the United States, with the advice and consent of the Senate. He holds office for four years and until his successor is appointed and approved.

34. U.S. Forces aboard Coast Guard-manned tank lighter moving in on Guam. (Official U.S. Coast Guard photo.)

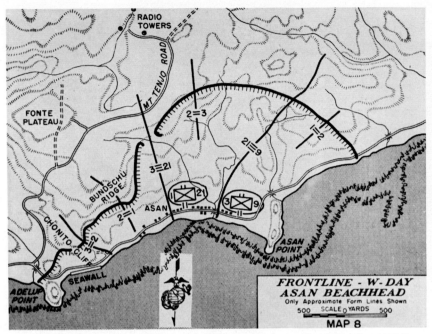

35. Strategic map of the front line at the Asan Beachhead on W Day.

36. Agana: Third Marines move through what was left of the city.

37. Old Pan-American clipper base at Sumay being used for unloading supplies after its recapture by U.S. Forces. Upturned, partially-submerged Japanese seaplane at left. (Official U.S. Marine Corps photo.)

38. Guamanian employee assembling records in 1945 from the ruins of the shattered Countz Building which housed governmental and Bank of Guam Offices. (Official U.S. Navy photo.)

39. U.S. House of Representatives committee hearing for Guam legislators at Agana in 1959. (Sanchez Studio photo.)

40. Postwar Agana, capital of Guam. The Post Office Building is in the left foreground; the Legislative Building, behind it and to the right; and at the extreme right, the Dulce Nombre de Maria Cathedral, built on the site donated by the first Chamorro convert to Catholicism. In front of the cathedral is the Plaza de Espana with its "Kiosko" bandstand. (Sanchez Studio photo.)

41. Among the first of the Chamorro and last of the Spanish priests. Left to right: Fr. Duenas, Fr. Manibusan, Bishop Olano, Monsignor Calvo, and Fr. Roman.

42. Delegation of Guamanian leaders express appreciation for their liberation by the U.S. Forces. (Official U.S. Marine Corps photo.)

His salary was originally set at $13,125 a year but was later increased to $19,500. It is paid by the U.S. government.

During the latter part of 1949 and the early part of 1950 Governor Carlton Skinner performed his duties under the supervision of the Navy Department. This was a transitional period during which naval personnel in the government were replaced by civilians. By July 1, 1950, the replacement had been completed, and the new government began operations with a staff composed entirely of civilians, including a Guamanian as agriculture director. Some of the governor's powers and duties are as follows:

1. He has general supervision and control over all executive departments and agencies of the government of Guam.

2. He is required to enforce all the laws of Guam and the laws of the United States that apply to Guam.

3. He may grant pardons and reprieves and set aside fines for offenses against the local laws. Moreover, he may postpone action for offenses against the laws of the United States until the decision of the President can be determined.

4. He may veto any bills passed by the Guam Legislature.

5. He may call upon the armed forces of the United States in Guam and may call out the militia to prevent or suppress violence, insurrection, or rebellion. In case of rebellion or the threat of invasion, the governor may suspend the writ of habeas corpus and may place the island under martial law.

6. At least once a year he must send a report on the activities of the government of Guam to the Secretary of the Interior. The secretary must then forward it to the Congress of the United States.

7. The governor may send recommendations to the legislature concerning laws which he thinks should be passed.

8. With the advice and consent of the legislature, the governor appoints the heads of all departments of the government of Guam. In making such appointments, he is required by law to give preference to qualified Guamanians.

9. He may, in general, remove from office all department and agency heads in the government of Guam.

10. From time to time the governor is required to examine the organization of the executive branch of the government. He may then make such changes as are necessary to promote the smooth and effective operation of the government.

In the performance of his duties, the governor is assisted by the secretary of Guam. With regard to this official and his duties, Section 7 of the Organic Act states:

> The President shall appoint a Secretary of Guam, who shall have all the powers of the Governor in the case of a vacancy in the office of Governor or the disability or temporary absence of the Governor. He shall have custody of the seal of Guam and shall countersign and affix such seal to all executive proclamations and other executive documents. He shall record and preserve the laws enacted by the legislature. He shall promulgate all proclamations and orders of the Governor and all laws enacted by the legislature. He shall have all such executive powers and perform such other duties as may be prescribed in this Act or assigned to him by the Governor. He shall hold office for four years and until his successor is appointed and has qualified.

The first secretary of Guam was Mr. Randall S. Herman. Herman came to Guam in 1946 as a Navy officer attached to the naval government of Guam working directly with the civilian affairs of the island. He resigned his commission to accept the secretary's position. An able administrator, Herman was the key man in the transition from naval to civilian government and was the stabilizing hand in the first half decade of civilian administration.

The office of secretary is similar to that of the secretary of state in the various states on the mainland. Additional duties, however, require the secretary to act in much the same capacity as the lieutenant governor of a state. If both the governor and the secretary are temporarily absent from Guam, an acting governor may be appointed by the Secretary of the Interior.

Mr. Carlton Skinner, Guam's first civilian governor, was a young man of thirty-nine when he first came to Guam. Most of the heavy burden of organizing the new government fell on his shoulders. Throughout his administration he was compelled to render decisions affecting many phases of the island's social, economic, and political life. The aggressive and intelligent leadership which he provided during a confused transitional period established the new government on a firm and solid foundation.

At the close of his administration in January 1953, Governor

Skinner personally delivered a message to the Second Guam Legislature on January 12. At that time he outlined briefly five major accomplishments of his administration. He said:

> I do want to point to the things which our territory long needed, now has and must keep.
>
> First, we have a judicial system cast in the finest American tradition. It is a working judicial system—one which gives justice to all alike, promptly and without great expense. It is a system which allows a final appeal to the highest court of our nation and yet can be revised by our legislature from time to time to fit the needs of the community.
>
> Second, we have a Legislature with full legislative power—not an advisory body, not a group which acts by petition to an all-powerful executive. We have a Legislature which, in its first term, enacted more positive, sound, basic legislation for the welfare of its constituents and for the progressive development of its territory than any other state or territorial Legislature has ever enacted in a similar term in the history of our country. We have a Legislature which has organized itself for the efficient conduct of its business in a simple, unassuming, and effective manner.
>
> Third, we have an executive branch which is serving the people as the people themselves determine. This service is organized and provided in accordance with the annual budget adopted by the Legislature. Through this budget, the people's representatives determine what the government shall do and how it shall be done. Perhaps more than any other development of the past three years this budget brings government most closely under the direction of the people of Guam. For well over three hundred years the activities of the Government of Guam and the services which the people received were decided arbitrarily at some remote point ... first, Madrid; then, Mexico City; then, Manila; then, Washington; for a short time, Tokyo, and then, Washington again. Now if the people of Guam want a service, they put it in the budget. No longer do they write a petition and mail it off to some remote and disinterested national or regional capital.
>
> Fourth, we have a building program, authorized by the Legislature and financed with our own funds, so that we, the people of Guam, can decide what is to be built, where, and how ... decide the relative needs of the community as between schools, roads, hospital, utilities, and the other many necessary public facilities.
>
> Fifth, although by no means only fifth in importance, we have equality —equality of opportunity, equality of treatment, equality among races,

371

equality between every person on the island no matter what his origin, status, or rank.

These are the basic gains of the past three years.

Upon the election of Dwight D. Eisenhower as President of the United States in November 1952, Governor Skinner, a Democrat, submitted his resignation. It became effective on February 20, 1953. From that time until the arrival of the new governor, Secretary Randall S. Herman served as acting governor. In the meantime the President appointed Ford Q. Elvidge, a Seattle, Washington, lawyer and an ardent Republican, to be the second civilian governor of Guam. Governor Elvidge assumed the duties of his office on April 23, 1953. His administration was marked by a determined effort to reduce government spending. Moreover, he concentrated his efforts on a program for improving the territory's medical facilities and school system. Like most governors before him, he also called on farmers to cultivate more land and produce more food. In this he was not too successful. Throughout his administration government organization remained pretty much the same as it was during Skinner's administration. Governor Elvidge's administration was hampered by an unfriendly and unco-operative legislature. Unlike Skinner, Elvidge and some of his appointees were subject to verbal attacks by members of the legislature.

Elvidge resigned early in 1956. Secretary William T. Corbett, a Pittsburg, Pennsylvania, Republican attorney, who replaced Herman as secretary, served as acting governor until the appointment of Richard Barrett Lowe in November 1956. Governor Lowe, a Republican from South Dakota, was serving as governor of American Samoa when he was nominated by President Eisenhower for the governorship of Guam. Lowe brought to Guam a background of experience in island government which proved very valuable to the territory. One of his first tasks was that of reorganizing the executive department. He made the secretary's office a part of the day-to-day administration of the government and gave to the secretary an assistant secretary to help him in his new role in governmental affairs. To the new position of assistant secretary, Governor Lowe named Manuel F. Leon Guerrero, a

372

Guamanian who had been for several years the deputy director of the Department of Land Management.* Whenever the occasion arose, Governor Lowe never failed to appoint qualified Guamanians to responsible positions in his administration.

During his three years as chief executive, Lowe initiated many capital improvement projects, among them the new and permanent administration building, the territorial College of Guam, several elementary and secondary schools, and a number of village municipal buildings.

Lowe came to Guam shortly before the 1956 election. The election brought to the legislature a majority of new congressmen untrained for and inexperienced in the work of the legislature. Lowe immediately initiated an executive-legislative conference where legislative matters were discussed. This proved helpful in many aspects although it did not check the introduction of legislation unacceptable to either the legislature or the executive department. Except in isolated cases, the cooperation between the legislature and the executive department was markedly better than that experienced during the Elvidge administration. Lowe remained aloof from local politics.

Lowe took definite stands which at various times incurred for him opposition from several sources. On two major issues he took a stand against some elements of the business community. The first of the issues concerned the question of income tax. For all the years since the Organic Act became effective on Guam, the legality of income taxes collected by the government of Guam under Section 31 of the Organic Act was a subject of debate. The District Court of Guam and the U.S. Ninth Circuit Court of Appeals maintained that the Organic Act of Guam provided for a territorial income tax. Some of the business elements, hopeful of a big windfall, contended that the income tax collected by the government of Guam was collected illegally and in violation of the federal income tax laws, which, they claimed, were applicable to Guam. When it

* Guerrero was later to become the first Guamanian secretary of Guam (1961–63) and the second American of Guamanian ancestry to be appointed governor of Guam. The first was the Honorable Joseph Flores, who was appointed governor by President Eisenhower in July 1960.

appeared that the issue was to be debated once more in the Court of Claims in Washington, D.C., Governor Lowe started the machinery rolling which ended the controversy. The Congress of the United States, repeating its intent when Section 31 was included in the Organic Act, declared in a bill that the income tax collected on Guam was a territorial tax. This was a major victory for the government of Guam, and Lowe deserved a great deal of the credit for carrying it through to its final conclusion.

Another issue of some importance in Guam concerned public utilities. Throughout most of its modern history, public utilities in Guam had always been a government venture. In recent years, there had been some discussion about turning over all public utility functions to private enterprises. During the Fourth Guam Legislature the matter was discussed, but no action was taken. During the early days of the Fifth Guam Legislature, a committee headed by Congressman Lorenzo Ramirez, an able legislator, proposed to the governor that the government get out of the public utility business and turn over to private enterprises all the capital, supplies, and facilities belonging to the Public Utility Agency. Governor Lowe objected to the proposal since it would, in effect, turn over to private individuals over seven million dollars' worth of government property without any guarantee of repayment. Lowe succeeded in checking what he called a "give-away program," although his action did not end the discussion of private versus public control of utilities.

During the last few months of Lowe's administration, another major issue arose. The United States Immigration Department issued a ruling limiting the employment of all Filipino contract laborers working for the civilian community to a three-year period. The ruling further forbade the importation of additional laborers. Lowe objected to the ruling because he felt that it would undermine the economic development of the territory. Both the legislature and the business community joined Lowe in his efforts to get the ruling rescinded or at least modified. In a meeting with representatives of the Chamber of Commerce, other businessmen, and the Guam Legislature, Governor Lowe proposed a seven-year "phase-out" program. This, he felt, would allow the government of Guam and business firms enough time to train replacements for Filipinos in skilled areas for which there were no Guamanian or permanent residents qualified. The Immigration Department disapproved the scheme and allowed the island three years to find replacements from local sources. Under the ruling, one third of all the Filipinos working in nonmilitary or nongovernment projects were to return each year to the Philippines. The year 1961 was declared to be the last year of the "phase-out" program.

Guam, under Lowe's administration, started receiving federal aid in such critical areas as education, public health, vocational rehabilitation, library, and medical services. He also secured the services of a full-time auditor general, paid for by federal funds, to provide a continuous audit of government funds and accounts. An economic survey of the island was conducted. Before Governor Lowe left the island, he succeeded in getting under way a personnel survey of the government of Guam, the first of its kind since 1950.

For most of the three years of his administration, Lowe was subjected to considerable pressure from various sources. The first instance of this came early in 1957 from the newly elected Fourth Guam Legislature. He quickly checked attempts, on the part of some legislators, to take on the functions of his administration. He drew the line between legislative and executive functions and strongly defended his position during all the time that he was governor. Pressures from a small segment of the business community, whose efforts might have undermined the taxing powers of the territory, forced him to take a positive stand on the income-tax issue. His stand resulted in the passage of a bill and the signing into law of an amendment to the Organic Act strengthening the taxing authority of the government of Guam. An important result of these and other pressures was that Lowe, because of his stand on many issues affecting the government, established the independence and the integrity of the government of Guam. While the contributions of his administration were numerous, this was perhaps his greatest contribution to the territory.

When Governor Lowe resigned in November 1959, the territory

was considered to be in such fine shape that appointment of a Guamanian as governor was considered a strong possibility. Seven months later, indeed, the Honorable Joseph Flores, publisher-editor of the *Guam Daily News* and the *Territorial Sun* and one of the island's outstanding Guamanian leaders, was appointed by President Dwight D. Eisenhower as the territory's first native Guamanian governor. Lowe had left American Samoa in the hands of a native governor, and a native Guamanian governor following in his footsteps was indeed a credit to the manner in which he had administered the affairs of the territory.

## THE LEGISLATURE

The Organic Act created a unicameral (one-house) legislature that was to consist of not more than twenty-one members. Members of the old Guam Congress remained in office until the first election under civil government was held on November 7, 1950. All persons who had established residence in Guam and had lived there for at least two years were eligible to vote. About 65 per cent of the registered voters participated in the election. The first twenty-one candidates receiving the highest number of votes were elected. Members of the legislature hold office for two years. They are paid $15.00 a day for each day that the legislature is in session, regular or special. Regular sessions are held annually for a period of not more than sixty days. Such sessions convene in Agana on the second Monday in January. Special sessions may be called by the governor but they cannot continue for more than fourteen days. All sessions of the legislature must be open to the public.

To be eligible for election to the legislature, a person must be a citizen of the United States, must be at least twenty-five years of age, and must have lived in Guam for at least five years immediately preceding the sitting of the legislature in which he seeks to become a member.

The legislature has complete lawmaking powers. However, its enactments may be vetoed by the governor. A bill vetoed by the governor may be passed a second time by a two-thirds vote of the legislature. The bill is then sent to the President of the United States for final action.

Two bills were sent to the President during the first decade of civilian government. The President in each case upheld the governor's veto. All laws passed by the legislature must be reported by the governor to the Secretary of the Interior, who must forward them to the Congress of the United States. The Congress has the power to annul any law passed by the Guam legislature. If Congress fails to annul such a law within one year after receiving it, the law is deemed to have been approved.

In view of the fact that the legislative body under naval rule had been referred to as the Guam Congress, the body elected in 1950 was called the Eleventh Guam Congress. It took its number in sequence from previous congresses. The new congress began its first regular session on the second Monday in January, 1951. One of its first acts was to change its name from Guam Congress to Guam Legislature. Members of the First Guam Legislature were Vicente B. Bamba, Baltazar J. Bordallo, Eduardo T. Calvo, Antonio C. Cruz, Antonio S. N. Duenas, Leon D. Flores, Jose D. Leon Guerrero, Manuel F. Leon Guerrero, Francisco B. Leon Guerrero, P. B. Leon Guerrero, Manuel U. Lujan, Jesus C. Okiyama, Frank D. Perez, Joaquin A. Perez, Joaquin C. Perez, Jesus R. Quinene, Ignacio P. Quitugua, Florencio T. Ramirez, James T. Sablan, Joaquin S. Santos, and Antonio B. Won-Pat, speaker. Standing rules adopted by the legislature were patterned after those of the senate of the state of California. Under the new rules the legislature's annual session was divided into two sessions of thirty days each. In general, bills introduced during one half of the session are not finally acted upon until the next half of the session. This gives members of the legislature time to study and, if necessary, to hold hearings on the bills. In 1950 the standing rules of the legislature provided for the following standing committees: agriculture and natural resources; education and labor; governmental affairs; finance and taxation; judiciary; transportation and housing; and the committee on rules.

One of the most important tasks begun by the First Guam

Legislature was that of revising the codes of Guam—civil, civil procedure, probate, and penal. These codes had been adapted from the codes of California by the naval government. Because of the change from naval rule to civilian administration and self-government, the codes were badly in need of revision. Moreover, under the naval government a number of orders and regulations having the force of law were issued as letters, proclamations, and executive orders. Some of them were still in force. To remove obsolete laws and bring some order out of chaos, revision of the codes was an absolute necessity. In addition to the revision of the codes, the legislature was faced with the gigantic task of creating new laws affecting all phases of the island's political and economic life. These included legislation in the fields of business, health, justice, law, public welfare, and reconstruction. During the period from June 30, 1951, to July 8, 1952, a total of 198 bills were introduced in the legislature. Sixty-four of them were passed and became public laws. In addition to these, the legislature considered during the same period a total of 69 resolutions and adopted 41.

The election of members of the Second Guam Legislature was held on November 4, 1952. Nineteen Popular Party candidates and two independent candidates won election to the 21-seat legislature. At that time Guam was unique among the states and territories of the United States in that it had only one political party—the Popular Party. It was not connected in any way with either of the major political parties on the mainland. All candidates not members of the Popular Party were lumped under the heading of independents and ran for office as such. Political differences between the two groups were along strictly local lines. National political affairs played only a minor part in local elections.

The first regular session of the Second Guam Legislature convened on June 8, 1953, and ran continuously until July 7, 1953, thus completing the period of sixty calendar days allotted for each annual session under the provisions of the Organic Act. In the course of the two half-sessions mentioned above, a total of 119 bills were introduced in the legislature. Of this total, 51 became public laws, 59 failed of passage, and 9 were vetoed by the governor. During the period from January 11 to July 13, 1954, the governor vetoed 7 of the 120 bills considered by the second regular session of the Second Guam Legislature. Among the bills vetoed was one calling for the establishment of movie censorship in the territory. After due consideration, the legislature passed the bill a second time, over the governor's veto. This was the first time in territorial history that a governor's veto had been overridden. The bill was then, by the terms of the Organic Act, sent to the President of the United States. The President upheld the governor's veto. The governor, meanwhile had introduced a substitute bill (Public Law 97), penal in nature and designed to control immoral movie exhibitions in the territory. The legislature acted favorably upon this measure.

Among the most significant bills passed by the Second Guam Legislature was one affecting codification of the laws of Guam. It enacted a new penal code for Guam, a new civil code, probate code, and code of civil procedure. Prepared under the direction of Attorney John A. Bohn, legislative counsel for the first three legislatures, the new code represented a compilation of all acts of the Guam Legislature, previous Guam Congresses, and all executive orders, memoranda, and letters having the force and effect of law in Guam. It repealed old statutes and enacted a new code into law. With the codification, all statutory enactments were henceforth made in the form of amendments, repeals, or additions to the codes. All statutes enacted by each legislature appear in the *Statutes and Amendments to the Code,* which is published after each legislative term.

Another important bill passed by the Second Guam Legislature extended suffrage to all citizens of Guam over eighteen years of age. "This law," according to Governor Elvidge, "places Guam among the foremost States of the Union in its program of social and political advancement, and makes it unique among the territories of the United States in this respect." At that time, only Georgia permitted eighteen-year-olds to vote.

Other laws authorized the investment and deposit of money from the general fund of the government of Guam, enacted a new business and trades license system, and provided for workmen's compensation.

Members of the Third Guam Legislature were elected in November 1954. As a result of the voting the Popular Party won eighteen seats in the legislature. The three remaining seats were won by independents, two of whom were Mrs. Lagrimas L. G. Untalan and Mrs. Cynthia J. Torres, the only women elected to the legislature during the first ten years of civil government. In a surprise election, the officers of the Third Guam Legislature changed hands at the beginning of the new legislative term in January 1955. Francisco B. Leon Guerrero, known as "Mr. Organic Act" because of his efforts in behalf of the Organic Act of Guam, replaced A. B. Won-Pat, who was generally expected to be re-elected speaker. Baltazar J. Bordallo and Antonio S. N. Duenas were elected vice-speaker and secretary, respectively. The various committee chairmen for the new term through 1956 were Eduardo T. Calvo, Committee on Rules; Vicente C. Reyes, Committee on Judiciary; Frank D. Perez, Committee on Finance and Taxation; Felix T. Carbullido, Committee on Governmental Affairs; Manuel U. Lujan, Committee on Education and Labor; James T. Sablan, Committee on Agriculture and Natural Resources; and Eduardo T. Calvo, Committee on Housing and Transportation.

One of the most important bills passed by this legislature was Public Law 42. It established trial by jury in certain cases within the jurisdiction of the District Court of Guam. For the first time the people of Guam acquired a basic right that had long been taken for granted among other citizens of the United States. "This is unquestionably a step along the road of progress," wrote Governor Elvidge in his 1955 annual report.

Among other important pieces of legislation passed by the Third Guam Legislature was a bill concerning funds for the conversion of the nursing-school building, then in process of construction at the Guam Memorial Hospital area, into a general hospital building. The debate over the matter was bitter in many respects, causing a major split in the once solid ranks of Popular Party legislators. The conversion bill finally passed and was signed into law by Governor Elvidge. He had requested the conversion when it became apparent to him that the original plans for the multimillion-dollar Guam Memorial Hospital would require more time and money than the government could afford.

Other laws passed during the first year included a retirement law for public employees of the government of Guam, a law relating to absentee ballots, a law relating to the Administrative Adjudication Law relative to service, a law relating to foreign corporations doing business in Guam, and a law relating to investments and deposits in savings and loan associations.

During the second regular session and second and third special sessions, the Third Guam Legislature enacted legislation which covered the fields of business, rehabilitation, public welfare, education, operation of the government and capital improvements projects. Among the bills passed into law were those concerning legal rates of interest, jury service by employees of the government, filing and recording of documents in the Department of Land Management, extradition proceedings, juries and trial by jury in civil cases within the jurisdiction of the District Court of Guam, laws relating to a tax appeal board, jaywalking, registration of leases of real property, procedure for processing and payment of claims against the government of Guam, student loan and scholarship funds, and many others.

The Third Guam Legislature met for the last time in a special session called by Acting Governor William T. Corbett. The session was held in October 1956 to consider a liquid fuel tax and an excise tax on gasoline sold on military reservations. Both bills were passed and signed into law.

The election of 1956 saw three political parties vying for control of the legislature. They were the Popular Party, the Territorial Party, and the Guam Party. The Guam Party, organized and composed primarily of stateside Americans, presented five candidates and endorsed sixteen other candidates from the two leading parties. Few people gave the Guam Party candidates any chance of winning, and both the Popular Party and the Territorial Party ignored the Guam Party during their campaigns.

The Territorial Party grew out of a split among Popular Party legislators during the days of the third legislature. Organized around a nucleus of eleven members of the third legislature, headed by Speaker F. B. Leon Guerrero, and supported by some of Guam's leading citizens, the Territorial Party was favored to win the election.

During the campaign, the Popular Party, taking the role of the underdog and calling itself the "party of the poor," conducted a hard and sometimes bitter campaign. The party was well organized at the village level and included among its supporters a great majority of the village commissioners. When the votes were counted, the Popular Party won by a landslide complete control of the 21-seat legislature. After the election, the Guam Party ceased to exist. The Territorial Party, however, started reorganizing almost immediately after its defeat.

The Fourth Guam Legislature experienced considerable difficulty during its first year. Although twenty-one were elected, only twenty served. Juan M. Tuncap declined a seat in the legislature in order to retain his position as legislative staff director, a position he had occupied since 1952. Of the twenty legislators, nine had no legislative experience whatsoever. Consequently, the burden of the legislature fell on the shoulders of only eight experienced congressmen. It wasn't until the close of the first year that some of the freshmen legislators began taking on a greater share of the burden.

Several important pieces of legislation were passed by the fourth legislature. Among these was a law providing for the free use of textbooks in the public schools of Guam, one of several campaign promises made good. Other bills which eventually became law included those providing for the establishment of a free public employment service, acceptance of the Vocational Education Act of 1946, and establishment of vocational rehabilitation services in the territory. In 1958 this legislature passed six laws affecting public employment, six affecting public safety and protection, six concerning business and professions, two on public health and sanitation, three on education, six affecting the courts, two on public highways and transportation, four on legislature and elections, one on public housing, and two classified as miscellaneous laws.

In the election of 1958 the Popular Party, campaigning against the Territorial Party, again won all twenty-one seats in the legislature. The margin of victory was closer than in the election of 1956, and the Territorial Party felt it had won a moral victory for its efforts. For the first time, too, a non-Guamanian was elected to the Legislature. He was Alfred Ching, a former resident of Hawaii. Of those elected, seventeen were holdovers from the fourth legislature, three had no legislative experience, and one had been a member of the second legislature.

The fifth legislature, like its predecessors, displayed real concern for the problems of education. A generous scholarship bill was enacted into law. It authorized the establishment of over 150 professional scholarships for students wishing to study in mainland colleges and universities. Other scholarships were authorized for use in the Territorial College of Guam. The law on the free use of textbooks was amended so as to enable students attending private schools to benefit from the act. At the close of the first session in 1960 several congressmen showed concern over the matter of teachers' salaries. Two bills were introduced providing for salary increases for educational employees.

Other measures passed had to do with the courts and the laws, with parks and recreation, business, commerce and taxation, public works and public utilities, public health and welfare, streets and zoning, agriculture, and miscellaneous matters. The legislature also appropriated funds supporting Governor Lowe's request for a personnel survey of the government of Guam and passed several measures affecting the executive and legislative branches of the government.

The record of the Guam Legislature during its first ten years of existence was an impressive one. Although the United States Congress had the right under the Organic Act to annul local legislation, it did not, during the first ten years, find it necessary to exercise that right.

## THE JUDICIARY

The judicial branch of the government of Guam was established by Section 22-a of the Organic Act, which follows:

> There is hereby created a court of record to be designated the "District Court of Guam," and the judicial authority of Guam shall be vested in the District Court of Guam and in such court or courts as may have been or may hereafter be established by the laws of Guam. The District Court of Guam shall have, in all causes arising under the laws of the United States, the jurisdiction of a District Court of the United States as such court is defined in Section 451 of Title 28, United States Code, and shall have original jurisdiction in all other causes in Guam, jurisdiction over which has not been transferred by the legislature to other court or courts established by it, and shall have such appellate jurisdiction as the legislature may determine. The jurisdiction of and the procedure in the courts of Guam other than the District Court of Guam shall be prescribed by the laws of Guam.

The judge of the District Court of Guam is appointed by the President of the United States, with the advice and consent of the Senate. He holds office for eight years and until his successor is chosen and qualified. However, he may be removed sooner by the President for cause. His salary, paid by the government of the United States, was at first the same as that of the governor. However, in 1959 the salary was increased to $22,000, higher than the governor's salary. The Honorable Paul D. Shriver of Colorado was appointed to serve as Guam's first district judge. He was relieved by the Honorable Eugene Gilmartin in 1959. Upon Judge Gilmartin's death in office in 1961, Judge Shriver returned to the bench to succeed him.

Organization of the District Court of Guam made it possible, for the first time, for certain cases arising in Guam to be appealed to the federal courts. As with any other state or territory, such cases may finally be appealed to the Supreme Court of the United States.

In 1950 Guam's court system was badly in need of reorganization. Consequently, a judiciary act was drawn up to revise and modernize the island's judicial system. The judiciary act was pre-

384

pared with the assistance of Judge Albert B. Maris, chairman of the United States Judicial Conference, judge of the Third Circuit Court of Appeals, and chief judge of the Emergency Court of Appeals. Upon its passage by the legislature, the act defined the jurisdiction, composition, and powers of the island's courts. It placed the courts under the supervision of a judicial council. The council was composed of the judge of the District Court of Guam as chairman; and the chief judge of the Island Court, the chairman of the Committee on Judiciary of the Guam Legislature, the attorney general of Guam, and the president of the Guam Bar Association as members. At the same time the Justice Court and the traffic branch of the Police Court were abolished. The Court of Appeals, as such, was also abolished. Its duties were assumed by the District Court of Guam, which was authorized to hear appeals from decisions of the Island Court. Before passage of the Organic Act the courts of Guam were four in number, namely: the Court of Appeals, the Island Court, the Justice Court, and the Police Court. After the reorganization, they consisted of the District Court of Guam, the Island Court, and the Police Court. In addition to reducing the number of courts, the Judiciary Act defined the powers, qualifications, and disqualifications of judges. It defined the duties of court clerks, reporters, marshals, the attorney general, and the island attorney or prosecuting attorney. Moreover, it set up requirements for admission to the practice of law in Guam. It also established a probation system and created commissioners' courts. Presided over by the commissioner of each municipality, the commissioners' courts handled petty offenses for which punishment was not more than a fine of five dollars. The District Court was given jurisdiction in civil cases having a value of more than $2,000 and, in criminal cases, jurisdiction over all felonies. The Island Court was given jurisdiction over misdemeanors and civil cases having a value of less than $2,000. The Honorable Jose C. Manibusan became the first senior judge of the Island Court, under civil government. He retired in January 1960 after more than forty years of service. Criminal misdemeanors in which the penalty was not more than a fine of $100 or imprisonment for six months, or both, were assigned to the jurisdiction of the Police Court. In a reorganization in 1960, following the retirement of Judge Francisco L. G. Lujan, the Police Court was abolished. Judge Cristobal C. Duenas, a law graduate of the University of Michigan, relieved Judge Joaquin C. Perez when the latter was elevated to senior judge of the Island Court.

## VILLAGE AND MUNICIPAL GOVERNMENT

After passage of the Organic Act, many changes occurred in the governmental structure of Guam. This was especially true at the territorial level. At the village and municipal levels, however, few changes occurred. Village affairs, in large part, continued to be supervised by the commissioners. The organization, authority, and responsbilities of the chief commissioner and the village commissioners continued to follow the pattern outlined in Guam Congress Bill No. 16, passed in 1948. By the terms of that bill, commissioners were elected by the people of their districts. Their election took place at the same time as that of the members of the legislature, and they held office for four years. The chief commissioner, however, was appointed by the governor, with the advice and consent of the legislature. He acted as the head and advisor of all commissioners on the island and held office at the pleasure of the governor. The commissioners were the direct administrative representatives of the people living in the areas from which they were elected. They were required to perform the following duties:

1. Co-operate with members of the Department of Public Safety and other law-enforcement agencies in maintaining peace, order, and tranquillity in the area.
2. See that sanitary and health standards set by the Department of Medical Services are maintained by the villages.
3. Maintain a census of all residents in their areas.
4. Co-operate with all officials in the Government of Guam in order to promote health, education, peace, and economic and social welfare of the people of their areas.
5. Make monthly written reports to the chief commissioner of Guam covering conditions of the area they represent, and making recommendations for the amelioration of certain problems.[2]

According to Governor Sinners annual report, submitted to the Secretary of the Interior in June 1951, the authority of the commissioners was as follows:

1. Act as executive heads for administration of the laws of Guam in the municipalities they represent.
2. Authority of a peace officer.
3. Authority to fine violators of sanitary regulations. Any decision in this regard may be appealed to the Police Court of Guam by either party within 30 days.
4. Issue building permits within their own area, with the exception of the new cities of Agana and Agat, in compliance with the provisions of existing zoning, building, health, and sanitary laws of Guam.[3]

The chief commissioner of Guam was the direct administrative representative of the governor. He had the following authority and duties:

1. Shall make not less than one personal inspection per month of the municipalities and villages of Guam to the end that he may thoroughly know and understand the problems of each.
2. Hold monthly meetings of all commissioners, or a general public meeting in any commissioner's area.
3. Work jointly with all officials of the government of Guam toward the attainment of peace, order, justice, and the general economic and social welfare of the people of Guam.
4. Make a monthly written report to the Governor of Guam which shall be, in substance, a codification of the comments and recommendations contained in the monthly reports of the village commissioners, together with the comments and recommendations of the chief commissioner.
5. As the direct representative of the Governor of Guam, he shall convey to the commissioners of Guam such information as may be required by the government of Guam.[4]

The position of chief commissioner was occupied during the first ten years of civilian government by Mr. Vicente Zafra, who retired early in 1960. He was succeeded by Frederico Gutierrez.

In 1951 the regular monthly meetings of the commissioners were held on the first Wednesday of each month. Representatives of other government departments attended such meetings to discuss and propose solutions for village problems. In addition to the monthly meetings, each commissioner held periodic public mass meetings in his district. At such meetings the people were told about new official orders and notices and were given other general information.

## DEPARTMENT OF LAW

As it had been since passage of the Organic Act, the Department of Law was one of the busiest departments in the government of Guam. It was faced with the task of handling all legal matters in which the government of Guam was a party. Moreover, it had to draw up new laws affecting almost every phase of island life. During fiscal year 1953, for example, the department drafted twenty-nine bills which were passed by the legislature and signed into law by the governor. Of the twenty-nine, the following were major pieces of legislation:

1. An act establishing a uniform warehouse receipts law.
2. An act regulating the practice of nursing and the licensing of nurses for the territory.
3. An act to provide for absentee voting in Guam elections.
4. An act to provide for the payment for injury, disability, or death to employees arising out of and in the course of their employment. (This is known as the Workmen's Compensation Law.)
5. An act setting forth the powers, qualifications, responsibilities, and duties of notaries public.
6. An education code to provide for the regulation of education in Guam.
7. An act to provide for the investment and deposit of public funds in the treasury of Guam.
8. An act to provide for the licensing of all businesses on the island.
9. An act setting up an approved military code in preparation for the establishment of a National Guard unit in Guam.

In addition to drafting new laws, the Department of Law had to devote a great deal of time to a number of tax problems. These arose as a result of the provisions in the Organic Act regarding income tax laws in Guam. These provisions are stated as follows:

Sec. 30. All customs duties and federal income taxes derived from

Guam, the proceeds of all taxes collected under the internal revenue laws of the United States on articles produced in Guam and transported to the United States, its territories, or possessions, or consumed in Guam, and the proceeds of any other taxes which may be levied by the Congress on the inhabitants of Guam, and all quarantine, passport, immigration and naturalization fees collected in Guam shall be covered into the treasury of Guam and held in account for the government of Guam, and shall be expended for the benefit of the government of Guam, in accordance with the annual budgets.

Sec. 31. The income-tax laws in force in the United States of America and those which may hereatfer be enacted shall be held to be likewise in force in Guam.

Before passage of the Organic Act, income taxes were not paid in Guam. After passage of the act, however, the island's resident and nonresident population became subject to the income tax laws then in force on the mainland. Within a short time these laws were contested in the courts.

One of the most important cases was that entitled *Laguana v. Ansell.* Laguana worked for a corporation doing business in Guam. In 1951 he brought suit against Ansell, who was the acting commissioner of revenue and taxation and treasurer of Guam. Laguana demanded the return of funds withheld from his wages by his employer. He contended that the manner in which federal income tax laws were applied to Guam was illegal. The government contended that Section 31 of the Organic Act set up a separate income tax system for Guam that was a duplicate of the federal income tax system. As such it permitted collection of the tax by territorial officials. The District Court of Guam decided in the government's favor. Laguana then appealed the decision to the United States Court of Appeals for the Ninth Circuit in San Francisco. On April 15, 1954, the Court of Appeals upheld the decision of the District Court of Guam. Other cases followed. The income tax issue was finally settled in 1959, when the U.S. Congress defined, in an amendment to the Organic Act, that Section 31 was a separate territorial tax system.

The most important legal development in the criminal field during 1954 involved a case entitled *Government of Guam v.*

*Hatchett.* In December 1952 Hatchett had been arrested on a felony charge of involuntary manslaughter. He was arraigned, by information, before the District Court of Guam. Since the island had no jury system, he was not indicted by a grand jury. On January 15, 1953, Hatchett was found guilty as charged. Shortly thereafter he asked the Court of Appeals, Ninth Circuit, to review the decision of the Guam court. The question before the appeals court was whether or not a person accused of a felony could be tried by information, or whether an indictment by grand jury was required under the Organic Act. The Court of Appeals decided that the prosecution of a felony must be brought by grand jury indictment unless the accused person waives such right. Thus the decision of the District Court of Guam was reversed. As a result, the Third Guam Legislature passed Public Law 42, which provided a jury system for the island.

## SELECTIVE SERVICE

Upon passage of the Organic Act, selective service was extended to Guam under the Universal Military Training and Service Act.

On May 10, 1951, Colonel Juan Muna took oath of office as Guam's first territorial director of selective service. The oath was administered by Brigadier General Louis Renfrow, deputy director of the Selective Service System. At the same time he administered the oath of office to members of the draft and appeal boards. The first few months after establishment of the system were spent in organizing headquarters. A great deal of time was also spent in explaining selective service to the islanders. Registration began on September 6, 1951. The first induction was held on January 25, 1952, with a call of ten men—three for the marines and seven for the United States Army. The following are figures on the number of registrants and volunteers as of June, 1952.[5]

| | |
|---|---:|
| Total living registrants | 6,148 |
| Total living registrants under 18½ years | 139 |
| Total classified registrants | 1,917 |
| Total inducted | 66 |
| Total volunteered for enlistment in Army, Air Force, Marines, and Navy | 189 |
| Total canceled, all ages | 89 |
| Total deceased, all ages | 2 |

By 1953 the islands' selective service system was organized after the pattern that prevailed on the mainland. At the top of the organization was the "State" headquarters, staffed by the director and his deputy. Two officers of the Guam Militia, Colonel Juan Muna and Major Raymondo Camacho, became the first director and deputy director, respectively. Under the headquarters division were two local boards of five members each. Of the ten board members, five were appointed to serve as an appeal board. A government appeal agent and a medical advisor to the director rounded out the system staff.

## CIVIL DEFENSE

From the time of its establishment, the civil defense program in Guam was closely co-ordinated with the activities of the United States military forces stationed on the island. Moreover, the Guam Militia, reactivated in December 1950, played an active and useful role in the program. The militia was composed of over 1,000 officers and men who served on a voluntary basis. As part of the executive branch of the government, the civil defense program was supervised by the governor through an appointed director of civil defense. Mr. Peter C. Siguenza served as the first director, followed by Mr. Frederico T. Gutierrez in 1952. The director co-ordinated the agency's activities and maintained close contact with the armed forces through Commander Naval Forces Marianas. In addition to the director, there was a civil defense council of which the governor was chairman. Members of the council included the heads of the departments of education, public safety, agriculture, and public health. The chief commissioner and the commanding officer of the Guam Militia also served as members. The rest of the council was

391

made up of citizens representing private business, welfare, and civic organizations, and two representatives of the armed forces. The two military members were nominated by the Commander Naval Forces Marianas and appointed by the governor.

The chief purpose of the civil defense program was to prepare the civilian population for any emergency resulting from flood, fire, typhoon, other disasters, or from enemy sabotage. By 1953 a total of 5,648 volunteers were enrolled in the program or awaiting training. The general public was given needed information through lectures, radio, and demonstrations. Real progress was made through the use of a civil defense plan for the schools. Mimeographed copies of the plan were distributed to all schools. In co-operation with the American Red Cross, the police, fire department, public works, and civic organizations, civil defense sponsored classes in first aid, home nursing, and disaster relief. As part of the civil defense program, the first Guam blood bank was established in 1953. Governor Elvidge officially opened the bank with a civil defense employee as the first donor. In view of Guam's climatic conditions, typhoons are common occurrences. On October 26, 1953, Typhoon Alice passed near the island. Damage was severe in some sections, especially in the Yigo district. There civil defense officials and volunteers removed a number of persons from a badly flooded area. Three other persons were swept out to sea when they tried to swim the flooded Talofofo River. Civil defense volunteers, in a joint rescue attempt with the Navy rescue teams, searched the area without success. At Tamuning, Piti, and Asan a number of families were evacuated by civil defense teams. In view of Guam's strategic location, civil defense is an unusually important and necessary phase of government activity.

## LAND MANAGEMENT

On October 12, 1950, the Office of Land Management was created by Government of Guam Order No. 14–50. The office was established for the purpose of administering the government's land program. It assisted in the relocation of people displaced from their land by the war and by the increased land requirements of the military forces. Moreover, it administered about 30,000 acres of the public domain which was transferred to the territorial government during fiscal year 1952. With the passage on August 29, 1951, of Public Law 33, First Guam Legislature, the Office of Land Management was raised to a departmental level. By the terms of the same act, the Territorial Planning Commission was created. The commission was composed of five members who were appointed by the governor with the consent of the legislature. The principal duty of the commission was to prepare a long-range plan for the physical and economic land development of Guam. Besides land use, the plan included public buildings, community design, and housing. As reorganized, the Department of Land Management contained three major subdivisions: Land Administration, the Land Transfer Board, and Land Planning. The Land Administration Division co-ordinated all activities of the department. The Land Transfer Board reviewed all applications for lease or purchase of government land. A total of 1,375 applications were processed during 1952 alone. Actual planning and engineering work was done by the Land Planning Section. At a later date a Land Survey Section was added to the department.

## COMMERCIAL DEVELOPMENT

Upon the establishment of civil government, a determined effort was made to develop private enterprise in Guam. This was done for two reasons: first, to make goods and services available to the people so that government would not have to take on more and more services and grow ever larger; second, to provide a sound, job-giving, tax-paying economy so that the island might be able to support itself when military spending and construction should decline. As a first step in this program, large American companies doing business in the Far East were encouraged to locate their Far Eastern headquarters in Guam. One of the first to do so was Bireley's, Inc., a soft-drink bottling firm. In 1951 it moved its Far East company from Manila to Guam. By this move it, and other American companies as well, secured the advantages offered by an American territory. Among these advantages were American

currency and banking, protection and security for capital investment, nearness to Far Eastern markets, and a federal court system.

A major development project of 1950 was the opening of the
commercial port in Apra Harbor. Since the entire harbor area
was a military reservation, the commercial port was established
on land belonging to the Navy. The government's initial investment
was $300,000. In the beginning, 13 acres of fenced land were set
aside for the port. Port facilities included 20,000 square feet of
warehousing and 1,200 linear feet of dock area. Depth of the water
at the docks was 32 feet. The new port, limited in space at first, was
modern in every detail. It was equipped to unload merchant ships
over a 24-hour period, seven days a week. Many of the stevedores
were Guamanians drawn from the districts of Talofofo, Yona,
Umatac, Merizo, Agat, and Santa Rita.

> ... The Commercial Port was established by Public Law 3 of the First
> Guam Legislature as a separate entity within the Department of Com-
> merce, and it operates essentially as a separate function of the govern-
> ment. The Commercial Port had a modest beginning, but has been in-
> creasing steadily in size and importance since its inception. It has taken
> its place as one of the most vital and important functions of the govern-
> ment, and its services to the community are invaluable. Although the
> Commercial Port has suffered many growing pains, it must be remem-
> bered that the port is a completely new operation, and that the local
> government is inexperienced in this field of activity. Although experi-
> enced administrators have been employed to assist in the operation of
> the port, the problems and difficulties occasioned by the unique situa-
> tion of a governmental port being operated within the jurisdiction of
> another government, has made the operation considerably more difficult
> than would be normally expected. The docking, warehousing, and un-
> loading facilities of the Commercial Port compare favorably with those
> used elsewhere in the United States, and there is a program of steady
> improvement of all phases of the work.[6]

During the fiscal year ending June 30, 1950, two important
transfers of facilities occurred. The first was the sale of the Bank
of Guam by the naval government. It became a private enterprise
when it was purchased by the Bank of America. The second transfer was the sale of the *Guam News*, published as a daily newspaper
by the Navy. It was purchased by Mr. Joseph Flores and became

known as the *Guam Daily News*. At this writing, it is the only daily newspaper in Guam. On July 16, 1950, the *Guam Daily News* published the first free privately owned newspaper on the island. Later Flores published the *Territorial Sun*, a Sunday newspaper.

By 1952 private commercial interests were becoming firmly established on the island. In that year the *Guam Daily News* moved into a new $250,000 plant in Agana. Other established business houses remodeled and expanded their facilities in order to better serve the people of the territory. A modern ice plant was built, and two new construction companies began operations. The Radio Corporation of America, already established on the island, extended its telephone and radiogram services to the Philippines. Prior to that time such services were available only between Guam and the mainland. Steamship companies, too, added to the commercial development of the island. By June 1953 Guam was a port of call for two major shipping lines, the Pacific Far East Lines and the American President Lines. Ships of the Pacific Far East Lines called at Guam on an average of four times a month. They carried freight and passengers between the west-coast ports of the United States, Guam, and the Orient. American President Lines ships called at the island about twice a month, bringing freight, mainly from the American east coast. The agreement between the American President Lines and the United States Maritime Commission with regard to calling at Guam was on a temporary basis. However, the company was seeking to add Guam to its regular, permanent transpacific trade routes for the purpose of carrying freight to the island from both the east and west coasts.

On March 8, 1954, the Bank of America began operations in a new building in Agana. The structure was of reinforced concrete and was modern in every respect. It had twelve commercial and savings windows, four for notes and collections, and a special enclosed space for handling export and import documents and large deposits. The bank also had more than 1,000 safe-deposit boxes. About four months after the Bank of America moved into its new building, the Guam Savings and Loan Association began operations. Established on July 7, 1954, it confined its activities to home building and improvement loans. The association was a member of the Federal Home Loan Bank of San Francisco. Each of its savings accounts was guaranteed up to $10,000. It was organized by local businessmen, headed by Mr. Joseph Flores, publisher-editor of the *Guam Daily News,* and was capitalized at $115,000.

The Hood Construction Company opened a branch in Guam in 1954. It specialized in tank pipelines, plant piping, steel erection, general welding, and conduit construction. At about the same time, a ceramics plant was opened. Ceramics manufactured included novelties, dishes, vases, lampshades, and statuettes. The plant also produced building bricks for use in the construction of local homes and business structures.

Guam's first commercial broadcasting station began operations on March 14, 1954. It was called KUAM, a privately owned 1,000-watt radio station with a wave length of 610 kilocycles. On an average of 126 hours a week it broadcast music, news, advertising, and special events. It proved to be a valuable asset in promoting the commercial and social development of the territory. In 1956 it added a TV Station bringing in programs from three major American stations.

SUMMARY: The complete history of the first ten years of civil government on Guam has yet to be written. The attempt in this chapter has been merely to give, in bare outline, the more important events and happenings between the years 1950 and 1960. Even a cursory look at the record will reveal, however, that Guam has made great strides forward in virtually every phase of life.

Economically, the people of Guam continued to enjoy the benefits of full employment opportunities. Every able-bodied man and woman could find jobs if they looked. The per capita income was higher than it was during the previous ten years. This resulted in a better standard of living. The American method of buying on installment made it possible for more people to enjoy the comfort of modern and easy living. By 1960 Guam was enjoying a standard of living higher than ever before in the history of the island and perhaps the highest in the Pacific west of Hawaii.

The program of rehabilitation, following a disastrous war, continued. Many Guamanians and other residents took advantage of loans made available by both the government of Guam and two private banking and loan institutions to build modern homes or to improve existing homes. Modern shops and shopping centers grew up. New and modern churches replaced wartime and temporary buildings in virtually every community. Among those erected was the beautiful and modern Catholic cathedral of Dulce Nombre de María, in Agana. The government, too, embarked on a ten-year capital improvement project which resulted in the building of several schools, municipal buildings, roads, water and power lines, and public buildings throughout the territory. Among the more important buildings were the Guam Memorial Hospital, the Administration Building in Agana, and the Territorial College in Mangilao. Rehabilitation still had a long way to go in 1960, but progress had been made.

The government of Guam, under three governors and five legislatures, made a ten-year record which received the praise of important officials in Washington, D.C. Secretary of the Interior Fred A. Seaton, following a trip to the island in November 1959, told newsmen of his sastisfaction with the administration of the island. Speaking before members of the Fifth Guam Legislature, United States Congressman Wayne Aspinall, chairman of the House Committee on Interior and Insular Affairs, expressed satisfaction with the manner in which the affairs of the island had been handled since the passage of the Organic Act of Guam.

Self-government cost the island over one hundred million dollars in ten years. The island continued to move toward more self-government. By June 1960 a native Guamanian had been appointed governor, and the election of a local governor became a topic of island conversation. Governor Lowe had urged it in a hearing in Washington. Governor Joseph Flores had publicly endorsed the idea and gave that as one of the major goals of his administration. With a Guamanian chief executive, Guam entered into a new era. President Eisenhower included in his 1961 budget request a sum of money to pay for a Guamanian delegate in the national Congress. Several pieces of legislation for a Guamanian voice in the national Congress were introduced in both houses. Such was the progress the island had made in the first ten years of civil government.

Guam under civil government, of course, continued to move ahead. However, except for an occasional entry, this chapter has attempted to present only those events which occurred through the year 1960. The decade of the sixties, only three years old at this writing, ushered in a new era for the territory—an era already full of important and unprecedented events—which someday must be written about as part of the history of a growing and developing people. The splendid administration of Governor Joseph Flores, the first Guamanian governor, followed by the administration of Governor William Patlov Daniel of Texas, as well as the administration of Governor Manuel F. Leon Guerrero, the second native governor—which at this writing has made an excellent beginning—will someday find a place in the pages of Guam's history books.

## NOTES

1. Governor of Guam, *Annual Report, 1951*, p. 6.
2. *Ibid.*, p. 30.
3. *Ibid.*
4. *Ibid.*
5. Governor of Guam, *Annual Report, 1952*, p. 33.
6. Government of Guam, Papers and Correspondence.

## CHAPTER ELEVEN

# DEVELOPMENT OF RELIGION AND EDUCATION

No HISTORY of Guam would be complete unless it contained a section dealing with the growth of religious institutions and with the development of the island's educational system. No institutions have exerted greater influence on the lives of the Guamanian people than have the church and the school. In view of the fact that the history of religious developments in Guam has been discussed extensively in an earlier chapter, this chapter presents a brief overview of the development of religious and educational institutions in Guam since 1900.

### RELIGION

After World War II Guam experienced a great religious revival. The Roman Catholic Church and a number of Protestant denominations intensified their efforts in many fields of activity. A better understanding of recent developments will be achieved by looking back on past events in the religious history of Guam.

As mentioned in an earlier chapter, the Spanish Augustinian priests were deported from Guam by order of Governor Leary on September 6, 1899. Only the Guamanian priest Padre Palomo was permitted to remain. In August 1902 three Spanish Capuchins from the Caroline Islands arrived in Guam. Although they had no passports, Governor Schroeder, the second American governor, allowed them to stay. From that time to the present the religious life of the overwhelming majority of the Guamanian people has been guided by Capuchin priests. These priests are members of the Order of Friars Minor, Capuchin. The order is an independent branch of the Franciscan order founded by St. Francis of Assisi in 1209. An Italian friar, Matteo da Bascio, is generally thought to have been the founder of the Capuchin order. Two other friars, Louis and Raphael of Fossombrone, Italy, were closely associated with him. The name of the Capuchins is derived from the Italian word *capuche* and refers to the distinctive "cap" or hood attached to the Capuchin habit. Pope Clement VII recognized the independent status of the order on July 3, 1528.

In the same year that the Capuchins arrived, Congregationalist missionaries established themselves in Guam. The mission was headed by Reverend Francis Price, a graduate of Harvard University. He was accompanied by his wife, two married daughters with their husbands, and a Miss Channel. This group erected the island's first Protestant mission buildings at Adelup Point on land bought from William Coe. A few natives were converted, including Jose Aguon Flores, who later became the first Guamanian Protestant minister. For lack of financial support, the mission was abandoned in 1910. In September 1911, Americans representing the General Baptist Foreign Missionary Society arrived in Guam. They took over the mission abandoned by the Congregationalists. The first Baptist missionaries were Reverend Arthur A. Logan and his wife, Edith. During the eleven years the young couple worked in Guam, they gained a number of converts in the northern part of the island and in Inarajan. They also moved the mission from Adelup to Agana, where, in 1921, they started construction on Guam's first modern Protestant church. In 1922 Mr. Logan was relieved by Reverend David R. Thomas. He, in turn, was relieved in 1925 by Reverend A. I. Luttrull. Mr. Luttrull established mission stations at Sumay and Agat. In 1925 he built a permanent Baptist church in Inarajan. It is still in use. Mr. Luttrull was relieved in 1928 by Reverend Dale Tenison, who, because of illness, remained on the island only a short time. During Mr. Luttrull's ministry, Joaquin Flores Sablan, a Guamanian convert, decided to become a Baptist minister. In 1928, at the age of fifteen, he left Guam for the United States to study for the ministry. From 1930 to 1935 no trained missionaries were sent out from the mainland. The work of the mission was carried on by Mr. Flores, mentioned earlier, who was ordained in Guam sometime during the early 1900's. In 1935 Mr. Sablan, now an ordained minister, returned to the island. Under his aggressive leadership the mission grew and expanded. Today there are Baptist churches in Agana Heights, Agat, Mt. Santa Rosa, Talofofo, and Inarajan. The total Guamanian membership is approximately 1,000.

After World War II the Seventh Day Adventists became active in Guam. Their first work was done by a Navy chief named Henry Metzker. He arrived on the island during or shortly after the American reoccupation in 1944. His first group consisted of Adventists in the armed forces and the family of Mrs. Maria A. Ulloa of Dededo. The church had no regular pastor until May 1948, when Reverend R. E. Dunton arrived on the island. After Mr. Dunton's arrival, the church grew rapidly. In 1949 he was joined by Reverend Raymond Turner. During the same year an Adventist church and school were built in Dededo. In late 1950 a branch school was opened in Talofofo, and churches were established in Talofofo and Inarajan. During 1953–54 the Dededo school was moved to Agana Heights and enlarged to twelve grades. Pastor V. E. Kalstrum served as president of the Adventist mission from November 1956 to July 1957, followed by Pastor J. L. Pogue. The church has about 200 members, of whom about one-half are Guamanians. The mission operates a medical clinic in Agana Heights.

To return to the Catholics, serious trouble developed in the local church in 1909. At that time Guam was placed under the spiritual jurisdiction of the German Capuchins in Saipan. Monsignor Paulus von Kirchausen, the newly appointed prefect apostolic of the Marianas, tried to replace Spanish priests with German priests. The Germans, who could not speak English, Spanish, or Chamorro, were resented by American authorities in Guam who were suspicious of them. Consequently, the German missionaries were compelled to leave the island. Shortly thereafter Monsignor Kirchausen made a pastoral visit to Guam, but he was not permitted to land. Through the good offices of Padre Palomo, he was allowed to remain on Cabras Island until the return of the schooner which took him back to Saipan.

On April 30, 1915, the first bishop of Guam arrived from Spain. He was Monsignor Felipe Joaquin Olaiz y Zabalza. As a young priest he had worked as a missionary in Ecuador. For almost twenty years (1915–34) Bishop Olaiz guided the affairs of the church in Guam. He encouraged Guamanians to study for the priesthood and sent a number of boys to San José Seminary in Manila. On July 5, 1919, about four years after the bishop began his reign, the venerable Padre Palomo died at the age of eighty-three. His passing was a severe loss to the bishop and to the Guamanian people as well. For his services to the church he had been raised to the rank of monsignor in 1909. In 1934 Bishop Olaiz was forced to leave the island because of ill health. He was succeeded by Bishop Miguel Angel de Olano y Urtega. Bishop Olano first came to the island in 1918. For a number of years he served as the parish priest of Sumay. He was chosen to be bishop while serving as the superior of the mission in Guam. Shortly after his selection he returned to San Sebastian, Spain. There, on May 5, 1935, he was consecrated Titular Bishop of Lagina and Vicar Apostolic of Guam. He returned to the island in August 1935.

During Bishop Olano's reign a campaign was begun to replace the Spanish Capuchins gradually with American priests of the same order. The Spanish priests were strongly opposed to the new policy. Some felt they were too old to start missionary work in a new field. Nevertheless, two American priests began work on the island in 1937. During the following year all the Spanish priests were replaced by American priests of the Capuchin order. Only Bishop Olano and his secretary, Brother Jesús, were allowed to remain. When the Japanese invaded Guam in December 1941, there were ten American priests on the island. They, along with Bishop Olano, were sent to Japan as prisoners. After the defeat of Japan, the bishop returned to Guam in March 1945. About seven months later, on October 25, 1945, he was relieved by the Most

Reverend Apollinaris William Baumgartner, O.F.M., Cap., the first American Bishop of Guam. On the day following Bishop Baumgartner's arrival, Bishop Olano left the island and went into semi-retirement in Manila. His departure brought to an end the 277-year period of Spanish spiritual rule that began with Father Sanvitores in 1668.

Bishop Baumgartner was born in College Point, New York, on July 24, 1899. He was professed as a Capuchin in 1920 and was ordained in 1926. On September 18, 1945, he was consecrated Titular Bishop of Joppe and Vicar Apostolic of Guam. The ceremony of consecration, performed by the Most Reverend Amleto Giovanni Cicognani, apostolic delegate to the United States, was held in St. Patrick's Cathedral, New York City. Just over a month after his consecration, he arrived in Guam to take up his duties. Throughout the long history of the church in Guam, no spiritual leader had ever had to cope with a situation like that which confronted the new bishop. Most of the island's churches, rectories, and other buildings were in ruins. Moreover, the people were morally and physically weakened as a result of hardships suffered during the war. An adequate number of priests was not available, and labor and materials for rebuilding were almost nonexistent. Church services were held in tents and other temporary structures. Despite the difficulties, the bishop began his reign with a determined campaign to rebuild and expand the war-shattered church. His determination to rebuild the church over the ashes and ruins of war was symbolized by the legendary phoenix emblazoned on his coat of arms.

Immediately after the reoccupation, Father Oscar Calvo was the only resident priest on the island. He began at once to minister to the needs of the people in the refugee camps. He was assisted by Catholic chaplains of the United States Army, Navy, and Marine Corps. In June 1945, two American Capuchins arrived from the mainland. About a year later, on March 19, 1946, a number of the prewar missionaries returned to the island. After the defeat of Japan, they had been released from prison and were sent back to the United States. Upon their return and after the arrival of

Bishop Baumgartner, the work of rehabilitation began in earnest. On April 13, 1947, the first permanent postwar church on the island was dedicated. It was the church of San Vicente in Barrigada. In the course of the next few years, churches were built at Dededo, Asan, Agana Heights, Agat, and in almost every village in Guam. The great church of Saint Joseph at Inarajan, badly damaged during the war, was repaired and rededicated in 1952. On September 18, 1955, the tenth anniversary of his consecration, Bishop Baumgartner announced the start of work of rebuilding the Dulce Nombre de María Cathedral in Agana. It occupies the historic site on which the first church was built by Father Sanvitores in 1669.

In addition to building churches and rectories, Bishop Baumgartner sponsored the establishment of religious communities and schools in Guam. At the invitation of the bishop, the Sisters of Mercy of Belmont, North Carolina, established a native community on the island in November 1946. In 1948 Guam's first Catholic school was established. It was named the Father Duenas Memorial High School in honor of the Guamanian priest and hero beheaded by the Japanese during World War II. The school was staffed by American priests of the Stigmatine order. After the establishment of the Father Duenas School other Catholic schools were built in Agana, Yona, Dededo, Barrigada, and Sinajana. By late 1960 the bishops rehabilitation program had achieved a remarkable degree of success.

## EDUCATION

Under Spanish rule, education was available to only a select few. Despite this limitation an ever-increasing number of Guamanians were able to secure a fair amount of education. With the beginning of American rule, educational opportunities became more widespread. Children of the poor, like those of the well-to-do, were able to attend school. They did so in such large numbers that the schools became permanently overcrowded. As the school expanded, its influence grew. School buildings became community centers. Teachers, moreover, gained a degree of influence and prestige that could not be matched in any other American possession. The role that teachers have played in the life of Guam has been of the utmost importance. A truly astounding fact about present-day Guam is that an unusually large number of its most responsible citizens, top government leaders, judges, members of the legislature, and business and professional men have, at one time or another, served as teachers in the island's public schools.

Under Spanish administration, education of the Guamanian people was "limited to the merest rudiments."[1] The "merest rudiments" included Spanish, elementary arithmetic, reading, and writing. By and large, Spanish priests on the island bore the greater share of the burden of educating the Guamanians. A few Guamanians received a fair amount of education and used their training to advantage during the early days of American occupation. Notable examples were Joaquín Pérez; Juan Torres and his brother Luis Torres, who served as judges; and Joaquín Díaz, who served as island treasurer until his death in 1915. Some Spanish governors were opposed to too much education for the natives, not because they felt that they were unable to learn but because they felt that the islanders could be more easily governed without it. This sentiment was shared by some early American governors. In spite of the official attitude, however, the Spanish priests managed to make approximately 50 per cent of the Guamanians over seven years of age literate in Spanish and about 75 per cent literate in Chamorro.

In 1898, at the time of the capture of Guam by American forces, there were schools in every major town and village on the island. These schools, operated by the Roman Catholic Church, included the Colegio de San Juan de Letran and the Colegio de Las Niñas, intermediate grade schools for boys and girls respectively.

The first English class in Guam was started in 1899 by Lieutenant William Edwin Safford, Guam's first American "lieutenant governor." Safford was greatly concerned about the inability of the natives to speak English and attempted to remedy the situation. He described his first class as follows:

I myself have started a night school for teaching English three nights a week. I have about fifty pupils, ranging from the age of five to fifty years. Among them, besides the natives, are a number of bandsmen (Italian) and Chinese servants of the officers' mess. I usually begin by pointing to various objects and pronounce the corresponding English names. My pupils repeat the words after me; then I teach them a few adjectives, such as long, short, thin, thick, hard, soft, illustrating the meaning by objects having these attributes; then a few verbs, such as walk, sit, stand, fall, catch, see, hear, speak. Most of my pupils do pretty well but the youngest do the best.[2]

Three private schools for the teaching of English were opened in Agana between 1900 and 1901. The first of these was opened in late 1900 and was taught by Miss Rosa Custino. She was the daughter of a Guamanian whaler who had returned to the island about the time of the American occupation. Among her students were many of Guam's outstanding leaders.* The second school was started by Lieutenant Albert Moritz, chief engineer of the station ship USS *Yosemite*. At about the same time a third private school was opened under the auspices of American missionaries of the American Board of Missions. Meanwhile, the Roman Catholic Church continued its Spanish schools, with an average enrollment of about a hundred students. These schools were gradually replaced as English teachers became available.

ELEMENTARY EDUCATION: On January 22, 1900, Governor Richard P. Leary issued a general order placing education "under the supervision and exclusive control of the Government."[3] His general order also contained four other provisions, namely:

1. All necessary expenses for the maintenance of the public schools will be defrayed by the Government.
2. Religious instruction in favor of any particular church or creed is prohibited. . . .
3. All children between the ages of eight and fourteen years must attend school, unless excused therefrom by competent authority for good reasons that interfere with their attendance.

* They included Francisco Taitano, John Taitano, Vicente and Pedro Martinez (businessmen), Don Jose Roberto (former secretary to the governor), Jose Cruz, Manuel Flores, Manuel Torres, Joaquin Perez, Mrs. Conchita Elliot, Mrs. Ana Underwood, Mrs. Ana Gay, Mrs. Rosalia Ojeda, and others.

406

4. Instruction in the English langauge will be introduced in the public schools as soon as suitable teachers can be provided.

Public instruction in English began in three schools in Agana on October 1, 1901. The schools were under the general supervision of Mr. H. H. Hiatt, a graduate of Iowa State University. Hiatt was assisted by his wife and daughter. Shortly thereafter, English instruction was started in a fourth school in Agana and in Asan as well. The instructors were two marine noncommissioned officers and a Guamanian. Agat school began English instruction a short time later.

The public schools were immediately popular with the local people. They wished to learn American ways as well as the English language. Attendance was so great that the schools were uncomfortably crowded. In all these schools, "everything [was] . . . subordinated to English and arithmetic."[4]

The small and feeble beginnings of the public school system met with two sharp setbacks in 1902. In July of that year the government, for lack of funds, was unable to continue the employment of Superintendent Hiatt. Accordingly, he and his family returned to the United States. Hiatt would have departed earlier had it not been for the generous assistance of the Civil Club, which paid his salary for several months.

The second major setback came in September 1902, when Guam was rocked by a severe earthquake. According to the governor's annual report of 1903, almost every stone building in Agana, including the public schools, was destroyed. Immediate repairs were made to one school in Agana, but it operated for only a short time. Earthquake damage and lack of funds forced the closing of all public schools. They remained closed for almost two years.

When Commander George L. Dyer became governor of Guam in 1904, the schools were still closed. He was shocked by the entire lack of public education and felt that "some means to lessen, if not overcome, this unhappy state of affairs seemed an imperative necessity."[5] He was especially concerned about the 2,300 children between the ages of six and fourteen who were receiving no schooling.

On June 13, 1904, Dyer reopened public schools in Agana and Asan. He diverted two American clerks and a marine from their regular duties for a part of the day in order that they might teach in the public schools. Three Guamanian girls "who knew enough English to teach the beginners" were appointed teachers. By the time Governor Dyer wrote his annual report for 1904 there were approximately "two hundred ninety-seven pupils of both sexes in Agana and twenty-six in Asan. There was a private school of about thirty, in English . . . attended by the children of the more well-to-do. The Roman Catholic priests . . . had small schools in Spanish, in several towns, averaging about one hundred children in all."

The year 1904 marked the beginning of continuous operation of the public school system. In that year there were schools only in Agana and Asan. The following year, however, schools were opened in Agat, Sumay, Piti, Umatac, Merizo, and Inarajan. Besides these an agricultural school, under the supervision of the agricultural experiment station, was opened at the same time. Its students consisted of twenty-nine selected boys. In addition there was opened in Agana a class for the Chamorro band and a night school for adults. A system of apprenticeships was begun, and boys underwent training in the Naval Hospital as aides to the medical officers, and in the Department of Public Works as carpenters, blacksmiths, and plumbers. Girls were sent to a class "to learn the cutting and making of garments, plain sewing, and such elementary embroidery as will be useful. . . ."[6]

By the close of Governor Dyer's administration there were eight schools in operation. They had an enrollment of 1,592: 865 boys and 727 girls. In his annual report for 1906 the governor requested a sum of $49,140 from Navy Department funds for the operation of the schools. His request was denied.

Between 1906 and 1910 four more schools were opened, including Dorn Hall School in Agana. Dorn Hall cost $2,600 to build. It served "as a public hall for various purposes."[7] Yigo School was built in 1913, and a permanent school building was erected in Umatac in 1914.* In the same year the "high school"—

* This building was used continuously as a school, including the period of the

408

in reality an intermediate school—was removed to the hill overlooking Agana at a spot about where Government House is now
located. Francis Lee Albert has described it.

> Since its removal to the hill overlooking Agana, the high school has
> demonstrated practically the Governor's ideal of industrial education.
> Under supervision of their teachers the boys have cleared away with
> their machetes and fusinos the rank growths of weeds and bushes, re-
> moved the debris, built a cascajo walk, and painted the floors and seats
> of the building. Spaces about the fort and on the crest of the hill have
> been prepared for vegetables and shrubbery. Each boy brought a tree
> or flower which he planted.
> The situation, 171½ feet above sea level, is ideal for a school in the
> tropics. If all the books were destroyed, the fundamentals of education
> might be illustrated on this hill. The sea stretches before us. In the
> distance are the headlands. Island bays and capes are visible. In the
> valley nestles the city into which trails and scientifically constructed
> roads lead. The remains of venerable Spanish forts are suggestive re-
> minders of a Historic past, and the hospitals themselves, reminiscent
> of the Humanitarian American occupation.[8]

In 1915 Yona School opened with an enrollment of fifty-three
pupils. This was followed in 1920 with the opening of the Talofofo
School. During 1921–22 the George Dyer School was built in Piti
and the Maxwell School in Sumay. Additional classrooms were
added to the schools at Asan, Merizo, and Inarajan. A school
opened in Barrigada in the spring of 1924 and a "one-room school
was opened in a rented building at Sinajana." In Agana a five-
room reinforced concrete building, the Althouse School, was
erected in 1923. Padre Palomo School, formerly located near the
naval cemetery in east Agana, was built the same year at a cost
of $14,492. The following year a temporary building of light
frame, bamboo, and *sawale* siding was built in Anigua. In 1926
a concrete building named the Roy C. Smith School replaced the
temporary structure. When Japanese forces captured Guam in
1941, there were thirty-two public schools on the island. These
schools had an enrollment of 5,084 pupils. There were also two

Japanese occupation. When the Francisco Q. Sanchez School was built in 1953, the
building became the Umatac village hall.

schools for American dependents and one private school, the Guam Institute. The institute was owned and operated by Nieves M. Flores, for whom the Nieves Flores Memorial Library was named.

Just prior to World War II, there were eight elementary schools for Guamanians in Agana. Padre Palomo School was under the principalship of Luis P. Untalan. Althouse School had Joaquin C. Torres as its principal. The Roy C. Smith School in Anigua was under the supervision of the late Mrs. Maria R. Flores and the Congressional School in Bradley Park had Mrs. Maria Garrido as its principal. Around the Plaza de España were located Dorn Hall School under Mrs. Remedios L. G. Perez; Richard P. Leary School, the only intermediate school in Agana prior to the war, under the principalship of Jose L. G. Rios, later vice-principal of George Washington High School; and the Post Office School under Mrs. Maria G. Brunton. The Seaton Schroeder School was a junior high school under Mrs. Agueda I. Johnston. It also housed the Department of Education offices. All of these schools were destroyed during the American reoccupation of Guam in 1944.

Expansion of the school system was accompanied by a steady increase in pupil enrollment. In 1904 Governor Dyer estimated that there were about 2,300 school-age children on the island. Of these, only 323 were enrolled in school. By 1906–7, when the number of schools had increased to 8, a total of 1,592 pupils were in school. Within a decade school enrollment went up to 2,000, and by 1930 there were 3,683 children attending classes in 25 schools. When the last school census was taken before Japan invaded Guam, a total of 5,084 pupils were enrolled in 32 schools. The postwar expansion, to be seen later, was even greater.

Financing the schools was one of the major problems encountered during the early history of the system. The first superintendent of schools had to return to the United States after only a year on Guam because of the lack of funds. No record of expenditures was kept before 1907–8. At that time, however, the government reported the expenditure of $5,619 for education. This went up to $7,335.21 in 1908–9 and to $9,660.75 the following year. The amount remained at about $9,660 during the next eight

410

years. During 1918–19 school expenses increased to $12,871.57 and to $19,136.67 in 1919–20. By 1930 the money spent for education amounted to $60,083.51. By the time of the Japanese invasion, the island government was spending $65,727.00 for its 32 schools and 5,084 pupils.

Financing the schools of Guam took approximately one-fourth of the naval government's annual revenue. This had to be augmented with funds from the Navy Department and from congressional appropriations. Inadequate funds between 1911 and 1926 made it necessary to establish half sessions in most of the island's schools. Between 1904 and 1923, some help from the Navy Department's appropriation for the naval station was made possible. This was done through an order of the Secretary of the Navy to use "clerical special laborers" as teachers in the public schools. After 1923 Guam received annually from the United States Congress an appropriated sum varying from $12,000 to $16,000 for the care of lepers. When the lepers were sent to the Culion Leper Colony in the Philippines, the money was diverted to education. The "leper fund" supplemented local revenues, which by 1941 amounted to approximately $50,000 annually for education. Postwar expenditures for education will be discussed later.

In 1900, when American public schools were first established in Guam, Superintendent Hiatt was the only person trained in education to be found on the island. The shortage of qualified teachers that prevailed at the time has continued to the present. In 1902 James H. Underwood, a young marine noncommissioned officer who later became a permanent resident of the island and its prewar postmaster, became one of Guam's first public school teachers. Two years later, Jose Charfauros and Miss Carmela Manalisay were employed to teach in the public schools. By 1907 a total of 33 Guamanians and about 10 Americans were employed as teachers. Among the Guamanian schoolteachers of this period were Jose Roberto, who later became the governor's secretary, Francisco Taitano, Jose V. Cruz, Antonio L. G. Perez, Pedro Martinez, Mrs. Carmen Leon Guerrero, Mrs. Ana Underwood, and Mrs. Agueda Iglesias Johnston. Among the American teachers were

411

such well-known island residents as James H. Underwood, William G. Johnston, Arthur W. Jackson, Albert P. Manley, and Jacques Schnabel.

By 1919, 50 Guamanians and 9 Americans were teaching in the public schools. The number increased to 104 Guamanians and 19 Americans by 1929 and to 111 Guamanians and 24 Americans in 1930. It soon became the policy of the naval government to employ only Guamanian teachers in the native schools. As a result, by 1933 not one American was employed in the local schools except for those who taught in the schools for American dependents. At the time of the Japanese invasion, there were 155 Guamanian teachers in the island's native schools. There were also 6 Americans teaching in 2 schools for American naval and civilian dependents.

The problem of obtaining trained teachers for the island's schools dates back to the very beginning of the public school system. Guamanian teachers hired during the initial years of the system were only a few English words ahead of their pupils. For the immediate task, namely the teaching of English, they, the marines, and the "clerical special laborers" were considered adequately trained. As the school system grew, however, the problem of obtaining educationally trained teachers became urgent.

Part of the educational program of almost every island governor included plans for training Guamanian teachers. Besides providing trained teachers, such plans were advanced in order to relieve the island treasury of the expense of importing teachers from the United States. Since the passage of the Organic Act, this matter has become a vital issue. An imported teacher costs the government thousands of dollars for travel and transportation expenses, as well as a 25 per cent territorial post differential in pay. Yet, until there is an adequate supply of qualified Guamanian and stateside (American) teachers residing on the island, the problem will continue to plague administrators.

The first attempt to improve the training of Guamanian teachers came in 1907, when all teachers were required to attend evening classes. No systematic program, however, was provided until September 1914, when a special normal-school course was offered. "The poor teachers were warned or dropped, and the educationally ambitious were advanced."[9] In 1916 a course in simple weaving, sewing, lacemaking, and embroidery was required of women teachers. In 1919 Saturday morning normal classes were started. By 1922 they were well established under the leadership of Commander M. G. Cook, aide to the governor. Cook obtained the services of doctors from the Naval Hospital and other officers with backgrounds in mathematics, history, and other subjects as teachers for the Saturday classes.

The first summer session was begun on June 4, 1923, under the direction of Dr. Thomas Collins. In addition to the summer session, he established a two-year normal school with instruction in college-level subjects. Many Guamanians took advantage of the program, but only four completed the two-year course. They were Nieves M. Flores, Miss Maria P. Leon Guerrero, Mrs. Remedios L. G. Perez, and Simon A. Sanchez, superintendent of schools for thirty-one years until his retirement in June 1959.

The summer normal-school program eventually replaced Saturday classes. It offered courses in methods of teaching, physiology, hygiene, psychology, English, mathematics, history, geography, and practical subjects such as weaving, slipper-making, and dress-making. Attendance was compulsory for all teachers and candidates for teaching positions. Promotions were based partially on grades received. The summer teachers' institute, as it was later called, has been part of the in-service training of Guamanian teachers since that time.

From the beginning of the school system, English, arithmetic, agriculture, health instruction, and vocational training were emphasized as being most adapted to the actual needs of the Guamanians. Next to English, health instruction was the most important part of the curriculum. In 1905, Governor Dyer wrote:

> One of the principal efforts on the part of the school administration has been to insist upon habits of order and cleanliness. Each child is inspected daily by the teachers, and if found soiled in person or dress,

is sent at once to the lavatories, separate buildings for each sex, in the rear of the school building. In these are stationed a man and a woman, respectively, to see that the children wash themselves thoroughly, and attend to their necessities after the manner of civilized people. If their clothes are soiled they are sent home to have them changed. This matter of personal cleanliness, neatness of attire, and proper habits, has been very carefully insisted upon. At the same time, the children while in school have been provided with distilled water to drink. It is believed that this intimate physical supervision of one thousand five hundred children has had sensible effect upon the general average of health in the community.

The children have made excellent progress in the acquiring of English during the year. The present policy aims to give them a practical speaking, reading, and writing knowledge of this language. It is not the intention to carry instruction of the mass beyond that.[10]

Health was considered to be so important that two governors even went so far as to dictate how girls should be dressed at school.

The Governor [Dorn] has ordered that, hereafter, girls attending the public school must wear skirts, the lower edge to be at least four inches above the ground. This new order will be received with some dissatisfaction on the part of parents who adhere to the custom of dressing their small daughters in the long trailing skirts which sweep the ground, but will be strictly enforced, for sanitary reasons.[11]

Again, in 1917, Governor Roy C. Smith, in Executive Notice 106, wrote as follows:

The order of March 10, 1910, requiring that school girls shall not wear long skirts is not being observed. Long skirts serve to trail dirt and germs, and should not be worn.

The skirts of schoolgirls should not reach lower than four inches from the ground. All teachers will report any violations of this order.[12]

As part of the health program, school children were given periodic physical examinations by doctors from the Naval Hospital. Each year, down to 1941, students were vaccinated regularly and inoculated periodically. Worm treatment was given each year by the public health nurses either in the schools or in the hospital in Agana. Inspection of students was part of the regular day's routine.

The school curriculum under the naval government was a practical one. From the beginning, apprenticeships were encouraged and practical arts were taught. In 1916 a Filipino industrial arts teacher was brought to the island to teach basketry, mat-making, lace work, slipper-making, and loom weaving. In time, he was replaced by Guamanian instructors. By 1941 classes in carpentry, fish-net making, weaving, cooking, and sewing were well established. Mrs. Josefa Aguon Perez taught weaving for many years in the weaving school at the foot of San Ramon Hill in Agana. Vicente G. Palomo and Francisco P. Cruz taught carpentry. Juan R. Unpingco, a member of the naval insular force attached to the Department of Education, taught fish-net making. Mrs. Ana Gay and Miss Jane Gutierrez specialized in teaching cooking and baking for girls. Along with these, agriculture was also stressed in the schools. Annual agricultural fairs gave students the opportunity to compete for prizes. The 4-H Club flourished prior to 1941, and almost every school had a garden of some sort. Agricultural extension agents worked very closely with the schools.

Basically, the school's academic program consisted of reading, writing, and arithmetic. History, geography, and hygiene completed the elementary program. Classes were held from 7:15 a.m. to 12:15. In the outlying schools, afternoons were devoted to nonacademic activities.

In 1922 Dr. Thomas Collins adapted the California school curriculum to the local system. New textbooks were secured, courses of study were revised, and pupils were graded in a manner to conform more closely to the pattern in the California schools. In later years, this basic curriculum was changed to fit the standards established by the United States Office of Education.

Between 1916 and 1926 the school day was divided into two parts. In most cases, boys went to school in the morning while girls attended in the afternoon. Between 1939 and 1941, overcrowded classrooms made double sessions in Agana a necessity. In general, the island's schools opened in July and closed for a three-month vacation at the end of March.

One of the most important events in the prewar school system

415

was the closing-day competitions. These were annual affairs held in Agana in March. The Department of Education, which sponsored the competitions, awarded prizes on the basis of points received during various contests. Contests consisted of solo singing, group singing, spelling bees, declamations, instrumental music groups, and a most popular event, close-order marching. The activities were held in Dorn Hall School, Leary School, and the Post Office School, all located near the southeast end of the Plaza de España.

Close-order marching consisted of complicated drills performed by groups of brightly uniformed boys from each school. The best team from the outlying districts as well as the best team from Agana were awarded first-prize banners. Magellan School, Umatac, was a perennial favorite. During the immediate prewar years, Gilmer School, Talofofo, under Ignacio P. Quitugua, and Maxwell School, Sumay, under Baltazar P. Carbullido, Antonio B. Won-Pat, and later Thomas Santos, were frequent winners. In Agana, Leary School, under Frederico Gutierrez, and Post Office School, under James T. Sablan, always provided tough competition. Attempts were made to revive these events during the immediate postwar period. School and government officials, however, discouraged them because they felt they were wasteful of time, money, and effort.

Before World War II, the last day of school was one of the most important days of the year in the towns and villages of Guam. It was surpassed in importance only by the traditional fiestas in honor of the communities' patron saints. Graduation exercises were so scheduled that the governor and other island leaders could attend the ceremonies in each village. Besides the governor, the official party usually included the Bishop of Guam, the governor's aide, the director of education, the superintendent of schools, and other leaders. Ordinarily three or four days were needed for the official party to visit all the schools. In each village the governor inspected exhibits, delivered speeches, and congratulated students and teachers. Besides the school exercises, the entire village joined in presenting games and plays and in serving food to students, parents, and guests. Graduation exercises at George Washington High School were usually last on the schedule.

In 1944, after the defeat of Japanese forces on the island, Guam's school system was almost completely destroyed. Earnest attempts were made to restore the system, but a year and a half elapsed before the schools approached their prewar levels. With the educational program restored, reading, writing, and simple arithmetic were once more emphasized in the schools. This was deemed necessary because both the returning students and new enrollees needed grounding in these subjects. Less emphasis was placed on nonacademic learning than was the case before the war. A serious attempt was made, however, to give junior high school students experience in the practical and industrial arts.

Immediately after the assault phase of the American reoccupation of Guam, military government officers were attached to various civilian "refugee" camps. There they remained until Island Command, under Major General Henry L. Larsen, took control of the island. By the early part of September 1944, the various branches of military government, as planned before the invasion, were operating.[13] Originally, there was no provision for a native welfare department. This was established later, however, and within a few months it became the Welfare and Education Department, under Lieutenant Commander Votow. As soon as food and housing needs were under control, the department began to consider the educational program and the emergency conditions under which the schools would have to operate. With the aid of the prewar superintendent of schools, Simon A. Sanchez, the former teachers and principals living in each community were located and assembled. By October five schools had been opened in buildings least damaged during the assault on the island. Paper, chalk, and pencils were furnished in quantity to each school as it opened. A small number of textbooks, saved during the war, were available. These were supplemented with mimeographed materials, magazines, journals, and other written materials. Since desks were not available, many pupils had to bring their own boxes or makeshift stools to school.

In areas which had seen much hard fighting and heavy bombardment, notably Agana, Asan, Piti, and Dededo, the opening of schools involved the building of temporary structures. These were crudely constructed of coconut palm logs and covered with tarpaulins or coconut thatched roofs. Many communities built their own schools rather than wait for military government to build for them. Hence it was possible to open schools earlier than would otherwise have been the case. In the greatly expanded villages of Agat, Sinajana, and Talofofo, new school buildings were included as part of the community plans. Damaged prewar buildings in Yona, Inarajan, Merizo, and Umatac were repaired. These were the only school buildings not completely destroyed during the war, since fighting had been slight in the area.

When the island had been declared secured from organized enemy resistance, the people began moving back to their homes. Since many villages had been destroyed, new civilian communities grew up. In time schools were built in Mongmong, Tamuning, Agana Heights, Santa Rita, and Chalan Pago. These were villages where schools had not existed before. By 1946 there were twenty-one schools in operation on the island.

At the beginning of World War II, there were 5,084 pupils in the public schools of Guam. By 1946 there were 7,150 pupils in grades one to twelve. Increased enrollment resulted from the fact that old students returned to complete their interrupted education at the same time that new students crowded into the schools. By 1951, at the close of the first year under the Organic Act. elementary school pupils alone numbered 8,083. Enrollment increased every year as a result of the normal increase among the Guamanian population and also because of the great influx of military and stateside civilian dependents. Students from trust territory families and the Filipino community in Guam added to the pupil load.

The Department of Education's annual report for 1955 showed a total enrollment of 8,762 pupils, grades one to eight, in 22 schools. This included 15 in the institutional school of the Guam Memorial Hospital. Of this total, 4,588 were girls and 4,174 were boys. Among them were 6,590 Guamanian students and 1,974 dependents of persons attached to the military and federal agencies or stateside businesses. At the same time, 46 foreign nationals, all of whom except one were Filipinos, were included in the total figure. The remainder of the students were from the trust territory and Samoa. By the beginning of the school year 1959–60, the total number of pupils enrolled at all levels in the schools of Guam numbered over 18,000.

One of the important advances in the education of youth during the postwar period was the establishment of a junior high school program. In 1953 the first postwar junior high school was established in Agana under the principalship of Pedro C. Sanchez. Its students consisted of seventh and eighth graders from Adelup Point, Agana Heights, Agana, and Asan elementary schools. In 1954 the ninth grade was added, making it a full junior high school. Two reasons were given for the establishment of the junior high school program: one, it would reduce the load at George Washington High School, and two, it would permit students of about the same age and maturity to work together in a separate school. Because of the program's success, plans were made for expanding the junior high school system. Inarajan opened a junior high in 1958, Agat in 1960, and others were being planned.

Before World War II the amount of money spent for education in Guam constituted 25 to 30 per cent of all local revenues. This was supplemented by federal funds amounting, since 1923, to approximately $12,000 to $16,000 annually. The cost per pupil ranged between $12 and $15 per year. Postwar expenditures for education increased tremendously. This was due largely to an increase in prices for supplies and equipment and in salaries for teachers. Teachers' salaries immediately before the war ranged for $0.60 to $3.08 a day. The largest amount ever expended for education in prewar years was $66,610.32 in 1937–38. No figures are available for the immediate postwar period. The first figures available are those of 1947–48, when $323,923 was spent for education. For the six-month period ending December 31, 1948, $315,029 was expended for educational purposes. Of this figure,

$82,506 came from local revenues. Direct and indirect federal appropriations furnished the balance. Payments for personal services accounted for approximately 82 per cent of this amount. During the first year of operation under the Organic Act, the Department of Education operated on a budget of $880,700.[14] The following year, 1952, the cost of education passed the million-dollar mark for the first time. Educational expenditures in that year were $1,754,434. By 1953–54 the educational budget exceeded two million dollars. The appropriation for the year was $2,270,400, of which 70.26 per cent, or $1,595,160, was spent for personal services, $117,560 for travel and transportation, $210,320 for equipment and supplies, $60,000 for student loans, and the remainder for other necessary items. Based on average enrollment, the amount spent was approximately $165.35 for each elementary pupil as compared to approximately $300.94 for each high school pupil. The gap was narrower in 1955–56, with $155.05 per elementary and $243.77 per high school pupil. By 1960 the operations budget amounted to nearly three and a half million dollars. These figures, however, did not include the cost of bus transportation and a few other items of expense for education. Slightly over a third of the government's operating budget went for education by 1960.

Because of the high regard in which education was held by the Guamanian people, the executive and legislative branches of the government gave wholehearted support to the development of the school system. This was especially true after the passage of the Organic Act in 1950. After that date the amount of money spent for education became the largest single item in the government's budget. The following table compares recent expenditures of various departments of the government:[15]

COMPARATIVE EXPENDITURES, FISCAL YEARS 1953, 1954, 1955

| DEPARTMENT | 1953 | 1954 | 1955 |
|---|---|---|---|
| General Government | $1,572,400 | $1,295,000 | $1,218,700 |
| Public Safety | 814,900 | 794,700 | 696,000 |
| Public Works | 708,200 | 581,900 | 611,200 |
| Medical Services | 1,723,600 | 1,721,200 | 1,621,000 |
| Education | 1,738,600 | 1,898,500 | 2,152,000 |
| Commerce and Agriculture | 276,300 | 217,500 | 202,000 |

The Guam Legislature consistently approved Department of Education requests for funds and in some instances actually increased budget requests. The budget for fiscal year 1957, however, was an exception. That year, after public hearings, the legislature's Committee on Taxation and Finance recommended cuts of over $180,000. The proposed cuts were opposed by a group of legislators composed of Congressmen Manuel U. Lujan and James T. Sablan and Congresswomen Cynthia J. Torres and Lagrimas L. G. Untalan. All were veteran educators of both the prewar and the immediate postwar periods. After lengthy and heated debate on the floor of the legislature, most of the proposed budget cuts were restored.

Since 1951 the Guam Legislature has appropriated several millions of dollars for the maintenance and repair of temporary school buildings and for the building of new and modern school plants. The first of the completely new schools was built in Piti at a cost of $154,624. Adelup Point School followed at a cost of $439,500. The Francisco Q. Sanchez School in Umatac cost $190,000, and the Inarajan School was built for $238,400. A new school in Santa Rita cost $180,500, and a new junior-senior high school at Tumon Heights involved an appropriation of over $1,500,000. With federal aid, new schools were erected in Tamuning, Sinajana, and Agana Heights by the 1958–59 school year. Agat Junior High School went under construction in 1959, and, as of 1960, plans were under way for building new junior high schools in Barrigada and in at least two other communities.

SECONDARY EDUCATION: Official records of the Department of Education contain several references to a "high school" in Guam as early as the first decade of American control. The "high school" then in existence, however, was not a high school in the modern sense. In reality, it was an intermediate school. Regular high school courses were first offered on the island in 1917.[16] The courses were primarily for teachers in the public schools. Other students who had completed the eight grades at the "high school," then located on the hill overlooking Agana, were admitted. The courses were offered in the intermediate school in the Armasen Building, located beside the governor's palace in Agana. Classes were taught by naval officers and by John A. Pearson, who at that time was principal of the school referred to as the "high school." Guam's first full-fledged high school was organized in 1923. The first class consisted of only nine students. This school was discontinued in 1925.

The Guam Evening High School was organized in 1925. Among the first instructors were Lieutenant W. O. Hiltabidle, USN, and Ramon M. Sablan. The school opened with two classes totaling 55 pupils, 41 in the freshman class. In 1928 it graduated its first class of seven members. The graduates were Luis P. Untalan, Vicente C. Reyes, Jose C. Torres, Edward T. Calvo, Maria P. Leon Guerrero, Lagrimas L. G. Untalan, and Teresa P. Sablan.

The evening high school offered courses similar to those of a regular high school in the United States. It was strictly an academic school. Instructors were officers attached to the naval station, naval dependents, and a number of Guamanians, including Jose Roberto, secretary to several governors; Joaquin C. Guerrero, first Guamanian director of agriculture; Simon A. Sanchez, superintendent of schools; and Dr. Ramon M. Sablan, a physician who later served as the school's principal. Classes were held in the post-office building until 1930, after which time the school was moved to the Seaton Schroeder Junior High School. In 1936 it was moved to the George Washington High School building, where it remained until the Japanese capture of Guam. After World War II, several unsuccessful attempts were made to re-establish the school.

The year 1930 marked the establishment of the first modern junior high school in Guam: the Seaton Schroeder Junior High School located in the San Ignacio district of Agana. Mrs. Agueda I. Johnston became the school's first principal. With the establishment of the Seaton Schroeder School, the intermediate school was discontinued. The new school's student body consisted of seventh, eighth, and ninth graders. On March 27, 1931, the new junior high school awarded ninth-grade diplomas to the 17 members of its first graduating class.

The Seaton Schroeder School was primarily academic. It did, however, offer some recreational and industrial activities. Courses offered were patterned after those in stateside schools. The school operated for only a brief period. It was replaced in 1936 by George Washington High School.

George Washington High School had its beginning on Friday, October 30, 1936, when it was officially dedicated. Its opening coincided with one of Guam's worst earthquakes. The new high school was situated in the San Nicolas district of Agana, near where the congress building is now located. It was built at an estimated cost of $12,000. The building was of reinforced concrete with a corrugated iron roof. It had eight classrooms and space for about 350 students.

First classes were held on the Monday following the dedication ceremonies. The school was under the principalship of Mrs. Johnston, who was transferred from Seaton Schroeder School. Like its predecessors, the prewar Washington High School offered only a limited number of nonacademic subjects. In the academic field, a standard high school curriculum prevailed. Admission to the seventh grade—since the school was in reality a junior-senior high school—was based on scores received on Stanford achievement tests. These tests were administered to the island's sixth-grade graduates during the summer vacation. Approximately 30 to 35 new students were admitted to the high school each year. The first twelfth-grade graduation exercise was held in March 1940. Members of the graduating class were Rosa B. Santos, Mercedes R. Leon Guerrero, Ana Q. Gogue, Jose P. Cruz, Jose L. Rosario, Aleandriana A. Manibusan, Richard Taitano (valedictorian), and Consolacion San Nicolas (salutatorian). A second class graduated in March 1941. The third class, however, did not graduate until 1945, after the Japanese occupation had ended.

For some time before World War II began, overcrowded conditions in the high school made it necessary to operate on double sessions. The morning session was held from 7:15 to 12:15; afternoon classes met from 1:00 to 5:00. School was in session from July to March.

423

Until the Territorial College of Guam was established in 1952, the overwhelming majority of Guamanian students could expect no formal education beyond the twelfth grade. Few could afford to pursue further studies in mainland colleges and universities. As a result, graduation from Washington High School was considered to be an outstanding achievement. In view of that fact, the school and its teachers were highly regarded by the Guamanian people. In the forefront of the people's esteem was Mrs. Johnston, often referred to as the "first lady" of Guam. Associated with her in the school's program were such respected teachers as Maria P. Leon Guerrero, Lagrimas L. G. Untalan, Cynthia Johnston Torres, Carmen Ojeda Herrero, Reverend Joaquin Sablan, James T. Sablan, Vicente R. Palomo, Juan M. Guerrero, Manuel U. Lujan, and William U. Lujan. Before World War II the high school was staffed entirely by Guamanians.

The immediate postwar period was a difficult one for the high school. During the war the school building was almost entirely demolished; only a few walls were left standing. A temporary canvas roof was erected, and tents were set up on the playground. Returning students and teachers found that they had almost nothing with which to work. There were no library books or texts, and equipment was almost totally lacking. However, Mrs. Johnston, with the help of her teachers and pupils, succeeded in rounding up old books and makeshift equipment. In a relatively short time, the school was operating once more at almost its prewar level.

During the school year 1945–46, the high school was moved from Agana to Sinajana. A large auditorium was built, and enough Quonset huts were erected to care for the students in double sessions. Textbooks became more rapidly available, and supplies and equipment began to arrive from the mainland. At the close of school in 1946, Mrs. Johnston was transferred to the Department of Education offices as an assistant superintendent. At that time, all the teachers who had started in the high school with her in 1936 resigned their positions and retired from teaching. Norbert Tabery, a mainland educator, became the new principal. New teachers, including a number of statesiders, were added to the

424

faculty. Tabery was principal of the school for only one year, since he was promoted to the position of director of education. Christian P. Zeien became principal in 1948 and remained with the school until 1952. It was during Zeien's administration that the high school was moved to Mongmong.

During the prewar and the immediate postwar periods, the high school's curriculum was strictly academic. Under Tabery, however, the curriculum was greatly expanded. A teacher-training program was begun by 1949, and home economics courses were started. In 1951 physical education was included in the curriculum, and a regular vocational department was established. During the principalship of Paul E. Gettys, who replaced Zeien in 1952, the high school became fully accredited by the North Central Association of Colleges and Secondary Schools.

Within a period of ten years the high school had changed from a highly selective, strictly academic school to one that was truly democratic in its aims and methods. Today, George Washington High School and the new Tumon Junior-Senior High School can be favorably compared with high schools of comparable size anywhere in the United States.

In 1951 the Guam Legislature appropriated $500,000 as the first increment for building a new and permanent high school. Because of difficulties in site selection, however, the funds were not used. In 1957 $1,500,000 was appropriated for the construction of Tumon Junior-Senior High School. The new high school, with 1,300 students, 55 teachers, and 6 administrative staff members, headed by Principal Alfred Fain, opened its doors for the first time in September 1959. It achieved the distinction of being accredited during its first year of operation.

ADULT AND VOCATIONAL EDUCATION: Private English schools which flourished during the early years of American occupation were largely for adults. In the main, throughout the first four decades of American rule, adult education classes were concerned with the teaching of English as well as some arithmetic and writing. The first real attempt to present a systematic program of adult education came during the middle 1930's, when almost all schools in Agana conducted night classes for the adult population. Attendance was quite large during the first few months. As the program continued, however, attendance lagged, and the whole scheme was dropped. In consequence, adult classes, except in isolated cases, were practically nonexistent by the time of the Japanese invasion. During the immediate postwar period, the Department of Education was more concerned with the problem of educating Guam's children than with that of educating its adults.

A significant step in the adult education program came in January 1952, when the Department of Education established the Guam Evening Vocational School. One of its principal objectives was to provide adults with new additional skills that would enable them to meet the pressing needs of the island.[17] Such courses as business English, shorthand, cabinetmaking, radio repair, appliance repair, motor repair, accounting, blueprint reading, bookkeeping, clerk-stenography, office management, and others were offered. Courses offered were determined by means of an occupational survey of the island. In 1954 administration of the program was placed under the control of the Territorial College of Guam.

Vocational education has been a part of Guam's school program for many years. As early as the first decade of American rule a system of apprenticeship training was in operation in the Agana schools. In 1917 an industrial arts teacher from the Philippines was employed, and local crafts and practical arts became an integral part of the school curriculum, notably in Agana. An agricultural school, established in 1905, became part of the public school system in the 1930's. By 1941 vocational education, operated in conjunction with public works and other departments, was an important part of the islands' educational program.

After World War II vocational education was re-established on both the elementary and the high school levels. Local handicraft techniques were taught, and school gardens became "productive as well as instructive."[18] At George Washington High School, an on-the-job training program was established by Norbert Tabery in 1947. When he became director of education, Paul Carano, one of the authors of this book, was appointed vocational co-ordinator. Carano, who was among the first small group of contract teachers recruited for the island's schools in 1947, supervised the apprenticeship training of 432 students in military, government, and civilian business establishments. In 1951 a regular vocational education department was established at Washington High School. At that time, all vocational instruction and activities were confined to the school campus. Industrial arts teachers from the mainland were employed under the supervision of Robert Meran, vocational consultant of the Department of Education. Attempts were made to secure federal assistance for the program, but because of legal technicalities none was obtained until 1958, when an omnibus bill was passed by the U.S. Congress and signed into law by President Eisenhower.

In 1956 the U.S. Navy opened an apprentice school at the naval station. Planned to enroll at least 200 students a year, the apprentice school expected to graduate its first four-year students in 1960. Meanwhile, the government of Guam opened a trade school in the old Tamuning Elementary School area. A night school program started early in 1960 and a regular daytime program was scheduled to begin in September of 1960.

Enrollment in the vocational and adult program has averaged about 450 students a quarter. An important phase of the adult program is the Americanization course offered on a semester basis in co-operation with the Department of Immigration of the United States government. In its first year of operation, the Americanization program enrolled an average of fifty foreign nationals a semester. In view of the intense interest shown in vocational education, it is expected that the program will continue to expand.

HIGHER EDUCATION: From the beginning of American rule in Guam, the island was plagued by a critical shortage of professionally trained college graduates. This was especially true in the field of education. In an attempt to remedy the situation, the government of Guam, in 1919, awarded scholarships to a small group of promising Guamanian students. Four young men were sent to the Oklahoma Agricultural and Mechanical College at Stillwater. They were Jose L. G. Rios, Ramon M. Sablan, Antonio I. Cruz, and Juan R. Rosario. At about the same time, Vicente Reyes and Henry Herrero were sent to the University of California—Reyes to study law and Herrero to study dentistry. All except Herrero eventually returned to Guam. In spite of government scholarships, there were relatively few Guamanian college graduates just prior to World War II. As late as 1940 there were only two Guamanian part-time teachers who held college degrees. They were Dr. Ramon M. Sablan, M.D., and Reverend Joaquin Sablan, a Baptist minister. College graduates not associated with the island's schools were Fathers Oscar L. Calvo and Jesus Baza Duenas, Sister Ines, Antonio I. Cruz, James Butler, Paul Palting, and Jose R. Palomo. It was not until 1949 that the first professionally trained Guamanian teacher was employed in the island's schools. He was Pedro C. Sanchez, one of the co-authors of this book.

Chaotic conditions of the postwar period dramatized the need for well-trained Guamanian teachers. Accordingly, in 1946, the Department of Education established the Adelup Point Normal School. The school, which was highly selective, had an enrollment of about twenty high school graduates who were being prepared as teachers. Standard freshman college courses were taught by stateside members of the high school faculty. Because of inadequate enrollment—only three students enrolled at the beginning of the second year—the school was closed in 1947.

To fill the void left by the closing of the normal school, the naval government, at the suggestion of Superintendent Simon A. Sanchez, invited the University of Hawaii to conduct summer sessions in Guam. The invitation was accepted, and summer sessions were held in 1946, 1947, and 1948. University of Hawaii professors, as many as five each summer, conducted the program on the island. Classes were held at Washington High School, then located in Sinajana. Standard University of Hawaii courses were offered, and credits leading toward graduation from that institution were granted. Because of misunderstandings concerning transportation, housing, and other arrangements normally made with the local government, the university summer session was not held in 1949. During that same year, however, the government of Guam proposed that the University of Hawaii sponsor a full year's educational program on the island. After serious consideration, University of Hawaii officials turned down the proposal for fear that it might impose a financial burden on them. With this rejection, higher education in Guam temporarily ceased.

In 1951 an arrangement was made between the extension division of the University of California and the government of Guam for the in-service training of teachers. Military authorities, under whose contract the university was already operating in Guam, co-operated to make courses available to the local teachers. Classes were begun in September 1951, with 126 teachers enrolled. The government of Guam exercised no control over the program or the staff. Because the staff was chosen originally to serve the needs of military personnel, course offerings were rather limited. Teachers, however, continued to enroll in the program until 1952, when the Territorial College of Guam was established.

Establishment of the Territorial College of Guam marked an important advance in the island's educational system. Need for an institution of higher learning was long recognized, but it was not until 1952 that the Guam Legislature authorized establishment of a territorial college. Under authority granted by the legislature, Dr. Jose R. Palomo, the first Guamanian director of education, contacted various colleges on the mainland with a view to obtaining help in establishing a junior college in Guam. Among institutions he contacted and later visited was Ohio State University, his alma mater. Ohio State agreed to undertake the project on the following terms:

1. The College of Education [of Ohio State] will co-operate with the staff of the Department of Education of the Territory in the development of an educational program at the college level for the preparation of elementary school teachers for the Territory and will assist in the evaluation and modification of the program as it develops.

429

2. The College of Education will select and release at least one staff member at a time continuously throughout a five-year period.

3. After consultation with the Director of Education of the Territory the Dean of the College of Education will designate one staff member of the College who will be nominated to serve under the Director of Education of the Territory as a Co-ordinator of Teacher Education and Higher Education.

These and other terms were agreed upon by the government of Guam and Ohio State. In 1957 the contract was modified. The appointment of the dean of the college was left to the director of education. Dr. Pedro C. Sanchez, co-author of this book, became the first Guamanian dean of the college. OSU agreed to help the college for a three-year period by sending two consultants the first year and one each year for the next two years. The consultants were to spend one quarter at the college. In 1960 Dr. Donald P. Cottrell, dean of OSU's School of Education, came to Guam as the OSU consultant. He was the main speaker at the dedication of the new territorial college buildings at the new campus in Mangilao.

Shortly after the contract had been signed, Dr. Edwin E. Lewis, Ohio State's first co-ordinator of higher education for Guam, arrived on the island and began the work of organizing the territorial college. The primary purpose of the college was to prepare teachers for the public elementary schools.

On June 30, 1952, the college opened its doors for the first time. A total of 191 students enrolled for the first summer session. Of the total, 110 were admitted as regular students. The remainder were admitted as special students pending review of their high school credits. Most of the students were elementary school teachers taking their annual in-service training. While the first summer session was still in progress, appointment of four additional faculty members and a registrar was approved. They arrived by September, in time to begin the first full-time program of public higher education in Guam since the closing of Adelup Point Normal School in 1947. The college's first year of operation, 1952–53, was largely a period of exploration and trial. Emphasis was placed on courses for teacher-education students. By the end of the first year, however, Dr. Palomo and Dr. Lewis suggested a possible change in emphasis when they wrote:

> The new college is, in essence, a Community College created to serve everyone in Guam and the Western Pacific area who needs and desires to extend his or her education beyond high school graduation and others who need short-time courses for vocational and self-improvement. Though feeble in its present offerings, and lacking in its immediate facilities, it will expand rapidly in its curriculum, in the quality of its instructional staff, and in the adequacy and convenience of the library and laboratory equipment.[19]

During the college's second year, 1953–54, the change in emphasis was reinforced by the new director of education, Dr. John S. Haitema, who also favored a community-college concept.

> The community-college concept is a point of view which has been gaining acceptance in the States and became the basis for the expansion of services and program which took place here. This concept is based upon the proposition that a local college should provide any type of education or training that is desired by groups of adults in the community which the staff is able to provide and the community able to support. Under this philosophy the community college offers everything from college credit courses to reading and writing, high school courses, general adult education, trade and apprentice training—in short, any type of instruction which can be provided.[20]

In September 1953 the territorial college enrolled approximately thirty-five students in a regular day-school college program. Adult vocational education became part of the college's program, and a regular college library was established. By the fall of 1955, fifty-seven full-time students were enrolled in the school's elementary teacher curriculum or in a two-year academic program leading to the degree of associate of arts. Furthermore, through the arrangement with Ohio State University, it became possible for graduates of the college to transfer credits to mainland institutions. In its arrangements with the government of Guam, Ohio State had made the following agreement:

> The College of Education, through the Entrance Board, will establish a basis for evaluating credit earned by students in the institution to be

organized in the Territory, and in so doing will take full cognizance of the service of the College of Education personnel in the Territory and of the responsibility which they carry for selecting instructors and maintaining high academic standards. The College of Education will attempt to facilitate the transfer of credit, up to a maximum of 96 quarter hours, for students from Guam who wish to continue their college work toward the completion of a degree in an American institution.

By 1955, credits earned at the Territorial College were being accepted by some ninety to one hundred mainland colleges and universities. By 1959 the college, under the directorship of Dr. Pedro C. Sanchez, was fully accredited as a junior college by the Western College Association. It became a four-year college in 1961, and Dr. Sanchez was appointed its first president.

After its first full year of operation the college had an average enrollment of about 250 students per quarter. Its first graduating class of three students received associate of arts degrees in the summer of 1953. By August 1958 approximately ninety Guamanian and stateside students had received the degree. By September 1960, when the college was moved to its new and modern plant on a new campus overlooking Pago Bay, over 250 full-time students were enrolled in its regular daytime program. Another 1,200 were enrolled in late afternoon and evening classes.

From its small beginnings as a teacher-training institution the college has expanded both in program and in enrollment. Today it offers courses leading toward the baccalaurcate degree in business, general academic, and teacher education. With an accredited college program comparable to any found anywhere in the United States and with a new home on a new campus and an ever-increasing enrollment from Guam and the neighboring islands, the Territorial College by 1960 had developed into a center of American higher education for the western Pacific islands.

## Administration of the School System

Throughout Guam's long period of naval administration, the governor was legally the director of education. In reality, however, his duties were delegated to a naval officer who was called the Head of the Department of Education. Between 1900 and 1919 the head of the depatment was usually the officer assigned to the governor as his aide. After 1919, chaplains assigned to the naval station were required to administer the affairs of the department as extra duty. Normally these officers were college graduates. They were given a six-week course in educational administration at San Diego State College or another institution before reporting for duty in Guam. Such directors were not always satisfactory, since they were first and foremost naval officers and chaplains, not school administrators. Moreover, their two-year tour of duty made it difficult for them to plan and carry out sound educational programs. This situation was relieved somewhat during the immediate postwar period, when naval officers with backgrounds in professional education were assigned as heads of the Department of Education. The first of these officers was Lieutenant Edward G. Lewis, a college professor who later taught at the University of Texas and the University of Illinois. Lewis's most important task was that of reorganizing and rebuilding Guam's war-damaged schools. He did a creditable job until relieved of his duties in 1945.

In 1947 a civilian school administrator became director of education. He was George V. Hall, an officer in the naval reserve who resigned his commission to accept the appointment. This change placed a professionally trained school administrator at the head of the Department of Education. However, the problem of frequent changes in leadership was not solved. Indeed, under civilian directors the problem became more acute. Whereas the naval officer directors served for at least two years, no civilian director remained on the job for two years until Dr. Haitema became head of the department in 1953. Between 1947 and 1953, a period of six years, no less than four directors and three acting directors served as heads of the Department of Education. Dr. Haitema himself was replaced in July 1957 by Mr. John R. Trace of Ohio. Trace resigned in July 1962.

SUPERINTENDENT OF SCHOOLS: The office of superintendent of schools was established in Guam during the early years of American rule. Superintendents were appointed to assist various education directors in the performance of their duties. The first superintendent was H. H. Hiatt, who was appointed in 1901. In 1913 Jacques Schnabel, an American resident of the island and one of Guam's early teachers, was appointed superintendent. He held the position until 1922, when he was relieved by Dr. Thomas Collins. Collins remained two years and was relieved by R. E. Hall, who in turn was succeeded in March 1925 by the first woman superintendent, Miss Alice V. Wall. Miss Wall came to Guam as a teacher. She was replaced by another woman, Mrs. Esther M. Riddle. Mrs. Riddle remained on the job until 1927, when her position was assigned to a Guamanian educator, Simon A. Sanchez. At the time of his retirement in June 1959, Sanchez had been superintendent of schools for over thirty years. As a Guamanian and a permanent staff member, he was able to give the department stability and continuity. These things could not be provided by directors who came and went in rapid succession. Because of his long tenure of office, members of the legislature and other government leaders turned to Sanchez for advice and guidance on all matters related to education. Director of Education John R. Trace referred to Sanchez as "Mr. Education" on Guam. Sanchez was succeeded by Mr. Oscar L. Musgrave of Ohio.

BOARD OF EDUCATION: Throughout most of the period of naval administration, Guam's schools were under the complete control of the governor. He formulated school policies, made key appointments, and decided how all the funds were to be spent. In 1923 the Guamanian people, through their leaders, sent a petition to the Secretary of the Navy requesting the establishment of a board of education. Their request was denied. It was not until 1938 that the first board was established.

> In 1938 [wrote Thompson], at the request of the Guam Congress, an advisory board of education was created, which made demands for more academic training for Guam's youth and for a voice in educational

policy. The board consisted of the head of the department of education and several Guamanian members: two elected from the Guam Congress, one from the Guam Teachers' Association, and one from the Parent-Teacher Association. The Guam Congress requested that the board adopt and recommend to the governor policies, rules and regulations for the conduct and administration of schools. But the governor limited its strictly advisory function to matters pertaining to buildings and grounds, material equipment, new school districts, sessions and socioeconomic conditions affecting the school program.[21]

Members of the first advisory board of education were appointed by the governor and served for two years. They had no real authority. The head of the Department of Education was the chairman, and the superintendent of schools usually served as secretary. After the re-establishment of naval government in 1946, organization of the board was altered by the governor. In May 1948 the Guam Congress made further changes in the composition of the body. In 1949 the board was composed of one member from each of the two houses of the Guam Congress; three members, elected at large; three representatives of the armed forces, appointed by the governor; and one representative from temporary residents not members of the armed forces, also appointed by the governor. The director of education and the superintendent of schools were ex-officio members, without voting powers. The board was still largely advisory, and it remained so until passage of the Education Code by the first Guam Legislature in 1952.

With the enactment of the Education Code, the board of education became, in reality, a policy-making body. Its authority was established in Section 11101, as follows: "The Department of Education shall be under the general cognizance of the Governor and shall be administered through: (a) the Territorial Board of Education which shall be the governing and policy determining body of the department." The code further provided for a board which "shall consist of five members, all citizens of the United States of America and residents of Guam, who shall be appointed by the Governor with the advice and consent of the Legislature." Members of Guam's first real board of education were Albert Bronson, Lagrimas L. G. Untalan, Paul Souder, Jesus Barcinas, and Vicente S. A. Benavente. The code also provided for "a maximum of three advisors from the armed forces who shall be without vote." The director of education served as the board's secretary.

Under the new law the board of education was empowered to "adopt reasonable rules and regulations, not inconsistent with the laws of the United States and this territory (a) for its own government, (b) for the government of the Department of Education, and (c) for the purpose of carrying out all other duties, powers and responsibilties herein conferred." It was permitted, "with the written consent of the Governor," to negotiate contracts and enter into necessary agreements. Moreover, it was authorized to establish and supervise released time for religious instruction that was not to exceed more than one hour per week during the school year.

By 1955 the board of education was regularly exercising its policy-making powers. Most of its efforts were devoted to matters concerned with the physical operation of the school system. In general, up until 1955, the board was able to give only limited consideration to the philosophy, objectives, and curriculum of the public schools.

SUMMARY: Education in Guam dates from the time of the arrival on the island of the Sanvitores mission in 1668. In 1669 the island's first school, the College of San Juan de Letran, was built in Agana. Its students consisted of a carefully selected group of boys who were trained for service to the church. At the same time centers were established for instructing the native children in the Catholic doctrine. Later, separate schools for boys and girls were established in a number of villages. The curriculm was expanded to include Spanish, elementary arithmetic, reading, and writing. Throughout the entire Spanish period, however, education was generally neglected. Only a small part of the total population received any schooling whatsoever, and that was "limited to the merest rudiments." With the beginning of American rule, a system of compulsory public education was instituted.

In the early American public schools, stress was laid on the teaching of English and elementary subjects. Religious instruction

436

was forbidden. In 1902, for lack of funds, all schools were closed. They were reopened in 1904. Except for a brief period during the Japanese occupation, the schools have been in continuous operation since that time. During the period from 1904 to 1922, the school system was greatly expanded. New schools were built in Agana and in the outlying districts as well. A night school was established, and vocational education became an important part of the curriculum. Under the leadership of trained American educators, a reorganization of the school system was begun in 1922. School regulations, procedures, and curriculum were patterned on the California school system.

Secondary education on the island dates from 1917, when regular high school courses were offered for the first time. Such courses were instituted in an attempt to raise the educational standards of native teachers in the public schools. In 1923 the island's first full-fledged high school was organized. It was discontinued in 1925, however, and was replaced by the Guam Evening High Shool. This school, in turn, was replaced by George Washington High School, which opened in October 1936. In 1956 George Washington High School, the only public high school in Guam, had an enrollment of more than 2,000 students.

Education beyond the high school level was not attainable in Guam until after World War II. The first attempt to provide such education occurred in 1946, when the Adelup Point Normal School was established. Because of inadequate enrollment, the school remained in operation only one year. During the summers of 1946, 1947, and 1948 the University of Hawaii conducted summer sessions on the island. Classes held during these sessions were primarily for Guamanian teachers. The sessions were not resumed in the summer of 1949. Consequently, opportunities for higher education ceased until 1951. At that time an arrangement was made with the extension division of the University of California for the in-service training of Guamanian teachers. Although course offerings were limited, teachers continued to enroll in the program until 1952, when the Territorial College of Guam was established. By 1959 the two-year college was accredited by the Western College

Association. Two years later it became a four-year degree-granting institution. Such was the progress of education in Guam.

## NOTES

1. Francis Lee Albert, "History of the Department of Education in Guam during the American Administration," *Guam Recorder*, Vol. VIII, p. 373.
2. *Ibid.*, p. 373.
3. General Order No. 12, Naval Government of Guam.
4. Governor of Guam, *Annual Report, 1902*.
5. Governor of Guam, *Annual Report, 1904*.
6. Albert, *op. cit.*, p. 380.
7. Governor of Guam, *Annual Report, 1910*.
8. Albert, *op. cit.*, p. 382.
9. *Ibid.*, p. 382.
10. *Ibid.*, p. 379.
11. *Ibid.*, p. 382.
12. *Ibid.*, p. 383.
13. Edward G. Lewis, "Experience in the Pacific Islands as Illustrated by Guam," in Carl J. Friedrich and Associates, *American Experiences in Military Government in World War II* (Rinehart and Company, Inc., New York, 1948), p. 300.
14. Department of Education, Guam, *Annual Report, 1951*.
15. Governor of Guam, *Annual Report, 1955*.
16. Albert, *op. cit.*, p. 383.
17. Governor of Guam, *Annual Report, 1952*, p. 28.
18. Lewis, *op. cit.*, pp. 306-7.
19. Department of Education, Guam, *Annual Report, 1952*.
20. Governor of Guam, *Annual Report, 1954*, p. 21.
21. Thompson, *Guam and Its People*, p. 219.

# BIBLIOGRAPHY

## BOOKS

Arago, Jacques Étienne Victor: *Narrative of a Voyage Round the World in the Uranie and Physicienne Corvettes, Commanded by Captain Freycinet*, Treuttel and Wurtz, London, 1823

Beaglehole, J. C.: *The Exploration of the Pacific*, A. C. Black, Ltd., London, 1934

Bemis, Samuel Flagg: *A Diplomatic History of the United States*, 3rd edition, Henry Holt and Co., Inc., New York, 1950

Benedetto, L. F.: *The Travels of Marco Polo*, translated by Aldo Ricci, The Viking Press, Inc., New York, 1931

Betagh, William: *A Voyage Round the World, Being an Account of a Remarkable Enterprize, Begun in the Year 1719, Chiefly to Cruise on the Spaniards in the Great South Ocean*, London, 1728

Blair, Emma, and Robertson, J. A., eds.: *The Philippine Islands, 1493–1898*, 53 vols., Arthus H. Clark Co., Cleveland, 1903

Brookes, Jean Ingram: *International Rivalry in the Pacific Islands*, University of California Press, Berkeley, 1941

Brown, J. MacMillan: *Peoples and Problems of the Pacific*, T. F. Unwin, London, 1927

Burney, James: *A Chronological History of the Voyages and Discoveries in the South Sea or Pacific Ocean*, 2 vols., London, 1806

Campbell, Thomas: *The Jesuits, 1534–1921*, The Encyclopedia Press, New York, 1921

Clyde, Paul H.: *Japan's Pacific Mandate*, The Macmillan Co., New York, 1935

Coon, Carleton S.: *The History of Man, from the First Human to Primitive Culture and Beyond*, Lowe and Brydone, Ltd., London, 1955

Coontz, Robert E.: *From the Mississippi to the Sea*, Dorrance and Co., Inc., Philadelphia, 1930

439

Corte y Ruano Calderón, Felipe de la: *A History of the Marianas Islands from the Time of the Arrival of the Spaniards to the 5th of May 1870, with Continuation by Padre José Palomo,* translated by Gertrude Hornbostel, manuscript, Bishop Museum, Honolulu

Dampier, William: *A New Voyage Round the World,* London, 1729

Dulles, Foster R.: *America in the Pacific: A Century of Expansion,* Houghton Mifflin Co., Boston, 1932

Forbes-Lindsay, C. H.: *America's Insular Possessions,* John C. Winston Co., Philadelphia, 1906

Freeman, Otis W.: *Geography of the Pacific,* John Wiley and Son, Inc., New York, 1951

Freycinet, Louis de: *Narrative of a Voyage Round the World,* London, 1823

Friedrich, Carl J., and Associates: *American Experiences in Military Government in World War II,* Rinehart and Co., Inc., New York, 1948

García, Francisco: *Vida y Martirio del Venerable Padre Diego Luis de Sanvitores de la Compañío de Jesús, Primer Apóstal de las Islas Marianas,* Madrid, 1683; translated by Margaret Higgins in the *Guam Recorder,* September 1936 to July 1939

Guillemard, Frances H. H.: *The Life of Magellan,* George Philip and Son, Ltd., London, 1890

Hobbs, William H.: *The Fortress Islands of the Pacific,* J. E. Edwards, Ann Arbor, 1945

Hough, Frank O.: *The Island War,* J. B. Lippincott Co., Philadelphia and New York, 1947

Hume, Martin, *Queens of Old Spain,* McClure, Phillips, and Co., New York, 1906

Josephy, Alvin M.: *The Long and the Short and the Tall,* Alfred A. Knopf, Inc., New York, 1946

Keesing, Felix M.: *Native Peoples of the Pacific World,* The Macmillan Co., New York, 1945

———: *The South Seas in the Modern World,* John Day Co., Inc., New York, 1945

Kotzebue, Otto von: *A Voyage of Discovery into the South Sea and Bering's Straits,* 3 vols., translated by H. E. Lloyd; Longman, Hurst, Rees, Orme, and Brown, London, 1821

La Pérouse, Jean François Galaup de: *A Voyage Round the World in the Years 1785, 1786, 1787, 1788,* 2 vols., London, 1798

Le Gobien, Charles: *Histoire des isles Marianes, nouvellement converties à la religion Chrestienne, et de la mort glorieuse des premiers missionaires qui y ont prêché la foy,* Paris, 1700

Leslie, Robert C.: *Life Aboard a British Privateer in the Times of Queen Anne, Being the Journal of Woodes Rogers, Master Mariner,* Chapman and Hall, Ltd., London, 1889

Linton, Ralph: *Ethnology of Polynesia and Micronesia,* Field Museum Press, Chicago, 1926

Lodge, C. R.: *The Recapture of Guam,* Historical Branch, G-3 Division, Headquarters, U.S. Marine Corps; U.S. Government Printing Office, Washington, 1954

Mahan, Alfred T.: *The Interest of America in Sea Power, Present and Future,* Little, Brown and Co., Boston, 1911

Morison, Samuel Eliot: *History of United States Naval Operations in World War, II,* Vol III: *The Rising Sun in the Pacific, 1931—April 1942,* Little, Brown and Co., Boston, 1948

——: *History of United States Naval Operations in World War II,* Vol. VIII: *New Guinea and the Marianas, March 1944—August 1944,* Little, Brown and Co., Boston, 1953

Pomeroy, Earl S.: *Pacific Outpost,* Stanford University Press, Stanford, California, 1951

Pratt, Fletcher: *The Marines' War,* William Sloane Associates, New York, 1948

Raynal, Abbé: *A Philosophical and Political History of the Settlements and Trade of the Europeans in the East and West Indies,* translated by J. O. Justamond, London, 1783

Riesenberg, Felix: *The Pacific Ocean,* Whittlesey House, New York, 1940

Roberts, S. H.: *Population Problems of the Pacific,* G. Routledge and Son, Ltd., London, 1927

Robson, R. W.: *The Pacific Islands Handbook, 1944,* The Macmillan Co., New York, 1945

Rochon, A. M. de: *Crozet's Voyage to Tasmania, New Zealand, the Ladrone Islands, and the Philippines in the Years 1771–1772,* translated by H. Ling Roth, London, 1891

Roosevelt, Theodore, Jr.: *Colonial Policies of the United States,* Doubleday, Doran and Co., New York, 1937

Roscher, William: *The Spanish Colonial System,* translated by Edward G. Bourne, Henry Holt and Co., Inc., New York, 1904

Safford, William Edwin: *The Useful Plants of the Island of Guam, with an Introductory Account of the Physical Features and Natural History of the Island, of the Character and History of Its People, and of Their Agriculture,* contributions from the U.S. National Herbarium, Vol. IX, U.S. National Museum, Washington, 1905

San Agustin, Gaspar de: *Conquista de las Filipinas,* Madrid, 1698

Schroeder, Seaton: *A Half Century of Naval Service*, D. Appleton and Co., New York, 1922

Schurz, William L.: *The Manila Galleon*, E. P. Dutton and Co., Inc., New York, 1959

Sherrod, Robert: *History of Marine Corps Aviation in World War II*, Combat Forces Press, Washington, 1952

Stevens, Russell L: *Guam, U.S.A.: Birth of a Territory*, Tongg Publishing Co., Ltd., Honolulu, 1953

Thompson, Laura: *Guam and Its People*, Princeton University Press, Princeton, New Jersey, 1947

Wagner, Henry R.: *Sir Francis Drake's Voyage around the World*, John Howell, San Francisco, 1926

Walter, Richard: *Anson's Voyage Round the World*, Martin Hopkinson, Ltd., London, 1928

## REPORTS AND PUBLIC DOCUMENTS

*Annual Reports of the Governors of Guam, 1901–1941*, file microcopies of records in the National Archives, The National Archives of the United States, Washington, 1950

Beers, Henry P.: *American Naval Occupation and Government of Guam, 1898–1902*, Administrative Reference Report No. 6, Office of Records Administration, Navy Department, Washington, March 1944

Carleton, Philips D.: "The Guam Operation," in *Campaign for the Marianas*, Historical Division, U.S. Marine Corps, Washington, 1946

Cloud, Preston E., Jr.: *Reconnaissance Geology of Guam and Problems of Water Supply and Fuel Storage*, prepared by Military Geology Branch, U.S. Geological Survey, for Intelligence Division, General Headquarters, Far East Command, 1951

*Colección de Documentos Inéditos Relativos al Descubrimiento, Conquista, y Organización de las Antiguas Posesiones Españolas de Ultramar*, Segunda Serie, Tomo Num. III, Madrid, 1887

*Congressional Record*, Vol. XCVI, 81st U.S. Congress, 2nd Session, Washington, 1950

Department of Education, Guam: *Annual Reports, 1951, 1952 Federal Register*, Vol. XIV, No. 174, The Natonal Archives of the United States, Washington, September 9, 1949

Hopkins, Ernest M. (chairman); Tobin, Maurice J.; and Ryerson, Knowles A.: *Report on the Civil Governments of Guam and Samoa*, U.S. Navy Department, Washington, 1947

442

McMillin, G. J.: "Surrender of Guam to the Japanese," Official Report to Chief of Naval Operations, September 11, 1945

Reed, Erik K.: *General Report on Archeology and History of Guam,* National Park Service, U.S. Department of the Interior, Washington, 1952

U.S. Bureau of the Census: *United States Census of Population, 1950* U.S. Department of Commerce, Washington, 1951

U.S. House of Representatives, *Hepburn Report,* House Document No. 65, 76th U.S. Congress, 1st Session, Washington, 1938

———: *Providing a Civil Government for Guam and for Other Purposes,* Report No. 1677, Committee on Public Lands, 81st U.S. Congress, 2nd Session, Washington, 1950

U.S. Navy Department: *Reports to the United Nations on Guam, American Samoa, and Other Island Possessions Administered by the Navy Department,* Series OpNav-P22-100 A through K, Washington, July 1946 to June 1950

U.S. Senate, Committee on Interior and Insular Affairs: *Hearings on S. 1892 and H.R. 7273, An Act to Provide a Civil Government for Guam,* 81st U.S. Congress, 2nd Session, Washington, 1950

## ARTICLES, BULLETINS, AND PERIODICALS

Albert, Francis L.: "History of the Department of Education in Guam during the American Administration," *Guam Recorder,* Vol. VIII, No. 8, November, 1931

Bruce, Andrew D.: "Administration, Supply, and Evacuation of the 77th Infantry Division on Guam," *Military Review,* December 1944

Carano, Paul: "The Old Order Changeth," *Guam Examiner,* Vol. I, No. 2, October 1951

Cox, L. M.: *The Island of Guam,* U.S. Navy Department, Washington, 1926

Cushman, Robert E.: "The Fight at Fonte," *Marine Corps Gazette,* April 1947

del Valle, Pedro A.: "Guam, the Classical Amphibious Operation," *Military Review,* April 1947.

———: "Massed Fires on Guam," *Marine Corps Gazette,* December 1944

Embree, John F.: "Military Government in Saipan and Tinian," *Applied Anthropology,* Winter 1946

Fink, Stanley: "Co-Prosperity on Guam," *Marine Corps Gazette,* October 1944

Frances, Anthony A.: "The Battle of Banzai Ridge," *"Marine Corps Gazette,* June 1945

*Guam Daily News,* July 21, 1952 and July 21, 1953

*Guam Echo,* Vol. I, No. 3, Institute of Ethnic Affairs (date and place of publication unknown)

"Guam: Operations of the 77th Division, 21 July—10 August 1944," Bulletin, *American Forces in Action* series, Historical Division, U.S. War Department, Washington, 1946

Haswell, William: *Remarks on a Voyage in 1801 to the Island of Guam,* Historical Collections of the Essex Institute, Vol. LIII, No. 3, Salem, Massachusetts, July 1917

James, Roy E.: "Military Government: Guam," *Far Eastern Survey,* Vol. XV, No. 18, September 11, 1946

——: "The Guam Congress," *Pacific Affairs,* Vol. XIX, No. 4, December 1946

Johnson, L. W.: "Guam Before December 1941," *U.S. Naval Institute Proceedings,* Vol. LXVIII, No. 7, July 1942

Kaufman, M.: "Attack on Guam," *Marine Corps Gazette,* April 1945

Larsen, Henry L.: "Rehabilitation of Guam," *Marine Corps Gazette,* June 1945

Leigh, R. W.: "Dental Morphology and Pathology of Prehistoric Guam," *Memoirs of the Bernice P. Bishop Museum,* Vol. XI, No. 3, Honolulu, 1929

McIntosh, K. C.: "War Provisions for Guam," *U.S. Naval Institute Proceedings,* Vol. XLII, No. 2, March–April 1916

Mead, Albert R.: "The Giant Snails," *Atlantic Monthly,* Vol. CLXXXIV, No. 2, August 1949

Nelson, F. J.: "Guam: Our Western Outpost," *U.S. Naval Institute Proceedings,* Vol. LXVI, No. 1, January 1940

——: "Why Guam Alone Is American," *U.S. Naval Institute Proceedings,* Vol. LXII, No. 8, August 1936

"Pictorial Review and Historical Sketch of the Island of Guam," *Guam Recorder,* Agana, 1928

Rowcliff, G. J.: "Guam," *U.S. Naval Institute Proceedings,* Vol. LXXI, No. 7, July 1945

Safford, William Edwin, "Our Smallest Possession: Guam," *National Geographic,* Vol. XVI, No. 5, May 1905

Thompson, Laura: "Archeology of the Marianas Islands," Bulletin No. 100, Bernice P. Bishop Museum, Honolulu, 1932

——: "Crisis on Guam," *Far Eastern Quarterly,* Vol. VI, No. 1, November 1946

———: "The Function of Latte in the Marianas," *Journal of the Polynesian Society*, Vol. XLIX, Polynesian Society, Wellington, 1940

———: "Guam: A Study in Military Government," *Far Eastern Survey*, August 9, 1944

———: "The Native Culture of the Marianas Islands," Bulletin No. 185, Bernice P. Bishop Museum, Honolulu, 1945

*Twenty Years of Progress: History of the Pacific-Alaska Division, Pan American World Airways*, Public Relations Department, Pan American World Airways System, 1955

Walker, Anthony: "Advance on Orote Peninsula," *Marine Corps Gazette*, February 1945

# INDEX

447

crafts of, 26–30; racial origins of,
14–17; *see also* Spanish-Chamorro wars
Charles I, king of Spain, 40
*China Clipper*, 247
Choco, 65, 66, 67
citizenship (U.S.) 232–33, 242–43, 319
348–62, 365–66; *see also* civil rights
City Planning Commission, 323
civil administrator, 320–21
civil defense, 391–92
civil government, 351–62, 365–93
civil rights, 232–34, 238, 319
climate, 4–5
Clipperton, John, 90–92
codes of Guam, 378, 379
College of San Juan de Letran, 68, 75,
102, 405
colonial system, *see* Spanish colonial
system
Columbus, Christopher, 38
commerce, *see* trade and commerce
commercial aviation, 246–48
commercial development, *see* trade and
commerce
communications, *see* postal system, transportation and communications
Congregationalists, 400
convict labor, 151, 153–54
Coontz, Robert E., governor, 171, 212–16
copra industry, 239–40, 261
*Cormoran* incident, 224–27
Corte, Felipe de la, *see* de la Corte,
Felipe María
Cottman, Vincendon L., 178, 181
Council of the Indies, 54
Court of Appeals, 253–54, 321, 385
courts, 253–54, 321, 384–85; *see also* judi-
cial system, legal system
Crozet expedition, 109–13
Crusades, 33, 36–37

da Gama, Vasco, 38–39
Dampier, William, 83
de la Corte, Felipe María, governor, 141,
155–59
Department of Agriculture, 255–57, 312,
314, 321, 337–38

Department of Civil Police, 322, 332–33
Department of Commerce and Industry,
313
Department of Economics and Labor,
312–13
Department of Education, 192, 312, 321,
435
Department of Health, 321
Department of Internal Affairs, 321–22
Department of Justice, 192
Department of Public Health, 314–15
Department of Public Safety, 315
Department of Public Works, 315, 322
Department of Records and Accounts, 322
development programs, *see* public works
discovery of Guam, 33–42
District Court of Guam, 384–85
Dorn, E. J., governor, 208–12
Drake, Francis, 33, 48
Duenas, Jesús Baza, 284–86
Duenas, Edward Camacho, 286
d'Urville, Dumont, 139–40
Dutch explorers, visits by, 33, 49–51
Dyer, G. L., governor, 201–8, 407–8

earthquakes, 151, 200, 407
Eaton, John, 82–83
economy, 106–9, 121, 125, 140–49, 155–56,
157–58, 180, 217–19, 239–40, 250–51,
255–57, 313–14, 335–46, 393–96
education, 109, 191, 312, 321, 383, 404–36;
adult and vocational, 425–27; elementary, 406–21; higher, 427–32; secondary,
421–26; Department of Education, 192,
312, 321, 435
Education Code, 435
elections, 236, 238, 240–41, 347, 378, 381–
82, 383
elementary education, 406–21
Elvidge, Ford Q., governor, 372
*encomendero*, 55
*encomienda*, 55
English explorers, visits by, 47–49
España, Damian de, governor, 74–75,
80–82, 84, 85
European explorers, 33, 35–36, 37–51
Executive Department, 254–55, 368–69

449

M